Appalachian
Ecocriticism
and the
Paradox *of*
Place

Appalachian Ecocriticism *and the* Paradox *of* Place

Edited by **Jessica Cory**
and **Laura Wright**

The University *of*
Georgia Press
Athens

© 2023 by the University of Georgia Press
Athens, Georgia 30602
www.ugapress.org
All rights reserved
Designed by Kaelin Chappell Broaddus
Set in 9.5/13 Dolly Pro Regular by Kaelin Chappell Broaddus

Most University of Georgia Press titles are
available from popular e-book vendors.

Printed digitally

Library of Congress Cataloging-in-Publication Data

Names: Cory, Jessica, editor. | Wright, Laura, 1970– editor.
Title: Appalachian ecocriticism and the paradox of place /
   edited by Jessica Cory and Laura Wright.
Description: Athens : The University of Georgia Press, [2023] |
   Includes bibliographical references and index. |
Identifiers: LCCN 2022052886 (print) | LCCN 2022052887 (ebook) |
   ISBN 9780820363943 (hardback) | ISBN 9780820363950 (paperback) |
   ISBN 9780820363929 (epub) | ISBN 9780820363936 (pdf)
Subjects: LCSH: American literature—Appalachian Region—
   History and criticism. | Appalachian Region—Intellectual life. |
   Appalachian Region—In literature. | Appalachian Region—
   In motion pictures. | Ecocriticism.
Classification: LCC PS286.A6 A5924 2023 (print) | LCC PS286.A6 (ebook) |
   DDC 810.9/974—dc23/eng/20230124
LC record available at https://lccn.loc.gov/2022052886
LC ebook record available at https://lccn.loc.gov/2022052887

Contents

Compass
Where Are We Headed?
JESSICA CORY AND LAURA WRIGHT 1

Trailhead Our Point of Origin

Perception and the Nature of Ethics
How to Learn about the Ethics of Place from Literature
M. JOSEPH ALOI 13

Walking in Woods Learning the Lay of the Land

Mountain Georgics
Appalachia and Everyday Nature
ETHAN MANNON 29

"The Grit of the Land Was in Them"
A Post-pastoral Reading of John Ehle's The Land Breakers
SAVANNAH PAIGE MURRAY 45

Deja Views Familiar Terrain with New Vistas

"Lives Slip Away Like Waters"
Drowned Communities in Rash's One Foot in Eden *and* Raising the Dead
ELISABETH AIKEN 61

"Little Porcelain Shepherds and Shepherdesses"
The Female Pastoral Archetype and Version of the Appalachian Pastoral
MICHAEL S. MARTIN 81

The Nymph's Reply
Kathryn Stripling Byer and Pastoral Romance
EVAN GURNEY 102

Uphill Both Ways *Struggle on the Sojourn*

"This River of Crazy Women"
Subversive Motherhood and the Affrilachian Landscape in Crystal Wilkinson's The Birds of Opulence
CAMERON WILLIAMS CRAWFORD 115

An Ecofeminist Reading of Robert Gipe's *Trampoline* as Insight into Appalachian Oppression
JESSICA CORY 129

Hidden Gems *Finding the New in the Familiar*

Ecosexuals in Appalachia
Identity, Community, and Counterdiscourse in Goodbye Gauley Mountain
CYNTHIA BELMONT 147

Seeing Queer Oddkin in *The Prettiest Star*'s Appalachia
CALEB PENDYGRAFT 171

Trail Magic *Seeking Guidance along the Journey*

Raven, Woman, Man
A/Religious Ecocritical Reading of Jim Minick's Fire Is Your Water
THERESA BURRISS 191

"Forest Christian," a Poet of the River Lands
Wendell Berry in Appalachia
LUCAS NOSSAMAN 204

Conflict and Resolution
Eco-environmentalism in Charles Frazier's Antiwar Novel Cold Mountain
SYLVIA BAILEY SHURBUTT 225

A New Overlook *Seeing the Forest Beyond the Trees*

Wallace Stevens's "Anecdote of the Jar"
Modernist Poetics and the Industrial Logging of the Great Appalachian Forest
KEVIN E. O'DONNELL 241

A Sense of Place
The Rhododendron as Regional Identification on the Covers of Appalachian Local Color Literature
STEWART PLEIN 252

What Lies Beyond the Summit The Future of Appalachian Ecocriticism
    Toward a Post-Appalachian Sense of Place
        ZACKARY VERNON   271

    For Further Reading   291
    Contributor Biographies   293
    Index   299

Appalachian
Ecocriticism
and the
Paradox *of*
Place

Compass

Where Are We Headed?

JESSICA CORY AND
LAURA WRIGHT

The idea of Appalachia has existed in the American imagination for centuries, though these musings are often political or derisive in nature, frequently due to mischaracterized portrayals of the region in a variety of media. However, if we examine depictions of Appalachia's landscapes, a much different narrative begins to appear. Lush trees and majestic mountains rise up against a backdrop of gray sky. Hills blaze with the oranges and golds of early autumn. Creeks crumple over rocks before widening into expansive rivers captured between steep granite. Grassy fields nourish the soil beneath. It is these images and imaginings of Appalachia that bring the leafers in autumn and the vacation home buyers year-round. While the region and its landscape have been overrepresented as agrarian, often due to depictions in historical novels, as Zackary Vernon explores in this collection's final chapter, the more nuanced realities of Appalachian landscapes undoubtedly influence the writers who conjure such settings in film, fiction, literary nonfiction, and poetry, bringing the hills, coves, and rivers to audiences who may have never witnessed the environmental diversity found in the region.

While such beauty fills Appalachia, environmental hazards and their consequences are widespread throughout the region as well. Writers have long been able to capture public sentiment and share such concerns through film, poetry, fiction, and creative nonfiction works. In Appalachian literature, writers are often engaging with mountaintop removal, flash flooding, and deforestation, among many other environmental issues. These environmental themes that are often a hallmark of Appalachian literature are found in many texts produced by Appalachian writers, from William Bartram's *Travels* (1791) to more contemporary works, such as Beth Stephens and Annie Sprinkle's documentary film *Goodbye Gauley Mountain* (2014) and Charles Frazier's *Cold Mountain* (1997), both of which are examined in this collection. Environmental writer Ian Marshall expands on the importance of environmental engagement in Appalachian writing: "The Appalachians are the only American mountain chain for which we have written accounts of encounters with the land from the earliest days of European settlement to the present. As a result, in the body of literature set in the Appalachians one can trace our evolving legacy of landscape aesthetics and our changing attitudes toward nature and the wild" (3). It is this intentional inclusion of the natural world in Appalachian literature that makes it ripe and overdue for ecocritical analysis. Viewing Appalachian texts through an ecocritical lens invites scholars and readers to challenge outdated ideas of Appalachia and to reimagine the region, its environments, and its artistic renderings.

Ecocriticism and environmental literature have always been conceptualized as uniquely associated with the United States, even as an increasing body of ecocritical work over the past decade has explored postcolonial contexts. William Rueckert coined the term "ecocriticism" in 1978 in "Literature and Ecology: An Experiment in Ecocriticism." Initially ecocritics focused on the works of eighteenth- and nineteenth-century East Coast writers like Ralph Waldo Emerson, Henry David Thoreau, and Walt Whitman. As a social movement in the 1960s, environmentalism was a specifically American phenomenon, heralded by the publication of Rachel Carson's *Silent Spring* in 1962. Cheryll Glotfelty claims that ecocriticism is the study of literature "as if the environment mattered" (Mazel 1). In the introduction to her foundational coedited 1996 volume *The Ecocriticism Reader*, Glotfelty characterizes such study as different from other theoretical modes of inquiry:

> Literary theory, in general, examines the relations between writers, texts, and the world. In most literary theory "the world" is synonymous with society—the social sphere. Ecocriticism expands the notion of "the world" to include the entire ecosphere. If we agree with Barry Commoner's first law of ecology, "Everything is connected to everything else," we must conclude that literature does not float above the material world in some aesthetic ether, but, rather, plays a part in an immensely complex global system, in which energy, matter, and ideas interact. (Glotfelty and Fromm xix)

Ecocriticism: The New Critical Idiom, Greg Garrard's 2012 overview of the field, maps the various "positions" that underscore environmentalism more broadly and inform ecocritical readings of literary texts. These positions include mainstream environmentalism, adopted by people who believe in science and in human-made environmental degradation but who largely seek to maintain the status quo; more radical deep ecology, the tenets of which are, first, that human life and nonhuman life have intrinsic value (that is, nonhuman life matters in and of itself, not in terms of its relation to humans) and, second, that there need to be fewer humans in order to sustain a balance between human and nonhuman life; and ecofeminism, the theory that all oppressions—in terms of nature, gender, race, and social class—are interconnected and based upon a binary system that devalues all things associated with femaleness and the natural world. Since the 1970s, ecocritics have been exploring the ways that the natural world and social influences upon it shape narrative, identity, and reality for both characters and authors, but ecocriticism's engagement with Appalachian literatures has been a more recent phenomenon.

Fred Waage notes in "Exploring the 'Life Territory': Ecology and Criticism in Appalachia" that both ecocriticism and Appalachian studies share a "history of definitional ambiguity and diversity" (136). As Chad Berry declares in Ashley York and Sally Rubin's 2019 documentary *Hillbilly*, "Appalachia [is] a construction. It was a social and cultural invention. For example, Iowa is a construction, too. The difference between Iowa and Appalachia is you know when you're in Iowa because there is a sign there that says 'welcome to Iowa.' There's no such sign with Appalachia." Despite such a shared history of mutable constructions, in-depth examinations of how the environment is portrayed in Appalachian literature are somewhat limited. This limited scholarship is likely due to a combination of several factors. Because of U.S. colonization patterns, Appalachia was peopled by white Europeans early on, and lands inhabited by these European people were consequently not viewed as "wilderness," in the same ways that the western part of the country was considered to be (though there are early nature writings about western mountainous areas as well). Early preservationists viewed humans (really white Europeans) as separate from the natural world and therefore saw areas inhabited by these people as somehow "marked" by human progress and therefore not part of "nature."

Enter the early nature writers. Certainly Bartram wrote an early account of the Appalachian landscape, published in 1791, and nearly fifty years later Thoreau penned his experience on Ktaadn (the Appalachian trailhead, though not part of the official Appalachian Regional Commission's boundaries). However, much early American nature writing focused on coastal areas or places easily accessible by river but not yet heavily peopled by white Europeans, such as the many travels up the Mississippi by Louis Hennepin and the Lewis and Clark expedition.[1] The rugged Appalachian terrain, therefore, was not so easily explored and recorded. However, the Louisiana Purchase in 1803 and Thomas Jefferson's determination for westward expansion led many white European settlers to move toward the Rocky Mountains and beyond. The 1838 Indian Removal Act, and the associated money to be made in slaughtering Native peoples, particularly in the West in the years following the California Gold Rush, made the region even more inhabitable for white European settlers.[2] And with more Europeans inhabiting this "new wilderness" came a plethora of nature writing, including John C. and Jessie Benton Fremont's impressions of Oregon and Northern California in 1845 and Howard Stansbury's thoughts on the Great Salt Lake area in 1852. Because of the expansiveness of the western landscape, with its many deserts and wide-open spaces, it was imagined as less peopled and therefore more akin to "real wilderness." This fascination with such western landscapes, particularly in the desert, never really dwindled, producing such twentieth-century writers as Michael P. Branch, Edward Abbey, and Terry Tempest Williams.

Since nature writing brought endangered environs to the forefront, it held significant influence in early preservation movements, and where better to preserve than "unpeopled" open spaces in the West? Certainly environmental efforts were made elsewhere as well; Appalachian scientist and environmental writer Rachel Carson's *Silent Spring* certainly brought about change, though changes in policy are not necessarily akin to designating millions of acres of land as national parks. The U.S. interest in preserving "nature" focused most of its efforts west of the Rockies; of the sixty-one current national parks in the United States (or in U.S.-held territories), only eight on the U.S. mainland are east of the Mississippi.[3] One of those eight is Great Smoky Mountains National Park, which opened to the public in 1934 and was championed by former Missouri-based librarian turned chronicler of Appalachian landscapes and peoples Horace Kephart in his 1913 book *Our Southern Highlanders: A Narrative of Adventure in the Southern Appalachians and a Study of Life among the Mountaineers*. According to Carlos C. Campbell, the "creation of the eighteen national parks prior to 1924 had been accomplished by the setting aside of lands which already belonged to the federal government" (12). Such was not the case with the Great Smokies, as "the 515,225.8 acres constituting this park were thin in private ownership, in more than 6,600 separate tracts" (12). Therefore, in order to get Congress to accept the idea of a park in the Smokies, "the spectacular beauty and scenic grandeur of the region had to be described repeatedly. But to get the land at reasonable prices, the owners had to be shown that their mountain land was relatively worthless for other purposes" (19). Kephart's writings and photographs taken by James E. Thompson were instrumental in this endeavor, which established the park and consequently displaced people who for generations had lived on land designated for it.

This representation of what was considered a "wild" or "natural" space played heavily in the development of ecocriticism. Even though Rueckert coined "ecocriticism" in 1978, it is important to note that scholars were certainly exploring connections between literature and the environment prior to the term's invention, as Glotfelty's bibliography was "about twenty single-spaced pages long" in the 1980s. However, as ecocriticism grew from the study of nature writing and early American environmental efforts and nature writing focused on preservation of wilderness, it becomes easy to see why early ecocritics (and many still today) examined areas that were less densely populated and home to myriad environmental landmarks.

From the initial study and critique of nature writing, a great number of subsets of ecocriticism have formed, allowing scholars to question and analyze environmental writing in a variety of ways. Included in this volume are methodical and theoretical examinations of environmental engagement, representation, and functionality within Appalachian literature. This collection includes interpretations and analyses of Appalachian texts based on ecotheological, pastoral, post-pastoral, ecofeminist, and additional environmentally focused theories that allow readers and scholars to more fully appreciate the depths of Appalachian texts and the region they have come to represent. Analyzing Appalachian works through these lenses allows for the full breadth of Appalachian environments to be examined and, upon critique, to enter the larger discussion on literature and the environment.

The study of Appalachian literature is marked by a paradox of place. While Appalachian literature may have first won audiences over with travel writings and "local color" literature in the "Southern Mountain Fiction" genre that originated in the 1870s (Batteau 40), writing from the region has evolved steadily to move past the stereotypes and embrace diversity in class, gender, sexual orientation, race, and other identity markers. Additionally, as we enter the Anthropocene, Appalachian writers—particularly women—have continued to reflect the Appalachian tradition of activism, especially related to environmental degradation, such as mountaintop removal and water pollution. Engaging with Appalachian literature through the larger context of literature and the environment will increase its visibility, helping readers to move beyond their mischaracterizations of Appalachia, its inhabitants, and its landscapes.

One of the benefits of utilizing ecocriticism to explore Appalachian texts is that doing so challenges the antiquated depiction of the region as largely rural. As Emily Satterwhite notes in *Dear Appalachia: Readers, Identity, and Popular Fiction since 1978*, novels, films, news coverage, and television shows have all contributed to erroneous depictions of Appalachians. Statistically, most people living in the region reside in midsize or large metropolitan areas, and many large cities exist within its boundaries, such as Pittsburgh, Pennsylvania, and Knoxville, Tennessee.[4] There are fine-dining restaurants, luxury resorts, sprawling metro areas, and condos, theaters, orchestras, museums, universities, and art galleries. Fortunately, as ecocriticism has evolved from the study of nature writing to embrace both the rural and the urban, it now offers a means to help scholars counter problematic representations of the region, its inhabitants, and its literature.

Increased visibility of Appalachian texts via ecocriticism and discussions of landscape also invite connections between Appalachia and other areas of the globe, as the Carpathian-Appalachian conference seeks to do in the Ukraine and the recent Mediating Mountains conference in Innsbruck, Austria, at which several of our colleagues presented. A broader readership may aid in building connections beyond mountainous terrain, over social ills and possible solutions, as historian Elizabeth Catte points out: "There's not a single social problem in Appalachia that can't be found elsewhere in our country" (8). David Joy embraces the idea of expanding the readership of Appalachian literature as well, noting that he could have set *Where All the Light Tends to Go* anywhere other than western North Carolina because "it's a human story, it's not an Appalachian story." Joy adds, "I think maybe that's one of the roles of literature more than anything else is to get that humanity. It's to illuminate some aspect of the human condition." If we are to broaden our understanding of the human condition, Appalachian literature needs to be acknowledged, read, and critiqued not only by those who live within the region but also by those who live beyond it, a goal that ecocritical analysis can help achieve by broadening the scholarly audience.

Certainly there has been discussion as to whether Appalachia should be seen and written of as a single region with a "unified culture" shared by a unique and collective people or as a collection of places that have more in common with their geographical neighbors (particularly in the South) than with one another. *Appalachian Ecocriticism and the Paradox of Place* presents Appalachia as a region, not unlike many other U.S. regions, where connections exist even among cultural differences. This work does not paint the varying Appalachian areas as the same but illuminates a shared sense of identity rooted in place and body of work that comprises a wide breadth of people, histories, and experiences that make up, along with the natural world, the Appalachian environment. This collection does not determine what is or is not Appalachian but rather enters into a larger dialogue about what the multifaceted environments within Appalachia can tell us and what we can learn from them as we traverse the paths they offer.

This collection is arranged to reflect the experiences and trajectories one might encounter while sojourning through a natural environment. The first and last parts include only one essay each, to reflect how journeys often occur, even if they take meandering paths along the way. As Our Point of Origin, we begin with M. Joseph Aloi's "Perception and the Nature of Ethics: How to Learn about the Ethics of Place from Literature." Aloi's essay positions us to examine how we think about what we read, particularly in regard to the values and ethics that accompany discussion of a region as complex as Appalachia. As a point of origin for our journey, Aloi's essay heightens our awareness of place, so that we may be fully immersed in the environments and essays to come.

From there we begin to learn the lay of the land with Ethan Mannon and Savannah Paige Murray's works, which focus on earlier canonical works of Appalachian literature and, in particular, the role of labor in environmental engagement. This section, "Walking in Woods," situates us within the pastoral and post-pastoral writings of Appalachian authors and provides solid groundwork on which to continue to build our knowledge of Appalachian environmental literature. Just as a sojourner learns the lay of the land by walking it and through close, intimate engagement, Mannon and Murray's essays center on the experiences of protagonists who struggle with and eventually learn to live in connection with, instead of against, the land.

Even if one is traveling familiar terrain, it can change, and sometimes abruptly. As Elisabeth Aiken explores in the case of Lake Jocassee, flooding in the name of "progress" has changed many of the region's landscapes permanently. Michael S. Martin and Evan Gurney explore this theme through the transition between contemporary and much older landscapes and via comparisons between historical European works and contemporary Appalachian ecological literary traditions. Their essays show us not only the usefulness of an ecocritical lens to bridge centuries and oceans but also how these historical criticisms can help us locate ourselves in contemporary Appalachian literatures. After our jaunt carries us a bit farther, we may begin to see similarities with the landscape we find ourselves in and other environments we have experienced. Perhaps we get lost and wind up doubling back on familiar terrain.

Thinking of familiar terrain, it's important to consider how what may seem familiar to us is not necessarily the experience shared by others. Cameron Williams Crawford and Jessica Cory address ways in which intersectionality through class, gender, race, and other identity markers can create barriers and difficulties for Appalachian people, particularly women. Their essays ask us to consider the ways in which we struggle or benefit from our identities and acknowledge that others may be facing obstacles of which we are unaware. Throughout journeys, struggle is inevitable, and it is important to consider how this struggle takes many forms.

Building on our awareness of one another's experiences and finding new approaches to familiar landscapes, Cynthia Belmont and Caleb Pendygraft provide queer readings of Appalachian environments that question the dominant narratives of who and what belong in the region, allowing us to refigure our relationships to the land and those who inhabit it. When sauntering, and particularly when struggles slow us down, our changes in speed and focus allow us to find hidden gems—perhaps a trail seldom taken, a unique rock outcropping never before noticed, or a small stand of wildflowers that captures our entire attention, even for just a few moments. These gems, then, allow us to understand and appreciate seemingly familiar environments in new ways, queering how we see and appreciate the world and our place within it.

Part of such appreciation and connection might be through a spiritual aspect, as explored by Theresa Burriss and Lucas Nossaman, or by communion with the land and those humans who commune with us, as Sylvia Bailey Shurbutt explores. These three essays show us a variety of ways in which Appalachian people and those who write about them find hope and make meaning of life. In Appalachian Trail terminology, "trail magic" is the kindness of strangers that increases a traveler's wonder. While this collection does not focus on AT narratives, this connection to land, wonder, and humanity is echoed in the essays in this section. In response to difficulties or in trying to gain new insights, whether in life or on a trail, often we seek guidance from or through an otherworldly connection.

Considering the perspective of otherworldly kin, and the ways in which we can see familiar areas anew, the essays in "A New Overlook: Seeing the Forest Beyond the Trees" examine Appalachian texts broadly. Kevin O'Donnell's piece explores the ways that Appalachia crosses boundaries as it influences non-Appalachian writers and brings in perspectives of the region that display firsthand how Appalachian ecocriticism can be helpful to understand texts not traditionally considered "of the region" and how our perspectives might shift to include them. Stewart Plein's examination of the rhododendron, used as a marker of place for local color literature, applies ecocritical analysis in a unique way, by looking *at* the text rather than *within* it. These essays are indicative of that point on our journey when our comfort with the landscape increases and we are able to envision the broader picture, seeing the forest as a whole instead of individual trees.

Our final destination is Zackary Vernon's "Toward a Post-Appalachian Sense of Place." Vernon's work shows us, by making a comparison to post-southern literature, where we can go from here to further develop our understanding of Appalachian literature. Vernon's discussion is forward-thinking and hope-giving as he describes change but not homogeneity, evolution but not extinction. It is from this place that we are better able to consider the legacy of environmental writing in the region and how scholarship and readership influence its future.

This collection examines, and dispels, what Henry Shapiro called the "myth of Appalachia" by bringing this region into the larger conversation of ecocritical scholarship. By illuminating studies of the Appalachian environment, examining the literature and criticism that result from such studies, and analyzing the intersections of these areas, we have created a collection that fills this gap in the literature.

NOTES

1. Prior to 1700, there was a fair amount of nature writing focusing on New England as well, since it was not overly populated by Europeans at that point. Michael P. Branch's *Reading the Roots: American Nature Writing before Walden* (2004) covers nature writing about what is now the United States from 1498 to 1853 and includes many early Italian and Spanish colonizers' writings as well as a bit of Native American writing and one freedom narrative (sometimes called the slave narrative).

2. Benjamin Madley's *An American Genocide: The United States and the California Indian Catastrophe, 1846–1873* (2016) covers the massacre of Native peoples in the U.S. West, particularly in California.

3. See the National Parks Trust website for a map: https://www.parktrust.org/map-of-national-parks/.

4. King, "Urban Appalachia?" The Southern Appalachian Vitality Index and ARC support these data as well.

BIBLIOGRAPHY

Batteau, Allen W. *The Invention of Appalachia*. Tucson: University of Arizona Press, 1990.

Branch, Michael P. *Reading the Roots: American Nature Writing before Walden*. Athens: University of Georgia Press, 2004.

Campbell, Carlos C. *Birth of A National Park: In the Great Smoky Mountains*. Knoxville: University of Tennessee Press, 1993.

Carson, Rachel. *Silent Spring*. 1962. New York: Houghton Mifflin, 2002.

Catte, Elizabeth. *What You Are Getting Wrong about Appalachia*. Cleveland: Belt, 2018.

Garrard, Greg. *Ecocriticism: The New Critical Idiom*. New York: Routledge, 2012.

Glotfelty, Cheryll. "The Formation of a Field: Ecocriticism in America—An Interview with Cheryll Glotfelty." *PMLA* 127, no. 3 (2012): 607–16, https://doi.org/10.1632/pmla.2012.127.3.607.

Glotfelty, Cheryll, and David Fromm, eds. *The Ecocriticism Reader*. Athens: University of Georgia Press, 1996.

Kephart, Horace. *Our Southern Highlanders: A Narrative of Adventure in the Southern Appalachians and a Study of Life among the Mountaineers*. New York: Outing, 1913.

Joy, David. "The 'Human Stories' of David Joy." Interview by Cory Vaillancourt. *Arts & Performance*, BPR News, August 7, 2018. http://www.bpr.org/post/human-stories-david-joy.

King, Niki. "Urban Appalachia: Who, Where, and What is It?" *The Hillville*, December 12, 2011. https://thehillville.com/2011/12/12/urban-appalachia-who-where-and-what-is-it/.

Madley, Benjamin. *An American Genocide: The United States and the California Indian Catastrophe, 1846–1873*. New Haven, Conn.: Yale University Press, 2016.

Marshall, Ian. *Storyline: Exploring the Literature of the Appalachian Trail*. University Press of Virginia, 1998.

Mazel, David, ed. *A Century of Early Ecocriticism*. University of Georgia Press, 2001.

National Parks Trust. "Park Preservation." https://www.parktrust.org/map-of-national-parks/.

Rueckert, William. "Literature and Ecology: An Experiment in Ecocriticism." *Iowa Review* 9, no. 1 (1978): 71–86.

Satterwhite, Emily. *Dear Appalachia: Readers, Identity, and Popular Fiction since 1978*. Lexington: University Press of Kentucky, 2011.

Waage, Fred. "Exploring the 'Life Territory': Ecology and Criticism in Appalachia." *Journal of Appalachian Studies* 11, no. 1/2 (2005): 133–63.

Trailhead
Our Point of Origin

Perception and the Nature of Ethics
How to Learn about the Ethics of Place from Literature

M. JOSEPH ALOI

> Fine and just actions ... admit of much variety and fluctuation. ... We must be content, then, in speaking of such subjects ... to indicate the truth roughly and in outline. —*Nicomachean Ethics*, 1094b15–23

> Poetry is something more philosophic and of graver import than history, since its statements are of the nature rather of universals, whereas those of history are singulars. —*Poetics*, 1451b5–8

> Place must indeed rank first; for place does not perish with the perishing things in it. —*Physics*, 209a1–2

These three observations of Aristotle's, taken together, constitute the background of my essay. Works of literature set in Appalachia teach us about the importance of considerations of this place to ethics, to the pursuit of the good life. Following Aristotle, I argue that the pursuit of the good life—ethics—is an endeavor that requires astute attention to the details of one's character, one's situation, one's relationship to others, and many other concrete details. The same action in a different context can carry a different ethical meaning. Accordingly, general rules for ethics have a very limited utility. The lessons we can gain from narrative—what Aristotle calls "poetry" above—are tied to very specific characters and actions and are, in that way, more instructive to the pupil of ethics than general rules. Further, because all actions—ethical or not, fictional or not—happen in specific places, and because these places usually precede and outlast the actions, attention to place is one of those things in life to which the ethical actor must pay constant and astute attention.

I begin by examining what ethics is and why good literature can help cultivate it. Next, I move on to examine the concept "place" and the role it plays in environmental philosophy broadly understood. After this, I briefly explain why literature is useful for cultivation of the good life. Finally, I conclude by way of example, seeking to learn about Appalachian places and the ways they're intertwined with our ethics from Scott McClanahan's 2013 *Crapalachia: A Biography of Place*, a chronicling of his youth in rural West Virginia in the 1980s and 1990s.

The argument that attention to place is an important ingredient of ethical action is not a new one, although I believe that my characterization of "place" and of "attention to place" is unique in important aspects that will become clear as this chapter unfolds. Neither is the argument that good literature makes us better persons new. But literature that is attendant to places and the concerns of place generally offers specific lessons, including ethical lessons, that we cannot learn in any other manner, excepting raw experience. The ethical heft of our relations to place, or in place, cannot be learned through attention only to historical sources or ecological sources. There is a class of lessons we can learn nowhere else than through experience and narrative. In particular, in an Appalachian context, there is a human history of struggle and deprivation, perseverance and resilience that lingers in the landscape, and this history is tied to the region's geography in hyperspecific, local ways. The importance of these lessons in understanding how to create and live the good life in Appalachia seems vital to attaining an ethical understanding of the region. McClanahan's work offers us an interdependent cluster of examples of these specifics, tied to a personal narrative.

The Limits of Rule-Following as a Guide for the Good Life

According to Aristotle, the goal of ethics—both the reflective study of ethics and the lived striving to be ethical—is to help people reach happiness and live the good life (1097a15–1097b23).[1] As he tells us, the study of ethics is not an abstract deriving of principles and an applying of these principles to actions; rather, it is the concrete study of the character of the good person in the complex situations of everyday life. We study the characters of good people in order to cultivate virtuous habits similar to theirs, knowing that this will lead to the fulfillment that Aristotle refers to as "the good life" (1103a16).

The underlying assumption of Aristotelian ethics is that overall characters—not individual actions—are the type of things that we can judge as good or bad. More precisely, we judge character as good or bad based on the picture we get from observing a person's habits. The good person does not merely do the right act but does it "at the right times, with reference to the right objects, towards the right people, with the right motive, and in the right way" (1106b20–23). Right action flows naturally out of the person of good character, and this good person becomes so through the hard work of cultivating his or her character in various ethical situations.

Listen to how Martha Nussbaum frames the problem: "Aristotle has no objection to the use of general guidelines . . . for certain purposes. . . . Rules and general procedures can be aids in moral development. . . . But Aristotle's point . . . is that the rule or algorithm represents a falling off from full practical rationality, not its flourishing or completion" (73). Nussbaum is here alluding to one of our epigraphic observations; because of the "variety and fluctuation" inherent in all ethical actions, the rules about ethics we can invent, deduce, or observe are nothing more than rules of thumb. They may guide the development of the right sort of habits, but we can fairly judge someone's character only once these good or bad acts have accreted into character traits—once these types of actions become instinctual and natural.

In particular, Nussbaum argues, dogged reliance on principles blinds people to certain important factors of moral life. To do the right thing, one needs to learn to perceive more acutely the "context-embeddedness of relevant features" than generalized rules are able to do (38). There is so much that is ethically relevant in any given situation that one's full attention must be directed to the event; one needs to soak in and synthesize these elements rather than step back and analyze their agreement with a general principle or two. When we have cultivated as rich of a character as possible through rule-following, we will need to build ethical habits through careful and thoughtful attention to our everyday actions and surroundings. This is particularly relevant to our ethical relations to place; because different places gather different things, and even gather the same things differently, it is important to allow careful perception to the elements of place to play as large a role as possible in our ethical deliberations.

In an Appalachian context, we can take as an example of an ethical rule the dictum that "the voices and perspectives of people inside the region ought to be prioritized over those of people from outside the region." This rubric allows us to distinguish thoughtless hillbilly stereotypes from clear-eyed assessment of regional problems by people working to solve them (Fisher and Smith 47). Furthermore, it's a rule that has a basis in an accurate historical analysis of power relations in Appalachia; "outsiders" actually did often enter the region in order to exploit it (Gaventa, esp. 50–75). But if we don't learn when to abandon this rule, "it conceals and exonerates *internal* exploiters ... [who] have used the rhetoric of insiders and outsiders—for example, in Friends of Coal" (Fisher and Smith 49, emphasis original).[2] In other words, to tell whether an insider or an outsider has the richest perspective, or has the best interests of the community in mind, one needs to pay attention to much, much more than their nativity or foreignness.

Casey on Place and Perception

Studies about place, and especially about the relationship of place to literature, are inherently interdisciplinary, so it's important to note that I approach this study through the disciplinary lenses of philosophy—specifically, hermeneutic philosophy. This tradition argues that our understanding of particulars is shaped by our background understanding of the general principles or abstract forms of which these particulars are examples or instantiations (Gadamer). Accordingly, I argue, our relations to individual places cannot be understood apart from our more abstract understanding of what place itself is.

Of course, hermeneutics also holds that the reverse is true; that our abstract or general understanding of concepts like "place" are largely formed by our understandings of specific places. But the interdisciplinary work of novelists, ecologists, bioregionalists, anthropologists, landscape architects, geographers, and environmental activists tends to focus on specific places and the specifics of these places. For this reason, there is an abundance of good work on the characters of specific places. And since discussion of the abstract and universal has traditionally been the domain of philosophers, I feel like it's our responsibility to shoulder the intellectual burden of this abstract half of the hermeneutic circle—to discuss the character of place itself. What is the essence of place; what is place such that we ought concern ourselves with it?

This question is all the more important for those of us who are students of the place called Appalachia. If we are able to study something about a place—its history, literature, or foodways—we must somehow recognize this place. We must be able to see it as a place, even if only in a cursory fashion, as a background. A better understanding of the general characteristics of place can only enrich the work we do as scholars of Appalachian places.

Phenomenological philosopher Edward Casey notices that moderns are likely to "assume that human experience begins with space and time and then proceeds to place" (13). As irresistible as it might be, this assumption is phenomenologically inaccurate; it does not describe our actual lived experiences of the world. Historically considered, Casey notes, the assumption that space proceeds place is peculiar to the modern era, becoming canonized in the works of Newton and Kant (14). From this modern perspective, "human experience starts from a mute and blank 'space' to which placial modifiers such as 'near,' 'over there,' 'along that way,' and 'just here' are added" (15). Moderns describe and explain the world as if it is first of all empty of meaning, and human action and decision bring this meaning to it, turning sections of space into different places along the way.

This is, surely, not the way we experience place in our everyday lives. Rather, as Casey notes, "we always find ourselves in particular places," never simply in an undetermined space (17). Even when we find ourselves in an unfamiliar place, we still recognize it as a specific, unknown, place—perhaps with curiosity, perhaps with apprehension. Going further, he claims that "knowledge of place is not ... subsequent to perception ... but is ingredient in perception itself" (18). A placeless perception would be no perception at all; it would be a "blooming buzzing confusion," as William James says of the experiences of a baby (*Principles of Psychology*, vol. 1, chap. 13).

The placed nature of each of our experiences is due to the fact that perception is "an affair of the whole body sensing and moving" (Casey 18). Bodies are always placed somewhere—neither everywhere nor nowhere. Furthermore, these placed, embodied perceptions are "always meaningful" and "constituted by cultural and social structures that sediment themselves into the deepest level of perception" (18). We move past the blooming, buzzing confusion of infancy by learning to recognize patterns and meanings of all sorts. These meanings are as essential to our perceptions as are the raw sense data moderns tend to think of as determinative. Accordingly, part of the power and importance of place is the rich cultural, personal, and emotional meanings brought forth by our perceptions in places.

But, to be clear, I should emphasize again that places are not constituted out of meaningful, embodied perceptions in an otherwise blank area of space. Rather, places precede—ontologically and experientially—our placed perceptions. The world is there before our perceptions of it, both in its raw materiality and with the thick layers of meaning it has accrued through tradition. Place itself does much of the work needed for our perception, making us, at most, only "actively passive" (18). As Casey writes, "Places gather things in their midst. ... Places also gather experiences and histories, even languages and thoughts. Think only of what it means to go back to a place you know, finding it full of memories" (24). As place itself gathers meanings and things, it unites the many into one world, one place. Were it not for these attributes of place, perception as we are familiar with it would be impossible. All action, ethical action included, would be impossible as well; action is, after all, utterly dependent on perception.

In addition to the gathering character of place and its inextricable relation to the living body, place is also "constituted by cultural and social structures that sediment themselves into the deepest level of perception" (18). Our bodily perception of places and within places is permeated with meanings derived from the culture or cultures that have formed us and the place. When I enter a room, whether I see the long, flat structure in front of me as a table or as an alter depends on cultural knowledge that has sedimented itself into my perception. Experiences where we enter a room and wonder whether an object is either a table or an alter are very rare, both because of the depth of this cultural sedimentation and because we always experience an object as ingredient to a place.

Even the ineffable moments of our experiences are indebted to our culture; "to be not yet articulated in concept or word is not to be nonculturally constituted, much less free from social constraints" (19). These cultural structures have embedded themselves not simply into our discussions of our perceptions but into our perceptions themselves. As cultures move and grow, so, of course, do the places of these cultures; "a place is more of an *event* than a *thing* . . . places not only *are* they *happen*" (26–27). An Appalachian place is not simply constituted by mountains, rivers, valleys, flora, fauna, and buildings. Rather, in its full thickness, an Appalachian place gathers these physical elements as well as cultural, traditional, and emotional elements into a concatenated event in which all these elements are participating.

Attention to the elements of place, then, is important because it is a way of attending to that event in which we are participating and which continuously creates us. Aristotle tells us that we must not only perform the right actions but perform them with "the right person, to the right extent, at the right time, with the right motive, and in the right way" (1109a.27). Clearly, we cannot do all of this without careful attention to the place in which we are acting. As with a dance or a game, attending to our coparticipants allows for more agile, astute, and fine-tuned participation in the event. Because it is an event that has, in some sense, formed us as the agents we are, attending to the elements of place allows us to engage in ethical action at a level more nuanced and appropriate than we could otherwise manage. This Aristotelian framework makes sense of why we are advised by environmental thinkers to learn the types of soil and birds of our areas; we learn about them so that we might be better equipped to interact with them.

Ethics and Literature

Now that we have a more robust understanding of the character of place, and of the role it plays in our ethical lives, we can begin to look at why literature can be a helpful partner in our place-based ethical development. The crux of Nussbaum's argument for the importance of literature for ethical development is that one can cultivate ethical perceptiveness through an engagement with good works of literature. Nussbaum uses the term "perception" to refer not to the automatic actions of the senses but to "the ability to discern, acutely and responsively, the salient features of one's particular situation" (37). To be perceptive is to "pay attention" in the normative—not merely in the descriptive—sense of that phrase.

Novels and memoirs depict concrete characters engaged in rich, particular, ethical contexts in particular settings. In these idealized situations, the complex, intertwined, morally relevant features of our relations to place shine forth as they seldom do in the haze of everyday life, making our edification more likely. This is why Aristotle claims that poetry is more philosophical than history, as we saw in the epigraph; history chronicles everything, while fiction helps us focus on perceiving only the important elements. Although we will seldom learn particular facts about the places we inhabit through these texts, we learn to recognize the complexity of place, the variety of ethical concerns these complexities give rise to, and the level of nuance and perceptiveness necessary for right action.

For the remainder of this essay, I examine a specific work of literature to see how it portrays, in addition to specific characters interacting in specific places, the general characteristics of place as described by Casey. According to Nussbaum's arguments, we ought to be able to gain a type of quasi-experiential wisdom about the relation of place to our ethical actions as readers of novels and, I argue, other narratives. But I make the further claim that critical reflection on such texts can show the work that places do; reflection on the role of place in narratives and novels shows the universal characteristics Casey describes of the event called place through the specific characteristics of the specific places of the text(s). Even if this further claim of mine is incorrect, Nussbaum's arguments offer additional reasons to advocate for the importance of Appalachian literature to persons pursing the good life in Appalachia. But if this further claim of mine is correct, we have a much stronger argument: someone who attempts to understand the place, or places, of Appalachia in order to live a richer life cannot do so without attending to the manner in which the character of place is revealed in narrative.[3]

Crapalachia and the Lessons of Place for the Good Life

In spite of its subtitle, "A Biography of Place," *Crapalachia* seems, on first glance, a book more about people than about place—a book about people and about their deaths. Yet all throughout, there are interspersed examples of how attention to place is essential to the good life. On the very first page, as we're being treated to "a short history of the McClanahan family," we're told that "they all grew up in Danese, WV, eating blackberries for breakfast and eating blackberries for lunch and watching the snow come beneath the door in the wintertime" (1). From this first page, we learn that this family is what it is, and the members are who they are, because they grew up in an Appalachian place, with snowy winters and blackberries in the summer. These elements of place are touchstones that allow them to orient themselves toward the good life, and, as the story moves on, this power of place to provide a context of meaning becomes an important theme.

Before we've gotten ten pages into the book, we're greeted with another of the book's major themes, the centrality of death to life. While grandma Ruby is feeding the hogs, a cat wanders up to the slop bucket and eats some of the hogs' food: "So finally the big daddy hog had enough and reached up and bit AIDS cat's head plumb off—gulp. The cat's body fell back jerked and jimmied and jerked some more, and the big daddy hog stood gobbling it on down. Ruby didn't say anything. She kept feeding the hogs and the pigs and then we went and sat on the front porch and watched the hummingbirds hum around. It felt peaceful" (9). From this anecdote, we can gather two things. The first is alluded to in the title of the chapter; we are told "A Story about Ruby That Will Shed Light on Her Character." This title is important for the overall narrative, but perhaps not so much for our current discussion of place.

More important for this discussion is how we also get our first glimpse at the way that the McClanahans are continually surrounded by death, often brutal, often close by. The death of AIDS cat is only the first of many in the narrative. In spite of this nearness of death, the McClanahans seem to be able to enjoy what life has to offer, feeling "peaceful" and at home. For another example, when the narrator is discussing a dream of a family dinner, one that he imagines will recur in his last moments alive, he writes that "it will be the feast of death and it will taste so delicious" (57). The vision of the good life that emerges here is one that does not exclude or avoid death, but rather respects it, accommodates it, and dwells with it. This vision of the good life—dwelling with death—has at least two place-based instantiations in the work.

First, throughout the text, this close relation between the dead and the alive has a placial analogy in the relation between the bottoms of valleys and the tops of mountains. At Uncle Nathan's funeral, our narrator writes, "I felt darkness because I had been deep in the hollers, and I knew glory because I had stood on top of the beautiful mountaintops" (70). The import of this metaphor is that life and death, glory and darkness, are tied together and make each other possible. The light and glory of the mountaintops are available only to those who attend to the darkness of the valleys just as the mountaintops themselves cannot exist without creating valleys. The value of attentiveness to this tied-togetherness seems to be the chief moral lesson we can gather from the narrative. And this lesson is one that can be read in the Appalachian landscape itself.

Second, one of the more uniquely Appalachian lessons of the text is the way in which living towns, living personal relationships, and living institutions are surrounded, haunted, and girded by dead ones. Let's begin with this extended excerpt from the text:

> [Ruby] looked out over the river and said: "Oh look out there. That river is nothing but a river of blood." . . . I drove up the mountain towards Prince and past all the old places. We drove past where Elgie sold moonshine and Ruby used to wash her clothes in the river. And we drove past the old mine, which had a church in front of it now. She told me about how she used to sit on the front porch and blow a whistle when the cops were coming. She blew the whistle and screamed, "The revenuers are coming. The revenuers are coming." Then Elgie would hear her on the mountain and blow up the still. She pointed to the hillside and said, "There used to be houses all over." Then she pointed to the side of the hill and said there used to be houses there too. Then she pointed beside the creek and said there used to be houses over there too. There used to be houses anywhere you could put a house. . . . As we drove through the holler I could see the whole place. There was a moment when it felt like it was 1930 and I was traveling through time. I could see the mine. I could see people walking. There were houses everywhere. It was all gone now. There were only mountains and a twisty turny-road. . . . There was only a train station nobody stopped at and the New River rushing all red and full of river mud. (89–92)

We can see in this scene the way in which, as Casey says, place is an event more than a mere collection of entities. Most, if not all, of the houses are gone, as are Elgie and the revenuers, but, as Aristotle says, "place does not perish with the perishing things in it" (209a1–2). The river is not merely the movement of water. It is that place where Ruby washed clothes, and, for our characters, it remains that place years after the washing has stopped. The melancholy nature of this scene stems from the fact that the place is recognizably the same in spite of the loss of many of its elements.

This insight into the often melancholic character of places remaining the same as their elements change is an especially fecund insight for those of us who dwell in Appalachian places. In an Appalachian context, there is a sense of permanence around the creeks, the rivers, and the hillsides—and perhaps something like permanence around the train tracks. But we know, in our most lucid moments, that the creeks can be dammed, the valleys can be filled, and the mountaintops can be removed. And we can only speak of the places as changed, as damaged or destroyed, because the places remain recognizable as the same.

Earlier in the book, there is a classroom scene where the characters read their "Crappalachia history book[s]" and find out about "the accidents of history" (34). The context that this scene provides to the scene with all the old places is important. In the history book scene, we—both the readers and the characters of the narrative—learn about political corruption, about the travesty of Hawk's Nest, and about the continual devastating force of coal mine deaths. In speaking of Hawk's Nest, McClanahan sardonically writes, "That's the best way to do anything—get a bunch of poor people to do it.... The men started dying by the tens and then the twenties and then the hundreds and then—the thousands? Since they were poor the company just buried them" (35–36). This is the import of the entire section; Appalachian places are what they are because of the efforts of innumerable unknown people who were taken advantage of and who've now moved on.

In this brief section, we get a clear picture of the region as a place full of working people taken advantage of by rich and powerful world makers. This objective sociological fact about the place is no more important, for the point of this essay, than is the fact that we see how this fact influences the narrator's understanding of issues of justice, politics, and economic class. We see how, in Casey's words, place is "constituted by cultural and social structures" (18). When we follow the narrator into his vision of "all the old places" in 1930, we understand that the people walking back from the mine, the people waiting to board the train, are low-income individuals working deadly jobs. Ruby's vision of the river as "nothing but a river of blood and hearts" now has a political weight; it's not just surreal (89). This metaphor shows how living places are haunted by the power and presence of the dead, and it strengthens the connection between darkness, death, and the valleys.

Later in the book, in another school scene, our main character "read about how everything changes even in Crapalachia. I read about how the miners became machines and the loggers became machines" (132). This later narrative, the narrative of technological advance in the twentieth century and the automation it brings in its wake, alters our understanding of "all the old places" from that earlier scene. We understand that there were so many houses on the hillsides because there were so many people needed to work at the mine above the New River. We also understand that the houses have disappeared because those people were no longer needed as they were replaced by machines. The contrast between the present day and the imagined 1930, which earlier evoked a mild melancholy, now evokes a more profound sense of loss; it becomes a narrative about the destruction of a community, not merely its dissipation, and about a place changed as much as a river is by being dammed. This strengthens the metaphor of the river as "a river of blood and hearts"; the river is full not only of the blood and hearts of individual miners and their families, but of the heart of the community itself. In turn, this strengthens the idea of the valley as darkness and death, even as it's intimately tied to the good life that was possible on the hillsides and on top of the peaks.

From these specific, unique facets of particular places as revealed in narrative, we can gather several general lessons, or principles, about the importance of place to our pursuit of the good life. First, being constantly surrounded by mountains is an important way to stay focused on how life and death, beauty and depravity, are joined at the hip. Next, although a place can retain identity as it loses some of its elements or constituents, these changes can infect a place with an air of melancholy that's difficult to shake in our ethical engagements. And, third, tradition and habit—especially family and narrative traditions—play at least as strong a role as geography in maintaining the identity of places. They can change this air of melancholy into a trenchant political analysis.

The Memoir as an Aid to Understand Place

In these three short scenes, we see exhibited a vision of the good life where Appalachian places—with their tragic histories and their contrasting mountains and valleys—can help us adjust to the proximity of death to life. McClanahan is far from didactic about it, but this is the type of specific, pointed ethical lesson about the importance for the good life of attending to place that is able to be detached from the plot of the narrative. It's certainly an Aristotelian insight; we cannot get precise rules about how, specifically, life and death ought to be intertwined and exactly which mountains can help us to adjust to it. But it isn't, necessarily, the type of moral insight that one can gain solely from a narrative. One could imagine learning this insight from one's grandfather or from a philosophical essay.

But *Crapalachia* also teaches of the importance of place to the good life in ways that are less easy to detach from the narrative. For instance, let's look again at the scene where Ruby and the narrator cross the New River. As the characters drive through the "old places," memories tied to these places come to Ruby. This is one way in which places gather memories, as Casey says. It is not that these memories were lost to Ruby; perhaps she reflects on them often. But the manner in which they arose at this moment—how she points to the hillside and remembers *those* houses on *that* hill *right there*—requires her presence in the place itself. The place has gathered the memories inside itself, and as Ruby becomes a part of this place again, she shares these memories with the hills and the road. Ruby's narrative about all the old places synthesizes the facts into a whole, which allows Scott, the narrator, to experience it as if it were whole. But her narrative happens as it does, when it does, because she's bodily surrounded by the place. Here we are shown, rather than told, how place is thick with cultural meanings. This scene teaches Casey's lesson in a way in which Casey's philosophical prose cannot replace.

The text also makes clear the way in which tradition maintains a place as the place it is, in spite of the changes to its elements. In this case, the tradition is linguistic, or narrative, as well as familial and cultural. The narrator has never seen this holler as a thriving coal camp, he's never had to worry about the revenuers coming for Elgie's still, he's not familiar with a time when the station at Prince was at the center of a thriving community. Yet, he writes, "I could see the mine. I could see people walking" (91). As the narrator moves himself and his grandmother up the valley, he can see the world she describes. Partly, this is because of the stories that Ruby tells, and we should never underestimate how the power of place as we know it owes much to the strengths of narrative and to our linguistic nature. But being in the place while hearing the stories, knowing that the stories are not just any stories, but memories, and knowing that these memories of this place are part of the life of the family he comes from—all of this is gathered by this place, all of it intertwined in the event that is this place, and all of it is what makes this visualization possible. And, again, watching how this plays out, all these threads gathered together, shows us these lessons in a way that we cannot learn by merely being told these facts outside of a narrative.

Finally, *Crapalachia* gives us a chance to vicariously learn through the life experiences of the characters about how to navigate the decisions we make about place and the good life. The bodily details of the death of AIDS cat and the lack of a correspondent sense of repulsion from Ruby are what give depth and substance to the lesson of that scene. There is more than a simple relating of the fact "she watched a hog eat the cat." Likewise, although we clearly cannot imagine the drive past Prince having the melancholy character that it does apart from Ruby's interpretation of her memories, we also notice that her melancholy interpretation of the scene is partially indebted to the power of the rain and the flooding of the river. The manner in which the melancholy deepens into a more tragic story of the near loss of a place, and the manipulation of the poor by enormous economic forces, as the narrative progresses emphasizes the importance of narrative to our relations to place. The feedback loops between our impressions of a place, our memories of a place, narratives about a place, and the ephemeral details of a place in a given moment are complex, nuanced, and fleeting. Accordingly, our ethical assessment, reaction, and approach must be similarly finely tuned.

As people who care about the places of Appalachia, we know well the power of place. The way in which place is crucial to our lived, embodied experiences of things; the way that place gathers our bodies, memories, creeks, and buildings into a single event; and the way that our embodied perception and the gathering function are saturated by traditional social structures—all of this makes attending to the subtle and intimate details of place, as well as the big picture, crucial for the good life. This is why we are advised to learn about the ridges, soils, and birds of our home places. Cultivating habits of attentiveness to place does not happen without years of personal experience, and even if we are able to begin with general principles, we must continue our pursuit of rightness through this hard experience.

Yet well-written narratives have the ability to offer us a surrogate experience, where we can attend to the relations between place, ethical choice, and the good life, and have the space to meditate on these relations. Attending to narratives can bring to the foreground characteristics of place that remain backgrounded in our daily lives. Accordingly, if we want to better participate in the event we inhabit, our place, we ought to supplement the education we gain from our personal experiences and our role models and mentors with literature. We can learn there things about place that we can learn nowhere else.

NOTES

1. Although Aristotle argues that we should not attempt to be overly specific in laying out principles when discussing ethics, he does offer a general definition of the human good: "activity of the soul in accordance with virtue [or excellence]" (1098a17).

2. The trope of "outside agitator" is, perhaps, the oldest manifestation of the insider-outsider dynamic being exploited by local elites to oppress their neighbors. See Gaventa 161–63 and esp. 236–37.

3. The rest of the essay relies on the specific arguments of Nussbaum regarding novels. I am not allowing other narratives to do the argumentative work that I ascribed to novels above. So I choose the more general term "narrative" here—rather than the specific term "novel"—not as an attempt at sleight of hand. Rather, I simply want to avoid ascribing some metaphysically unique status to novels; there are other narrative mediums that can perform this function. Memoirs, folk tales, family histories, and films are a few examples.

BIBLIOGRAPHY

Aristotle. *Nicomachean Ethics*. Translated by W. D. Ross. In *The Basic Works of Aristotle*, edited by Richard McKeon. New York: Modern Library, 1941.

———. *Physics*. Translated by Richard Hope. Lincoln: University of Nebraska Press, 1961.

———. *Poetics*. Translated by Ingram Bywater. In *The Basic Works of Aristotle*, edited by Richard McKeon. New York: Modern Library, 1941.

Casey, Edward S. "How to Get from Space to Place in a Fairly Short Stretch of Time: Phenomenological Prolegomena." In *Senses of Place*, edited by Steven Feld and Keith H. Basso, 13–52. Santa Fe: School of American Research Press, 1997.

Fisher, Steve, and Barbara Ellen Smith. "Internal Colony—Are You Sure? Defining, Theorizing, Organizing Appalachia." *Journal of Appalachian Studies* 22, no. 1 (2016): 45–50.

Gadamer, Hans-Georg. *Truth and Method*. Translated by Joel Weinsheimer and Donald G. Marshall. New York: Continuum, 2012.

Gaventa, John. *Power and Powerlessness: Quiescence and Rebellion in an Appalachian Valley*. Chicago: University of Illinois Press, 1980.

James, William. *The Principles of Psychology*. http://psychclassics.yorku.ca/James/Principles/prin13.htm.

McClanahan, Scott. *Crapalachia: A Biography of Place*. Columbus, Ohio: Two Dollar Radio, 2013.

Nussbaum, Martha C. *Love's Knowledge*. Oxford: Oxford University Press, 1992.

Walking in Woods
Learning the Lay
of the Land

Mountain Georgics
Appalachia and Everyday Nature

ETHAN MANNON

In the essay that precedes this one, M. Joseph Aloi suggests that literature provides the opportunity to attend to and meditate upon the relations between place, ethics, and the good life. If reading Appalachian literature cultivates one's attention to place and increases the odds that one will find and enjoy the good life (as Aloi says that it does), then I would suggest that much Appalachian literature runs parallel to the georgic mode—a tradition of texts fixated on the notion of place, characterized by humans living and working on the land, and identified by ecocritic Scott Hess as one of the literary discourses that encourages recognition of and investment in "everyday nature" (102, 108). In "Imagining an Everyday Nature," Hess argues that Romantic constructions of the nonhuman world privilege untrammeled, sublime landscapes above the places where we live and where we work.[1] Because a focus on the familiar, common, and even mundane elements of nonhuman nature underscores the importance of the "literature of home, work, and community" (90)—themes embodied by many Appalachian texts—the concept of "everyday nature" builds upon an understanding of place to open the possibility for an ecocritical approach to Appalachian literature. While Hess's work broadens beyond the georgic mode, I focus my attention there because of the striking affinities between georgics and Appalachian literature. Recognizing the confluence of the georgic mode and Appalachian literature undermines much of the travel writing that historically (mis)characterized Appalachia. The idea of Mountain Georgics helps us view the region from within rather than through the eyes of seasonal visitors with metropolitan allegiances and identities. Before exploring the characteristics that a georgic perspective recovers—especially work, dwelling, and home—I begin by introducing the georgic mode via its more familiar counterpart, the pastoral mode.

Just Passing Through
Pastoral(ism) in Appalachia

As ecocritic and scholar of the pastoral mode Terry Gifford explains, the term "pastoral" can refer to "any literature that describes the country" (2). However, a more precise definition traces the mode back to its foundational texts: Theocritus's *Idylls* and especially Virgil's *Eclogues*. Each of these texts frames nature as a space for leisure and for literary creativity. Theocritus's title suggests a relaxed tranquility. And though the setting of the *Eclogues* is nominally agricultural, Virgil's shepherds spend the majority of their time lounging in the shade of beech trees while composing songs and playing lutes. These classics established a tradition of texts that echo this leisurely *otium*. Works that derive from the *Idylls* and the *Eclogues* also tend to replicate the mobility of the shepherd—a figure who glides fluidly across landscapes as he moves his livestock to fresh pasture—but on a larger scale. Rather than functioning as a permanent home, nature in pastoral literature more often provides a temporary retreat. After humans spend time in the purity of the natural world, they become rejuvenated enough to return to their normal lives. Gifford labels this pattern of "retreat and return" as essential to the pastoral literary tradition (1). Thus, when Walt Whitman "lean[s] and loaf[es] at his ease while observing a spear of summer grass" at the beginning of "Song of Myself," he demonstrates a quintessentially pastoral pose: his presence in and observance of the nonhuman world produces an emotional response that he later recollects (in tranquility, if he follows William Wordsworth's famous formula). His recollection becomes, in turn, poetry, but his interaction with the nonhuman world produces, so far as we know, nothing else.

Obviously, Whitman did not carry out his project in the context of Appalachia. However, other writers utilized a pastoral pattern of retreat and return to organize their literary representations of the region or moved back and forth between Appalachia and some other area during their own lives. Regarding the former, Kevin O'Donnell and Helen Hollingsworth's *Seekers of Scenery* carries out a careful examination of the travel writing industry constructed by periodicals like *Harper's* and the *Atlantic Monthly*. I view this body of writing as pastoral because these texts regularly juxtaposed an educated, affluent traveler against the wild, rugged mountains and mountaineers. The traveler would generally visit Appalachia only long enough to note the strangeness of the land and the peculiarity of the people and would then return (often with relief) to more "civilized" places.[2] As an author whose own life followed a pastoral pattern, Mary Noailles Murfree provides an example of the latter tendency. Born in Murfreesboro, Tennessee, in 1850, she spent the majority of each year in the more populated regions around Murfreesboro and Nashville. She also, however, summered in Beersheba Springs—a mountain resort located one hundred miles southeast of Nashville. There she gained the knowledge of mountain culture that enabled her to produce short stories and novels (initially published under the pseudonym Charles Egbert Craddock) for the burgeoning local color market. Though scholars disagree about the degree to which her fiction stereotyped Appalachia,[3] her travel patterns make clear that her relationship to the region was pastoral: the comparative pristineness and purity of Beersheba Springs provided a temporary escape for Murfree—one that prompted creativity and literary production.

In addition to the forms of *literary* pastoralism carried out by those producing travel writing and local color, Appalachia is not without examples of *historical* pastoralism. First, even though the Native American tribes occupying Appalachia did not have domesticated livestock, mobility constituted an essential characteristic of their culture. Much of the Appalachian region served as seasonal hunting grounds (sometimes claimed by multiple tribes), and "Warrior's Path" served as one of the names for the valley between the Blue Ridge Mountains and the Ridge and Valley formation (Williams 36). Environmental historians have also pointed out that the coalescence of poor travel infrastructure and abundant mast crops (acorns, hickory nuts, and especially American chestnuts) prompted the European colonists who settled in the Appalachian Mountains to utilize an agricultural system featuring livestock that could eat such mast (along with corn and other cultivated crops) and then walk their way to distant markets.[4] Though the livestock drovers who moved scores of pigs, cattle, and even turkeys and geese would not bring to mind Virgil's shepherds, the two groups share a common dependence on grazing and mobility—hallmarks of pastoral agriculture and literature. Finally, the onset of industrialization ushered in an era of "shuttle migration" when Appalachians moved back and forth between a distant (often industrial) job and a farm.[5]

These associations between Appalachia and the pastoral mode indicate an awkward relationship. Literature from the travel writing and local color genres has, by and large, come under fire for misrepresenting the region and for creating long-standing myths.[6] Further, the mobility of Native Americans, Appalachian livestock, and the mountaineers themselves did not take place within a pure and pristine nature. The livestock drives were dusty, smelly, and loud affairs; depending on the locale and the historical period the mountaineers might have traveled for seasonal work on farms, in timber camps, or in mines. Thus, even in its quasi-pastoral characteristics Appalachia did not resemble a mythic paradise like Arcadia. Indeed, a fundamental incongruity exists between the hardscrabble, gritty realities of Appalachian life in the nineteenth century on the one hand and the connotations of leisure that characterize the pastoral mode on the other.

The georgic mode, conversely, provides a more accurate description of the relationship between humans and nonhuman nature in Appalachia. As its namesake, Virgil's *Georgics* outlines the key features of the mode. First, the title translates to "earth worker," indicating an important distinction between the pastoral *Eclogues* and the *Georgics* (Conlogue 8). Namely, Virgil's second poem is notably more sweat-soaked. Anthony Low describes this aspect of the poems as the key difference between the modes they established: "pastoral celebrates play and leisure, georgic celebrates work" (4). The tenor of the *Georgics* is also distinct from that of the *Eclogues*. While the agricultural details fade into the background and go unnoticed in the latter, the *Georgics* makes a point of focusing on farming. In fact, some scholars regard the four books of the *Georgics* as treatises on horticulture, viticulture, animal husbandry, and beekeeping (Thibodeau 12). The *Georgics* is thus serious in tone and heaps up didactic detail regarding how to wrest food from the land. Finally, the focus on bodily labor that produces food from the earth means that the *Georgics* emphasizes dwelling rather than mobility. Compared to his pastoral cousin, the georgic farmer is rooted in place—the seasons rotate around him as he cares for fields, vineyards, and orchards that are immobile.

The differences between the pastoral and georgic modes are important in an ecological sense because each mode describes and inculcates a very different relationship between humans and the nonhuman world. As Dana Phillips has argued, an understanding of nature built on pastoral images of unsullied purity operates as mythology and thus is harmful: the "pastoral impulse will surely lead us [ecocritics] astray," warns Phillips (17). Along similar lines, I have argued at length elsewhere that the georgic literary tradition provides a valuable resource to ecocritics because of the way the mode presents a relationship with nature built on dwelling, observation, and work. Georgics insist that the studious farmer knows and appreciates more about the land than the holiday excursionist. In this way, georgic texts offer an environmental ethic for the land that we use: farms, mines, and working forests.[7] Because so much of Appalachia falls into those same categories of land use, and because so many Appalachian texts emphasize land use as part of a well-developed setting, I see a remarkable confluence between Appalachian literature and an ecocriticism cognizant of the georgic literary tradition. In what follows I offer three sketches focused on three themes common in Appalachian literature and that define georgics—agricultural didacticism, the tension between dwelling and displacement, and a commitment to a working relationship with one's homeplace—to illustrate the potential synergy between Appalachian literature, ecocriticism, and the georgic literary tradition.

Georgic Didacticism
The Details of a Mountain Farm

The publication of *Man with a Bull-Tongue Plow* in 1934 raised Kentucky poet Jesse Stuart to a place of national prominence. The collection of 703 irregular sonnets required a second printing within a month of its publication, eventually sold more than 10,000 copies, and led to Stuart's nomination for a Pulitzer Prize in poetry (Green 11). However, this wave of interest and acclaim did not translate to lasting national renown for Stuart. Though he continued to publish poetry (as well as fiction and nonfiction) throughout his life, one of his great regrets was that none of his work ever appeared in an anthology of poetry. In a 1961 letter to Robert Nathan, Stuart laments that even though he had published more than 1,600 poems, he "never made one of the big American Anthologies" (qtd. in Daughaday 42).[8] As Charles H. Daughaday explains, the form and aesthetics of Stuart's sonnets left him out of step with those writers who have come to represent American modernist poetry. Allen Tate and John Crowe Ransom—the driving forces behind New Criticism and editors of many of the American anthologies of poetry—simply ignored Stuart's verses.[9] And even after the New Criticism became old news and Appalachian studies gained legitimacy as a field, Stuart's poetry remained unheralded. Chris Green suggests that no revival of Stuart's poetry took place because his work, including *Man with a Bull-Tongue Plow*, affirmed Appalachian stereotypes in a way that Appalachian studies scholars, working several decades after the volume's publication, found objectionable. Because he presented the people of his region as racially homogenous, hardworking but illiterate, and often violent, Stuart gave scholars working in Appalachian studies "someone against whom to define themselves" (Green 97).

The objections of the New Critics and of Appalachian studies scholars bear up. Stuart's sonnets are coarse and haphazard and occasionally traffic in caricatures of mountain people. However, *Man with a Bull-Tongue Plow* also articulates a remarkable attention to detail. Stuart's subjects don't merely "observe" "grass": they plant, mow, or plow up timothy, clover, and wheat. In its attention to specificities, Stuart's volume describes the way that agricultural labor generates intense local knowledge—a vision that places Stuart within a succession of georgic poets.

Labor is by far the most popular theme in *Man with a Bull-Tongue Plow*, and much of that work involves the ground—turning the soil, as well as the labor of planting, hoeing, and harvesting crops. Stuart's speaker revels in all this work, but plowing occupies pride of place: "I plow the earth around my mountain shack," says the speaker of "156," "I work from dawn until the setting sun" (5, 8). Stuart celebrates the "hill-man" who knows only "work and work" ("52"; 2) and in sonnet "96" offers an image of the pride that comes from competent work. Speaking as Johnson Hailstrap, Stuart writes,

> I am a farmer and my cutter plow
> Makes furrows round the steep Kentucky hill;
> I make my living by sweat from my brow.
> . . .
> In Spring these hands go forth to sow the seeds,
> Through summer days they cultivate its needs.
> In autumn they go out and garner crops—
> These hands were made for work—they never stop
> From time they plant until they gather crop.
> I am a farmer and I love the plow.
> I make my bread by hot sweat on my brow. (1–3, 8–14)

In this and other sonnets, work forges a bond between the plowman, his tools, and, most important, the land. Working the soil leads to a deep knowledge of and intimacy with one's place.

Stuart demonstrates a farmer's local knowledge by infusing his poetry with seasonal information about farming. In fact, sonnet "204" functions as a kind of crash course on the crops and seasons of farming in Kentucky. Stuart's speaker explains that burley tobacco grows in "golden clay" and should be set out during an April rain once bloodroot has "donned white flowers" (1, 14). Corn follows three years of tobacco and should be planted "round the tenth of May" (12). Finally, oats and orchard grass complete the rotation of crops and should be sown "on thinner lands" "when the beech / Buds swell" (5, 11–12). Folded within this sonnet, a reader finds three kinds of folk knowledge. First, notice that Stuart outlines a crop-rotation regimen: corn follows three years of tobacco, and oats and orchard grass follow corn. Second, the sonnet indicates the annual timing for planting each specific crop. And finally, that annual timing is linked to the calendar—"round the tenth of May"; or "April"—but also to signals that will vary from year to year. Because Stuart preserves the wisdom of "old men" who plant according to local signs like the swelling buds on the branches of beech trees and the blooming of bloodroot, his sonnet archives place-specific knowledge.

In sonnet "204" Stuart also recommends practices that we might refer to today as sustainable agriculture and that were outlined by Virgil more than nineteen hundred years before either Stuart's poetry or the sustainability movement. On the one hand, Stuart's poem seems to assume the gradual decline of land: the "thinner" land suitable for oats and grass likely results from the erosion that occurred during three years of tobacco cultivation and then one or more crops of corn. On the other hand, Stuart's speaker instructs farmers to build fertility. On land "poor as a snake where pine trees grow," Stuart directs farmers to grow cowpeas (a legume) for grazing livestock since "Fodder stalks and cattle dung is better / Than all this fancy fertilizer you buy" ("253"; 1, 10–11). Such treatment restores depleted cropland to good tilth—"every year it will keep getting better" (8). Remarkably, Virgil included much of the same practical knowledge in the *Georgics*. Beginning with line 71 of the *First Georgic*, he recommends crop rotation—"sow yellow corn in lands whence you have first carried off the pulse that rejoices in its quivering pods"—because "by changing the crops the toil [of the soil] is light." Understanding the results (if not the scientific process) of sowing legumes that will fix atmospheric nitrogen in the soil thus represents a clear point of contact between Stuart's poetry and Virgil's *Georgics*.

The plowman's attention to the demands of his locale makes the timing of the seasons central in *Man with a Bull-Tongue Plow* but also distances Stuart from his own historical moment. Stuart's celebration of an agrarian existence requires a backward glance: "Stuart looks back at a golden age in which man was in harmony with the earth and wishes that this were so today" (LeMaster 35). Such nostalgia left Stuart's poems out of step with contemporary tastes—a fact he calls attention to with the first sonnet in the volume: "I do not sing the songs you love to hear; / My basket songs are woven from the words / Of corn and crickets, trees and men and birds" (5–7). Indeed, the themes of his "rugged" songs distance Stuart from many of his better-known American contemporaries—Wallace Stevens and T. S. Eliot, for example—and instead place him within an international tradition of georgic poetry that celebrates plowing and the land ("337"; line 14).

Perhaps because of the affinities between furrows and lines, fields and stanzas, the plow has attracted a long lineage of poets. In the *Georgics*—a veritable encomium of the plow—cultivating the soil enables a man to demonstrate his mastery over nature but also familiarizes him with his local terrain. The sense of place that plowing facilitates in the *Georgics* resonates in the eighteenth-century British "topographic" poetry of James Thomson and Oliver Goldsmith, among others.[10] In *Piers Ploughman*, the association between Piers (the character) and Christ suggests that William Langland wanted to emphasize the connection between agricultural labor and virtue. Finally, in "To a Mouse" Robert Burns implicitly argues for his own goodness. Only an empathetic person would be "truly sorry" that "Man's dominion / Has broken Nature's social union" (5–6). Thus, when Stuart invokes the plow as the facilitator of an intimate connection between person and place, he steps into a succession of poets who similarly suggested that working the land and coming to know a place inculcates morality and goodness.[11]

Georgic Displacement
Socioeconomic Class in the Appalachians

Writers of pastoral literature generally code human movement in positive terms. Those who travel to distant places and lounge in the restorative lap of Mother Nature enjoy such physical mobility as one of the many blessings that accompanies affluence. In short, a strong correlation exists between wealth and a "pastoral," upper-class life characterized by travel and leisure. Excursions to Appalachia by well-to-do outsiders have impacted the region's economy—both past and present. Asheville, North Carolina, for example, began as a retreat for wealthy Tidewater residents eager to escape the heat and malaria of lower elevations (Williams 132). The experiences of plantation owners and aristocrats had, of course, little in common with the lives of Appalachia's year-round inhabitants. Though the lives of the latter were not without movement, their limited resources meant that relocation was often the result of desperation rather than recreation. Reading Appalachian literature in the context of the georgic mode highlights the way that *displacement* often describes movement by Appalachians. Two iconic Appalachian novels—James Still's *River of Earth* (1940) and Harriette Arnow's *The Dollmaker* (1954)—feature Appalachian women with strong desires to put down georgic roots but who suffer displacement instead.

Set in Eastern Kentucky during the early decades of the twentieth century, Still's *River of Earth* captures the difficulty created as a subsistence farming culture gives ground to industrial mining and wage earning. The family at the center of the novel, the Baldridges, is pulled in two directions. The father, Brack, feels that he has no talent for farming and instead "was born to dig coal" (241). His constant pursuit of mining work means that the family lives in a series of mining towns: "Blue Diamond . . . Chavies, Tribbey, Butterfly Two, Elkhorn, and Lackey . . . Hardburly twice, and . . . Blackjack beyond counting" (179). His wife, Alpha, wants the opposite of this constant relocation. At multiple points in the novel she petitions Brack to stop chasing mine work. She argues that the mining towns are dirty, crowded, and dangerous, but she also stresses the positive aspects of having a settled home in the rural countryside: "Forever moving yon and back, setting down nowhere for good and all, searching for God knows what," she said. "Where air we expecting to draw up to?" Her eyes dampened. "Forever I've wanted to set us down in a lone spot, a place certain and enduring, with room to swing arm and elbow, a garden-piece for fresh victuals, and a cow to furnish milk for the baby. So many places we've lived—the far side of one mine camp and next the slag pile of another.... I'm longing to set me down shorely and raise my chaps proper" (51–52). In the final third of the novel, Alpha delivers a ringing endorsement of the place outside the coal camp where the family currently lives: "I'm a-mind to stay on here," she says, "It's the nighest heaven I've been on this earth" (176). Those familiar with Still's novel know that Alpha's agrarian desires never materialize. The novel concludes with the family about to sell their meager belongings and travel to a distant mine where there are rumors of work. Brack announces, "We've got to begin over again. We've got to start from scratch" (241).

In the novel's attention to the land, *River of Earth* aligns with the georgic literary tradition. First, the novel persistently links soil with sustenance. Alpha's mother (with whom the narrator spends the middle third of the novel) symbolizes the established life of subsistence farming being undermined by the coal industry. Because she believes in living "on the land, growing [one's] own victuals, raising sheep and cattle, beholden to nobody," her wish for her daughter's husband is that he "settle some place and grow roots" (130). Along with Alpha's gardening and homesteading, Uncle Jolly (Alpha's brother) also contributes to the novel's treatment of farming and food production as "certain and enduring." He chooses, at the end of the novel, to marry and imagines a future involving "a young mule, new ground cleared ... Bees to work my red apple trees, grapevines" (242). Alpha and her mother and brother, then, see the land of Appalachia as the perennial source of life rather than a short-term escape from it or as a store of mineral resources worth cash. The land's vulnerability further compounds the georgic resonance of the novel. Rather than investing in pastoral projections of untouched natural beauty, *River of Earth* documents the realities of a lived environment. This involves the pleasantries of deep woods and ferns as well as the satisfactions of farming labor but also the recognition of degradation. Near the coal camp, the narrator describes the creek: "The waters ran yellow, draining acid from the mines, cankering rocks in its bed. The rocks were snuffy brown, eaten and crumbly. There were no fishes swimming the eddies" (189). Here, Still's prose describes the consequences of careless land use; as in the georgic literary tradition, the land is a potential source of sustenance and livelihood, but misuse diminishes that potential.

Harriette Arnow's *The Dollmaker* echoes both the land's fragility and the human displacement that characterize *River of Earth*. Regarding the latter, Arnow's novel chronicles the outmigration from Appalachia during the World War II era; however, the first fifth of the novel nevertheless makes clear the importance of place to protagonist Gertie Nevels. Before she moves with her family (a husband, Clovis, and five children) to Detroit, Gertie bursts off the early pages of the novel as an earth worker as competent at raising food and at homemaking in general as Alpha Baldridge. Readers see Gertie splitting wood and digging potatoes and learn that her life's goal has been to own land of her own. She and her family have endured "the chaos of yearly moving" during a fifteen-year period of sharecropping on marginal land (54). Despite such hardship, Gertie managed to save enough money to buy a vacant farm that she imagines as "a little piece of heaven right here on earth" (71). Thus, the Nevels' perennial relocating pulls against Gertie's strong desire for a settled home much like Brack's pursuit of mining work frustrated Alpha's wishes for permanence in *River of Earth*. In fact, both women equate home and stasis with heaven on earth. Like *River of Earth*, Arnow's novel expresses a concern for the fragility of the land. While inspecting the farm she plans to buy, Gertie discovers a deep gully in an overgrown orchard. Because the "red wound in the hillside" is "stealing the earth," Gertie fills it with fallen limbs and brush that will "hold back a little dirt, an keep this hillside from bleeden to death" (47).

The Dollmaker and *River of Earth*, then, demonstrate a mindfulness of land use and misuse; the volumes validate dwelling and subsistence, but also recognize in the fragility of the land the potential for diminishment. These features indicate that Virgil's *Georgics* operates as a precursor text—not an *influence* on either Still or Arnow, but a work with which both authors' novels reach a *confluence*. Virgil's volume, too, celebrates living in place and mourns its inverse: the displacement (from the effects of war, mentioned in the *First Georgic*, lines 505–8) that precludes dwelling. The *Georgics* also recognizes the vulnerability of the land and warns against plowing fields that would be eroded by strong winds (I. 61–62). Recognizing the georgic characteristics of *River of Earth* and *The Dollmaker* links them with not only Virgil's second poem but also other texts in the georgic literary tradition. Such an association broadens the relevance of both *River of Earth* and *The Dollmaker*. Though these volumes are well-known as Appalachian masterpieces, they are little known beyond the region or outside the field of Appalachian studies.[12] My argument here is that the environmental conundrum the novels outline—the tension between cultivating a settled home and displacement—should be of interest to ecocritics. These novels illuminate working-class displacement as the dark side of the mobility that so characterizes modern society. That mobility, reinforced and in part created by the pastoral mode, pulls against a georgic valuing of place.

Georgic Homecoming
Rerooting in Appalachia

Gurney Norman's *Divine Right's Trip* (1972) and Thomas Rain Crowe's *Zoro's Field* (2005) urge an Appalachian homecoming that reverses the displacement within and beyond Appalachia articulated by Still and Arnow, respectively. Both Norman and Crowe point to agricultural work as integral to resettling Appalachia and returning home. As such, their literary projects sound calls with clear georgic undertones.

Though the protagonist of Norman's novel—known variously as David Ray, D. R., and Divine Right—pursues enlightenment and self-actualization through a postmodern, beatific, cross-country adventure, by the end of the novel he wants a homegrown life. When he returns to Trace Fork, Kentucky, to care for an ill uncle, D. R. finds that the landscape he encountered during the weekends of his childhood has been thoroughly degraded. Writing to a friend, D. R. describes the way that all the surrounding hills "were strip-mined a couple of years ago. I mean, man, they've been destroyed. Bulldozers pushed the tops of the mountains into the valleys so they could scoop the coal up with machines. About eighty per cent of my grandfather's farm here is under mud now, and out behind the house there's this incredible big mound of mud, this big wall of it, about fifteen feet high, waiting on a rain to loosen it enough to flow right on through this very kitchen" (254). Despite the precariousness of such a situation, D. R. chooses to remain on his family's land after his uncle dies. Further, D. R. decides to carry forward his uncle's project to redeem the land and rebuild its fertility, or, as D. R. calls the older man's plan, "my uncle's crazy scheme to save the world with rabbit shit" (255). Though readers never see D. R. reading Virgil, the younger man's plan to continue using rabbit manure and worms to create new topsoil atop the overburden left behind by mining carries out the poet's imperative to "feed fat the dried-out soil with rich dung" (I. 79–81). D. R. even imagines what it would mean to scale up his uncle's efforts, to "have a thousand hutches, one standing on every five square yards of that old ruined mountain, shitting pure worm food onto the ground, creating perfect lettuce beds and comfrey stands, and alfalfa fields galore" (281).

Along with its maniacal focus on manure, D. R.'s enterprise replicates the georgic focus on place and labor. First, his return to Trace Fork answers a very real need identified by the community news writer. In one edition of "The Trace Fork News" included in the novel, Barry Berry explains that "we need all of our young people to come back home to live" (252).[13] D. R.'s return to Trace Fork reverses the trend of people moving out from this place, "one by one, 'til they wasn't a soul living up there except Emmit [D. R.'s uncle]" (259). Thus, *Divine Right's Trip* echoes the georgic mode's emphasis on harmony between people and place over the course of generations. But even after D. R. takes up residence on family land, he must learn to labor in order to fully return and become an integral component of the place and the community. By regularly showing D. R. at work in Kentucky, Norman maps his protagonist's transformation. Shortly after his return, D. R. helps dig his uncle's grave, and must then take on responsibility for the needs of the deceased man's livestock. D. R. performs this work well enough, but his breakthrough comes while helping a neighbor construct a pig pen. Left alone to dig the post holes, D. R. is sorely tempted to abandon his work:

> D. R. wanted to quit. It wasn't his body that wanted to quit.... It was something else, some longing, some invitation from somewhere deep inside him to lay down the tools and just arbitrarily quit.
> Not stop to rest....
> But quit.
> For the day.
> Just stop right there where he was, ten inches deep into the seventh hole, and go down to the store and hang around awhile, or else go on back up to the homeplace for the afternoon.
> It was like some kind of sour bile swimming through his head.
>
> (269–70)

D. R. perseveres and learns the georgic satisfaction that comes from a job completed.[14] Later, the novel mentions a different day of work that "tired his body in that satisfying way he'd come to relish the last few days" (282). D. R.'s attitude toward labor has transformed: it remains physically taxing but is no longer mentally exhausting drudgery. He recognizes that labor is productive and fulfilling.

Thomas Rain Crowe, too, relishes the joy of rest from labor and also stresses the need for a georgic homecoming. In the early pages of *Zoro's Field*,

Crowe explains that his annual pattern for almost four years has balanced *labor* and *otium*. In fact, he describes his project as an endeavor to engage "the intellect... alongside the forearm" (23). The balance he seeks requires mindfulness of the seasons. "March through November," Crowe fills his days with georgic tasks: "Laboring with and in the earth. Sowing seeds.... Harvesting and laying by food for the winter. This is the work of living" (4). His winter activities—"reading, writing, pondering... exploring the wild world of image, symbol, and metaphor"—complement the bodily work that occupied him during the other seasons (5). With the writing he undertakes during December, January, and February, Crowe stresses dwelling and criticizes transience and mobility. He explains that his "ideology is based on the premise of living in one place for a long time and knowing that place well," which means that *Zoro's Field* breaks with the pastoral pattern of retreat and return (4). Christopher Camuto, in his foreword to the volume, makes this point clear when he distinguishes Crowe from "some hit-and-run city slicker or media celeb slumming in the country" (xiv).

Though his annual routine may sound bare, Crowe makes clear that his period of plain living in western North Carolina is sustaining and sustainable. He has no plans to abandon his lifestyle. Rather, he finds rhythm in his work and speaks back to another North Carolina writer who famously said *You Can't Go Home Again*.[15] Crowe, conversely, encourages readers to return, permanently, to rural spaces: "you *must* go home again" (119).

Coda
Appalachian Georgic Mutualism

The concept of a mountain home—whether celebrated (by Stuart), sought (by Still and Arnow's protagonists), or reclaimed (by Divine Right and Crowe)—positions Appalachian literature within the georgic mode. Cultivating a homeplace requires work that yields one or many products common to both Appalachian texts and georgics: knowledge, food, fuel, and attachment. In addition, all such work involves the *use* of nature—the conversion of resources into the stuff of life.[16] The georgic literary tradition embraces this inevitability; so, too, have the generations of Appalachian writers who address the realities of living. Neither the georgic mode nor Appalachian literature invests in a mythology of pristine, untrammeled nature. Instead, each discourse implicitly acknowledges that venerating some land as *sacred* denigrates the remainder and dooms it, in many cases, to *desecration*. Stated another way, the protection of some places situates those acres atop a hierarchy of land designations and also inevitably creates a bottom tier: lands not especially pristine or remarkable that are made more susceptible to degradation because they are not labelled special. In short, the preservation of wilderness in Yosemite National Park (or anywhere else) is part of a larger ideology that allows mountaintop removal in Appalachian coal country.[17]

What, then, are the implications of the interests shared between Appalachian literature and the georgic mode? The work of acknowledging and articulating that kinship would, I think, raise the profile of Appalachian literature and of georgic scholarship. First, "Appalachian" is too often applied as a modifier that dismisses texts and authors as merely regional. Approaching those same texts via the georgic mode (or as examples of post-pastoral literature, as Savannah Paige Murray does in the essay following this one) would amplify their significance. Developing the category of Appalachian georgics would signal the national and international ties of this literature and would invite attention from a broader audience. Ecocritics, in particular, should consider the history of land use and the folk ecology contained in Appalachian literature. Appalachian writers record and construct a vision of human life lived at the intersection of nature and culture—a practice also valued by ecocriticism. In the same way, the georgic mode, when not overshadowed by the pastoral, is often perceived as an archaic literary tradition—a dead mode of writing without contemporary relevance. Appalachian writing makes clear that place and labor remain primary concerns. Such texts, then, represent an active vein of georgic discourse. Taken together, the georgic mode and Appalachian literature strengthen each tradition's claims regarding one of the necessities of life: the ability to cultivate a sense of place through embodied work in the nonhuman world.

NOTES

1. Hess's article takes up and advances the work of two environmental historians: William Cronon's "The Trouble with Wilderness" and Richard White's "'Are you an Environmentalist or Do You Work for a Living?'" Both scholars note that wilderness apologists and environmentalists more broadly construct false dichotomies that venerate some landscapes and some human interactions with the nonhuman world while ignoring or condemning others. Complete bibliographic information for these and other sources can be found at the end of this essay.

2. I allude to a famous example of travel writing about Appalachia: Harney's "A Strange Land and a Peculiar People," published in an 1873 issue of *Lippincott's*.

3. See Pryse's article.

4. Wilma Dykeman's chapter on the livestock drives in *The French Broad* provides excellent detail. On the importance of chestnuts to Appalachia's economy, see Donald E. Davis, "A Whole World Dying."

5. On shuttle migration, see Phillip J. Obermiller and Jack Temple Kirby.

6. On the creation of a mythic Appalachia, see Shapiro's seminal volume.

7. See "Georgic Environmentalism" in *ISLE* 23, no. 2, 346–48 and 356–60.

8. The letter Daughaday quotes is part of Murray State University's Special Collection of Stuart papers located in the Pogue Library.

9. See Ruel E. Foster's letter to Stuart dated January 21, 1961, discussed in Daughaday's essay, 41.

10. See Vespa 18–22.

11. Thomas Jefferson's famous formulation in *Notes on the State of Virginia* expresses a similar sentiment: "Those who labour in the earth are the chosen people of God . . . whose breasts he has made his peculiar deposit for substantial and genuine virtue" (172).

12. For a fuller discussion of *The Dollmaker*, its georgic resonances, and the ways it transcends region, see my "Precluded Dwelling: *The Dollmaker* and *Under the Feet of Jesus* as Georgics of Displacement" in *Journal of French and Francophone Philosophy*.

13. Virgil also laments a depopulated landscape. At the end of Book I, he refers to land being "robbed of the tillers" and lying in "waste" because of battles elsewhere.

14. In an article involving the georgic mode, Thomas L. Altherr explains that "the farmer must work hard and rejoice in weariness as a worthwhile recompense" (110).

15. See the posthumous 1940 novel of the same title by Thomas Wolfe.

16. See Timothy Sweet's *American Georgics* for additional ideas on the economic dimension of the georgic.

17. Let me be clear: I am not opposed to the preservation of wilderness; my point is that our environmental protections are too all-or-nothing be able to safeguard from despoliation the land that we use. We need wilderness *and* everyday nature, now and in the future.

BIBLIOGRAPHY

Altherr, Thomas L. "'The Country We Have Married': Wendell Berry and the Georgic Tradition of Agriculture." *Southern Studies* 1, no. 2 (1990): 105–15.

Arnow, Harriette. *The Dollmaker*. New York: Macmillan, 1954.

Conlogue, William. *Working the Garden: American Writers and the Industrialization of Agriculture*. Chapel Hill: University of North Carolina Press, 2001.

Cronon, William. "The Trouble with Wilderness; or, Getting Back to the Wrong Nature." In *Uncommon Ground: Rethinking the Human Place in Nature*, edited by William Cronon, 69–90. New York: Norton, 1996.

Crowe, Thomas Rain. *Zoro's Field: My Life in the Appalachian Woods*. Athens: University of Georgia Press, 2005.

Daughaday, Charles H. "The Changing Poetic Canon: The Case of Jesse Stuart and Ezra Pound." In *An American Vein: Critical Readings in Appalachian Literature*, edited by Danny Miller, Sharon Hatfield, and Gurney Norman, 35–48. Athens: Ohio University Press, 2005.

Davis, Donald E. "A Whole World Dying." In *Homeplace Geography: Essays for Appalachia*, 177–84. Macon, Ga.: Mercer University Press, 2006.

Dykeman, Wilma. "The Great Drives." In *The French Broad*, 137–51. New York: Henry Holt, 1955.

Gifford, Terry. *Pastoral*. London: Routledge, 1999.

Green, Chris. *The Social Life of Poetry: Appalachia, Race, and Radical Modernism*. London: Palgrave Macmillan, 2009.
Harney, Will Wallace. "A Strange Land and a Peculiar People." *Lippincott's Magazine of Popular Literature and Science* 12, no. 31 (1873): 429–38.
Hess, Scott. "Imagining an Everyday Nature." *Interdisciplinary Studies in Literature and Environment* 17, no. 1 (2010): 85–112.
Jefferson, Thomas. *Notes on the State of Virginia*. 1785. Boston: Lilly & Wait, 1832.
Kirby, Jack Temple. "The Southern Exodus, 1910–1960: A Primer for Historians." *Journal of Southern History* 49 (1983): 585–600.
LeMaster, J. R. "Jesse Stuart's Poetry as Fugitive-Agrarian Synthesis." In *Jesse Stuart: Essays on His Work*, edited by J. R. LeMaster and Mary Washington Clarke, 19–39. Lexington: University Press of Kentucky, 1977.
Low, Anthony. *The Georgic Revolution*. Princeton, N.J.: Princeton University Press, 1985.
Mannon, Ethan. "Georgic Environmentalism in *North of Boston*: An Ethic for Economic Landscapes." *Interdisciplinary Studies in Literature and Environment* 23, no. 2 (2016): 344–69.
———. "Precluded Dwelling: *The Dollmaker* and *Under the Feet of Jesus* as Georgics of Displacement." *Journal of French and Francophone Philosophy* 25, no. 1 (2017): 86–104.
Norman, Gurney. *Divine Right's Trip: A Folk Tale*. New York: Bantam, 1972.
Obermiller, Phillip J. "Migration." In *High Mountains Rising: Appalachia in Time and Place*, edited by Richard A. Straw and H. Tyler Blethen, 88–100. Champaign: University of Illinois Press, 2004.
O'Donnell, Kevin, and Helen Hollingsworth. *Seekers of Scenery: Travel Writing from Southern Appalachia, 1840–1900*. Knoxville: University of Tennessee Press, 2004.
Phillips, Dana. *The Truth of Ecology: Nature, Culture, and Literature in America*. Oxford: Oxford University Press, 2003.
Pryse, Marjorie. "Exploring Contact: Regionalism and the 'Outsider' Standpoint in Mary Noailles Murfree's Appalachia." *Legacy* 17, no. 2 (2000): 199–212.
Shapiro, Henry D. *Appalachia on Our Mind: The Southern Mountains and Mountaineers in the American Consciousness, 1870–1920*. 1978. Chapel Hill: University of North Carolina Press, 1986.
Still, James. *River of Earth*. 1940. Lexington: University Press of Kentucky, 1978.
Stuart, Jesse. *Man with a Bull-Tongue Plow*. Boston: E.P. Dutton, 1934.
Sweet, Timothy. *American Georgics: Economy and Environment in Early American Literature*. Philadelphia: University of Pennsylvania Press, 2002.
Thibodeau, Philip. *Playing the Farmer: Representations of Rural Life in Vergil's Georgics*. Berkeley: University of California Press, 2011.
Vespa, Jack. "Georgic Inquisitiveness, Pastoral Meditation, Romantic Reflexivity: 'Nutting' and the Figure of Wordsworth as Poet." *Genre* 38, no. 1–2 (2005): 1–44.
Virgil. *Eclogues, Georgic. Aeneid I–VI*. Translated by H. Rushton Fairclough. Revised by G. P. Goold. Cambridge, Mass.: Harvard University Press, 1999.
White, Richard. "'Are You an Environmentalist or Do You Work for a Living?': Work and Nature." In *Uncommon Ground: Rethinking the Human Place in Nature*, edited by William Cronon, 171–85. New York: Norton, 2006.
Williams, John Alexander. *Appalachia: A History*. Chapel Hill: University of North Carolina Press, 2002.

"The Grit of the Land Was in Them"
A Post-pastoral Reading of John Ehle's
The Land Breakers

SAVANNAH PAIGE MURRAY

    For John Ehle's novels, chronicling the lives of the King and Wright families in Appalachian North Carolina, "the main character in these seven mountain novels is the mountains themselves" (Ehle, "Near and Distant Kin" 4). Ehle writes of the North Carolina mountains, "I was born under them, they cupped me as a boy, have shaded my own life, they've lorded it over me, and in my novels they lord it over my people. Their streams are the region's blood, their winds are deep breaths" (4). The interconnectedness between mountains and mountaineers in Ehle's fiction, particularly his novel *The Land Breakers*, set in the Appalachian backwoods of the late eighteenth century, makes the text a prime candidate for ecocriticism. Ecocriticism, or "the study of the relationship between literature and the physical environment" (Glotfelty and Fromm xviii), is a large and growing field, containing many schools of thought useful to investigate various themes in Appalachian literature, including ecofeminism, environmental justice, and animal studies. However, the post-pastoral offers a particularly valuable theoretical model for the examination of place in Appalachian literature and Ehle's 2014 exploration of eighteenth-century Appalachian life, *The Land Breakers*, in particular.

    The post-pastoral, as defined by ecocritic and John Muir scholar Terry Gifford, is "a cultural practice that seeks to reconnect our species and its home, reconnects our practical literary activities to help us represent John Muir's notion of a right relationship with nature that is hopefully not utopian in the idealized sense" (*Reconnecting with John Muir* 13–14). Post-pastoral texts can perhaps change the way human culture understands and interacts with the environment, inspiring increased environmental awareness and conservation that hopefully "reconnects" us with the earth. In *Reconnect-*

ing with John Muir: Essays in Post-pastoral Practice, Gifford suggests that post-pastoral texts pose six general questions for readers:

1. "Can awe in the face of natural phenomena, such as landscapes, lead to humility in our species?" (31)
2. "What are the implications of recognizing that we [as humans] are part of that creative-destructive process" that dominates the entire universe? (32)
3. "If the processes of inner nature echo those of outer nature in the ebbs and flows of growth and decay, how can we learn to understand the inner by being closer to the outer?" (32)
4. "If nature is culture, is culture nature?" (34)
5. "How... can our distinctively human consciousness, which gives us a conscience, be used as a tool to heal our troubled relationship with our natural home?" (34)
6. "How should we address the issue that the exploitation of our planet emerges from the same mind-set as our exploitation of each other?" (35)

These post-pastoral questions are particularly useful for ecocritics because they offer a flexible, instructive framework through which scholars can identify essential elements of post-pastoral texts. Scholars can use the post-pastoral as a way to understand the ways in which the natural landscape can call into being a moral response and the ways in which our cultural ideas impact how we attend to the natural word. The post-pastoral questions Gifford poses allow for the interrogation of intersectional power dynamics and ethical relations that operate all around us, both within and between nature and humanity. In *The Land Breakers*, the novel reflects post-pastoral theory as characters struggle for survival in the American Mountain South, the aim not only to survive in a landscape but to find a "right relationship" between people and planet, between humans and their natural home. In Ehle's fiction, the ability of his characters to find the "right relationship" with the natural world hinges on their humility, identity, and responsibility.

"The Mountain Wanted the Old Way Still"
Humility and Nature in *The Land Breakers*

Of the 2014 rerelease of Ehle's novel *The Land Breakers* (originally published in 1964), award-winning novelist and nonfiction writer Linda Spalding writes that the text begins "in 1779 with a man and a woman, hungry and young" who have been walking down the spine of the Appalachian Mountains "for two or three years looking for land on which to make a home" (vii). Spalding describes the landscape in which Mooney and Imy find themselves as one capable of evoking the awe and terror inherent in the natural sublime, describing the nearby "mountain covered by trees and clouds and the narrow trails of ancient beasts" (viii). It is a place where "no person has ever made settlement," where nothing lives except "wolves and panthers, and a great, wanton bear" (viii)." Although these circumstances could easily promote fear and bitterness toward the natural world, for Mooney the landscape inspires him to take a humbled approach to the surrounding environment.

As Imy and Mooney make their long journey from a life of indentured servitude in Philadelphia to owning a piece of land of their own in the mountains of western North Carolina, the pair is practicing the ancient pastoral tradition. Ecocritic and pastoral scholar Terry Gifford comments that the "pastoral" is "essentially a discourse of retreat which may ... either simply *escape* from the complexities of the city, the court, the present, 'our manners,' or *explore* them" (*Pastoral* 99). In their retreat from a life of servitude in a bustling city, Imy and Mooney are not only searching for a departure from urban life but also looking for a change in social status so that they can own property. The novel immediately complicates this pastoral narrative in its description of the rugged terrain that Imy and Mooney Wright encounter as they arrive in Morganton, North Carolina. Imy and Mooney "were interested" in the "blue wall" of mountains "rising from the hilly country" that they could see from town because "land was what they wanted, a place for a home" (11). But the pair quickly learns from others in town that "nobody lived up there . . . the wild animals owned it" (11). Mooney's desire to own land nearly overwhelms him when the couple wanders into a general store in Morganton. Perhaps noticing that Imy and Mooney looked road-tired and destitute, the shop owner begins talking with them, discussing the thousand-acre plot of land up in the "blue wall" of mountains to the east of town that he owns and would be willing to sell (11). Imy discloses the value of the couple's life savings to the merchant, and he begins selecting the essential items the couple should purchase in order to survive in the mountains. After gathering a variety of tools and supplies for the Wrights, the shopkeeper "fell into contemplation again; then his fingers folded as his hands came together, and he said quietly, 'For the little money that's left, I'll sell you six hundred forty acres of bottomland'" (15). The narrator says, "The answer burst out of Mooney, who for almost three years of wandering had sought a piece of land" (15). Mooney hurriedly agrees to the deal, leaves the shop with the couple's new wares, and "sought fresh air, relief coming over him, and he sank down on the porch step and began to chuckle and shake his head" (15).

Mooney is beside himself thinking of this new property and keeps repeating the conversation with the merchant in his head: "Good land, the storekeeper had said, river-bottom land" (15). Mooney's reaction to the purchase of his new land reflects the post-pastoral because he is immediately humbled by his new status as a landowner.

On the first night in their new landscape, the couple "lay in each other's arms near the fire and comforted one another, assured one another they had done right in this" (15). The couple's excitement regarding their new landscape transforms into elation as the Wrights reach the summit of their climb. Describing a scene nearly identical to Caspar David Friedrich's painting *Wanderer above the Sea of Fog* (1818), the narrator claims that below Imy and Mooney "was a sea of clouds that covered the lowlands"; they realized they "were above the clouds, above the world of Old Fort and Morganton, and doubtless of Virginia and Pennsylvania, too" (16). The view from the summit evokes the natural sublime in the couple: "They got caught up in exaltation, thinking about that, for it was all pretty as a picture and as fine as they had ever seen; they got to laughing and joking, hurling limbs and rocks down into the lowlands. They got to hugging each other, lost in pleasure to be up here and off to themselves, and they sank to the ground together and sought one another in this new place" (16). The transformative and transfixing natural sublime the pair encounter on the summit carries over into their emotions regarding their new life as they settled in for the night. Imy and Mooney, after experiencing the natural sublime, feel elevated geographically, as well as socially, in their new mountain home. Being high off in the hills, the pair seem to understand themselves as not only better than their previous indentured servitude but also better than those still trapped in the status quo of social hierarchies that dominate the culture of the valleys and lowlands. The Wrights are not alone in their connection of elevation with cultural superiority. Cian Duffy writes in *Landscapes of the Sublime* that mountain summits offered a similar paradigm shift as Europeans "discovered" the alpine sublime. According to Duffy, eighteenth-century travel accounts about mountaineering in the Alps feature a "discourse of ascent," a "discourse which links the physical ascent of mountains to a wide variety of ostensibly unrelated forms of elevation, moral, political, epistemological, etc." (18). This "discourse of ascent" is present as Imy and Mooney suggest that in their new mountain home they had "won out at last" over the "various misfortunes and handicaps of life down there, way off in the lowlands" (16). In these early encounters with their new mountain home, the Wrights have not yet embraced any sort of humbled response to the surrounding landscape.

Illustrating both the promise of the natural sublime and that of the post-pastoral, the story quickly robs its characters of their summit-induced superiority complex. On the night following their mountaintop exhilaration, the landscape that Mooney previously described as "unknown, untampered with, left but lately by the savages" quickly becomes incredibly crowded and unwelcoming (11). As the pair settle down to sleep, the "stock was quiet; the dog was cozy and content" and as the night approaches, "the darkness came on deeper; it seemed to be a deeper darkness than the lowlands knew" (16). The pair awaken with fear as "sharply, quaveringly, came a long cry" and then "another cry came from another way. It was a creature being tortured, sounded like" (16). This "current of cries began, a babble of screeches, screams, calls," and both Imy and Mooney are "wide-eyed with wonder and she with fear, and maybe he with fear, for he had never heard such terror-filled noise before" (16). In this moment, both experience the darker side of the natural sublime, one in which the natural world inspires fear and terror rather than awe and wonder. The "night passed slowly," the Wrights "hoped for dawn and welcomed it" (16). For Imy and Mooney, their first night on their land certainly produced a more fear-induced reaction to the sublime, but eventually that fear turns into humility, as also described in post-pastoral theory.

As dawn arrives, Mooney and Imy emerge from their camp incredibly humbled, providing and confirming the latent hypothesis of the first post-pastoral question, suggesting that the natural world can inspire humility. This fearful night also illustrates what philosopher Emily Brady suggests—"it is possible to recognize the element of humility running through reflections on the sublime in nature, through which we feel insignificant in the face of powers that exceed us" (179). As seen in both Brady's work and the post-pastoral, humility in the face of nature can, in fact, counteract some of the issues surrounding the natural sublime, such as the "discourse of ascent." On the morning after their fitful and terrifying night in the backwoods of eighteenth-century Appalachia, Imy communicates just how terrified she was the previous night, telling Mooney of the beasts from the night before, "I thought for a while they was going to come on in to congregate at our fire. They was none too welcome-sounding" (16). Mooney agrees with Imy about the threats inherent in their new environment, and this understanding, this awe in the face of a natural environment, prompts Mooney to question their entire mission. Mooney, standing beside Imy along the narrow road that would lead the couple back to the nearby settlement, thinks, "They could go on, or they could go back. If they went on into the mountain country, however, they might not find it easy to get out again"

(17). The Wrights are clearly not feeling as self-assured of their place in the world as they were while on the summit.

Nevertheless, at Imy's request the couple travels on, and after a few more days they arrive on their land with a much more complicated conception of the surrounding landscape. On their property the Wrights "could see mountains strewn in all directions, and it was awesome to consider the marvels and dens and torrents of this new country, to feel the loneliness of being here, yet at the same time the right of belonging here" (17). While Mooney may own the land, he an Imy are not the only humans present. Donald E. Davis writes in *Where There Are Mountains* that the Cherokee occupied massive hunting grounds throughout southern Appalachia that they used to hunt and trap furs for sale in the burgeoning North American fur trade (67–69). Not only does Mooney express a view of the landscape infected with his own notion of dominion, but his is also an anthropocentric view at that: "This is the land of the wolf and the bear, the panther, the snake, the eagle high above them, the buzzards following them—or so it had been since they arrived," meaning that now this was the land of man, in particular the land of the Wrights (17). Clearly in these early moments on their own land, Mooney is not experiencing humility.

Unfortunately, it takes losing Imy for Mooney to shed his pompous reaction to the natural world. Mooney's dramatic transformation from one who was exhilarated on a mountaintop to one terrified by the forest's nightly chorus, to recognizing himself as but a mere part of the mountain world and all of its processes, is apparent, and he stands over Imy's hillside grave. Even knowing that "Imy would not want him to be so low, would tell him if she could, to climb out of the hole and stand straight above it," Mooney could not help himself from contemplating all that he had lost, all that mountain had cost him (37). Mooney knows "there would be no more touching her . . . no more seeing her by the fire, no more holding her of a night" (37). As "the dirt was closing over her," Mooney realized he was not above the world around him, that the mountain had a say in his destiny. Humbly, Mooney acknowledges, "the mountain had received them with noisy challenges and now had taken her" (37). In this scene, Mooney affords the natural world much more agency than before, an admission he is capable of only due to his newfound humility, as Mooney realizes, "The mountain had wanted the old way still, and he who changes what is ordered and old and set is a man who grasps the lion's jaw" (37).

Mooney and Imy Wright display the wide range of emotions often associated with the natural sublime. At the realization that they had purchased their own land high in the North Carolina mountains, the pair are immensely excited. As they look out from the mountain summit, they experience the natural sublime's typical feelings of excitement and transcendence. Yet as Mooney is forced to confront Imy's untimely death, he sheds his pride in order to adopt a humbled and cautious approach to the landscape around him. This incorporation of humility into the sublime, as suggested by Emily Brady, involves feeling "insignificant in the face of the powers that exceed us," which can inspire us to be better stewards of the earth and to promote environmental conservation (179). In *The Land Breakers*, the transformation of awe in the face of nature into humility aligns with Gifford's first post-pastoral question. Mooney's humility stems from the awe and fear the landscape provoked and from his understanding that neither he nor his wife could escape the natural world. Mooney's humility in the face of the mountain world and his understanding of the interconnectedness of the ecosystem and all its inhabitants illustrate the novel's interaction with the first and second post-pastoral questions in terms of how the natural landscape can inspire humility in human beings and how interacting with the landscape prompts individuals to question the ethical ramifications of realizing they are intimately connected to the natural processes of the earth. Mooney's insight functions to make him a better steward of the earth, setting him on the path to finding a "right relationship" with the natural world.

"The Grit of the Land Was in Them"
"Everyday Nature" in *The Land Breakers*

The inner workings of the human mind and soul are shaped by the outer workings of the natural world, and coming to understand one helps us understand the other. Nature writer Barry Lopez, in "Landscape and Narrative," describes two landscapes—"one outside the self, the other within" (64). For Lopez, "the external landscape is the one we see" and the second, interior landscape is "a kind of projection within a person of a part of the exterior landscape" (64, 65). These two landscapes interact and inform one another: "The interior landscape responds to the character and subtlety of an exterior landscape; the shape of the individual mind is affected by land as it is by genes" (65). This depiction of an interior and exterior landscape ties directly to Terry Gifford's third post-pastoral question: "If the processes of inner nature echo those of outer nature in the ebbs and flows of growth and decay, how can we learn to understand the inner by being closer to the outer?" (*Reconnecting* 32). For both Muir and Lopez, studying and appreciating the external natural world can influence our sense of ourselves. The same sort of experiential environmental awareness and its role in connecting to one's emotional state is present in Ehle's *The Land Breakers*, as Mooney Wright grieves for his deceased wife Imy.

The narrator describes the connection between Mooney's inner nature and the outer nature of the environment around him in the blizzard that follows Imy's untimely death. As Mooney sits alone in his cabin, trapped inside with his livestock for fear of the rapidly accumulating snow outside, "his mind turned on the thoughts of what he was to do, and of the past, coming like mountain mist in morning, leading to this place, to this room where he huddled with animals in winter.... Half of me is in the ground, he thought" (43). As the storm rages outside, Mooney's own inner thoughts are just as turbulent—blaming himself for leading Imy "to this place" where she suddenly died. Even after the snow ceases to fall, Mooney's inner emotions echo those of the surrounding world. Mooney "took long walks along the riverbank and saw where the cold water from mountain springs washed down, making indentations in the ice before losing itself underneath. High above, the mountains were white; the world was white and without meaning to him" (43). For Mooney, life is devoid of color and meaning not simply because of the winter storm but because of his grief.

Gradually, as the seasons change, so does Mooney. He begins to contemplate what he will do without Imy, allowing the gravity of her death to sink in, but also allowing himself to plan ahead for a future without her. As winter starts to thaw, Mooney wanders outside, breathing in "the coldness and the tingling freshness of the pine sap. The air was clean and alive with frozen soundlessness and cleanliness, and it pained his chest to breathe the air for long. He crept back to his fireplace and ... waited for a thought, some idea of what to do" (43). Mooney's willingness to breathe the mountain air, the element of the natural world he was so convinced had been the cause of Imy's death, is astonishing. He no longer blames the smoke-filled air for killing his spouse but instead allows himself to experience the atmosphere, breathing it in and finding it clean. And just as Mooney finds the air painful to breathe "for long," he is also beginning to deal with the pain and grief caused by his wife's death. By hoping to generate "some idea of what to do," the narrative illustrates that although still grieving and still in pain, Mooney has not given up on his own life in the Appalachian woods.

Spring affords new life and growth to the landscape surrounding Mooney's cabin. One morning, Mooney "awoke to hear a thousand birds, all sorts of birds ... he went outdoors, pushing his long brown hair back from his bearded face, and saw great flocks of robins and bluebirds" (44). Mooney experiences "a profusion of life awakening" as "alders came to budding life," "the tops of maple trees put out red blooms," "azure butterflies darted about," "tiger beetles haunted the trails," and "lizards moved in frightening dashes" (44). Mooney is not immune to this seasonal renewal, but instead "he would come into the clearing and stare about and listen to the noises, not echoing noises, not fearful either at this season, but vibrant lively sounds, which were out of sorts with his own distraught temper" (44). But as "the sweep of spring crept up on the mountain," Mooney is not "distraught" much longer (45). Mooney's disposition eventually begins to reflect the levity of the season: "The mountain country came into life again, slowly, then with a swish of color and action that caught a spark in him, too" (45). Under the spell of nature's seasonal renewal, Mooney "awoke each morning to the first light with a fresh expectancy and lay smelling in the newness of the air" (45). It is remarkable that the air itself, which Mooney previously viewed as the culprit responsible for Imy's death, is now an element of the "exterior landscape" that Mooney gladly greets each day.

The rebirth of the natural world, as seen in the "exterior landscape," inspires Mooney to reorganize and restructure his own "inner landscape" as well. As he comes to appreciate the mountain atmosphere, Mooney is learning not only to accept the landscape, but also to accept himself. Mooney begins to enjoy his own company, as "he would take long walks . . . and he would chuckle to himself in this mad, busy world" (45). This reaction to the natural world is a stark contrast to Mooney's deep loneliness during the blizzard of the previous winter, when "the world was white and without meaning to him" (43). Mooney's inner transformation is clear as he ventures back to the "clearing he and Imy made, and he would feel softness come back to the earth, a freshness come to it as if it wanted seed, was ready to be done finally with autumn's ripeness and winter's death" (46). The similarities between Mooney's "exterior landscape" and that of his "inner landscape" are incredibly clear in this scene. Just as the mountain's clearing is "ready to be done" with the death of winter, Mooney, through his interactions with the "exterior landscape," is finally prepared to move forward from Imy's death.

Even in this harmonious moment between man and nature, the narrative is careful to avoid idyllic depictions of the environment that his characters inhabit, and he is careful not to allow Mooney's new serenity to drag the novel into a traditional pastoral depiction of place: "Even in the wealth of spring, he remembered the harshness of the place, he thought, a place of dangers, after all" (38). Mooney acknowledges that even as pioneers develop an appreciation for their new surroundings, they must not forget that it is still in many ways a wild place. This realization is similar to that of Henry David Thoreau at Mount Katahdin in his piece "Ktaadn," where he writes of his experience climbing the tumultuous summit of the northern Appalachian Mountains: "There was clearly felt the presence of a force not bound to be kind to man" (135). Both Thoreau and Ehle acknowledge that unlike humans, the natural world does not subscribe to a moral code that (hopefully) encourages the fair treatment of sentient beings. Ehle shows that the natural world can bring about both hardship and happiness. Depictions of nature in *The Land Breakers* illustrate the interrelationship between "exterior landscapes" and "interior" ones, while avoiding idyllic pastoral descriptions of the environment. In other words, in the contrast between the exterior and interior landscape, the narrative helps readers think beyond the bounds of the pastoral, seeing the mountain ecosystem as a much more nuanced and complex habitat, even a post-pastoral landscape.

"Everyday nature" is manifest in the novel, particularly surrounding Mooney's new wife Lorry and the couple's new family unit. In "Imagining an Everyday Nature," Scott Hess makes the case for a revised understanding of the environment, one in which we humans do not disconnect ourselves from the natural world around us but rather incorporate a respect and appreciation for nature into our daily lives and identity as a species. Hess writes that "nature in environmental writing and culture today often appears as a form of refuge . . . the place where we go, both imaginatively and physically, to escape from this modernity" (85). For Hess these divisions between nature and culture, between the environment and its human inhabitants, are problematic: "This tendency to locate 'nature' apart from ourselves skews our environmental awareness and priorities in ways that blind us to the devastating ecological impact of our own daily lives and incapacitate us from pursuing realistic alternatives" (85). Hess astutely questions readers about the futility of this self-versus-environment identity: "If we seek nature apart from our lives, how can we restructure those lives—not just individually, but socially, politically, and economically—in order to change the current patterns of environmental destruction?" (85). He suggests that because nature has been defined in literature and human thought as being "in opposition to the social, the economic, and the everyday," a restructuring of human identity that incorporates nature into our routine lives is absolutely necessary (85), and he argues the case for "redefining 'nature' to include also the everyday and, in so doing, reshaping also the senses of self, work, and society with which our ideas of nature are inextricably and interdependently defined" (85).

"Everyday nature" is apparent in the depiction of Mooney's family. Not long after Lorry's arrival on a neighboring plot of land, Mooney marries her, a skilled and hardworking woman from Virginia who was abandoned by her first husband. We see the Wrights' "everyday nature" as they work on taming Mooney's undeveloped land into a homestead. Each member of the family "knew what was expected of them now, and what could be expected of the work horse and of the chain and of the fires and ax, of all the tools and stock they used" (106). The interconnectedness of each human family member, as well as the animals, natural elements, and tools, mirrors the interrelatedness of the ecological community surrounding the family's landscape. This focus on the routine, daily tasks humans complete in connection to the natural environment is clearly indicative of "everyday nature."

The novel continues with an even more explicit reference to "natures of the everyday," as Ehle writes, "The family and the place were the same thing and could not be separated one from the other. One could not understand the family without knowing about the land and their work on it and plans for it, and one could not know the land without knowing this family of people" (107). In this passage, the text demonstrates what Hess calls for in an "everyday nature," an interdependency that "includes such everyday relationships and experience, even in its most common and untranscendent forms" (97). Mooney's new family is "dusty with the land; the grit of the land was in them" (107), and such an "everyday nature" breaks down the human/nature dualism and alters human identity so that nature can be perceived, respected, and incorporated into how we see ourselves in "our ordinary lives, work, actions, and relationships" (Hess 97).

"Everyday nature" is also present in the depiction of Mooney's new wife, Lorry. She has a clear understanding of the natural world, one that very much includes herself and her own family. For Lorry, "the falling of the rain, the growth and drying and breaking of green things, the cooking and eating and washing of the arms and hands and necks of the boys, the laughter in the firelight, the growth of the baby inside her were part of a pattern, as routinely and consistently drawn as the daytime light cast on the cabin floor" (227). Lorry's understanding of nature is an example of an "everyday nature" because her own identity, and that of her family, is indistinguishable from the natural world. Lorry's "everyday nature" "includes habitual as well as heightened experience, work as well as leisure, human as well as nonhuman relationships" (Hess 96). She also explores the third post-pastoral question regarding the interrelatedness of her experiences of inner and outer nature as Lorry, pregnant with Mooney's child, looks to her various tasks around the family home as a means of easing her anxieties about childbirth: "digging and cutting away, lengthening the open spaces, felling trees and skinning logs, chopping bark for the tanning trough, the daily chores—helped take up her mind so that the baby due to arrive was a relaxing thought" (227).

Not only is Lorry connecting the worry of her "interior landscape" to the business of her "exterior landscape" but her reality also illustrates the practical and grounded environmental experiences that Lorry has with the surrounding landscape in her day-to-day life.

The Land Breakers, with its emphasis on the parallels and connections between our inner and outer nature, provides an interesting commentary on the third post-pastoral question, and the work also explores the divide between nature and culture present in the fourth post-pastoral question in its use of an "everyday nature" as it prompts readers to question the arbitrary nature of the divide between nature and culture. These combined representations illustrate for readers that humans cannot view themselves as operating in a separate realm from the natural world but instead that our identity, our core values, must contain a respect for nature and an incorporation of the "exterior landscape" of the environment into the "inner landscape" of our minds.

In arguing for an "everyday nature," Hess suggests that "environmental thought and imagination needs this category of 'everyday nature' precisely because the legacy of Romantic and wilderness nature as a 'place apart' is so deeply embedded in Western assumption, often in ways that are impossible to see without close critical attention" (102). As Hess writes, the Romantic ideas of nature still promote "escapism and autonomous individualism," both of which negatively impact the relationship between humans and the natural world (102). In "The Trouble with Wilderness," William Cronon argues that in "idealizing a distant wilderness," a wilderness-oriented understanding of nature states that "the place where we are is the place where nature is not," meaning we often ignore or abandon our local landscapes in order to protect wilderness areas (81). Both Romantic ideas of nature and the idea of wilderness have allowed "Nature" in environmental writing and the public consciousness to be "defined in opposition to the social, the economic, and the everyday" (Hess 85). By redefining nature into an "everyday nature," we may come to realize that "we can imagine nature without having to escape our own lives, work, and relationships" (102). An "everyday nature," therefore, reintegrates nature "into the ordinary, returning value and spirituality into our everyday lives and relationships as part of a wider process of resacramentalization" (102).

Ehle's fiction offers readers a sense of a historic Appalachian "everyday nature," one in which early settlers, who must "break" the land to survive, come to realize that they cannot be separated from the land and the work they are doing to it. For the Wrights in *The Land Breakers*, this sense of a "nature of the everyday" allows them to more easily understand their "interior landscape" through their knowledge of the "exterior landscape" around them. For Mooney Wright, observing his outer nature with the birth of spring allowed him to see how his inner nature could heal and experience new life after the tragic loss of his wife Imy. Ultimately, these depictions of nature in Ehle's fiction allow readers to see the inherent value in an "everyday nature," an accessible inclusion of the landscape around us into our daily lives, one that can both give us a greater understanding of the environment and deepen our understandings of ourselves.

BIBLIOGRAPHY

Berry, Wendell. *The Unsettling of America: Culture and Agriculture.* Berkeley, Calif.: Counterpoint, 2015.

Brady, Emily. "The Environmental Sublime." In *The Sublime from Antiquity to the Present*, edited by Timothy M. Costelloe, 171–82. Cambridge: Cambridge University Press, 2012.

Cronon, William. "The Trouble with Wilderness; or, Getting Back to Wrong Nature." In *Uncommon Ground: Rethinking the Human Place in Nature*, edited by William Cronon, 69–90. New York: Norton, 1996.

Davis, Donald Edward. *Where There Are Mountains: An Environmental History of the Southern Appalachians.* Athens: University of Georgia Press, 2000.

Duffy, Cian. *Landscapes of the Sublime 1700–1830: Classic Ground.* London: Palgrave Macmillan, 2013.

Ehle, John. *The Land Breakers.* 1964. New York: New York Review of Books, 2014.

———. "Near and Distant Kin." *Iron Mountain Review* 3, no. 2 (1987): 4–5.

Friedrich, Caspar David. *Wanderer about the Sea Fog.* 1817. Oil on canvas. Hamburger Kunsthalle, Hamburg, Germany.

Gifford, Terry. *Pastoral.* London: Routledge, 1999.

———. *Reconnecting with John Muir: Essays in Post-pastoral Practice.* Athens: University of Georgia Press, 2006.

Glotfelty, Cheryll, and Harold Fromm. *The Ecocriticism Reader: Landmarks in Literary Ecology.* Athens: University of Georgia Press, 1996.

Hess, Scott. "Imagining an Everyday Nature." *Interdisciplinary Studies in Literature and the Environment* 17, no. 1 (2010): 85–112.

Lopez, Barry. "Landscape and Narrative." In *Crossing Open Ground*, 61–72. New York: Scribner's, 1988.

Ryden, Kent C. "'How Could a Weed Be a Book?' Books, Ethics, Power, and *A Sand County Almanac*." *Interdisciplinary Studies in Literature and the Environment* 15, no. 1 (2008): 1–10.

Spalding, Linda. "Introduction." In *The Land Breakers*, vii–xi. New York: New York Review of Books, 2014.

Deja Views
Familiar Terrain
with New Vistas

"Lives Slip Away Like Waters"
Drowned Communities in Rash's
One Foot in Eden and *Raising the Dead*

ELISABETH AIKEN

Much as a river guide might read a river's rapids and eddies, aware of subtle currents lying beneath the watery surface, a reader of Appalachian literature can plumb the depths of various works using the lens of ecocriticism, which, according to Richard Kerridge, "strives to see how all things are interdependent, even those apparently most separate" (6). In its purest form, this theory emphasizes the role of the natural world in literature, demonstrating "nature is not merely a setting or backdrop for human action, but an actual factor in the plot," as John Tallmadge writes (Buell 282). However, studying literary depictions of elements of the natural world in isolation yields an incomplete understanding of the growing body of works deemed Appalachian. Because this literature is not only of or about this bioregion but rather is inextricably rooted in both the physical geography of this resource-rich, verdant region as well as its diverse histories and contemporary cultures, ecocriticism as a theoretical approach must be expanded to include a study of the relationship between the individual characters and communities of Appalachia—and their histories—and the natural world surrounding them.

While Appalachia does not fit neatly into the colonial model,[1] elements of the colonial narrative of progress are applicable to the history of this region so rich in natural resources. Enter "slow violence." Incorporating what Rob Nixon refers to as slow violence into an ecocritical approach provides readers the opportunity to understand more fully the complex relationship between people and nature often depicted in Appalachian literature. According to Nixon, slow violence "occurs gradually and out of sight, a violence of delayed destruction that is dispersed across time and space, an attritional violence that is typically not viewed as violence at all . . . a violence that is neither spectacular nor instantaneous, but rather incremental and accretive, its calamitous repercussions playing out against a range of temporal scales" (2). In Appalachia, then, slow violence is the steady deforestation of the southern mountains in the early twentieth century, the continued use of mountaintop removal mining to extract coal and other minerals (though in some cases this violence can hardly be called slow), or—germane to my discussion in this essay—the drowning of lush valleys and subsequent removal of their inhabitants in order to establish hydroelectric dams. These offenses have been and continue to be carried out in the names of progress and profit, with little regard to effects on either the surrounding environment or local communities. Ron Rash is among many authors whose works incorporate destructive environmental events while emphasizing the toll on the natural world and its inhabitants.

In a 2003 interview with Joyce Compton Brown titled "The Power of Blood-Memory," Rash quoted Francis Bacon when he claimed that an "important value of art . . . is 'to deepen the mystery'" (29). Rash could have considered himself a successful artist at that point in his career according to this criterion, given his (then) recent publication of novel *One Foot in Eden* and his collection of poetry *Raising the Dead*, both released in 2002. Each of these works explores the complex relationship between land and people, tradition and progress, and the volatile role water often plays in shaping events. *One Foot in Eden* is Rash's first novel; well received, it won the *ForeWord* Magazine Literary Book of the Year, Novello Literary Award, and Appalachian Book of the Year, an honor bestowed by the Appalachian Writers Association. This multinarrator work details a fictional murder and its aftermath in an upstate South Carolina valley that, in both novel and reality, would be flooded to become the Jocassee Reservoir. One might consider, as Silas House does, Rash's Pulitzer-nominated collection of poems *Raising the Dead* as an accompaniment to *One Foot in Eden* (21); while this collection is largely autobiographical, in these texts Rash also plumbs the depths of history and bioregionalism.

DeLoughrey and Handley remind us that "nature . . . is the past's only true guardian." Appalachian literature—or, specifically related to this essay, *One Foot in Eden* and *Raising the Dead*—preserves the role of nature, linking past and present. To wit, the common bond between the two books is the actual flooding of the Jocassee Valley to create "Lake" Jocassee. In *One Foot in Eden* Rash refers to the actual Jocassee Valley and the Horsepasture River, which is one of four rivers that now run into Lake Jocassee, though he does create unquestionably fictional characters and renames Duke Power (now known as Duke Energy) as Carolina Power, likely based on Carolina Power and Light, an early twentieth-century electric company. In the novel, Rash uses the river as physical boundary between forces of capitalism and those treated as "uninhabitants,"[2] and his chosen multinarrator format allows for a variety of perspectives. This presentation of the river as a cultural boundary, an idea further explored later in this essay, invites readers to consider Mary Louise Pratt's definition of contact zones as "social spaces where cultures meet, clash, and grapple with each other, often in contexts of highly asymmetrical relations of power, such as colonialism, slavery, or their aftermaths as they are lived out in many parts of the world today" (34). The novel's poetic counterpart *Raising the Dead* serves as the poet's autobiographical record of the flooding of Jocassee Valley by Duke Power, documenting the cultural and personal changes wrought by the watershed event. In both works, Rash uses his platform as writer to preserve Appalachian culture, highlight the lasting environmental damage (most prominently through the loss of the Oconee Bell flower), and question the dominant narrative of progress as beneficial to all.

Rash addresses the role that the environment plays in his works, telling Richard Birnbaum that he is "certainly concerned with environmental issues" and, in a roundtable discussion at Emory and Henry College, elaborated on that idea: "I'm very interested in how landscape affects the way we perceive reality and perceive ourselves" ("Nature, Place" 21). An ecocritical reading of both *One Foot* and *Raising the Dead*, which so eloquently reflect both the natural world of Appalachia and its people with authenticity and compassion, proves that they function well on at least two levels: they depict arguments for and against environmental activism and offer rich natural metaphors for readers' consideration. More specifically, readers are encouraged to notice the significant role that water plays on both of these levels. *One Foot* and *Raising* reflect Rash's acknowledgment of the significance of water in his life: "Just being a southern Baptist, being immersed in water literally when I was baptized, that religious symbolism of water represents for Christians both death and resurrection. For me it's a very potent symbol, one I almost don't want to analyze too much, but I do know that water is something I'm obviously obsessed with, particularly in reservoirs, how that water can annihilate any human presence" (Brown 27).

S

The long history of the once-verdant Jocassee Valley begins with the Cherokee legend of Princess Jocassee, in love with Nagoochee, a hunter from a neighboring warring faction; when Jocassee's brother slayed Nagoochee, Jocassee, in her grief, walked across the waters of the Whitewater River to meet her lover's ghost. Because of this lore, Jocassee means, as Rash states, a "place for the lost" (*One Foot* 214). This legend predates the Cherokee War of 1760–61, a series of violent expeditions by British forces into southern Cherokee lands, after which the Cherokee people successfully negotiated a "permanent boundary line separating Indian lands from white settlers" (Williams 58). Of course history tells us that this "permanent" line was very much temporary, and the Revolutionary War would see successful military campaigns against the Cherokees of southern Appalachia, eventually resulting in the majority's inhumane removal in 1840.

Though many of its original inhabitants were removed, in the nineteenth century the valley itself supported settlers and attracted attention for its charming appeal. Thomas Addison Richards wrote in 1853 that "in South Carolina, ... there is the fair valley of Jocassee, dissected by the babbling waters of the sparkling Keowee; the very spot to ream in on a summer-morn: or, in moonlight-hours to dance with the woodland elf and the merry fay!" (728). Ironically, this very source also lamented the dearth of lakes in the region, stating that the natural valleys "take the place of the lakes in the North, and go far to compensate for the absence of that charming feature; the want of which, however, the tourist will sometimes feel in his Southern rambles" (727).

The area's remote location led to its inhabitants of European descent to continue the agricultural tradition well into the twentieth century: Importantly, in *One Foot in Eden*, Rash details the day before the Holcombe family is to leave permanently. Isaac Holcombe is at the family farm, harvesting the remaining cabbage crop before the field becomes lake floor. Perhaps it is this lack of urban development in addition to the geography that attracted the attention of energy giant Duke Power.

Duke Power's inception is credited to three "visionaries" who "founded the company to spur economic revival of the Carolina countryside" ("Our History"). Significantly, their first plant, the Catawba Hydro Station, provided energy to Victoria Cotton Mills; there is some irony in the electricity magnate's later building dams, dislocating Appalachian inhabitants from their land, to provide energy to the very mills where they would find employment. The years following World War II were profitable ones, and this "era was a true boom time for energy-related industries" ("Our History"). Duke Power became "one of the earliest adopters of nuclear power technology in the United States" (Murray) with the Keowee-Toxaway Project, which was begun in 1965, despite heavy competition from the federal government's proposed dams. According to Robert F. Durden, Duke Power had been planning for a project of this magnitude, in 1963 having formed the South Carolina Land and Timber Company, a subsidiary that quickly bought a parcel of 31,113 acres before the public announcement of the proposed dams and power stations (131). The name of this company may have inspired Rash's fictionalized name for Duke Power in *One Foot in Eden*. The project enjoyed strong political support in South Carolina: Durden quotes Congressman William Jennings Bryan Dorn as celebrating the Keowee-Toxaway Project as the "greatest single industrial announcement in the history of South Carolina . . . and industry the magnitude of which is fantastic and almost incomprehensible" (134).

The proposed project included what many would call environmental benefits to the surrounding communities. Duke Power purchased more than a hundred thousand acres in the surrounding area to protect the watersheds that flow into the proposed reservoirs. The need to safeguard these watersheds prompted Duke Power to maintain "scientific forest management" that would "continue to provide timber for local mills and jobs for people working in forest industries" (135). It also allowed the South Carolina Wildlife Resources Department to create the Horsepasture Game Management Area by leasing sixty-eight thousand acres, and master plans included free public-access areas on Lake Keowee and Lake Jocassee (136).

The result of the Jocassee Dam and Hydro Station is what is known today as Lake Jocassee, completed and dedicated in 1973. The dam is "385 feet high and 1750 feet long." Known as one of the deepest lakes in the system of lakes created by Duke Power, when full it reaches a depth of 1,110 feet ("Lake Jocassee"). As the company's first nuclear facility, it was heralded for coming in under budget and earning the company its first of three Edison Awards for "its outstanding engineering accomplishments in the integrated hydrothermal development of the Keowee-Toxaway Project, fully utilizing the area and its natural resources for electric generation and at the same time protecting and enhancing the environment of the Keowee Valley" (qtd. in Durden 141). In 1975, the American Society of Civil Engineers named the Keowee-Toxaway Power Project the nation's outstanding achievement in civil engineering.

One Foot in Eden is a novel in five sections that grew from Rash's image of a "farmer standing in his field, crops dying around him. He had a look of desperation of [sic] his face that transcended the drought" (Kingsbury 46). In a feature unique among Rash's works, each section of *One Foot* utilizes a different narrator who depicts the events of one hot, dry summer and its long-reaching aftermath. This technique easily situates *One Foot* among other southern novels, William Faulkner's *As I Lay Dying* being the quintessential multinarrator work. Set against the backdrop of the actual damming of the confluence of the Toxaway, Horsepasture, Thompson, and Whitewater rivers in South Carolina, *One Foot in Eden* details the fictional story of Billy and Amy Holcombe, the murder of Holland Winchester, and the actual impending flooding of the Jocassee Valley to create Lake Jocassee. As the characters navigate the precarious ground of marriage and sexual relationships, the presence of Carolina Power looms in the background. This faceless entity bought land on the other side of the river from the Winchesters, Holcombes, and Alexanders; indeed, each of these families is aware of the eventual flooding of their valley by this corporation. The constant threat that their valley will one day be entirely submerged adds an element of urgency at various points of the novel; they are all aware of the coming deluge, like being aware of some type of deadline, though they are not aware of precisely when it will occur. While water is a physical presence in the novel and its imagery permeates much of Rash's language, the work as a whole might be thought of as a river that is being dammed: it begins by assessing the surface, or known features, then plunges readers to deeper and deeper depths, sounding and articulating events that would come to first define and then obliterate the lives of these characters. Finally, the novel simultaneously serves as a metaphorical warning against the dangers of losing something that cannot be replaced and, according to Mindy Beth Miller, allows Rash to "prevent Jocassee from vanishing by writing about it" (201).

The novel opens with High Sheriff Will Alexander's narration, which provides for readers the surface of the body of water that defines the rest of the novel. Alexander journeys from urban, downstate Seneca back to his birthplace, Jocassee, to investigate the disappearance of Holland Winchester. In the next section, the narrative sounds the depths of these defining events, providing the backstory of the couple's courtship and early marriage in the section narrated by Amy. At the time of her exposition, the Holcombes are a young married couple whose poverty forces them to live close to the land. Amy's impotent husband Billy continues the narrative of events in the novel's third section, detailing first his struggle with infertility and deteriorating marriage and then his discovery of Amy's pregnancy via infidelity, noting that by that point in the hot, dry summer "that baby was about the only thing growing" (116). Amy's son Isaac's narration moves quickly through the early years of his life. Throughout his life, Isaac is aware of the impending damming of the rivers that would flood his valley home; the main action of this section occurs after the dam's completion, a month after the Holcombes leave their farm for life in a mill town and one mere day before the family's forced permanent exile. Billy is finally relieved of the burden of guilt as he tries to surrender to Alexander; the sheriff, however, tells him that the statute of limitations has passed and advises him to surrender Holland's earthly remains to the rising river. In returning to their truck to flee the valley one last time, both Amy and Billy (who cannot swim) drown in the deadly water. Isaac and Alexander survive to leave Jocassee forever. The concluding narration, provided by Deputy Bobby Murphree, who has been summoned by Carolina Power, invites readers to take one final dive to what is now the lake bed and, in doing so, consider objects that surface as evidence of its former existence as a river valley. He reflects this "wasn't no place for people who had a home. This was a place for the lost" (214).

The narrative highlights the river as a contact zone throughout the novel by emphasizing the significant role of the river in the lives of the inhabitants of the Jocassee Valley, pitting local farmers against the faceless corporation that will dam the downstream confluence of the Horsepasture, Toxaway, Thompson, and Whitewater rivers and flood their valley in the name of progress. By manipulating Horsepasture River's flow and consequentially flooding the valley, Carolina Power is exerting its considerable power against local citizens. As a contact zone, then, the river of *One Foot in Eden* functions environmentally as a boundary that characters must explore and navigate. They know that the flooding of the valley will obliterate their way of life, their physical legacy, and many irreplaceable elements of the natural world (such as the rare Oconee Bell flower). But the work does not depict the rising waters from a strictly environmental perspective. Perhaps more significantly, this river also represents a metaphorical boundary. Geographically speaking, the river provides a stark physical boundary between life and death. On one side of the Horsepasture River, an Appalachian River Styx, live the Holcombes and their farm, site of procreation and birth. On the other side is the land owned by Carolina Power, a symbolic entity that will facilitate the death of the valley. The hiding place for Holland Winchester's body is also on Carolina Power's side of the river. Though murdered on the Holcombes' land, his body could not rest there; rather than leave Holland's body on the same side of the river as the new life represented by Isaac's birth, Billy Holcombe instead uses the river almost as a protective barrier and moves Holland's body to the side of the river where all life is doomed. Indeed, almost everyone who visits the far side of the river is doomed as well: Sam, Billy's horse, does not return from carrying Holland's body across the river; the Widow Glendower (whom Billy sees on the banks of the river as he hikes to conceal Holland's remains) dies alone; and Billy himself eventually drowns in the swelling and powerful water. The only characters who survive are Isaac and Sheriff Alexander, who is conversely given a second chance at fatherhood, having barely survived his own encounter with the flooding river.

The idea that these characters exist in a contact zone is clearly reinforced by the novel's title. As the biblical reference insinuates, Billy and Amy exist in a state of looming exile, spending the majority of the text preparing to leave their home and land. The novel's prologue, by Scottish poet Edwin Muir, from whom the title is taken, reinforces the intensity of the boundary that Billy and Amy negotiate:

> One foot in Eden still, I stand
> And look across the other land.
> The world's great day is growing late,
> Yet strange these fields that we have planted,
> So long with crops of love and hate.

For the entirety of the novel, the Holcombes live with the knowledge that they will be removed from what they consider paradise, the land they know.

The river also provides delineation between farmers who rely on nature to support their existence and the impersonal corporations that destroy nature in the name of profit. These farmers must maintain a balance between supporting themselves and exploiting their resources. Implicit in any comparison of the farmer with the vast corporation is a stark distinction of social classes, what can be characterized as an often-impoverished lifestyle versus a progressive, technologically aggressive way of life. In this way, the threat of the rising water functions as a weapon wielded by the powerful against the marginalized farmer. The novel highlights this contrast as social stratification, emphasized when Sheriff Alexander notes that the Holcombes don't have electricity: "I smelled the wood smoke as I stepped inside and remembered I hadn't seen a gap in the trees for a power line. . . . That was enough to know they were poor in a way none of my people had been since the Depression. They got water from a well, and they still used an outhouse" (27). The poverty of the Holcombes is made clear through the divisive boundary of the river, which separates their land and social station, ironically enough, from the property and wealth of Carolina Power. The Holcombes cannot afford to bring the services of this corporation to their side of the river.

The idea of the river as a clean and unbreachable boundary does not hold up throughout the novel, however, and so readers are reminded of the folly of relying upon consistency from the natural world. Various key characters react differently to the slowly rising waters: Billy and Amy eventually move to town and struggle to acclimate themselves to their new life, while a teenage Isaac explains that "I'd grown up knowing there was no future here, that Jocassee would sooner or later be covered in water, so I'd never let myself get attached to it the way Momma and Daddy had" (168–69). In the final day before the valley is entirely submerged by Carolina Power, the banks of the river swell and its borders blur: it is no longer a natural boundary, but as the water is increasingly manipulated from its original course, it becomes a symbol of death. An elderly Mrs. Winchester refuses to leave her homestead, and by extension her son Holland; as a result, the arson and suicide that she commits are ironically quelled by the rising waters as the river completes its metamorphosis into a lake.

Mrs. Winchester, like Holland before her, and Billy and Amy Holcombe to follow, cannot leave the land, and so the flood sets off a sequence of events that, like the irreversible destruction of the river itself, is inevitable. The rising power of the river, though, swelling its banks and claiming the valley floor with unnatural strength, causes the drowning of Billy and Amy. Their deaths in the river suggest that though they moved to town and Billy procured a job at the local mill, they could never survive away from their land; indeed, they could never live anywhere but on the floor of the valley, on the side of the river reserved for life and growth. As the river grows into a lake, it also becomes the final resting place of the Widow Glendower. Finally, the water provides a window for Bobby, the deputy, to peer into the past as it is preserved on the lake floor. Bobby floats above the Holcombes' farm, now their eternal resting place, and notes that "the front door of the house was open and I couldn't shake the feeling that someone might step onto the porch at any second and look up at me the same way that I might look up at a plane—someone who didn't even know they was dead and buried under a lake" (213–14). Though nearly all of the actual structures of the town were razed by Duke Power, in leaving the fictional farmhouse intact for Bobby to observe from above the intended message is clear: the Holcombe farm is preserved in time, swallowed by the progress and growth demanded by Carolina Power—or, as Rash puts it, "a change big enough to swallow this whole valley" (11).

Raising the Dead, also published in 2002, is the poetic counterpart to *One Foot in Eden*; as such, the rivers and Jocassee Dam figure prominently in this collection. Mirroring the structure of *One Foot*, this work is also organized into five sections. As such, it reflects Rash's stated goal that the "poems, stories, and novels . . . inform and enrich one another" (Shurbutt and Hoffman). Unlike the novel, however, in *Raising the Dead* Rash does not mask the identity of Duke Power but instead refers to it by its actual name at that point in time. This decision may be due in part to the resonance of the real name: a duke is an aristocrat, a powerful social figure. This collection itself realizes its own title, evoking the memory of the dead throughout, while individual poems work through a literal movement of graves to symbolically represent the deceased. As Rash does with the coda of *Serena* and the first chapters of parts 1 and 2 of *Saints at the River*, the title and content of the last poem of each section are italicized. This emphasis creates an otherworldly and surreal effect, almost as if the reader is reading the poems underwater.

Raising the Dead is marked by a somber, elegiac tone. Sections I and V, which are especially relevant to this discussion, focus on the creation of Lake Jocassee by Duke Power in 1974. The collection opens, tellingly, with "Last Service," in which a congregation gathers at its church while the waters that would be Lake Jocassee rise. Here Rash describes the powerful action of cranes and bulldozers that would unearth graves, relocating deceased parishioners while their still-alive counterparts

> lit
> the church with candles and sang
> from memory deep as water
> old hymns of resurrection. (lines 17–19)

This poem mirrors "*The Men Who Raise the Dead*," the final poem of section V, which echoes Billy Holcombe's thoughts as he watches the bulldozers dig up graves on the valley floor in *One Foot*. Encased between these poems is section II, in which Rash dives into his family history of generations past, exploring, for example, nineteenth-century floods in Watauga County and the tragic Shelton Laurel massacre of the Civil War. In subsequent poems of sections III and IV Rash depicts his childhood in and around water with his cousin (Jeffrey Charles Critcher, to whom the collection is dedicated), then focuses on the painful and untimely passing of the same cousin.

The title and subject matter of the collection are made more evident when paired with the stunningly beautiful (and deceptively peaceful) cover photo of a lone fisherman silhouetted against the sunset on Lake Jocassee, taken by Bill Barley. The tranquility of the cover is immediately challenged by a stark black-and-white photo of the Jocassee Dam on the title page—provided courtesy of Duke Power. Like *One Foot*, this collection is reminiscent of diving below the surface to explore and chart aqueous depths. The poems, then, serve as an account of what such a dive discovered, a reading encouraged by the lines from Shakespeare's *Henry IV, Part 1* that serve as a prologue:

> Glendower:
> *I can call spirits from the vasty deep.*
> Hotspur:
> *Why, so can I, so can any man.*
> *But will they come when you do call for them?*

Read "more like a quilt than mere pieces of different-angled cloth on completely different designs" (Shurbutt and Hoffman), *One Foot in Eden* and *Raising the Dead* blur the distinction between past and present, dead and alive, submerged and surface. Read in coordination with the other, each work demonstrates Silas House's claim that regardless of genre, the writing of Rash "takes us to a place where the living and the dead coexist, a place where there is a thin line between the past and the present. Not only that, but he also creates a world in which times overlap and occasionally interrupt one another" (21). Rash is keenly aware of the importance of history, writing that when "novelists write historical fiction, they aspire to give the chaos of history coherence, for the nature of stories is to make events understandable" ("Facts of Historical Fiction"). As such, the history of the Jocassee Valley is a significant subject within both works. Mindy Beth Miller agrees that the "pages of the book act as a historical record, a kind of storehouse that can be revisited time and again" (205).

The narrative of capitalist progress and advancement contrasts sharply with the interests of valley residents; indeed, the building of Jocassee Dam to create Lake Jocassee easily supports a depiction of Duke Power as a neocolonizing force within the Carolinas. The end result of providing reliable energy to the region may be altruistic, but the company's methods had environmentally destructive and culturally subordinating effects. In a discussion of megadams, especially pertinent to any conversation regarding reservoir building in the Southeast, Rob Nixon notes that the "production of ghosted communities who haunt the visible nation has been essential for maintaining the dominant narratives of national development, a process that has intensified during the era of neoliberal globalization" (151). Sheriff Alexander comments on one such ghosted community and offers readers historical precedent for the coming displacement when he considers the settler communities that built their lives in the valley:

> I thought of how the descendants of settlers from Scotland and Wales and Ireland and England—people poor and desperate enough to risk their lives to take that land, as the Cherokees had once taken it from other tribes—would soon vanish from Jocassee as well. Fifteen years, twenty at most, and it'll all be water, at least that was what the people who would know had told me. Reservoir, reservation, the two words sounded so alike. In a dictionary they would be on the same page.
>
> There was a kind of justice in what would happen. But this time the disappearance would be total. There would be no names left, because

> Alexander Springs and Boone Creek and Robertson's Ford and Chapman's Bridge would all disappear. Every tombstone with Holcome or Lusk or Alexander or Nicholson chiseled into it would vanish as well.
>
> (*One Foot* 23)

Sheriff Alexander's reminisces reflect Rash's awareness of settler colonies within Appalachia as he both reflects upon the forced and violent removal of the Cherokee and anticipates the coming removal of the valley's current inhabitants. Though the musings of a single character, his forecast of the drowned valley rends the current inhabitants invisible, thus facilitating and justifying their removal. Nixon addresses the role that this imaginative displacement plays in aiding the physical removal of communities, thus creating spatial amnesia, wherein "communities, under the banner of development, are physically unsettled and imaginatively removed, evacuated from place and time and thus uncoupled from the idea of both a national future and a national memory" (151).

Stripping the valley community of its imagined presence and voice creates a silent void and, with that void, an opportunity for alternative and dominant narratives. Indeed, according to Alexia Jones Helsley, the "dominant narrative of national development" argues poetically, albeit patriarchally, that "man dammed the rivers of the Carolinas to produce electricity, reduce flooding, and create reservoirs. The lakes that flooded ancient burial grounds, Revolutionary battle sites, colonial homesteads, villages, mills, and churches bring recreation, waterfront living and tourism to the land-bound reaches of the Carolinas. In exercising his dominion over the earth, man forever changed the landscape of the Carolinas." Damming the rivers has effects that extend beyond the loss of historical sites—though that loss alone is immeasurable. The dominant narrative—represented here by the historical narratives of Duke Power, Durden, and Helsley—does not acknowledge the impact these dams had on local communities. Tellingly, Durden's history of Duke Power does not include any mention of the relocation of now invisible Jocassee Valley inhabitants.

Rash rarely allows his narrators to mention Duke Power by even its fictional name in *One Foot*. Early in his narrated section, Sheriff Alexander identifies land holdings of the energy giant and notes that residents "up here wouldn't like it worth a damn to be run off their land, but when the time came there would be nothing they could do about it" (11). Billy later recalls the "the power company didn't allow hunting or logging so there wouldn't be many folks poking around these woods" (132), and Isaac later recalls a conversation between his father and a Carolina Power employee (167).

Despite this general lack of physical presence, the coming inundation looms on every page of the novel.

In succinct "Notes" that follow the final section of *Raising the Dead*, Rash provides a brief history of the Jocassee Valley that contrasts sharply with the narrative provided by Duke Power, Durden, and Helsley: "Despite fervent opposition by the valley's inhabitants, Duke Power Company built a dam to create Jocassee Reservoir. Both the living and the dead were evicted, for hundreds of graves were dug up and their contents reburied in cemeteries outside the valley. The reservoir reached full water capacity in 1974. In Cherokee *Jocassee* means 'place of the lost'" (75). Rash's words demonstrate the loss of both place and history that Nixon addresses: "When refugees are severed from environments that have provided ancestral sustenance they find themselves stranded not just in place but in time as well. Their improvised lives in makeshift camps are lives of temporal impoverishment. When a megadam obliterates a flood plain whose ebb and flow has shaped the agricultural fishing, fruit, and nut harvesting—and hence nutritional—rhythms of a community, it also drowns the past" (162).

The creation of Lake Jocassee didn't only drown the past; it also forever redefined the valley. *Raising the Dead* reflects Rash's belief that "landscape is destiny" (Zacharias), a simple, definite statement that echoes DeLoughrey and Handley's explanation of place as having "infinite meaning and morphologies: It might be defined geographically, in terms of the expansion of empire; environmentally, in terms of wilderness or urban settings; genealogically, in linking communal ancestry to land; as well as phenomenologically, connecting body to place" (4). Indeed, this collection of poetry reflects each of these four potential definitions. The changing landscape of Jocassee represented within this collection, combined with the voices that Rash includes, demonstrates the implicit interconnectivity of this culture and the surrounding geography. *Raising* simultaneously supports Buell's claim that the "subject of a text's representation of its environmental ground *matters*—matters aesthetically, conceptually, ideologically. Language never replicates extratextual landscapes, but it can be bent toward or away from them" (33).

Read as a cohesive work, *Raising the Dead* reinforces the connection between environmental events and neocolonizing efforts. While nature would return to the reservoir, readers must be aware that it is a manipulation of nature—and its return is markedly more anthropocentric than biocentric. Val Plumwood notes that an "anthropocentric culture rarely sees nature and animals as individual centres of striving or needs, doing their best in their conditions of life. Instead, nature is conceived in terms of interchangeable and replaceable units (as 'resources'), rather than as infinitely diverse and always in excess of knowledge and classification" (55).

To best understand the ramifications of this manipulation, we must consider Buell's three-part definition of place: The "concept of place gestures in at least three directions at once: toward environmental materiality, toward social perception or construction, and toward individual affect or bond" (63). By stripping Jocassee Valley of its wealth of resources and inhabitants and planning to submerge it permanently under water, Duke Power has divorced the place from its history, thus reinforcing its status as neocolonizing force. As DeLoughrey and Handley note, the "decoupling of nature and history has helped to mystify colonialism's histories of forced migration, suffering, and human violence" (4). *Raising the Dead* subtly identifies the presence of capitalist entities behind the drowning of the valley and, through a focus on nature, strives to preserve the valley and record the effects of its demise.

Silas House notes that in "Rash's writing the dead represent the past while the living represent the present—or even the future. Appalachia is a place where these two forces—the past and the present—are constantly colliding" (21). These representations of past and present, dead and alive, are a constant theme in *Raising*. As Newt Smith notes, this collection is a "highly structured book with an underlying story of loss, premature death, submerged memory, and the burial by water of a valley of homesteads and graves" (19). In a similar fashion to *One Foot*, much of section I of *Raising the Dead* invokes an image of a river or water as a boundary that clearly delineates a distinction between life and death. The opening poem of both section and collection, "Last Service," describes the final worship services at a church quickly being submerged in the growing Lake Jocassee. The congregation had already lost their farms to the deepening water, and by the final Sunday

>   nothing but that brief island
>   left of their world as they lit
>   the church with candles and sang
>   from memory deep as water
>   old hymns of resurrection
>   before leaving that high ground
>   where the dead had once risen.   (lines 15–21)

That the congregants chose to sing "old hymns of resurrection" is significant to Rash's work; *Raising the Dead* itself may be considered one such hymn, reviving a culture that thrived in a valley that is now the floor of a lake. Within the poem, though, water physically separates the farmers' present from their past lives and divides the inhabitants into those living—those who "still congregated there, / wading then crossing in boats" (lines 11–12)—and those deceased, whose corpses were exhumed and moved to another graveyard. Importantly, Rash identifies with sharp insight both the environmental and cultural impact of the dam, noting the "quick-dying streams" and "soon obsolete bridges" (lines 9, 10).

"Under Jocassee" continues the theme of water separating life and death with a narrator who speaks directly to readers, intimately involving them in the fictional drama of *One Foot* and the historical spectacle of the creation of Lake Jocassee. Directing readers to rent a boat and

> shadow
> Jocassee's western shoreline
> until you reach the cove
> that was Horsepasture River, (lines 4–7)

the narrator commands them to

> cut the motor and drift
> back sixty years and remember
> a woman who lived in that house (lines 17–19)

before invoking the now-familiar image of the same woman, looking up. House writes that in this poem "we see the collision of two times: the image of a woman of Old Appalachia going through her hard working day in a natural setting is paralleled to a more leisurely day spent fishing on a man-made lake in New Appalachia. We also feel the sense of death always being present, floating above us" (21).

Rash imbues nature with a prophetic power in "Shee-Show." This brief poem provides a concise history of the scientific naming by Michaux of the Oconee Bell flower, a flower whose loss of habitat he laments in *One Foot*. In "Shee-Show" Rash alludes to the role that binomial taxonomy has played historically in contributing to colonizing efforts. As DeLoughrey and Handley note, "New taxonomies of flora and fauna instituted a hierarchy of human species through this episteme of difference, contributing biologically determinist discourses of race, gender, and nature" (14). Without dwelling on the colonial implications that this name represents, Rash continues to state that the Latin given name is rarely used by the white settlers who generally preferred to

> let place and shape
> inspire a prettier name. (lines 4–5)

He continues to invoke the colonizing experience in writing that the Cherokee name is

> a rich feel of syllables
> run off the tongue, merging two
> cultures for once without blood. (lines 6–8)

Perhaps the poet transfers knowledge of the "coming water" (line 14) to the plant because of the violent etymology inherent in both Latin and Cherokee names.

The concluding section of *Raising the Dead* presents readers with diverse depictions of nature; however, the theme behind each of them is the manipulation of nature for personal gain. Also, Rash uses nature to lament the passage of time as well as the deleterious effects that human nature has imposed on its environment. "Carolina Parakeets" recalls the species of bird that were

> once plentiful enough
> to pulse an acre field, green
> a blue sky. (lines 1–3)

The poet does not divulge what might have hunted these birds, though the implication is that their extinction is due not to natural prey but rather to the growing human population of the region. This poem harkens back to 1860, to the presumed last sighting of the birds. However, the theme of the poem revolves around the mountains as a safe harbor for such exotic fowl. Before the birds were "forever lost" (line 5), they were last seen in the mountains, when a farmer might

> look up from new-broken land
> and glimpse that bright vanishing. (lines 9–10)

Rash suggests here that the white settlers who populated the area after the removal of the Cherokee witnessed (and likely caused) the demise of natural species.

The majority of poems in this section, though, focus on the rising water. In a scene reminiscent of Mrs. Winchester's conflagration, a farmer in "A Homestead on the Horsepasture" watches helplessly the rising water. He then

> soaked
> house and barn with kerosene (lines 8–9)

and bitterly stands by as his house burns in order to leave only what he'd chiseled from river rock "for the water to reclaim" (line 15). "Bottomland" presents the image of scarecrows in crop-less, abandoned fields; the water rises to meet them, giving the impression that they

> stalked
> those vanished fields, raised arms spread
> like arms of the forsaken under the autumn moon. (lines 10–12)

In "Tremor" the pragmatic outsider (Duke Power) is positioned against the intuitive local when

> cups...shiver in the cupboards
> cows...pause. (lines 2–3)

One of the final poems in the collection is "The Day the Gates Closed," in which Rash depicts the absence of human and nonhuman nature from the valley:

> *We lose so much in this life.*
> *Shouldn't some things stay*, she said,
> but it was already gone,
> no human sound, the poplars
> and oaks cut down so even
> the wind had nothing to rub
> a whisper from, just silence
> rising over the valley
> deep and wide as a glacier. (lines 1–9)

Though the female speaker is not identified, the woman has suffered loss beyond the destruction she is surveying in the valley. Rash incorporates elements of deep ecology, which addresses almost exclusively nonhuman nature and attempts to place it at the center of concern, when he references the prehistoric glaciers that defined such geography and would eventually become a lake. This short poem represents a vacuum: the valley is vacant of all inhabitants, all forms of nature, and all sounds. In preparing the valley for the imminent flood, Duke Power has effectively annihilated each of the three elements of Buell's definition of place: "The Day the Gates Closed" represents a dearth of "environmental materiality," a destruction of "social perception or construction," and loss of "individual affect or bond."

What is Rash's role, then, as author of *One Foot in Eden* and *Raising the Dead*? Clues abound in scholarship on Rash, in interviews with the author, and within the works themselves. For example, Rash "depicts a distinct Appalachian culture, one that is marginalized, living, and fierce; he sets it up as existing in opposition to the mainstream" (Miller 198–99). Striking a similar note, Jesse Graves writes that Rash represents a generation of Appalachian writers who witnessed the shift away from a primarily agricultural livelihood first-hand, so [he] record[s] not only the work and ways of living, [he] also record[s] the change itself, and its attendant losses. One could call [his] work commemorative, and as memory is mother of the muses, that would be an accurate claim, but in another sense, these writers, and so many others in the region, give history a second life.... Ron Rash take[s] Eliot's claim about "the historical sense" seriously, and ... [he] invoke[s] the past as a deeper layer, a substrata, of life in the continuously evolving present moment. (85)

Rash himself claims that the explosion of Appalachian literature "has happened in part because Appalachian writers are seeing much of their culture disappear" (Biggers 14). Presumably Rash includes himself among the ranks of these writers, chronicling the demise of this beloved culture. As he stated in an interview, "I think that's part of an Appalachian writer's role—to remember that there's something here worth ... remembering ... : and if you honor and respect it, then it has a better chance of continuing" (Miller 209).

In addition to serving as records of a culture that is at best rapidly changing and at worst merely a memory, *One Foot in Eden* and *Raising the Dead* are aggressive attempts to reclaim both the land of the Jocassee Valley and the culture of the settler communities that thrived there. The presence of Duke Power's dam that would "cork this whole valley up and make them a lake" (*One Foot* 135) is an act of "geographical violence through which virtually every space in the world is explored, charted, and finally brought under control. For the native, the history of colonial servitude is inaugurated by the loss of locality to the outsider; its geographical identity must thereafter be searched for and somehow restored" (Edward Said qtd. in DeLoughrey and Handley 4). *One Foot* and *Raising the Dead*, then, preserve this locality and its geographical identity. Rash's inclusion of both the culture and the natural world within these works defiantly rebukes Duke Power's claim upon the physical valley.

"At Boone Creek Landing," included in the first section of *Raising the Dead*, offers readers a final glimpse into his reaction to the flooding of the valley. This poem, set on the banks of Lake Keowee, depicts a first-person speaker's attempt to envision the current location of the fort deep below the lake's surface. The speaker, seemingly Rash himself, traces his ancestry to "a captain named Candler" who

  wed
  Mary Boone   (lines 8–9)

at the fort before striking out for North Carolina. Rash depicts himself as a

> long-delayed
> wedding guest to this shore. (lines 13–14)

This image alludes to the Wedding-Guest of Coleridge's "The Rime of the Ancient Mariner," a man who "cannot choose but hear" the tale spun before him (line 18). Like the wedding guest held in a thrall by the Ancient Mariner, readers are invited to envision the weight of Jocassee's loss on Rash

> like one that hath been stunned,
> And is of sense forlorn:
> A sadder and a wiser man,
> He rose the morrow morn. (lines 622–25)

NOTES

1. Appalachia more closely resembles the definition of a settler colony; see Lawson and Ashcroft, Griffiths, and Tiffin.
2. Rob Nixon defines "uninhabitants" as politically insignificant inhabitants of "an area targeted for 'progress'" (153). They are also victims of what Nixon describes as an alternative form of displacement, which not only addresses the "movement of people from their places of belonging, [but] refers rather to the loss of the land and resources beneath them, a loss that leaves communities stranded in a place stripped of the very characteristics that made it inhabitable" (19).

BIBLIOGRAPHY

Ashcroft, Bill, Gareth Griffiths, and Helen Tiffin. *The Empire Writes Back: Theory and Practice in Post-colonial Literatures.* 2nd ed. London: Routledge, 2002.

Biggers, Jeff. "Out of Appalachia: New Writing From an Old Region, Including an Interview with Gretchen Laskas and Ron Rash." *Bloomsbury Review* 23, no. 4 (2003): 14–15.

Brown, Joyce Compton. "The Power of Blood-Memory: A Conversation." *Iron Mountain Review* 20 (2004): 21–35.

Buell, Lawrence. *The Future of Environmental Criticism: Environmental Crisis and Literary Imagination.* Hoboken, N.J.: Wiley-Blackwell, 2005.

DeLoughrey, Elizabeth, and George B. Handley, eds. *Postcolonial Ecologies: Literatures of the Environment.* Oxford: Oxford University Press, 2011.

Durden, Robert F. *Electrifying the Piedmont Carolinas: The Duke Power Company, 1904–1997.* Durham, N.C.: Carolina Academic Press, 2001.

Graves, Jesse. "Lattice Work: Formal Tendencies in the Poetry of Robert Morgan and Ron Rash." *Poetry in the South* 45, no. 1 (2007): 78–86.

Helsley, Alexia Jones. "History of Carolina Lakes—Manmade for Man." *Carolina Living.*

House, Silas. "A Matter of Life and Death: Old and New Appalachia Meet in *One Foot in Eden.*" *Iron Mountain Review* 20 (2004): 21–25.

Kerridge, Richard. "Introduction." In *Writing the Environment: Ecocriticism and Literature*, 1–10. London: Zed Books, 1998.

Kingsbury, Pam. "Language Can Be Magical: An Interview with Ron Rash." In *Conversations with Ron Rash*, edited by Mae Miller Claxton and Rain Newcomb, 45–48. Jackson: University Press of Mississippi, 2017.

"Lake Jocassee." Duke Energy Corporation, n.d. https://www.duke-energy.com/power-plants/pumped-storage-hydro/jocassee.asp.

Lawson, Alan. "Postcolonial Theory and the Settler Subject." *Essays on Canadian Writing* 56 (1995): 20–37.

Miller, Mindy Beth. "Long Remember, Long Recall: The Preservation of Appalachian Regional Heritage in Ron Rash's *One Foot in Eden*." *Journal of Kentucky Studies* 26 (2009) 198–209.

Murray, Jonathan. "Duke Power Company." North Carolina History Project. John Locke Foundation. https://northcarolinahistory.org/encyclopedia/duke-power-company/.

Nixon, Rob. *Slow Violence and the Environmentalism of the Poor*. Cambridge, Mass.: Harvard University Press, 2011.

"Our History." Duke Energy Corporation, n.d. https://www.duke-energy.com/our-company/about-us/our-history.

Plumwood, Val. "Decolonizing Relationships with Nature." In *Decolonizing Nature: Strategies for Conservation in a Post-colonial Era*, edited by William M. Adams and Martin Mulligan, 51–78. New York: Routledge, 2002.

Pratt, Mary Louise. "Arts of the Contact Zone." *Profession* (1991): 33–40.

Rash, Ron. "The Facts of Historical Fiction." *Publisher's Weekly*. https://www.publishersweekly.com/pw/by-topic/columns-and-blogs/soapbox/article/12786-the-facts-of-historical-fiction.html

———. *One Foot in Eden*. New York: Picador, 2002.

———. *Raising the Dead*. Oak Ridge, Tenn.: Iris Press, 2002.

Rash, Ron, et al. "Nature, Place and the Appalachian Writer." *Iron Mountain Review* 23 (2007): 18–24.

Richards, Thomas Addison. "Landscape of the South." *Harper's New Monthly Magazine* 36, no. 6 (1853): 721–32.

Shurbutt, Sylvia Bailey, and David O. Hoffman. "Interview with Ron Rash." Ron Rash: 2011 Appalachian Heritage Writer-in-Residence, Shepherd University. https://www.shepherd.edu/ahwirweb/rash/interview.doc.

Smith, Newton. "Words to Raise the Dead: The Poetry of Ron Rash." *Iron Mountain Review* 20 (2004): 13–20.

Williams, John Alexander. *Appalachia: A History*. Chapel Hill: University of North Carolina Press, 2002.

Zacharias, Karen Spears. "Interview with Ron Rash." *Authors 'Round the South*. September 21, 2006. https://authorsroundthesouth.com/southern-lit-news/author-news-interviews/139-ron-rash-speaks-with-karen-spears-zacharias.

"Little Porcelain Shepherds and Shepherdesses"

The Female Pastoral Archetype and Version of the Appalachian Pastoral

MICHAEL S. MARTIN

Writing in the 1838 travelogue collection *The Poetry of Travelling in the United States*, Anna Maria Wells, a little-known early nineteenth-century American poet, frames her experience on a mountain excursion along the French Broad River in North Carolina in decidedly gendered terms. Wells was a Boston-based antebellum poet who had a better-known sister in Frances "Fanny" Osgood, one of the most popular female writers in the first half of the nineteenth century. While gazing upon North Carolina's famous Mount Pisgah and admiring the "beautiful" "Blue Ridge" mountains, Wells lapses into transcendental revelry, as she recalls that the sunset over the mountains is comparable to God's "splendour" and the peaks reflect the golden sun as if they were a "continuous thread of light" (277). At this moment of digesting the symbolic import of the Appalachian wilderness, Wells includes an original poem, an ode called "To the Whippoorwill." In the poem, Wells includes several of the signature characteristics of the pastoral ideal: the "whispering mountain breeze" that allows for the mountain's idyllic quality; a Pan or Faunus figure, a "ploughman sing[ing] with rustic" skill; and the "woodsman's axe" that interrupts the pastoral idyll. But embedded within this seemingly simplistic ode is a feminized version of the Appalachian pastoral ideal. Wells imaginatively projects herself as being the mother whippoorwill who yearns for the domestic life ("my distant home") while in the wilderness and is concerned that her "Lov'd ones," that is, her "children," cannot hear her song calling to them (lines 17, 25). What differentiates Wells's pastoral framing of her experience in the Appalachian Mountains from those of some of her male peers is her rendering of a specifically gendered version of nature. She actively envisions herself as being a female archetype within the woods and can thus fashion the pastoral myth to her liking, here complete with the calming presence of the domestic house and her children's voices to assuage the solitude of her wilderness experience. Wells combines elements of sentimental literature (loss, sorrow, and domesticity) within her gendered version of the Appalachian pastoral ideal.

In Wells's example of Appalachian travel writing, the female pastoral ideal is reappropriated from its usual ideological use, that is, as a representation of male desire projected onto the landscape. Wells subverts and controls the fantasy—which really isn't purely a "fantasy" and instead has an aesthetic, referential dimension—by reconceiving her pastoral vision with a female figure serving as the protagonist in nature, here through the conceit of the female mother as a calling bird. Such unorthodox engagement with the pastoral goes against what may be a dominant and, to an extent, justified critique of this aesthetic trope that has had much currency in twentieth-century American studies: approaching nineteenth-century literary pastoralism as connected to male hegemony; a willful apolitical and ahistorical retreat into an idealized, platonic world; and even, as Lawrence Buell argues, "romantic naturism" becoming "an instrument of imperial conquest" (35). What these critiques of pastoralism presume is that literature and literary tropes primarily function as ideological arguments: pastoralism as colonialism, pastoralism as antifeminism, and so on. Instead, my argument reinvigorates and rethinks the role of pastoralism in a field of writing—antebellum, Appalachian nonfiction nature and travel narratives—as having a more complex, polyvalent meaning than merely serving as an ideological equivalent to national conquest. Further, very little scholarship exists in regard to pastoral devices within southern, antebellum Appalachian travel narratives. Finally, the female pastoral ideal, conceived by writers either from Appalachia or traveling through Appalachia, has been reappropriated both by women writers who include some alternate-gendered version of the pastoral myth and by male writers who have varying versions, both orthodox and nontraditional, of the female pastoral archetype. My argument, then, recognizes the political and social critiques that have been leveled at pastoral while putting forth examples of female pastoral literary types that challenge such a simplified, constructivist reading of these nineteenth-century Appalachian nonfiction texts; my work also reappropriates the category of the "pastoral" from its usual contemporary framing and applies its aesthetic ideas to mainly noncanonical women's eastern mountain travel writing from this time period.

Gendered approaches to the landscape have often been critically framed as moments when male authors enact fantasies of violence and sexuality upon the land, which acts as a substitute for the female body. Kate Soper summarizes this approach by suggesting that woman-as-land signifies that "'she' is nature conceived as spatial territory . . . which is tamed and tilled [as] in agriculture" (141). Soper further elaborates on this traditional gendered landscape approach by setting up two versions of it: "Nature is allegorized as either a powerful maternal force, the womb of all human production, or as the site of sexual enticement and ultimate seduction" (141). Soper and other critics, particularly Buell, have sought to reinvigorate and rethink approaches to nature in literature and pastoralism so that pastoral imagery isn't simplified to this formula of being either a protective "womb" or a sexualized landscape. It is in this space of critical intervention that I situate this project. That is, the following argument suggests that the sociopolitical components of the pastoral myth, perhaps best illustrated in feminized versions of it, are but one component of the antebellum female pastoral that was produced by Appalachian writers, both male and female. The antebellum Appalachian female pastoral is conceived of by writers such as Susan Fenimore Cooper, Charles Lanman, and Anna Maria Wells in multiple ways. This version of the pastoral functions as a useable, changeable literary trope that often revealed the limits of social conventions related to gender as well as a narrativized response to real-world nature, the Appalachian Mountains.

Male Writers and Female Archetypes in Antebellum Pastoral Imagery

Both male and female travel writers into the Appalachian region reveal similar usage of the female pastoral archetype, no matter the sex of the author. Philip Pendleton Kennedy's work reveals, for example, an idealized erotic dimension to the Appalachian female pastoral archetype. Kennedy creates a pastoral tableau whereby multiple goddesses and female water nymphs roam in the Appalachian Mountains: "Diana . . . nightly kissed the boy Endymion" in those wilds; the supreme water nymph Undine is seen "sitting in all her beauty by the foam" of the falls; and Bonny Kilmeney, the celebrated rural woman in James Hoggs's poetic "Elegy," is described by Kennedy in unambiguously erotic terms, with "her bosom heaped with flowers" (158). Diana, Undine, and Bonny Kilmeney are central figures in Kennedy's extended transcendental vision that is framed as a fleeting pastoral drama. The women are rendered in equal parts aesthetic description (Undine's "beauty") and erotic positions (Diana "kissing" Endymion, Kilmeney's heaping "bosom"). Clearly, Kennedy's female pastoral vision is one that confirms the American studies thesis that male writers sexualized the landscape as a "site of sexual enticement," to use Soper's description.

But Kennedy's varied poetic and mythological references also presume an audience of northern readership that had knowledge of a vast literary tradition of the female pastoral, from Greek stories of Undine and her transfixing beauty to the eighteenth-century Scottish poet Hogg, himself a shepherd, who valorized Kilmeney in his poetic elegy that celebrated her—Hogg calls her his rustic "bonny flower"—as the female pastoral ideal. Seemingly, Kennedy is acknowledging that vast literary tradition as an intertextual part of his female Appalachian pastoral archetype, a shared tradition that elevates his referencing of goddesses and women heroes above being pure erotica material. In the process, Kennedy seems to raise the female pastoral tradition to that of literary luminaries that he references equally as much in the book, including Shakespeare, Wordsworth, and Robert Burns. Kennedy's choice of the Allegheny chain of the Appalachian Mountains for furthering this component of the pastoral tradition implicitly suggests he considers this particular setting, the Blackwater Region, as its latest incarnation on the American continent.

Another antebellum writing on the female pastoral comes from Charles Lanman's *Adventures in the Wilds of the United States British American Provinces* (1856). Lanman conveys a unique version of the female pastoral figure. While traveling through the North Georgia Mountains, Lanman recalls the Cherokee legend, memorialized by an Indian mound, that surrounds the female namesake of the Valley of Nacoochee. As an avatar of Acadia, Nacoochee is figured as being outside of time and history: Lanman poeticizes Nacoochee as being a "maiden" who passed away on a perpetual "summer day" and for whom the waters of the Nacoochee River "seem to be murmuring a perpetual song in memory of the departed" (358). Lanman allegorizes the Cherokee girl in various ways here and further in his description: she is the human embodiment or avatar of the Arcadian idyll (the "maiden" who died on a "summer day"), not necessarily figured as a shepherd or shepherdess; she is likened to the water nymph of the European pastoral tradition, as her relationship with the Nacoochee River suggests she is an Undine-like figure; and she is finally emblazoned as a "newly born star [that] made its [first] appearance in the sky" on the evening after her death (358). What is unique about the Appalachian version of the female pastoral in its multiple forms and versions (water nymph, river conceit, virgin maiden) is that the fantasy is now centered on a Native American woman, yet transposed into what is usually a European literary convention and setting. For Lanman and others, a female Native American pastoral figure must have seemed an appropriate symbol for a literary framing of such an interior space, the wild, undomesticated landscape of the Appalachian Mountains, as Native American memory and culture were still pervasive within the North Georgia Mountains. Lanman's orientation toward the Cherokee maiden, undoubtedly, is an appropriating one; yet he has to delve into local history and lore to find his symbol rather than, as in the European model, relying on a figure from an imagined site somewhere in modern-day Greece.

But Nacoochee, the Cherokee woman, becomes something more later in nineteenth-century Georgia poet and future Confederate general Henry R. Jackson's poetic elegy, as she is rendered the most celebratory and permanent figure in nature, a being who has "vanished with her maidens" in a place where "the mountain echoes catch no more the strain" of the Native American's music and voice (lines 11–13). In her death, Nacoochee becomes the ultimate pastoral ideal, the figure who is in complete harmony with the surrounding environs, the "mountain[s]," "meadows," and "marshy stream[s]" (lines 12–17). But, in distinctly sexual terms, Jackson also renders Nacoochee the untouched virgin of the forest, a figure that corresponds with the sexualized landscape thesis: Rumbling "branches" can no longer "pluck [her] jasmine flowers," and the speaker imagines himself laying on her "green breast" in order to "forget" the world (lines 15, 23). The branches seem to be a conspicuously phallic object in Jackson's pastoral vision of the Cherokee legend; the "green breast" could alternate between a stereotypical landscape description and an eroticized version of the Cherokee woman that is centered on a part for the whole. What Lanman and Jackson's respective evocations of Nacoochee seem to suggest on a larger level is that the Appalachian female pastoral was a literary space where cross-racial fantasies could be enacted, a textual domain where cultural taboos of sexuality could be explored but done so in the familiar, "high art" mode of the European literary pastoral. In this respect, the pastoral mode does function in the traditional way of hegemonic appropriation and, in this instant, confirm the "hegemonic" narrative that is predominant in modern-day pastoral studies. Jackson ameliorates the more erotic components of this poem, however, by returning Nacoochee to the virgin pastoral archetype in the final stanza, as he pictures her in a permanent place in the Arcadian Georgia landscape:

> Unsullied Nature hold o'er thee control,
> And years still leave thee beauteous as they roll. (lines 40–41)

Nacoochee's bosom remains "unsullied," or untouched, the pure virgin that cohabits a poetic space that previously had the female protagonist imaginatively lending her green breast to the speaker. Jackson backs off from such overtly erotic components to his cross-racial poetic fantasy of the Cherokee girl and instead now relegates her to a permanent platonic state outside of time and history: Nacoochee is still "beauteous" through time immemorial because she is impervious to it. In returning to the ahistorical virgin version of the female pastoral archetype, Jackson seems self-conscious of his objectifying gaze leveled at the female Native American body, even if done imaginatively.

This North Georgia Appalachian region became idealized in travel narratives throughout the antebellum period, and George Cooke, a Maryland writer, also memorialized the same peak and river in his "Sketches of Georgia" (1840). "Sketches of Georgia" was published in the *Southern Literary Messenger* as part of the regional movement to sell Appalachia to a northern audience and therefore included pastoral imagery as part of a way to reach that erudite audience. Kevin O'Donnell, in "The Artist in the Garden," contends that Cooke's paintings, for which he was better known than his literary endeavors, were meant to "transmit the power and authority of European culture back to monied Americans" (79). The literary pastoral, particularly the female version of it, was therefore a code for European cultural prestige embedded within the Appalachian landscape. Cooke's travelogue continues the Nacoochee legend of the female rustic that Jackson and Lanman also invoked in their respective travelogue and poetry, though Cooke doesn't overtly eroticize the Native American woman specifically within his "Sketches." Cooke's version of the Nacoochee legend commends the "maiden" for heroism and bravery in offering herself on a "funeral pire [sic] to make atonement for her people" (776). Cooke's legend, as with Jackson, preserves "the bright and beautiful daughter" for time immemorial (776). In Cooke's literary framing, Nacoochee becomes an inverted form of the female pastoral: she is the sacrificial woodland figure that must be given up for preservation of the Cherokee culture and their environment, the Native American "hunting grounds" (776). Though Cooke doesn't explicitly mention Nacoochee again after the funeral pyre scene, he does create a gendered version of the Appalachian wilderness.

In memorializing a scene at Toccoa Falls for the reader, Cooke feminizes the landscape as part of his pastoral vision; in contrast, his description of the Tallulah River is figured as masculine. Cooke describes the falls as if they were something out of a pastoral painting or Shakespeare's *Midsummer Night's Dream*: The "beautiful cascade, is indeed a scene of enchanting beauty, where fairies might dance by its sparkling light" (776). Here, Cooke metonymically substitutes a female woman with the landscape, which becomes a substitute "enchanting beauty"; he also furthers the pastoral fantasy by imagining fairies traipsing across the waterfall's rocks. Cooke completes his feminization of the waterfall stating the cascading stream of water lands gently and "leave[s] unruffled the bosom of the reservoir," while the "lofty elms" above the falls shield "its beauty with a flickering veil" (776). Notably, the woman/waterfall's "bosom" is preserved in Cooke's fantasy, and her "veil" retains its modesty by being beyond the gaze of presumably other male suitors, or anyone who would taint Cooke's idealized virginal figure. In contrast, Cooke's literary typology for the Tallulah River is cast in unambiguously male-centered language, as he states that "the Tallulah is a more masculine scene" than Toccoa Falls (776). Cooke's gesture here is to equate the literary categories of the picturesque and pastoral, which are somewhat interchangeable, with the sublime, which he formulates as being masculine. For example, Cooke's third-person visitor to the falls, now given the pronoun "he," "approach[es] this scene [and] finds himself on the verge of a yawning chasm" (776). The "yawning chasm" is representative of the sublime's characteristic of having high mountain peaks and vast panoramas as part of the natural setting that solicits the highest emotion possible in the observer.

What may be happening in Cooke's two gendered versions of the Appalachian female pastoral is that he is offering dual competing ideals about nature and its domestication to his northern audience. In her reading of Washington Irving's stories, Annette Kolodny writes that Irving dichotomizes the environment in ways that I suggest are similar to Cooke's travelogue of northern Georgia: "Irving succeeded in preserving, intact, the maternal image of the American pastoral at a time when the aggressive, sexually assertive aspect of the impulse was coming more and more to dominate" (*Lay of the Land* 69). *The Land Before Her: Fantasy and Experience of the American Frontiers, 1630–1860* (1984) is Kolodny's landmark study of frontier women's writing from the Ohio Valley and other Appalachian and western areas. In her reading of Irving, Kolodny argues that his New York villages in "Sleepy Hollow" and "Rip Van Winkle" are "maternally oriented pastoral retreats" that represent a womb-like stasis and return to an uncomplicated American past. The implicit suggestion here is that the "sexually aggressive" part of Kolodny's formula is the male presence in the pastoral myth, what may be illustrated both in Cooke's figure of the male sojourner perilously hiking above the "yawning chasm" of Tallulah's lower waters and in his personification of the river's rushing waters as having "an angry brow and hoarse murmurings common to the rougher sex" (776). Meanwhile, the female pastoral would be represented in the womb-like interior setting of both Sleepy Hollow and Toccoa Falls, a soft, gentle environment where the pastoral imagination runs rampant and "fairies dance" by "sparkling light," to use Cooke's phrasing. Cooke deploys the female pastoral in his middle-ground vision of a domesticated pastoral wilderness as a way of preserving the landscape as a "retreat," to use Kolodny's phrase, a comforting vision of a pleasure-ground wilderness softened to the reader through feminine imagery. For example, Cooke alternates his vision from the "rougher sex," that is, the male version of the pastoral, to that of conspicuously feminine, domestic imagery: "Habersham [the resort]" is a place where travelers "can enjoy the sweets of domestic life... the hospitable hearth [and] social circle" (776). In Kolodny's words, Cooke deploys "the maternal image of the American pastoral" as a countervailing force to the masculine, aggressive component of his landscape description, here illustrated in his equating the Tallulah River with the "rougher sex."

The previous close readings of Kennedy, Lanman, Jackson, and Cooke all reveal that antebellum travel writing about Appalachia by male authors has a more varied story behind it than the "male psycho-sexual landscape thesis" allows. Kennedy, for example, is active in re-creating the female pastoral archetype; in this respect, he enacts what "post-pastoral" theory might suggest is the transference of individual consciousness into a conscience awareness of the ecosystem and the subject's relationship to that system. In Cooke's formulation, Nacoochee becomes the female pastoral sacrificial figure, a unique component to the feminized landscape as conceived by male antebellum writers. Finally, each writer, whether Lanman and Cooke referencing the Nacoochee legend or Kennedy's reference to the Scottish ballad tradition and folklore, utilizes some form of Appalachian oral tradition, whether European American or Native American, to base their own female pastoral version upon and transform it according to the dictates of place and circumstance. Kennedy's background in balladry has been noted by Timothy Sweet, editor of the latest edition of *The Blackwater Chronicle*, who writes that Kennedy was "a great student of songs and ballad" (xxi). Certainly, some of these ballads and songs would be from the Scots-Irish culture and tradition in South-Central Appalachia, just as Lanman, Jackson, and Cooke drew from the Native American oral legends particular to place, the North Georgia Mountains. In other words, an actual place, setting, and location helped form the antebellum female pastoral just as much as these male writers' imagination and capacity for mythological fantasies did.

Female Appalachian Writers, Female Pastoral Archetypes

As with male antebellum Appalachian writers and nonnatives writing about their travels through the Appalachian region, pre–Civil War women writers from this mountain region are no monolithic bunch, nor are they adherents to a particular version of the pastoral where they necessarily alter the mythos simply because a member of their sex is idealized. Anne Newport Royall is one early nineteenth-century writer who should be considered a native Appalachian writer, as she was grew up in western Pennsylvania and lived much of her married life in the Virginia mountains. Her 1827 novel *The Tennessean*, which features a first-person female narrator, is one of the earliest pieces of full-length fiction that features the Appalachian region, and her *Sketches of History, Life, and Manners in the United States* (1826) may be one of the first pieces of writing, fiction or nonfiction, to depict "the mountaineer" as a literary type. In this travelogue, one of the earliest pieces of travel writing composed by a woman that depicts the Appalachian region, Royall does not willfully enter into pastoral mythology and instead, as a devoted journalist, is more analytical in her approach to the region and the culture, dividing her sketches of each place under such rubrics as "general character" and "history."

Antebellum Appalachian women writers such as Royall do not seem, at least consciously, to insert their gender within a pastoralized mountain landscape as a deliberate rhetorical device, though Royall does incorporate components of the European pastoral nonetheless. As mentioned previously, Royall errs on the side of journalistic prose rather than poetic evocations; yet she does create a gendered version of the landscape. For example, Royall personifies a hanging rock in Greenbrier County, then in Virginia, as a woman's chest: "The main body of the rock reclines in the bosom of the mountain" (78). Nature as a concept is the classical version for Royall, that is, the antithesis to tainted culture and civilization, as well as being static, metaphysical, and female. She writes, for instance, of the climate and landscape near Staunton, Virginia, that "the fertility of the soil, and numerous streams of the purest water, may be ascribed [to] that exuberance of nature everywhere visible" (88). In Royall's version of classical nature, the mountains are shaped like a woman's bosom, and she notices that nature bears the same qualities of idealized nineteenth-century womanhood: the ability for pregnancy ("fertility") and virginity ("purity"). At multiple points, Royall notices streams or springs that are of the "purest" verdure, as if she, as with the majority of early nineteenth-century writers, male or female, transposes the body of nature with that of a woman.

In short, in Royall's 1826 travelogue account of the Appalachian Mountains, we see early, nascent versions of the female pastoral. Yet these versions are best understood through the lens of multiple, gendered traits related to the landscape, ones that were prominent in eighteenth- and nineteenth-century traditions, including the category of the "picturesque." The picturesque centers on finding beauty in nature's variety.[1] In one such description of the Blue Ridge Mountains around Staunton, Virginia, for example, Royall relates that language fails "to give even a glimmering of this grand spectacle" before her, a universalizing vision that gestures toward the category of the sublime (the spectacle is "grand") while also pointing toward the picturesque beautiful. But she doesn't develop this aesthetic approach to include herself imaginatively projected into the landscape, nor suggest a vast fantasy of nymphs traipsing along a vast waterfall or anything akin. She unconsciously considers nature to be a fertile, virginal female in multiple instances, judging from her language choices ("bosom," "impregnating"); her use of such language thus confirms part of Soper's landscape thesis on the pure, womb-like portrayals of nature, but this time proffered by a female writer. Finally, her gaze is indeed toward the central dramatic objects situated in the European pastoral—farms, valleys, meadows, those areas watched over by the pastoral shepherd—yet these objects stand in isolation to a totalizing myth and are often gender neutral.

Anna Maria Wells and the Poetic Pastoral Frame

Anna Maria Wells, by contrast, begins to develop an alternate version and more textured approach to the female pastoral in her poetry selections, based on her experience in the Southern Appalachian Mountains published in her 1838 book. Wells's prose is also more poetic than Royall's, and her personality and flourish as an author are more foregrounded than Royall's in *Sketches*. Wells begins sections with epigraphs inserted for dramatic effect ("we dashed thro' the rivers where bridge there was none"; 273), inserts colloquial jokes based on local dialect, and foregrounds her gender by mentioning two incidents: she is accompanied by a male fellow traveler and also mourning the loss of a mother alligator and her brood (an "unfortunate mother and her young one"; 272). The latter point, that is, that Wells overtly inserts herself and her gendered identity into her travelogue, is what makes her poetic rendering of the female pastoral archetype more varied and developed than Royall's.

As with Lanman's incorporating Jackson's poetry to memorialize an Appalachian Mountain scene, Wells inserts multiple poems that she authored in remembering Buncombe County in her "Sketches." There are four poems included in all: "The Mountain Church," "To the Whippoorwill," "Let Us Go to the Woods," and "Song" (of New England). Unlike with Royall's use of female metaphors for the landscape in her *Sketches*, Wells creates a sustained poetic conceit of landscape-as-woman throughout these four poems. In "The Mountain Church," which Wells states was occasioned by her finding country gravestones one evening while riding through the mountains, she bemoans the solitary existence of the graveyard "where the dead were laid" (line 22). The mountain church, by contrast, is a place where "the scattered families" can be figuratively baptized through prayer by the "mountains and deep forest shades" (lines 8–9). The grave mound is similarly given a spiritual rebirth through nature:

> The forest flowers
> Themselves had fondly clustered there,—and white
> Azalias [sic] with sweet breath stood round about
> Like fair young maidens mourning o'er the dead.
> In some sweet solitude like this I would
> That I might sleep my last long dreamless sleep! (lines 26–31)

On a general level, what stands out in these lines is that Wells is using the first-person pronoun to position herself within the poetic drama, the setting that she is vividly re-creating from her evening ride through the North Carolina mountains; she inserts herself as a decidedly female, not gender-neutral, figure within her poetic vision. Further, Wells incorporates particular characteristics associated with the nineteenth-century sentimental tradition—her mourning and remembrance of the dead through the "Azalia [sic]" flowers and vision of the young maiden, for example—that would have further indicated her authorship as being female. She fully incorporates the woman-as-virgin component of the pastoral myth with the untouched "maidens" analogized as flowers; in this respect, Wells incorporates and appropriates the female virgin component of the pastoral archetype and does so in an orthodox way. For Wells and many of the male writers (Jackson's "branches" that "pluck jasmine flowers"), landscape depictions instead are usually metonymically compared with bosoms or the curvature of a woman's body.

Wells's pastoral vision is not of a shepherd watching over the static, ahistorical world of a recreated Arcadia transplanted in the Appalachian Mountains: her myth instead recreates the mountain landscape as a female body, a metaphorical shepherdess, that watches over and "clasp[s]" both the deceased spirits and secluded, rustic church. Wells acknowledges that her poetic mourning for the mountain church and the deceased is within a pastoral frame likening the sacred rustic space to a perpetual Arcadian idyll: "Still shall sweet summer smiling, linger here" (line 35). Just as male Appalachian writers inserted themselves into the landscape, at least indirectly, in sexualizing it, Wells even more forcefully inserts herself, her femininity, into her pastoral vision by imagining the mountains as an extension of a woman's body, "giant arms" that enclose and nurture any suffering that occurs in her poetic spectacle.

In her third and most celebratory poem, "Let Us Go to the Woods," Wells furthers her poetic vision of the female pastoral by invoking images of domesticity and motherhood into the North Carolina mountainscape. According to Annette Kolodny in *The Land Before Her*, "Avoiding for a time male assertions of a rediscovered Eden, women claimed the frontiers as a potential sanctuary for an idealized domesticity. Massive exploitation and alteration of the continent do not seem to have been part of women's fantasies. They dreamed, more modestly, of locating a home and a familial human community within a cultivated garden" (xiii). Kolodny contends that female writers had a different orientation to the frontier than male writers had with the "sexualized landscape" thesis: Antebellum women writers instead fantasize about home and hearth and a "familial human community" when they incorporate the trope of the pastoral type as a literary device. Wells's "Let Us Go to the Woods" follows such a female-centered version of the pastoral and with the traits of "idealized domesticity" that Kolodny identifies with this subgenre. The poem's dramatis personae are, of course, women, as the speaker imagines herself heading for a sojourn into the woods in what is a conspicuously pastoral landscape. The first image from the landscape in Wells's poem is a tilled meadow—"They are mowing the grass, and at work with the hay" (line 2)—where farmers, a usual focal point in the pastoral myth, are working in the fields. Wells's two female protagonists, however, do not seem to be self-conscious that they encounter images of themselves, or idealized femininity, almost immediately in the farmland environment:

> Come over the meadow and scent the fresh air,
> For the pure mountain breezes are everywhere.   (lines 2–3)

That is, Wells has her female speaker and companion confront the virginal, "pure" Arcadian environment, encountering an allegorized version of the female body within it. Later, in line 25, she also portrays virginal "mountain-maids" who are gathering and naming various flowers and plants. In perhaps an unconscious way, Wells has her speaker and the companion confront the landscape as an allegorized female body, yet they don't seem to notice; this ideology of the pastoral landscape is so naturalized by the time of Wells's writing that this lack of conflict or self-consciousness toward such a depiction is to be expected, even when women writers insert themselves into the pastoral myth. Further, in the early stanzas, where Wells and her companion play with various plants, including "touch-me-not[s]" and "phlox" (lines 18–21), she poetically imagines such a nonaggressive (e.g., the antithesis to male-centered fantasy), "cultivated garden" natural paradise as Kolodny outlines for the female pastoral.

The final stanza of "Let Us Go to the Woods" situates the two female companions climbing the hillside for one final gaze over the landscape, both the grandiose and the miniature, the latter trait seemingly a hallmark of the antebellum female pastoral. For Wells's aesthetic of the miniature, for example, previous stanzas have the speaker find the smallest flowers ("the *Midsummer Daisy* is hiding here yet"; line 34), *clematis* petals that are positioned as tiny pearls in her companion's hair (lines 15–16), and other individual objects. The speaker even forewarns her companion "Nay—pause not to gaze at the landscape now" (line 9), as if their domain is instead relegated to those objects that are miniaturized in nature. In this final stanza, however, Wells's speaker finally compels her companion to abandon an aesthetic of the miniature instead for a grandiose vision of a pastoral valley, with tilled fields in golden sunlight: "But stay—We are now on the high hill's brow! How bright lie the fields in the sun light below!" (lines 35–36). When the speaker's gaze is extended to a panorama of the Appalachian Mountains, she sees not nymphs frolicking on waterfalls or shepherds playing flutes but instead a familiar symbol of the family: "those white chimneys that peep o'er the grove" are her friend's "own little cottage—the home that [she] love[s]" (lines 37–38). At the same time that the female speaker notes the "white chimneys" of her friend's domestic home off in the horizon, she returns to an aesthetic of the miniature and finds a parallel mother-children instance in nature: a "*black-bird* that [may] have flown with her brood" (line 44). Wells once again notices shared traits in the animal—a mother and her children in nature—just as she did with the alligator and her brood earlier in her narrative section. The poem ends with Wells trying to discern a moral lesson from nature, for from "the lowliest thing / Some lesson of worth to the mind can bring" (lines 47–48), as if she were considering the role of didactic instruction to pupils or even children. Wells's compendium of gendered characteristics within nature—noticing parallel mothers and children in nature, seeing the domestic home as the focal point of her hillside gaze, inserting herself and a female companion into her poetic vision—represents a sustained use of what might be recognized as a pastoral archetype, with some variation. Kolodny's argument from *The Land Before Her*, that is, that female frontier writers envisioned their pastoral dream as one that was a "sanctuary for idealized domesticity," is confirmed in the maternal images from "Let Us Go to the Woods" and "The Whippoorwill," poems that include Wells fantasizing about her distant domicile, her children, and even nature and morality in the Edenic, Arcadian Appalachian landscape.

Susan Fenimore Cooper and the Demythologized Shepherdess

Perhaps the most sustained piece of antebellum women's nature writing on the Appalachian landscape, however, comes from the pen of Susan Fenimore Cooper in her 1850 seasonal journal *Rural Hours*. Scholarship on Cooper and *Rural Hours*, her most famous piece of writing, has taken off in the past few decades, leading her to be on almost equal critical footing as her more famous father, nineteenth-century American fiction writer James Fenimore Cooper. *Rural Hours* reads similarly to Thoreau's *Walden* (1854), a nature journal composed by a gifted writer with a careful eye centered on the natural and cultural history of a particular place. Cooper's particular places are the woods and lake region that surround Cooperstown, New York, located in Otsego County, one of the northernmost counties included in the Appalachian Regional Commission's designated counties of Appalachia. Cooper's narrative lens in *Rural Hours* is generally that of an astute naturalist, with very few poeticized descriptions of nature; yet the cumulative effect of *Rural Hours* upon the reader is that the entire book is composed in the pastoral mood, written as if the vision of the perpetual Arcadian idyll is embedded in the prose as a narrative device. That is, while Cooper usually does not explicitly invoke pastoral mythology when describing the New York countryside, many of the natural vignettes in her diary entries replicate the drowsy, lazy idyll inherent within pastoral literary types.

For example, Cooper writes in an "Autumn" entry, "Monday, 16th—Charming weather; bright and warm, with hazy Indian summer atmosphere. They are harvesting the last maize-fields; some farmers 'top' the stalks, that is to say, cut off the upper half, and leave the lower ears several weeks longer to ripen" (214). Cooper's descriptive and analytical style relays to the reader the harvesting practices associated with maize cutting. Yet the opening lines read like something from a pastoral romance, with the extended "Indian summer" reminiscent of the pastoral idyll as well as the subsequent focus on the farmer in the landscape. Long moonlit walks within the woods;

"pleasant" traipses to local working farms, which she romanticizes; and first spring buds described on the trees and plants—the cumulative effect of Cooper's nature diary is an intoxicating one, a replication of the pastoral mood.

Cooper's complex stance toward gender and gender relations in *Rural Hours* also influences her vision of nature overall, her version of the pastoral myth, and proper farmland work roles in her rustic, village setting. In meditating upon men and women farmers working the fields in the "Summer" section, she mentions that she once saw "a woman ploughing in this county" and suggests that female farmers are a rarity in the New World (106). The farmer, or ploughman, is of course the typical human presence in the pastoral myth, with the precursor being the Shepherd Poet figure of Greek and Roman fame. Yet Cooper makes a double commentary on gender and farming here. On one hand, she makes a feminist critique in complaining that she had once "seen a woman and a cow harnessed together" in the fields, while a man was driving them (106). On the other, she maintains orthodox, conservative views on gender in her portrayal of the farmer as being inevitably male, as "woman's helplessness" and general bodily "weakness" (women don't have "the stronger arm") make them inappropriate farmer figures (106). As with Royall's depiction of a feminized landscape metonymically substituted for the female body, Cooper approaches figures in the landscape from an uncomplicated, tacit agreement with orthodox gender ideology, which presumes males to be bodily superior, in the nineteenth-century. Cooper's conformity to stereotypical gender roles in *Rural Hours* is confirmed earlier in "Summer" when she criticizes some female visitors to a rural farm, stating they "had their hair cropped short like men, a custom which seems all but unnatural" (100). Cooper's criticism of short-haired women in this passage perhaps aligns with Anne Perrin's argument on pastoralism, community, and male personages in Cooper's nonfiction. Perrin writes that this pastoral trait in Cooper's work is marked by "a father-figure," ranging from George Washington to her actual father, "engaged in land alteration," that is, planting or farming. The genealogy of the pastoral in Cooper's work is overtly masculine in Perrin's argument where this male pastoral functions as Cooper's gesture toward a symbol of community stability, the male forefathers. Cooper's explicit critique of gender roles, that is, farmers must necessarily be male and women must confirm to traditional standards of beauty, can be read in light of Perrin's genealogical approach to the male pastoral in her work. Cooper's orthodox approach to real female figures in the landscape—farmers stripped of the framing device of explicit pastoral mythology—shapes how she does approach explicitly pastoral narrative moments in *Rural Hours*.

Despite her traditional views on gender roles, Cooper nonetheless envisions a pastoral garden that includes both male and female figures tending the flock and immersed in the Appalachian landscape. With her discussion of changing artistic and literary depictions of the season "Autumn," Cooper shifts into a self-conscious meditation on the Americanized version of the European pastoral: "When writing a pastoral [writers] turned away from the little porcelain shepherds and shepherdesses, standing in high-heeled shoes upon every mantel-piece, and they fixed their eyes upon the real living Roger and Dolly in the hay-field" (208). Here, Cooper is offering a revised version of the pastoral that corresponds to "a more natural style in gardening" and eschews what she terms "mere vapid, conventional repetitions" (208). Her self-conscious commentary replicates Kennedy's several authorial interjections in his pastoral descriptions in *The Blackwater Chronicle*; but Cooper's explicit referent to the pastoral type here is even more geared toward demythologizing this artistic trope, what she labels the faux "porcelain" shepherds and shepherdesses, in lieu of "the real living" pastoral figures inhabiting the landscape. Unlike Wells, who incorporates the pastoral type but doesn't invoke the entire pastoral myth, Cooper comments on pastoralism as an artistic mode and considers its limitations, arguing that the American or Appalachian version of the Arcadian idyll should "seat Roger and Dolly," common names, "under a hawthorn ... [rather] than paint them beneath a laurel, or an ilex of Greece or Rome" (208). In seating her pastoral figures in the New York countryside, Cooper is deploying the European pastoral for her own purposes and in a new context: the myth is still a useable literary trope for her, but it has been demythologized and taken from the realm of "high art," the world of "Greece or Rome," and instead applied to the aesthetics of real-world farmers and pastoral figures who take their pose under a lowly, Americanized "hawthorn" tree. Cooper's revision of the pastoral mode here alters the way that her other farming references, which number in the dozens, function in *Rural Hours*: farming scenes in her nature journal are ways that Cooper attempts to enact her realist method of reframing the American/Appalachian pastoral, what she terms in this excerpt from "Autumn" "look[ing] at nature by the light of the sun, and not the glimmerings of the poet's lamp" (208).

One such reframing that Cooper initiates in converting this realist method to practice is in the "Summer" during her sojourn up an unnamed Otsego mountain, her most developed consideration of the Appalachian Mountains and, generally speaking, the concept of mountains. The passage begins with what should by now be a familiar literary flourish in antebellum Appalachian nature writing: the author's highly dramatic creation of her entry into the mountain region. Cooper writes, "After driving through a tame, uninteresting country, we come *suddenly* upon a wild nook, with its groves, and brook and rocks" (151, emphasis added). To be sure that Cooper is invoking the pastoral mode in her mountain description, she references the most famous pastoral elegy, "the Lycidas of [John] Milton," in comparing various individual, but revelatory, minutia in nature—"the mountain flower, the solitary bird, the rare plant," all natural symbols of the female Appalachian aesthetic of the miniature—to grandiose views of the natural world, particularly from the vantage of a mountaintop (152). From the elevated position, Cooper meditates in a quasi-transcendental aside on the way that mountains contribute to humankind's greater vision of the world: the mountains "add to the grandeur of the earth" and they vary "her"—nature is feminized here for Cooper—"character, climates, and productions" (153). Again, Cooper seems to be invoking the European pastoral only to demythologize it. For example, she compares aesthetic position from "below" or parallel to the ground level as being nothing but "pictures in one aspect only," while her view from the top presents an environment that relays discord, not stasis: from there, one "behold[s] the repose of power and strength after a great conflict" (153). Cooper's vision of a dynamic environment—"scars and furrows upon the giant Alps," as with the Appalachian Mountains, reveal "the record of earth's stormy history" (153)—signals a powerful shift in antebellum appropriations of the European pastoral: the pastoral is now historicized and "naturally" situated within a particular environment and setting.

Cooper seems to be corresponding that knowledge of place, which is framed through usual pastoral conventions, with both a cultural and natural history of the region; she sees the telltale signs of geologic conflict and dynamic processes when gazing at the Appalachian Mountains rather than a static, ahistorical setting. In demythologizing the European pastoral, Cooper also conspicuously leaves out the shepherd or shepherdess from her totalizing vision, thus suggesting through such an omission that gendered versions of the pastoral myth, including what critics may consider the sexualized landscape thesis, are part of the faux elements ("porcelain") of that artistic model; Cooper's landscape, besides a general notion of it being a "her," is devoid of particular gender designations.

The Appalachian Pastoral Female Archetype in Antebellum Nature Writing

In Cratis D. Williams's landmark dissertation "The Southern Mountaineer in Fact and Fiction" (1961), female writers and representations of women in Appalachia are not substantially analyzed until his analysis of Mary Noailles Murfee's mountain fiction in "Taking the Blue Ribbon" from 1876 (2:490–95). In other words, the historical timeline used here helps reset Appalachian women's writing and depictions of female archetypes to a much earlier time period, beginning with Royall's *Sketches of History, Life, and Manners in the United States* (1826), though there were even earlier such works. Antebellum men and women did not necessarily depict orthodox notions of the gendered pastoral in their travel and nature writing, though male writers such as Lanman did envision a sexualized version of Nacoochee through this literary trope, just as female writers such as Wells imagined images of quaint domesticity and motherhood while traveling deep in the Appalachian Mountains. The sexualized landscape thesis is therefore proven partially true, yet delimiting at the same time. Kennedy's depiction of a sexualized landscape in the Blackwater Region, for example, harkens equally to an oral history connected with place, and Scottish ballads passed on in Appalachia by immigrants from that country. Cooke's version of the female pastoral myth alters that literary type by making the protagonist both a purified virginal wilderness and a sacrificial figure. By 1850, when Cooper publishes *Rural Hours*, she imagines a female shepherdess tending the flock on equal footing with the male shepherd; yet her most extended mountain description alters the pastoral myth so that both gender and mythology are taken out of the equation. None of the authors covered passively re-create the European literary pastoral and the female archetype therein; almost all of these antebellum versions are instead at least partially alternative models of the pastoral trope.

Further, each of these writers was shaping their version of the female pastoral archetype according to an experiential encounter in the Appalachian Mountains; their choice of the pastoral as a useable metaphor did not precede their encounter in the wilderness, what Buell might call the "referential dimension" of language in literary texts. Writing in *American Incarnation: The Individual, the Nation, and the Continent* (1986), Myra Jehlen stresses that for early American exploration narratives, the concept of "America" was based on "the continent's physical reality" rather than a pure abstraction (9). The problem, according to Jehlen, is when "historical revisionists" work "to separate the idea and myth of America from its material reality" (10). Jehlen's formulation of the America myth suggests that both the "ideal and material (idealist and materialist)" perpetuate the story of democratic individualism, liberal selfhood, and so on (10). In the same respect, the materiality of the Appalachian Mountains emerges in such seemingly mythological narratives as Kennedy's *Blackwater Chronicle* and its depictions of woodland nymphs sitting under waterfalls. Kennedy, as with the other male and female writers from the time period, formulates the myth and metaphor at the same time he is creating a narrative response to a vast, immanent material reality: the Appalachian Mountains. Further, Cooke, Lanman, and Jackson all had to contend with oral legends connected with place in order to shape their female pastoral archetype in the North Georgia Mountains. In women's writing, even though Wells invokes the discourse of sentimentalism, a general nineteenth-century concept, in her poetic response to the Appalachian Mountains, she sees images of home and hearth only within the context of the Appalachian countryside; loss and mourning are equally shaped by sentimental literary expectations as they are by the actual space and place in the Buncombe countryside, particularly the solitary gravestones and country church she first encounters there, before subsequently transforming that experience into poetic reminiscence. Finally, there may be two reasons that the female pastoral archetype was such a prevalent literary symbol in these antebellum travel/nature narratives. First, the actual landscape that these writers encountered in North Carolina, Georgia, New York, and other Appalachian regions closely resembled the depictions of the European pastoral so prevalent in art, music, and literature; that is, the tilled farmland and settled, "middle-ground" landscape seemed like a real-world depiction of the Appalachia Arcadia, so the literary connotations associated with it—the female figure in the landscape or metonymically substituted for that landscape—were necessarily part of any literary re-creation. Second, the female pastoral archetype would have been an expected, accepted literary trope or symbol and therefore could allow for authorial exploration of controversial subjects through its frame; these could range from, within the male perspective, cross-racial desire embedded in the traditional pastoral depiction of the female virgin to, from women's perspective, the merging of the female desire for wilderness and outdoor freedom with an explicit gesture toward the domestic or maternal ideal.

NOTE

1. In terms of landscape aesthetics, Royall seems to be incorporating the philosophy of eighteenth-century British artist William Gilpin and his well-known definition of the *travel picturesque*: "In treating of picturesque travel, we may consider first its *object*; and secondly it's sources of *amusement*. This great object we pursue

through the scenery of nature. We seek it among all the ingredients of landscape—trees—rocks—broken-grounds—woods—rivers—lakes—plains—vallies [sic]—mountains—and distances. These objects *in themselves* produce infinite variety. No two rocks, or trees are exactly the same. They are varied, a second time, by *combination*; and almost as much, a third time, by different *lights, and shades*, and other aerial effects. Sometimes we find among them the exhibition of a *whole*; but oftener we find only beautiful *parts*" (16–17). Royall notices individual objects in her landscape visions of the Appalachian Mountains, ranging from farms to meadows to streams and more, and seems to be hinting at Gilpin's theory of seeing "infinity variety" in nature in her repeated descriptions of the vast panorama of the Blue Ridge Mountains. Finally, Royall's job as a journalist and her subsequent travelogue render her one of the first professional female writers, Appalachian or American, to enact the "travel picturesque" in her writings and help make it a regular feature for future nineteenth-century female writers (Caroline Howard Gilman and Margaret Fuller, for example).

BIBLIOGRAPHY

Buell, Lawrence. *The Environmental Imagination: Thoreau, Nature Writing, and the Formation of American Culture*. Cambridge, Mass.: Harvard University Press, 1995.

Cooke, George. "Sketches of Georgia." *Southern Literary Messenger*, November 1840, 775–77.

Fenimore Cooper, Susan. *Rural Hours*. Edited by Rochelle Johnson and Daniel Patterson. 1850. Athens: University of Georgia Press, 1998.

Gilpin, William. *Three Essays on Picturesque Beauty*. 2nd ed. London: R. Blamire, 1794.

Hogg, James. "Kilmeny." In *The Oxford Book of English Verse: 1250–1900*, edited by Arthur Quiller-Couch, 583–94. London: Oxford University Press, 1918.

Jackson, Henry R. "Mount Yonah—Vale of Nacoochee." In *Adventures in the Wilds of the United States British American Provinces*, edited by Charles Lanman, 358–59. Philadelphia: John W. Moore, 1856.

Jehlen, Myra. *American Incarnation: The Individual, the Nation, and the Continent*. Cambridge, Mass.: Harvard University Press, 1986.

Kennedy, Philip Pendleton. *The Blackwater Chronicle*. Edited by Timothy Sweet. Morgantown: West Virginia University Press, 2002.

Kolodny, Annette. *The Land Before Her: Fantasy and Experience of the American Frontiers, 1630–1860*. Chapel Hill: University of North Carolina Press, 1984.

———. *The Lay of the Land: Metaphor as Experience in American Life and Letters*. Chapel Hill: University of North Carolina Press, 1975.

Lanman, Charles. *Adventures in the Wilds of the United States British American Provinces*. Philadelphia: John W. Moore, 1856.

O'Donnell, Kevin. "The Artist in the Garden: George Cooke and the Ideology of Fine Arts Painting in Antebellum Georgia." In *CrossRoads: A Southern Culture Annual*, edited by Ted Olson, 73–96. Macon, Ga.: Mercer University Press, 2004.

Perrin, Anne. "Subversion and Narrative Style in Susan Fenimore Cooper's *Rural Hours*." In *James Fenimore Cooper: His Country and His Art. Papers from the 1999 Cooper Seminar (No. 12)*, edited by Hugh C. MacDougall, 79–84. Oneonta: State University of New York, College at Oneonta. https://www.jfcoopersociety.org/articles/SUNY/1999suny-perrin.html.

Royall, Anne Newport. *Sketches of History, Life, and Manners in the United States.* 1826. Carlisle, Mass.: Applewood Books, 2007.
Soper, Kate. "Naturalized Woman and Feminized Nature." In *The Green Studies Reader,* edited by Laurence Coupe, 139–43. London: Routledge, 2000.
Sweet, Timothy. *Traces of War: Poetry, Photography, and the Crises of the Union.* Baltimore: Johns Hopkins University Press, 1990.
Wells, Anna Maria. "Sketches from Buncombe, N.C., including Various Poems." In *The Poetry of Travelling in the United States,* edited by Carolina Gilman, 271–83. New York: S. Colman, 1838.
Williams, Cratis D. "The Southern Mountaineer in Fact and Fiction." PhD diss., New York University, 1961.

The Nymph's Reply
Kathryn Stripling Byer and Pastoral Romance

EVAN GURNEY

This essay starts out in Elizabethan England before it arrives in contemporary Appalachia, where Kathryn Stripling Byer situates her potent response to Christopher Marlowe's vision of pastoral romance. Although the world of *Wildwood Flower* (1992) and *Black Shawl* (1998) is clearly home to bucolic passion, with erotic desire emerging persistently and in a range of rural contexts, Byer offers a powerful corrective to Marlowe's seductive poetics, which stand in for a broader lyric tradition complicated by masculine and urbane privilege. Byer's Appalachian Mountains are insistently real; so too are the relationships Byer stages within that terrain. Indeed, by refusing to ignore the fraught politics of gender and region, Byer's lyric voice recalibrates the relationship between love and landscape, offering readers a fuller, more convincing vision of pastoral romance.

Perhaps the most famous lyric of the Renaissance period in England, "The Passionate Shepherd to His Love," is surely one of its most ludicrous too, as Marlowe adopts the persona of a lovesick shepherd who courts a would-be bride:

> Come live with mee, and be my love, And we will all the pleasures prove, That Vallies, groves, hills and fieldes, Woods, or steepie mountaine yeeldes.
>
> And wee will sit upon the Rocks,
> Seeing the Sheepherds feede theyr flocks, By shallow Rivers,
> to whose falls, Melodious byrds sing Madrigalls. (537.1–8)

The poem possesses an allure based in part on its vision of eternal springtime. It is a natural world that remains artificial, a bucolic pleasure dome that doesn't fade with time, one that intentionally forgets its seasonal rhythms and concomitant duties of tending a flock or harvest. The prospective couple will watch other shepherds work as birds "sing Madrigalls" and the landscape itself metamorphoses into objects of sumptuous refinement:

> And I will make thee beds of Roses
> And a thousand fragrant posies,
> A cap of flowers, and a kirtle
> Imbroydred all with leaves of Mirtle. (537.9–12)

Everything is based on some indeterminate future—we *will* live and love and prove pleasures—that also betrays the speaker's urge to enjoy his own willful desires: you *will* wear this, you *will* sleep here. The shepherd's "bed of Roses" takes for granted that any prick by its thorns will be wholly gratifying. And by linking the natural world to pleasure and evacuating any curse of labor, Marlowe's romantic vision ignores not merely rural workaday duties but also the looming specter of pregnancy and childbirth. This is the work of a hyperliterate male poet playing at shepherd. Marlowe's pastoral imagination—urbane, educated, and masculine—is born of and mediated by privilege, but it holds a mythic, dreamlike power. It certainly seems to demand an answer. The poem was a sensation even in its own time, prompting a host of replies and imitations. In "The Nymph's Reply," for example, Sir Walter Raleigh responds in the voice of a pragmatic maid, who sensibly confounds the shepherd's invitation with stern logic:

> The flowers doe fade, and wanton fieldes,
> To wayward winter reckoning yeeldes,
> A honny tongue, a hart of gall,
> Is fancies spring, but sorrowes fall. (16.9–12)

Raleigh's is a privileged male voice, too, of course, and part of the poem's power derives from its dramatized rivalry between two formidable writers, but both imaginations are overly simplistic, Raleigh's merely on the side of winter before spring, subordinating romance to more sterile priorities. It seems too great a cost to deny the shepherd in this fashion, as if one must forgo the magic and power of love altogether. In "The Bait" John Donne seems equally skeptical of Marlowe's romance, but he (unsurprisingly) reimagines the scene in frankly sensual terms, underscoring the erotic attractions motivating the shepherd's passionate declaration. Robert Herrick, meanwhile, responds to both of these writers as well as Marlowe when he writes "To Phyllis, to Love and Live with Him." Unlike Donne's angling temptress, Herrick's "shephardling" catches hearts with a "Sheep-hook," and his world is more convincingly rural than the rest, but he seems most concerned with engaging in poetic gamesmanship: he litters his poem with persuasive arguments as if to claim the laurel crown in this contest of seductive power (181–82). Thomas Carew nods toward Marlowe in his erotic poem "A Rapture," which envisions

> a bed
> Of Roses, and fresh Myrtles... spread
> Under the cooler shade of Cypress groves,

and so does John Milton in *Paradise Lost*, when Adam and Eve enjoy their first sinful embrace in Book 9:

> Flowers were the couch,
> Pansies, and violets, and asphodel,
> And hyacinth, earth's freshest softest lap. (lines 1039–41)

These are impressive, canonical figures, and there are others since them who have engaged Marlowe's lyric and all it represents. Many of these are powerful female voices working to contest or revise the poem's claims, not responding to Marlowe directly, perhaps, but chafing at the essentially male priorities hardwired into the language of love, those like Edna St. Vincent Millay who flips the dynamic by treating men themselves as pleasure toys, and others like Adrienne Rich who lay bare the violent politics of "the oppressor's language," and also those who offer a polite but firm refusal, as Annie Finch does in "Coy Mistress," though she's responding in this case to Andrew Marvell, who is admittedly easier to turn down.[1] It would do well to add a geographical as well as gendered complaint. Marlowe doesn't give "The Passionate Shepherd" a specific locale, but it is worth calling attention to his basic misapprehension of a countryside that was comparatively rural, poor, and uneducated. His celebrated lyric, in other words, betrays a conventional attitude among the educated and well-to-do city set that often idealizes the agrarian lifestyle. The tradition in which Marlowe's poem participates, pastoral romance, in its very name calls attention to this persistent habit of romanticizing rural landscapes. In sixteenth-century England that could have been just about anywhere but London, but in America for the last century and more, it sounds an awful lot like Appalachia, which has held a kind of mythic status as the country's backwoods capital, an easy victim of the glamorizing impulse of urban writers and readers along the East Coast.

This essay, which is focused on a specifically Appalachian female response to the lyric voice of pastoral romance, might have discussed the work of several other writers who have put Marlowe and his ilk firmly in their place. Think of Ron Rash's short story "The Trusty" and the slick-talking metropolitan man who is undone by his own (apparent) success at the seduction of a mountain woman. But no one to my mind answers Marlowe's shepherd, with its potent cocktail of fantasy and privilege, with as much complexity and nuance as Kathryn Stripling Byer, writing from her adopted home in the Smokies four centuries later. And by "answer" I don't mean that Byer gives an abstract or secondhand response, nor do I mention "The Passionate Shepherd" by accident. Byer wrote many of the poems of *Wildwood Flower* and *Black Shawl* with Lee Smith's *Oral History* "at the ready."[2] Marlowe's lyric plays a central role in Smith's novel, set down in full and functioning as a kind of poetic distillation of the romantic and intellectual aspirations of Richard Burlage, an aristocratic interloper from Richmond whose own seduction of mountain native Dory Cantrell meets with mixed success.[3] In this way, Byer's poetry emerges at a complex intersection, a meeting of the waters of literary influence: there is Marlowe's specific poem, which may or may not have set Byer's muse in motion; and there is also what his lyric represents, standing in for the more general tradition of pastoral romance, which is itself the artistic production of the passionate male artist, as likely to compose a gypsy ballad as an Elizabethan poem. Meanwhile, Marlowe's work and its broader resonances are embedded in the fabric of Smith's *Oral History*, the imaginative world of a fellow woman writer and a fellow Appalachian. In many ways, Byer's work in *Wildwood Flower* and *Black Shawl* provides an explicit answer to Marlowe (and Burlage) that Smith is content to leave unspoken in her work, one that further complicates and enriches the cultural conversation I have been laboring to describe, providing a reminder not to confine the scope and influence of Appalachian literature to its own geographic borders.

Much as Smith ventriloquizes a range of female voices in *Oral History*, Byer adopts a variety of female personae throughout her career, repeatedly responding to Marlowe's siren song of male desire: in some cases the shepherd is denied, perhaps with regret; other times he is accepted, but with qualifications. In each case Byer invests the female voice with wisdom and power, aiming for "a more realistic expression of the feminine" (interview 31) and lending her vision of this primal instinct for spring romance more texture than her poetic forebears, honoring "the womanly experiences that she feels need to be remembered," as Ann Richman notes, "including desire for the love and companionship of men, the suffering as well as the joy of motherhood, loneliness and disappointed love" (42). Much of this perspective is shaped, moreover, by the work of Emma Bell Miles, whose work *The Spirit of the Mountains* provides the epigraph to *Wildwood Flower*—"Solitude is deep water"—and whose ecological feminism (as it has been aptly described by Elizabeth Engelhardt) provides a template for engaging gender relations in Appalachia. Byer, in other words, dramatizes the complex rituals of pastoral romance in a specific Appalachian context, with its own native customs (many of them passed down, through English/Scots-Irish ancestry, from Elizabethan rural society), with its own vexed gender relations (this as a female poet in a region that has been largely dominated by male writers),[4] and its own powerful sense of place, a hard-fought understanding of what fruits the land will yield—and their cost. In *Black Shawl*'s "Dulcimer," for example, Byer presents the same mythic drama as Marlowe in compressed fashion, the shepherd's invitation to the female speaker pruned into a simple word, "Come," voiced by a gifted musician. The erotic temptation here is no less powerful than those earlier texts. Rather than Marlowe's

> beds of roses
> And a thousand fragrant posies,

Byer imagines a

> bed of leaves
> we'd gathered, wildflowers strewn
> on a pillow of moss. (6.18–20)

And though this mountain nymph stops her ears much like Raleigh's, it's a delicate dismissal, the refusal sugared with its own compliments:

> No, I'll not listen.
> The sound of it's too sweet,
> like honey I licked from the spoon. (6.1–3)

There's genuine lament in her voice as she acknowledges that springtime won't last forever, a recognition that brings responsibility but also nostalgic regret:

> But I sent him away,
> letting go of his hand
> without whispering as I do
> now when my wits fail me, *oh my sweet, nothing
> but sweet
> good for nothing man.* (6.21–27)

The poem's choice of instrument roots the song in a local tradition of musical craftsmanship—the dulcimer being native to Appalachia—but it also invokes universal images of the poet-artist, the "soul of the laurel shade" (6.16). The phrase, perfectly at home in classical Greece or in the Smokies, gestures at Apollo's mythic chase of Daphne (memorably depicted by Ovid), a story of how romantic desire metamorphoses into poetic power, symbolized by the laurel tree. Here, in contrast to the frenzied male passion of Apollo, Byer presents us with a woman who can restrain her desires even as she reckons with their power, who acknowledges and understands the whole spectrum of time and experience. Here she also presents us with a female poet responding in song—"singing," it might be said, as Byer does, becomes "a kind of dreaming forward, and backward, in time" ("Deep Water" 64)—to the authorial power traditionally vested in the male Orphic voice rather than the vulnerable song of Philomela or the old ballads of mountain women.

A similarly expansive scope enhances Byer's engagement with pastoral romance in her earlier volume *Wildwood Flower*, as she embeds that urgent invitation of Marlowe's shepherd within a broader temporal frame, gesturing throughout the book at the romantic narrative that unfolds in the life of Alma: her courtship, her marriage, and her eventual abandonment.[5] In this way the relational dynamic between shepherd and nymph is deepened, given space and time to flourish or, in this case, fail. That breadth of perspective lends poignancy to "Trillium," which can sweep the reader up in its initial charm. The drama unfolds as we might expect: it is April, land and love warming up, the very landscape burning with desire,

> as if the souls of all creatures
> with wings buried under the leaf mold had risen
> and . . . might take to the sky / singing praise. (22.8–11)

We hear the sound of

> bluejays
> rejoicing. (22.13–14)

And then the seductive song of male desire,

> his breath filling my ear
> with my name. (22.14–15)

As the erotic energy heightens, and the verbal and physical domains of love seem to blur and overlap, readers might be forgiven if they too desire a lyrical celebration of sexual union. But it all ends with loss:

> Though we spoke of love,
> I know now it means little
> but loneliness. (22.17–19)

That experience resonates later in "Sister," when Alma hears secondhand of another seductive call, this time directed at her sibling. Here the shepherd's song transforms into a lover's ballad—"Blackjack Davey" to be precise—but the central invitation remains the same:

> Come go
> with me, my pretty little miss,
> come go with me, my lady. (38.6–7)

In this case, however, Byer splits the female perspectives. The passionate sister succumbs to the gypsy lover's song, while the speaker retains her rational perspective but remains conscious of its romantic deprivations:

> I still envy
> you, tossing your hair in the sun
> and believing he'd love you forever. (38.18–20)

In similar fashion Byer provides in *Black Shawl* a counterpoint to the wise restraint of "Dulcimer" by including "The Devil's Dream" a few pages later, the voice of the dulcimer traded out for fiddle music, which

> filled
> up the green hollow
> come the first warm
> nights, (8.2–5)

and here the landscape conspires with the musician and his blithe romance, leaving the female speaker

> snagged forever on
> April, like me among
> blackberry briars, letting wind
> in these leaves tease
> my fancy. (8.28–32)

This fundamental ambivalence between passion and prudence is played out elsewhere with varying degrees of emphasis in "Sisters," "Gypsy," and "Let's Say." Byer makes it clear that both postures involve loss, as does a third alternative, dramatized in "Sea Change," when the female speaker discontinues her otherwise happy but unreliable relationship with a "true lover" (*Black Shawl* 39.10), the sexual intimacy of "his hands at the hooks of my bodice" (39.19) abandoned for the relational constancy and spiritual intimacy of God. Even "Diamonds," a profoundly beautiful scene of mountain courtship near the end of *Wildwood Flower*, is marked by absence,

> his open hands empty,
> his pockets turned inside out, (48.9–10)

and marked by loss as well if we attend to the whole breadth of the book's temporal frame.

Byer's double vision of the pastoral world, filtered through realistic as well as romantic lenses, lends her work a literary sophistication that remains persuasive in its depiction of lived experience. This is especially evident in the floral imagery she uses to texture her pastoral world, figuring forth with springtime wildflowers a world of romance, its natural beauty but also its impermanence. In some cases, the flowers seem to collude with male seduction, recalling Marlowe's rose-petals, but more often they serve as emblems of a woman's own emergence of sexual longing. Consider the speaker's wish to be ready for "whoever he is" (*Black Shawl* 19.5) in "Rose of Sharon," to be

> Rose
> Willing (19.10–11)

when that unnamed stranger

> comes with his silver
> axe swinging. (19.6–7)

At a more general level, the poem "Wild" gestures also at the unruly power of female desire, which is embodied in the sudden and ubiquitous presence in the landscape of Queen Anne's Lace:

> Come June
> in the Blue Ridge
> there's hardly a woman who hasn't herself longed for lace
> or to let fall its trappings
> among yellow milkwort and lowliest meadow rue. (42.9–14)

This desire, of course, can have consequences. In "Phacelia," for example, the so-called

> *Sheer*
> *Illusion* (25.26–27)

of romance gives way to the physical (and implicitly psychological) stains on the speaker's dress from lovemaking, and she is left with only a memory of the canopy of white flowers that served as an impromptu bed, how she too suddenly merged into the flower

> as she lay
> beneath him like trampled
> earth already trying
> to cover itself with a veil
> of such snowy white. (25.19–23)

And in "Ivory Combs," when Alma and her husband begin to make love—

> I watched him come after me,
> crushing the wildflowers under his feet (*Wildwood Flower* 23.30–31)

—his unconcern for the floral landscape foreshadows the relational violence of his wanderlust. The ecological imagery lends power to the gendered critique.

But Byer's women are hardly owned by such flings. Instead, these moments of passion are acknowledged like the wildflowers as a natural ornament of the spring, a season in which men blaze into view for a short while and bring equal measures of pleasure and regret. Even when romance blossoms into a loving marriage there is still a death waiting to nip its bud, as in "Drought Days":

> By then her man was gone,
> wrapped tight inside a dream of trees
> that leafed out every spring. (*Descent* 17.8–10)

Byer shows the influence not merely of Lee Smith but also Emma Bell Miles. In her essay "Deep Water," Byer calls attention to the continued reality in the Mountain South of what Miles described as "the rift that is set between the sexes at birth and widens with the passage of the years."[6] And in Byer's poetic imagination, as in Miles's observations of Walden's Ridge, the men are almost always gone or going, just as the mountain's wildflowers are briefly in bloom before fading, their presence an insistent reminder of beauty and pain, love and loss, past and future. When Richard Burlage remarks of Dory in *Oral History* that "such a sturdy mountain flower will surely flourish wherever she takes root," his prophecy is false in the particular—Dory commits suicide, a victim of Burlage's own complacency—but true in its general sense (Smith 162). The old prophetesses (as Miles calls them) who endure that springtime season, responding in their own personal and idiosyncratic fashion to the various forms of male courtship passed down through centuries of privilege, eventually inherit their own positions of cultural power and poetic wisdom.

Marlowe too, like the various men that populate *Wildwood Flower* and

Black Shawl, blazed out in his springtime, dead by a knifing at twenty-nine. He was no shepherd, but his lyric testifies to the passionate intensity of his life and work in the hubbub of late sixteenth-century London. Byer, for her part, counters this urgency with patience and wisdom, and if she has been influenced by Smith and Miles, Byer has provided her own model for Appalachian poets like Lisa Coffman or, more recently, Rose McLarney, who stage similarly complex romantic relations in their verse. Sir Walter Raleigh, as I noted, wrote "The Nymph's Reply," but if we keep the breadth of her work in mind, Byer has written a response that is much more powerful, one that honors the fullness of female experience in Appalachia but also, more generally, offers a healthy corrective to the masculine world of pastoral romance. Indeed, her nymph (if it is suitable to use the phrase) can listen with perfect equanimity to the lusty song of Marlowe's shepherd, not because she is situated far from the English pastoral in the rugged Smokies but because she can reply with equal vigor. Indeed, her nymph (if it is suitable to use the phrase) can listen with perfect equanimity to the lusty song of Marlowe's shepherd, not because she is situated far from the English pastoral in the rugged Smokies but because she can reply with equal vigor.

NOTES

1. See "The Burning of Paper Instead of Children."
2. Byer describes the central role of *Oral History* in her early work in "Deep Water."
3. Marlowe's poem appears in the first section of Burlage's journal (Smith 124).
4. Several recent anthologies have called attention to (and have begun to redress) this gender disparity. See, for example, *Bloodroot: Reflections on Place by Appalachian Women Writers*, *Her Words: Diverse Voices in Contemporary Appalachian Women's Poetry*, and *Listen Here: Women Writing in Appalachia*.
5. For a helpful guide to the patchwork of voices throughout *Wildwood Flower* and *Black Shawl*, see Lang (125–56) and Kennedy.
6. Byer, quoting Miles, in "Deep Water," 68.

BIBLIOGRAPHY

Ballard, Sandra, and Patricia Hudson, eds. *Listen Here: Women Writing in Appalachia*. Lexington: University Press of Kentucky, 2003.

Byer, Kathryn Stripling. *Black Shawl*. Baton Rouge: Louisiana State University Press, 1998.

———. "Deep Water." In *Bloodroot: Reflections on Place by Appalachian Women Writers*, edited by Joyce Dyer, 61–70. Lexington: University Press of Kentucky, 1998.

———. *Descent*. Baton Rouge: Louisiana State University Press, 2012.

———. Interview. *Mossy Creek Journal* 11 (1987): 31.

———. *Wildwood Flower*. Baton Rouge: Louisiana State University Press, 1992.

Carew, Thomas. *The Poems of Thomas Carew*. Edited by Arthur Vincent. New York: Charles Scribner's Sons, 1899.

Engelhardt, Elizabeth. *The Tangled Roots of Feminism, Environmentalism, and Appalachian Literature.* Athens: Ohio University Press, 2003.

Herrick, Robert. *The Complete Poetry of Robert Herrick.* Vol. 1. Edited by Tom Cain and Ruth Connelly. Oxford: Oxford University Press, 2013.

Kennedy, Sarah. "'That Little Gal's Not Going Anywhere': Kathryn Stripling Byer's Incremental Monologues." *Iron Mountain Review* 18 (2002): 9–15.

Lang, John. *Six Poets from the Mountain South.* Baton Rouge: Louisiana State University Press, 2010.

Marlowe, Christopher. *The Complete Works of Christopher Marlowe.* Vol. 2. Edited by Fredson Bowers. Cambridge: Cambridge University Press, 1973.

Milton, John. *Paradise Lost.* Edited by Alistair Fowler. London: Longman, 2007.

Raleigh, Sir Walter. *The Poems of Sir Walter Raleigh.* Edited by Agnes Latham. London: Routledge & Paul, 1951.

Rich, Adrienne. "The Burning of Paper Instead of Children." In *The Will to Change: Poems 1968–1970,* 15–18. New York: Norton, 1971.

Richman, Ann. "Singing Our Hearts Away: The Poetry of Kathryn Stripling Byer." In *Her Words: Diverse Voices in Contemporary Appalachian Women's Poetry,* edited by Felicia Mitchell, 38–48. Knoxville: University of Tennessee Press, 2002.

Smith, Lee. *Oral History.* New York: G.P. Putnam's Sons, 1983.

Uphill Both Ways
Struggle on the Sojourn

"This River of Crazy Women"
Subversive Motherhood and the Affrilachian Landscape in Crystal Wilkinson's *The Birds of Opulence*

CAMERON WILLIAMS CRAWFORD

In the introduction to her collection of short stories, *Blackberries, Blackberries* (2000), Crystal Wilkinson writes that "being country is as much a part of me as my full lips, wide hips, dreadlocks, and cheekbones. There are many Black country folks who have lived and are living in small towns, up hollers and across knobs. They are all over the South—scattered like milk—thistle seeds in the wind" (3). Wilkinson describes a doubly marginalized group of people—Black and rural—who are often rendered invisible in mainstream narratives about "the South," especially in discussions of Appalachia, a region typically and incorrectly assumed to be peopled almost exclusively with white "mountain dwellers" (K. Taylor). Although more recent scholarship has turned its critical eye toward the "Affrilachian" tradition—a term coined by Frank X. Walker in 1991—scholars largely continue to overlook the many contributions of Black artists, musicians, and writers to Appalachian studies. Wilkinson is one Affrilachian poet whose work has been the subject of some critical inquiry, notably as her fiction takes up particular concerns with the Appalachian environment and the rural African Americans who reside there.

Her newest novel, *The Birds of Opulence* (2016), offers a similar meditation on the lives of "black country folks" in Appalachia. More specifically, *The Birds of Opulence* follows four generations of the Goodes, a family of "crazy women" who have resided for decades in the fictional mountain town of Opulence, Kentucky. The Goode women are deeply and profoundly connected to the land. This connection, however, is fraught, marred by a history of slavery and violence. As Mama Minnie tells her children, "All this . . . been up under your people's feet since slave times. My mama and daddy worked this land, and their mama and daddy before them.... All y'all was raised up on money the tobacco brought in and the garden food we put on the table" (112–13). Mama Minnie's granddaughter, Lucy Goode-Brown, most literally embodies her family's vexed relationship with the land when she gives birth to her daughter, Yolanda, while harvesting squash from the family garden. After doing so, "she feels the squash vines growing up from her toes clean up to her head" (183), closing in on her, choking her, like "a sorrow cloaked around her head that she couldn't shake," unable to stop "the bad thoughts ... clotting in her brain" (12). These bad thoughts later cause Lucy to drop her baby on the floor in front of a roomful of visitors. She also "pinches the baby's nostrils together ... watches her daughter struggle for breath, watches her bright eyes widen until the legs kick" (34–35). Lucy is not the only character to disrupt assumptions about nature, women, and motherhood; ashamed of her daughter Tookie's impropriety, Mama Minnie—herself a victim of sexual assault—physically abuses Tookie, revealing a cycle of shame and violence against women and the ways in which that cycle becomes internalized. In connecting these women and images of subversive maternity to a vexed history of the land, *The Birds of Opulence* grapples with the larger relationship of African Americans to Appalachia in particular and the environment in general, steeped as it is in the legacy of slavery, exploitation, and violence, especially against Black women.

Women have been associated with nature for centuries, a common perception that, for better or worse, is rooted in the "parallels between the reproductive capacity of women and the reproductive cycles of the Earth"; women share with the Earth "the essential life-giving nature that links them as symbolic, spiritual, and physical mothers" (Stearney 152). From the outset, *The Birds of Opulence* works to establish the traditional gender roles of the Opulence community—nestled somewhere in the Kentucky foothills of the Appalachian Mountains—that similarly link women with nature and, therefore, also with nurturing and motherhood. Mama Minnie, for instance, is described as inherently maternal. As her name implies, she is the matriarch of the Goode family line who, from the time at which the narrative begins in 1962, has been serving as the sole familial authority figure ever since her husband died. In addition to occupying the role of matriarch, Mama Minnie is endowed with some kind of preternatural knowledge about how to care for babies. She can "read signs," can "spot a woman in the family way, before anyone else, sometimes even before the mother knew herself" (6). She knows "what sign of the moon to cut a baby's hair, when to wean it from its mother's nipple, whether the ball of a woman's belly contained girl or boy" (5–6). For a time, Mama Minnie served as a midwife, helping to "catch babies" for other women. She can even "gauge the weight of a reaching child on a woman's hip, squeezing sweet fat knees around a mama's waist." "Nothing like a young un in this whole world," she says (6). Apparently, Mama's Minnie's affection for babies is typical of women in Opulence. At the gathering to celebrate the birth of Lucy's baby, Yolanda, one anonymous male guest—observing the women going "wide-eyed at the baby"—muses to the other men, "You know how the women are" (29–30).

It is important to note the place where Lucy gives birth to Yolanda: the family garden. This particular patch of land has been in the Goode family for generations and is imbued with meaning. Not only is it the place where Lucy gives birth, it is also the place where Mama Minnie was born: Yolanda recalls how "Mama Minnie pointed toward the field where she had been born, like she knew the exact spot, like she remembered" (12). These women quite literally come from the land. The men in the novel, on the other hand, are more closely aligned with industrial urban life. Once grown, Mama Minnie's sons, Butter and June, leave Opulence and move to the city (6). Joe Brown makes the unusual move from city to country, though he never fully integrates into the bucolic lifestyle. Joe is more mechanically than agriculturally minded, spending his days repairing broken appliances and tinkering with old cars.

But the Goode women's connection to the environment around them is complicated. They care greatly about and love the land they live on; they respect and understand it, yet they are also tormented by it. In the garden, right before Lucy gives birth, Tookie, Mama Minnie's daughter, is overwhelmed by a feeling of "something shifting." The land triggers a wave of memories for Tookie: Ma Teke's pie, a whittled "play-pretty" from Pa Green, games of tag with girlhood friends. Then, memories of "girlish frolic" give way to something more unpleasant, something "entombed somewhere deep within the walls of . . . Tookie's chest. She put her hands to her throat and coughed hard, but nothing came up" (9). That something is a memory from 1943, when Tookie was twelve years old and went with Bruce Harrison out into the cornfield where he "kissed her so hard she thought she would die." Bruce then "took her clothes off, promised it wouldn't hurt. Promised he'd take it out before anything bad happened. But when he climbed on top of her it had hurt like nothing she had ever known, and then he mounted her and put all his weight into her chest and pushed inside her and began to move faster and faster, like he was trying to kill something, and wouldn't stop" (139–40). Based on this description, it seems that Tookie's encounter with Bruce was not consensual. As if that memory is not painful enough, there's what comes next: "She knew it was wrong then. Knew it was the 'anything bad' that he had talked about that was happening.... Minnie hadn't told her about babies, but Tookie knew she was pregnant the way any woman knows" (140). Tookie turns to her mother for help and comfort—"Who else but a mama would understand this?" she thinks to herself—yet instead of kindness and understanding, Tookie is met with "the strap of the belt":

> Minnie Mae said, "I didn't raise you to be no whore!" ... Each word came with a lash on her back. With her back turned to protect the baby, she couldn't see her mother's face, but she could hear her labored breathing. Heard the shuffle of footsteps behind her when her daddy tried to pull the belt from her mama's hands. Could see her brothers cowering in the corners of the kitchen and see their scared faces begging their mother to stop. She remembers her father finally pulling her mother away, her brothers slinking off grateful that the beating had finally stopped. Remembers being in a house full with two adults and two children and having nobody to comfort her. Remembers pulling her own bruised and bloodied body up and going to the bathroom, taking a bath and crawling, sore and marked for life, into the bed. (140–41)

Clearly, Tookie carries the weight of these traumatic experiences with her into adulthood, though the burden is not hers alone. Tookie's encounter with Bruce seems to parallel a similar time when Mama Minnie, also at age twelve, was nearly raped by Macon Jones, "wrestling him for her own honey pot," a euphemism that links Mama Minnie's female body to the environment by relating her genitalia to the natural product derived from the land (26).

Tookie passes down her family's history of women's trauma to her daughter, Lucy, who, like Mama Minnie and Tookie before her, also has a problematic relationship with the land. Ominous signs portend trouble even before she goes into labor while harvesting squash from the garden: "The raw smell of freshly turned dirt churned her stomach, made her head swim" (10). After safely delivering Yolanda right in the middle of the squash patch, Lucy is unable to "stop bad thoughts from clotting in her brain. There was already a sorrow cloaked around her head that she couldn't shake" (12). Yolanda remarks that, once safely delivered of a child, "Mama didn't look like our mother at all," but looks "feeble" and "whispered incoherently through chapped lips" (13). Once back home, Lucy has a kind of flashback wherein she suddenly smells squash and feels the vines closing in around her head. It bears mentioning that Lucy has given birth once before to her older child, a son named Kevin (affectionately nicknamed Kee Kee), and after giving birth suffers a bout of postpartum depression that eventually "slipped away." Things are notably different this time around after delivering a daughter. After giving birth to Yolanda, Lucy cannot shake the "dreariness" that has overtaken her. She observes that her belly, "the taut mountain that had cradled her child," is now "hollow, a drained riverbed," the language here likening her maternal body to her Appalachian environment (19). The version of motherhood offered through Lucy is complex, a direct challenge to the notions that inseparably link together women/nature and nurture/maternity. Lucy really disrupts expectations of mothering when she drops the infant Yolanda, only a few days old, on the floor in front of a houseful of guests: "The baby rolls from Lucy's lap, rolls like a can of lard, like a wad of fabric or a cumbersome quilt, like a rolling pin or a small sack of new potatoes, and makes a light thud on the plank floor like something being cast away" (32). The scene is upsetting, and guests who witness the incident are shocked and visibly disturbed: "There is one wide-eyed look on every face in the room. A great communal hush rises up, and for a few seconds, no one says a word." Several women "grab the hands of their children," as if to assert themselves in contrast to Lucy as good mothers, then "lower their heads, and leave quietly" (32). The remaining guests simply stare in silence, too stunned by what they have witnessed to do anything else. The last onlookers eventually depart and Joe helps Lucy to bed, where that night the baby rests with them. Joe sleeps as Lucy nurses the child, and she weeps while she "touches the child's face . . . and then pinches the baby's nostrils together" on and off, knowing that she "could starve the child of air and even Joe, who is snoring gently in her ear, would never know" (34). Lucy continues to suffocate her baby, "watches her daughter struggle for breath, watches her bright eyes widen until the legs kick and she lets go of the nipple," again and again "until she can feel the baby trying to fling her head free, then she releases and listens to her child settle into being able to breathe again" (34–35). Lucy's behavior flies in the face of acceptable motherly conduct. Tookie articulates the standard societal expectations for motherhood when, before revealing the news of her pregnancy to Mama Minnie at twelve years old, she thinks to herself, "And who else would a child turn to but her mama—the one who had been there to nurse her cuts and bruises, the one who had stayed up with her for three days when she had the fever and changed the ice rags on her head and sung her songs" (140). In other words, a mother's hand is supposed to heal, not harm, her child.

Lucy's treatment of her baby is tied to her postpartum symptoms of feeling like "a drained riverbed" and being strangled by squash vines. Her mothering is therefore also linked to the other Goode women's relationship with their Appalachian environment, which is tainted by their family's personal and painful history of violence and exploitation. This relationship is further complicated by the racial history of the land. Mama Minnie, "placing one hand on her hip and the other one spreading far and wide from one edge of the knob across the creek to the other side," explains to her children how the town of Opulence was established in 1878, when "just one hundred years after Daniel Boone blazed a bloody trail through here, killing every Indian he saw, Old Man Hezekiah (he was freed from Virginia) paid one hundred and fifty-six dollars for eight acres of land right here" (112). He named the town Opulence after getting "fighting mad" at the "white folks" who called it by a hateful racial slur (112). At the same time that Mama Minnie is proud of this legacy, telling the story of Old Man Hezekiah with a certain reverence, she carefully draws attention to the kinds of violence and mistreatment that people of color faced in making America "America." Notably, Mama Minnie makes a reference to Old Man Hezekiah coming to Opulence after being freed from Virginia, placing the reality of slavery safely outside the borders of Opulence, but it's important to understand that Appalachia was not immune to what Dwight Billings calls "the blight of slaveholding," which is a common misperception. According to Wilma A. Dunaway in *Slavery in the American Mountain South*, "The prevailing scholarly view is that slavery was largely absent from the Mountain South and that the region's few slaveholders were more kindly than their Lower South peers.... As a result, Mountain slaves have remained a *people without history* because too many researchers have claimed that 'the "peculiar institution" never influenced Appalachian culture and society'" (5, emphasis original). Opulence is presented as a sort of paradise, a veritable Garden of Eden for African Americans; yet, as Mama Minnie herself makes conspicuous, the specter of slavery hovers in the background nonetheless. It is necessary to recognize the very real history that provides a backdrop for this novel, particularly for the larger point it illustrates: that for African Americans, in particular those living in the South, no place—not even the very land itself—is safe from the lingering effects of slavery.

It is this conundrum with which the novel wrestles. It is a means through which *The Birds of Opulence* taps into a narrative tradition of African American literature that "provide[s] testimony of a people for whom the environment has often been theirs to suffer, occasionally to shape, and seldom to own" (Bostian 42). In *Black on Earth: African American Ecoliterary Traditions*, Kimberly N. Ruffin contends that "for as long as Africans have been Americans, they have had no entitlement to speak for or about nature," explaining that "the history of racialized slavery and its continuing aftermath are factors in African Americans' access to the natural world and their perceptions of nature" (1, 4). Dianne D. Glave, in *Rooted in the Earth: Reclaiming the African American Environmental Heritage*, also traces the complex history of African Americans and their perceived "ambivalence" about the land:

> In the years after enslavement, African Americans began to move to Northern cities in a series of mass migrations that continued into the 1970s. This relocation to the increasingly urbanized North distanced them from the rural experiences of their parents and grandparents, who lived and worked in fields, gardens, and woods. Scorn, distaste, and fear of nature became the emotional legacy of a people who had been kidnapped from their homelands and forced to make the long journey across the Atlantic Ocean to pick cotton and prime tobacco for often violent and abusive masters; they were finally subjected to losing legally owned land to the whites who continued to victimize them long after slavery was banned. (5)

According to Glave, these "terror-filled experiences" were inevitably inherited by subsequent generations of Black people living in America.

For African Americans living in the Appalachian Mountain South, adding to this already fraught relationship with the environment is the general erasure of people of color from Appalachian history. Part of the impetus behind Frank X. Walker coining the term "Affrilachia" in 1991 was his discovery that *Webster's Dictionary* defined those who identified as "Appalachian" as "white residents from the mountains" (qtd. in Colley 89). More "astonishingly," Erica Abrams Locklear points out, "in 2006 a search for 'Appalachian' on the Merriam-Webster web site yielded the following result: 'a white native or resident of the Appalachian mountain area'" (111). The myth of Appalachia as primarily white is a carefully constructed one that emerged after the Civil War as a form of propaganda, an effort to secure northern sympathy (and financial assistance) during Reconstruction. In a chapter from *Appalachia in the Making: The Mountain South in the Nineteenth Century*, John C. Inscoe describes the recent scholarly approach that traces the evolution of the myth of a "pure white" Appalachia. Citing James Klotter and Nina Silber, Inscoe explains that the image "provided northerners with identifying links less apparent in poor whites elsewhere in the South, still unreformed rebels caught up in the biracial complexities of the lowland South" (106). William H. Turner and Edward J. Cabbell's seminal 1985 work, *Blacks in Appalachia*, disputes the notion of a "pure white" Mountain South and describes the "very serious dilemma" that such a myth creates for Black Appalachians. Cabbell writes that the erasure of African Americans in the Mountain South "provides strong support to the myth that the number of Black people in the mountains is inconsequential." It furthermore "supports the myth that Appalachia is a land of 'poor white hillbillies,' beset solely with 'white problems' and not the 'color problems' that plague the rest of America. In reality, the 1.3 million Black people in Appalachia suffer worse economic status than white Appalachians, and their problems are compounded by racism and discrimination" (3). African Americans living in Appalachia have long been rendered invisible and therefore largely isolated from their environment.

Black women faced their own unique set of difficulties in negotiating their attachment to the land. According to Rachel Stein, "In this system of agricultural slave labor, the negative association of African women and nature was reinforced as black women were 'put in the ground' to perform arduous field labor" (88). Citing Paula Giddings, Stein explains that as slavery became increasingly widespread, field labor "became the distinguishing division between black slaves and white servants, a sign of the innately bestial character of black women" (88). Compounding this abuse was the fact that such myths as the "innately bestial character of black women" were used to justify the sexual exploitation of Black women by white men. In *The Birds of Opulence*, more often than not, this "double-edged" subjugation "of racism concerning land" is acted out on the bodies of Black women (Glave 9). As a child, Tookie is presumably taken advantage of by Bruce Harrison; Mama Minnie is almost raped by Macon Jones. These are far from the only instances in which women's bodies become sites from which to interrogate the link between racial trauma, gender, and the environment. Minnie has memories of "knocking out that boy, Possum Briggs, that time when he'd called her out of her name and slapped her when they were swimming in the creek, and how scared her mama was that she'd hang for giving that old white boy a black eye" (26). This incident makes most apparent the double bind of gender and racial oppression particular to women of color.

Mona, though not one of the Goode women, similarly endures a sexual assault that is at once motivated by race and gender when she and Yolanda take a walk to the Simpson place to look for duck eggs by the pond. The pond sits on the Simpsons' land, "but the girls have never seen any of the Simpsons here. They see them in town. Nice white folks that their parents know.... The land, the girls are convinced, is not Simpson land at all, just land, free for the coming and going of rabbits and birds and girls" (68). The Simpsons' son, Obie, believes differently. Yolanda and Mona have seen Obie in passing at school, and while they don't know him well, they do know that, "like some of the other white boys in town, there is a certain way he looks at them that they don't like" (68). No sooner do the girls step foot on the Simpsons' land than they are confronted by Obie, who accuses them of trespassing. Yolanda immediately runs, but "Mona stays still, and Obie Simpson grabs her arm," then he pushes her to the ground, "grabs her legs and drags her toward him" (69). He "sits straggle-legged on Mona's stomach, he brings his hand up as if he will strike her, but when his hand comes back down he slides it up under her shirt and grabs the skin where her breasts will be" (70). Despite Mona's struggle, Obie removes both of their pants and rapes her. Mona eventually frees herself and runs away. As she does so, Obie yells after her and Yolanda, "And don't come back. Damned black bitches" (71).

Obie's threat is a clear attempt to return Yolanda and Mona, two young Black girls discovering a newfound independence in their adolescence, to their "place," a reminder of his—and by proxy white patriarchy's—power and authority over all space, both public and personal. The incident embodies the particular difficulties surrounding Black women's relationship with the environment and the ways in which white supremacy continues to justify the sexual exploitation of Black women by regarding them as "bestial" and therefore in need of being put "in the ground." These difficulties are perhaps even more pronounced in the Appalachian Mountain South, where the intersecting oppressions of race and gender are compounded by the marginalization of place, thereby making the complexities of rural Black women's lived experiences even more subject to erasure. However, Mona's response to being raped by Obie is remarkable:

> Something soft slaps against her legs, and somewhere in a moment when she should be most panicked, Mona sees a weakness rising in Obie's face, a slight, vulnerable instant. She has never seen a boy's penis, and wants to see it. Even through these thoughts, she fights him. His penis grows hard, and she feels it slip into her spread thighs—not for long, just one time and only halfway, but she feels it—and a little, tiny feeling of glee replaces her fear and anger. Not because of the pleasure, because there is none, but because she recognizes something iniquitous. She becomes curious about this new thing, this certain kind of weakness she has not known that men and boys have until now. The tiniest grin forms behind her lips before she squirms loose, joins Yolanda, and runs across the fields toward the safety of home. (70–71)

During the struggle, she remains acutely aware of what's happening to her and its implications. Her resistance to the assault is at once physical, as she fights back against Obie, and psychological in the sense that, while being raped, she still manages to locate in the act a source of power for herself. Some of that power seems to also come from a kind of generative agency tied to the land. The motivation behind Obie's attack on Mona is largely territorial; he assaults Mona in a gross demonstration of his ownership over both the environment and her body. Yet the Simpsons' land, the girls are "convinced," does not truly belong to the Simpsons—it is "just land," free and as much theirs as anyone else's. Mona is one of the ways through which *The Birds of Opulence* "offer[s] an affirmation of black identity rather than simply a protest against white racism" (Fowler qtd. in S. Taylor). In this regard, Wilkinson's novel exemplifies one of the hallmarks of "the works of Affrilachian women," which "ultimately tie back to place, the lull and call of location, intimately shaping how they view both gender and race." For Wilkinson and other Affrilachian women writers, "Appalachia is their home," and through her fiction—through Mona—Wilkinson shows that Black women "claim just as much ownership as any 'white native or resident'" (S. Taylor).

Mona's mother, Francine, likewise plays a significant role in *The Birds of Opulence* despite not being part of the Goode family line, particularly as Francine provides another iteration of a subversive woman who challenges conventional narratives that link motherhood to the environment. In fact, the novel goes out of its way to distance Francine from the land, making her the most pointed example of Black women's displacement from the Appalachian environment. Francine is not a native of Opulence but rather moved to the small country town when she married Sonny Clark, a kind and loving husband who died unexpectedly ten years before Francine's story takes place. Unlike the Goode women, Francine is decidedly removed from the land; she is considered "citified," though she admits that she does not enjoy the company of other people and has trained herself to become country: "She has spent ten years since Sonny died training herself to enjoy the occasional rustlings of some creature, or a twig scratching the window, a little bit of low music, even the company of the tomcat she feeds on the back porch, but no people" (38–39). One afternoon, while in the kitchen making fudge, Francine feels "a sharp pain" in her stomach that "takes her to her knees" (43). It turns out that Francine is pregnant, a condition that comes as a surprise to her and the rest of the Opulence community, which does not see her as fit for motherhood. Even Mama Minnie, so skilled at detecting women "in the family way," dismisses the "something funny" she observes about Francine "as a sign of melancholy," not maternity (45). When Francine does give birth, "Mona's entrance into the world will make men's heads tilt in confusion, and cause old women to gossip with their hands on their hips. Over tea in one another's kitchens for the rest of winter they will speculate that a woman like Francine Clark is apt to run off or give the baby up" (46). Indeed, Francine does not appear to fit the image of a typical nurturing, maternal figure. Shortly after Mona is born, Hazel Sloan remarks on "the awkward way Francine Clark grips [her] child: around the chest, slumped like a dog, her head wagging" (57). As Mona grows up, Francine seems largely absent from her life and maintains a careful distance between herself and her daughter, leaving Mona to grow into adulthood contending with "the loneliness that she feels with her own mother" (125).

In addition to serving as another figure that complicates assumptions that associate nature with nurturing/motherhood, Francine—and Opulence's collective response to her pregnancy—is another vehicle through which the novel explores the link between racial trauma, gender, and the environment. Because Francine is considered "citified," deliberately disconnected from Opulence and its surrounding Appalachian environs, she is regarded as an outsider and is treated as little more than fodder for gossip and prurient speculation. Upon learning of Francine's pregnancy, "each resident in town puts her where they want her": "There are women who do this all the time, women who don't know where their babies came from, who have menstrual cycles all through their pregnancies, women who refuse to remember tragedy, women who were raped. Then there are women who live one life by day and another by night. It is not known which category Francine Clark is in. . . . Some will shift her to the double-life category, others will place her neatly in the box labeled *Rape*, but nobody knows for sure" (44–45). The community's salacious speculation, whereby they inscribe upon Francine's body their own narrative, is itself an example of the systemic violence of erasure that denies Francine's agency. That the prevailing assumption is that Francine was raped also underscores the harsh realities of the town's sexual politics. The threat of rape—even just a rumor—looms heavy over the women of Opulence, so real a possibility as to become part of the fabric of everyday life. The father of Francine's baby is never named, nor are the true circumstances surrounding her pregnancy; however, the sexual politics of Opulence, along with the "shame" she has "buried beneath the folds of soft tissue around her stomach" and the careful distance that Francine intentionally keeps between herself and the Opulence community and her general distrust of other people, suggest that the townspeople might be right in their suspicions. Despite their differences, Francine and the Goode women are links in a chain of sexual violence against Black women. The system of politics in Opulence that has normalized Black women's sexual exploitation is surely derived from the historical treatment of Black women in the South. In evoking this history, *The Birds of Opulence* also asks us to consider the ongoing and national problem of sexual violence against Black women, who continue to be at a higher risk of sexual assault than women overall. According to results of the 2011 National Intimate Partner and Sexual Violence

Survey, "21.2 percent of black women are raped during their lifetime, compared with 19.3 percent of all women aged 18 and older" (qtd. in DuMonthier, Childers, and Milli 120).

The experiences of Francine and Mona, along with those of the Goode women, are undoubtedly tragic: Mona leaves Opulence and moves to the city, but she finds herself forever drawn back to her hometown; Francine's health declines as she continues to live in isolation; Tookie and Mama Minnie pass on, and eventually Lucy joins them when she commits suicide. Still, their stories are not without hope. As Lucy, in her increasingly deteriorating mental state, continually mutters to herself, "Mama gone, Granny gone, roots still here" (183). These roots are strong, and they endure no matter what, as evidenced most pointedly in a scene that treats the exploitation of the land as a metaphor for the exploitation of Black women's bodies. After Mama Minnie's death and Lucy's suicide, the Goode homestead is sold off to "city white folks" who have let the land and the house—that Mama Minnie tended so carefully and always kept neat and kempt—grow over with weeds. Joe stops by to pay his respects and encounters the new owner, who is hostile and more or less shoos Joe off the property, brusquely explaining that they are "digging out a pond" on the land. A week after, Joe learns that the men working on the pond left their bulldozer parked "in that spot where some of them old-time people had found that underground spring years ago," just in time for "the awfulest rain you ever did see." John Turner regales Joe with the news: "When them old boys come back on Monday all they could see is the tip top of the seat of that dozer. Said the man that bought the place had to pay double to have somebody come out there and pull that dozer our before they could start up again" (198). John jokes that "Miss Minnie's people done come back and gave them folks a piece of their minds," and Joe laughs at this because he knows instinctively that it's true, that Mama Minnie, Tookie, and Lucy were in some supernatural way responsible for the bulldozer's flooding. In death, the Goode women are finally able to enact the control, over the land and over their own bodies, that had been denied to them in life.

The Birds of Opulence offers another glimmer of hope through Kee, the sole male character in the novel with the unique ability to negotiate gendered spaces. He grew up in the Goode household, "learning the ways of women" early on (5). He shares with them a similar connection to the land; not only is he with Mama Minnie, Tookie, and Lucy on the day Yolanda is born in the squash patch, but he watches his mother give birth, witnessing firsthand a ritual of femininity in its rawest form. As an adult, "he realizes that he's as good in the kitchen as any woman in his family. He can kitchen dance like any Goode woman with a skillet." Kee (a childhood nickname that, notably, as his wife Nadine observes, "sounds like a girl's name") "can also do a mean dance with the inside of a car's engine" (166). Like his father, Kee Kee is skilled in the area of mechanics. Also like other men in Opulence, Kee participates in the system that treats Black women's bodies as little more than "spit cups" (Stein 89). Over the years, Kee has been with a lot of women—Trudy, Athena, Ina, even Mona, to name but a few. However, when Kee is married to Nadine, the two of them expecting their first child together, he reflects on the ways in which he has been complicit in perpetuating this cycle: "It was bragging rights to some of the cats he hung with, but it made him uncomfortable. He thought about what Mama Minnie or Granny Tookie would say. Disrespecting women. At least that's how'd they see it. That much he knew for sure" (171). It seems as though Kee would at least agree that he "disrespected" Mona, "still the one he was most ashamed of." It is worth remarking on the way that Kee ruminates on his encounter with Mona, assuring himself that "it wasn't rape, but he knew she'd been too damned young," a remark that indicates an awareness of how men often treat women within the Opulence community (171). He also remembers Ina, a sophomore at a college in Indianapolis. One night, Ina calls Kee and tells him that she is pregnant. Although he wants to respond "it ain't mine," as he had "seen brothers do," he instead insists on helping her. However, Ina's parents have other plans; they want her to "go away and have it and put it up for adoption" (170). This conversation is the last Kee has with Ina, and it haunts him into adulthood. In fact, now that Nadine is pregnant, he begins to have visions of a "ghost girl," the imaginary daughter he might have fathered with Ina. Kee is aware of his complicity in perpetuating the cycle of violence against women and knows his responsibility in ending it. His "ghost child" is a symbol of hope that represents the possibility of breaking that cycle.

Ultimately, by inscribing the fictional story of the Goode women onto a factual history of Appalachia, *The Birds of Opulence* challenges monolithic narratives about Black women, maternity, and the Appalachian Mountain South. One of the primary goals of Affrilachian literature is to counter the erasure of African Americans in Appalachia, to assert the prevalence and the centrality of Black lives to the culture of the Appalachian Mountain South. The real, lived experiences of Black women in Appalachia are rendered even more invisible, yet in *The Birds of Opulence* Wilkinson demonstrates that "this conversation, this celebration, belongs to them, not only to 'say' but to show they are indeed 'here.'" For Wilkinson, "the strong sense of 'here-ness' ties directly back [to] sense of place—a place finally beginning to accept their existence" (S. Taylor). The relationship of African Americans to Appalachia might indeed be fraught, tarnished by a history of slavery, exploitation, and violence, especially against Black women, but, as Lucy Goode-Brown knows to be true, "roots still here," and those roots are strong.

BIBLIOGRAPHY

Bostian, Patricia Kennedy. "Brown, Sterling (1901–1989)." In *Encyclopedia of the Environment in American Literature*, edited by Geoff Hamilton and Brian Jones, 42. Jefferson, N.C.: McFarland, 2013.

Cabbell, Edward J. "Black Invisibility and Racism in Appalachia: An Informal Survey." In *Blacks in Appalachia*, edited by William H. Turner and Edward J. Cabbell, 3–10. Lexington: University Press of Kentucky, 1985.

Colley, Sharon E. "Beyond Black and White: Ethnic Complexity within the Affrilachian Poets." In *Seeking Home: Marginalization and Representation in Appalachian Literature and Song*, edited by Leslie Harper Worthington and Jürgen E. Grandt, 89–104. Knoxville: University of Tennessee Press, 2016.

DuMonthier, Asha, Chandra Childers, and Jessica Milli. "The Status of Black Women in the United States." Institute for Women's Policy Research. https://iwpr.org/iwpr-issues/race-ethnicity-gender-and-economy/the-status-of-black-women-in-the-united-states/.

Dunaway, Wilma A. *Slavery in the American Mountain South*. Cambridge: Cambridge University Press, 2003.

Glave, Dianne D. *Rooted in the Earth: Reclaiming the African American Environmental Heritage*. New York: Lawrence Hill, 2010.

Inscoe, John C. "Race and Racism in Nineteenth-Century Southern Appalachia: Myths, Realities, and Ambiguities." In *Appalachia in the Making: The Mountain South in the Nineteenth Century*, edited by Mary Beth Pudup, Dwight D. Billings, and Altina L. Waller, 103–31. Chapel Hill: University of North Carolina Press, 1995.

Locklear, Erica Abrams. "Consenting to Create: Crystal Wilkinson and the Affrilachian Movement." In *Seeking Home: Marginalization and Representation in Appalachian Literature and Song*, edited by Leslie Harper Worthington and Jürgen E. Grandt, 105–19. Knoxville: University of Tennessee Press, 2016.

Ruffin, Kimberly N. *Black on Earth: African American Ecoliterary Traditions*. Athens: University of Georgia Press, 2010.

Stearney, Lynn M. "Feminism, Ecofeminism, and the Maternal Archetype: Motherhood as a Feminine Universal." *Communication Quarterly* 42, no. 2 (1994): 145–59.

Stein, Rachel. *Shifting the Ground: American Women Writers' Revisions of Nature, Gender, and Race*. Charlottesville: University Press of Virginia, 1997.

Taylor, Kathryn Trauth. "Naming Affrilachia: Toward Rhetorical Ecologies of Identity Performance in Appalachia." *Enculturation*, June 21, 2011. https://enculturation.net/naming-affrilachia.

Taylor, Shaina D. W. "Gender, Race, and Place: Plurality and Diversity in the Writings of Affrilachian Women." Marshall University, n.d. https://www.marshall.edu/woodson-dev/plurality-and-diversity-in-the-writings-of-affrilachian-women/.

Wilkinson, Crystal. *Blackberries, Blackberries*. 2000. Seattle: Lake Union Publishing, 2011.

———. *The Birds of Opulence*. Lexington: University Press of Kentucky, 2016.

An Ecofeminist Reading of Robert Gipe's *Trampoline* as Insight into Appalachian Oppression

JESSICA CORY

Elizabeth Engelhardt notes in *The Tangled Roots of Feminism, Environmentalism, and Appalachian Literature* that "feminism, environmentalism, and Appalachia have existed in a complicated relationship to each other at least since the turn of last century" (32). Robert Gipe's debut illustrated novel *Trampoline*, released in 2015, provides contemporary insight into this complicated relationship as it showcases ongoing challenges and struggles that many women in Appalachia experience alongside the environmental degradation for which Central Appalachia is well known. Through an ecofeminist lens, it is apparent that in this region women and nature inhabit one side of a false binary while capitalist economics and men share the opposite side. Numerous ecofeminists, including Engelhardt, have explored "the binary relationship between man and nature" and found it "remarkable how often Nature becomes gendered as female" and considered by many (even still) to be "unexploitable because her resources seem never-ending" ("Nature-Loving Souls" 343). Gipe's novel, through his portrayal of women and environmental destruction, displays this imbalance in power and illustrates how oppression of the natural world extends to the female body and experience, resulting in negative impacts on not only the book's female characters but also the landscape of Blue Bear Mountain and its surrounding community. Engelhardt goes on to suggest that "feminist ecocriticism's questions can be organized into two categories: how does an author talk about—in rhetorical terms, 'construct'—nature in his or her text? and how does the author's discussion of race, class, and gender intersect with that construction of nature in the text?" (343). This essay seeks to answer those questions as they relate to Gipe's novel.

For clarity, "ecofeminism" throughout this essay is used interchangeably with the term "ecological feminism." This is an important distinction to make, as Engelhardt has declared that "although many people use 'ecological feminism' and 'ecofeminism' interchangeably, I do not, because this working definition [of ecological feminism] is closer to the environmental justice movement in its anti-essentialism than it is to some ecofeminism."[1] Some scholars and critics have found ecofeminism (particularly early ecofeminism) to be overly broad or essentialist in its calls to action, as the editors at *Signs* wrote in 1992 "ecofeminism seems to be concerned with everything in the world ... [as a result] feminism itself seems almost to get erased in the process" (qtd. by Adams and Gruen 23). However, to sum up the theory and its current breadth, Gaard describes ecofeminism as "a theory that has evolved from various fields of feminist inquiry and ... calls for an end to all oppressions, arguing that no attempt to liberate women (or any other oppressed group) will be successful without an equal attempt to liberate nature" ("Living Interconnections" 1). Gaard's use of "other oppressed groups" clearly addresses claims that ecofeminism is anthropocentric or misandrist and that attempts to use alternate terms for ecofeminism, such as "ecological feminism," effectively seek to erase early ecofeminist scholarship. To make clear that these ideas are the based on the same ideals and theories, and to avoid confusion that they differ widely, I use the term "ecofeminism" here, as it speaks to a lens that examines the intersections of human (often, but not exclusively, female) identity and the environment and how these entities are affected by systemic oppression.

The exploitation of the Appalachian landscape by its (often European) settlers through strip mining, underground mining, and hydraulic fracturing has been well documented. Because many residents in the areas affected by the oil extraction industry are employed in these sectors, there has existed a continual controversy over the value of Nature versus the importance of local economy. In many Appalachian areas, particularly in the Kentucky coalfields where *Trampoline* is situated, the latter has won, both in reality and in the early stages of the novel. This fictional representation of conflict is largely based in reality, as Gipe states in an interview with Zackary Vernon that the activism regarding Blue Bear Mountain is modeled after protests surrounding the strip mining of Black Mountain, protests that Gipe was a part of and resulted in "a hollow [victory], because it [was] just one mountain that's saved and because the people had to pay for it."[2]

In addition to systemic oppression resulting in this value of currency over environment in Appalachia, the lives of Appalachian women are systematically devalued through the same patriarchal capitalist oppression.

Appalachian women are statistically more likely to be financially impoverished and experience a higher rate of intimate partner violence and social control than women elsewhere in America (see Davidov et al.), particularly if they are single mothers like Tricia Jewell, who struggles with substance abuse following the death of her husband. What Gipe uniquely achieves in *Trampoline* is that he exemplifies the ways in which the system that oppresses and opposes the natural world extends this oppression onto the female inhabitants of the region.

At Western Carolina University's annual literary festival in 2017, Laura Wright asked Gipe as well as his fellow presenter, photographer Roger May, if either gentleman intentionally and consciously focused on the connection between the oppression of women and the oppression of nature in their work. Gipe responded that he hadn't created *Trampoline* while consciously considering the manuscript from an ecofeminist perspective, but Gipe did make it clear that the story of Dawn Jewell is loosely based on the experiences of many of the students he encounters through Southeast Kentucky Community and Technical College's Appalachian Program, which he has been the director of for some time. In an interview with David Joy, Gipe explains, "I work at a community college in Harlan County, and I hear Dawn every day—young women striving, figuring how to stay themselves but get smarter, grow into their potential, and make a living—all while dealing with life challenges that would have reduced me to tears when I was their age. A big motivation in writing the book was to amplify that voice, in all its feistiness, despair, hope, humor, and anger." These voices to which Gipe bears witness are the oral histories of real Appalachian women and the strength with which they overcome their obstacles is evident both in day-to-day life as well as in the pages of Gipe's work of fiction. While Gipe may not have intentionally created *Trampoline* as an ecofeminist critique of Appalachia, his understanding of the region as influenced by the oral histories of local women gives the voice of Dawn an authenticity that speaks to the systems of oppression at work in the region to devalue the region's women and the environment they inhabit.

Through the examination of Dawn Jewell, her mother Tricia, her maternal grandmother Cora, and friend Decent Ferguson, as well as other minor female characters, it becomes evident that these Appalachian women and the Appalachian environment share a common dynamic that contrasts the dualism of patriarchal culture and capitalism. What is important to keep in mind is that the denigration of women and the environment in Appalachia is not solely a work of fiction, as portrayed in the illustrated novel. Specifically, women fighting for environmental justice in the region, as Dawn and

Cora do, face serious threats to their families and their own well-being, as multiple scholars have pointed out.[3]

It is curious that Gipe chose to make many of those protesting the mining of Blue Bear Mountain female, as Gipe stated that the protest in *Trampoline* was modeled after a protest in which he, as a male, had participated (the Black Mountain protests mentioned earlier). However, I posit that Gipe's creation of a female protagonist and numerous strong female characters acknowledges the grassroots organization and struggle that has "largely been initiated, led, and sustained by working-class women," as Shannon Elizabeth Bell discusses her in her work, which focuses on interviewing women engaged in the fight for environmental justice in the Central Appalachian region (2). Bell also mentions that often "those with the least political and economic power . . . bear a disproportionate share of the waste, pollution, and environmental destruction" (2). While it is painfully clear that the Central Appalachian natural environment is largely sacrificed in order for the rest of the nation to enjoy affordable energy, even in Appalachia there are demographics that are disproportionately affected by this sacrifice, and women are most certainly one of those demographics.

It is important to be aware that the majority of people employed in coal and oil extraction and processing within Appalachia self-identify as male (Bureau of Labor Statistics). While women are certainly legally allowed to be employed in the energy sector, including in the extraction industry, most of the occupations employing women in the region involve waiting tables or running cash registers, as Patricia Gagné observes. These employment possibilities often result in the woman, if unmarried, living in a state of poverty that does not allow for extra funds to protect her home or health from the potentially devastating effects of land degradation, such as flooding, earthquakes, water and soil contamination, and poor air quality. Being in a position of poverty also disallows the woman to miss work in order to engage in activism that might result in the companies being held accountable for these damaging effects. Also, due to the communal nature in many of these areas, where neighbors may know one another's families for generations, it would undoubtedly be a risk to social capital, namely future upward mobility, for any woman (regardless of marital or relationship status) to speak out against the companies and industries that employ many of her neighbors.

As is the reality in Central Appalachia, many of Dawn Jewell's neighbors and family members work for the local mining company and find her assistance in her grandmother's goal to end mining on Blue Bear Mountain personally problematic. Dawn is bullied at school, and her grandmother Cora is threatened by community members with ties to the local mine. Even folks who associate with Cora and Dawn are at risk for retribution from their neighbors. Cora visits the home of their neighbor Duane to gain information on property damage he has experienced due to nearby mining. At first, Duane is happy to meet with Cora and aligns himself with her cause; however, shortly before Cora and her supporters are to meet with industry officials, someone murders Duane's dog as a method of intimidation to silence Duane and his family. The intimidation works and Duane refuses to participate further in the efforts to save Blue Bear Mountain. Dawn later finds "broken glass sitting on a Styrofoam tray like meat comes on at the grocery store" (31) at her cousins' home, leading her to hypothesize that perhaps her cousins are directly responsible for the murder of Duane's dog, who was "fed...broken glass mashed up in hamburger" (10). The father of these cousins, Denny, "work[s] on the strip job Mamaw's petition was about" (28). This realization is clearly a terrifying and repulsing thought for Dawn, as shown in the accompanying image of her face: mouth slanted and eyebrow downturned in an arc of concern.

The murder of a man's dog seems to be a popular method of intimidation or retribution in Appalachian literature. In fact, the recent (and controversial) *Hillbilly Elegy* by J. D. Vance also mentions dogs being threatened or killed due to disagreements between humans, and Larry Gibson, an environmentalist who lives on Kayford Mountain, not far from Whitesville, West Virginia, shared in a recent interview that his coal-loving neighbors "[have] shot one of his dogs and tried to hang another" (Schnayerson). It is as if killing man's best friend is the next best thing if one can't kill the man himself. One commonality between Gipe's *Trampoline* and Gibson's interview is that both of the perpetrators have sided with "Big Coal," a term used especially by Joyce Berry as it is "more encompassing and reflective of the current political-economic hegemony in relation to the production and consumption of coal" (4). This connection illuminates the superiority the perpetrators feel over both the land and nonhuman animals. Even if a creature has been commodified as someone's pet, because of the few legal repercussions for killing a nonhuman animal, one may be more likely to murder an animal than a human. However, this threat implies that someone callous enough to injure a dog would likely be callous enough to end a human life as well, whether the implication is true or not.[4] When Gipe's work and the works of many other Appalachian writers are viewed through an ecofeminist lens, a pattern emerges in which a character who believes himself capable, even potentially, of causing deliberate and perhaps even fatal harm to another often offends on a female or feminized "other." One example of this can be found in domestic offenders who abuse not only their female or feminized partners but also the pets of the partner, as noted by Carol J. Adams, Frank Ascione, and many other scholars (Cudworth).

In *Trampoline*, while there may not be much overt intimate partner violence, there is certainly social control enacted against women and feminized others, such as children and animals, by select men of the community. When Dawn attends a party with her Aunt June and wanders away from her aunt, Dawn finds herself at the mercy of "a bald man who... said twice 'You got a feller'?" (213) and proceeds to suggest "me and you should think about getting married" (214). When Dawn tries to remove herself from the man's presence, he grabs her wrist and she fears "his grip was tight and I wasn't sure if I could whip him. And I was in the wrong spot to knock him out of the barn loft" (214). The man, whom we come to know by his nickname, Billy Goat Gruff, repeatedly asserts his masculinity during his interaction with Dawn, referring to himself as "a man [sic] man... somebody not afraid to be a man," feminizing Dawn's "feller" because Willett is not present at the party and insisting that Dawn "ain't got no man... because you don't know how to appreciate" (214). Billy also highlights the link being capitalism and patriarchy when he showcases his alleged financial stability in an attempt to impress Dawn: "I made a fortune in the seventies.... We all had helicopters and cocaine, and everybody wore big gold chains" (214). This capitalist patriarchy is the root of the oppression that keeps some women in Appalachia reliant on their partners' incomes, a fact clearly known to both Billy and Gipe, and noted by Betty Parker Duff as being a historical (and therefore generational) truth as "exclusion of women from waged labor... made them totally dependent on male support" (159).

Interestingly, Gagné's research, which studies the prevalence of domestic violence, its presentation, and its causes among families in the region, revealed that women in rural Appalachia are more likely to be the main breadwinner for their families despite their low wages. However, it bears mention that Gagné's research included many male subjects unwilling to work in the mines because of the risk of physical danger. As one subject explained, "Yea, I could go work in the mines. But I ain't goin' to. The way I figure is why should I die makin' somebody else rich?" (397). Though several male subjects refused local mining work and thus were reliant on their partner's incomes, which contradicts many Western ideas about masculinity, Gagné's research shows that their female partners were frequently the victims of domestic abuse and controlling behavior. The men in these heteronormative relationships often limited the socialization of their female partners, particularly around other men. The men also limited the social mobility and earning potential of their partners by forced pregnancies, coupled with the men's refusal to provide child care to the children they fathered. As one subject notes, "My third child wasn't planned by me, but it was planned by my husband because he threw my birth control pills away" (405). Because of the isolated rural areas wherein many Appalachian women live, withholding transportation is another method of male domination and can easily be linked to the stunting of social mobility mentioned earlier if the men refuse to allow their partners to attend school or seek better wages. Gagné's research illustrates that even when men are un- or underemployed, patriarchal oppression is still at work, including by forcing women to maintain traditional roles against their wishes.[5]

Many of the female background characters in Gipe's novel portray stereotypical gender roles. When Cora visits Duane, the local man mentioned earlier who she's hoping will contribute to the next meeting, he shares with her the details of the damage to his home's foundation caused by "the blasting" as his wife "set[s] down a plate of sliced pound cake, a bowl of strawberries, and a tub of Cool Whip" (4). Dawn, who has accompanied her grandmother, notes that "people always fix pound cake when Mamaw comes to talk about their troubles with the coal company" (4). It is also mentioned in the same scenario that the man's wife has "china plates" that were "stood up in a cabinet and they busted all over the place" due to the nearby dynamite usage (5). These images portray Duane's wife as a silent caretaker engaged in traditional feminine gender roles. Continuing to portray Duane's wife as a victim of oppression, Gipe does not name her throughout the interaction, even when the woman answers a statement directed toward her: "'Look at that Christmas cactus,' Mamaw said. 'So beautiful.' 'Thank you,' the man's wife said. 'It likes that spot.' The wife had a northern accent. She moved through the room making things straight" (4). Dawn, as the narrator, constructs the woman as an "outsider" based on her manner of speaking, a common trait of Appalachian literature. However, the effect in this case serves only to further ostracize the woman from the other females around her. Gagné discusses how women may avoid certain women they have "Othered" because of preconceived notions based on stereotypes and a lack of trust (402). This avoidance then results in isolation from one's own gender. We later see the distrust that grows between Dawn and her once-best-friend Evie, after Evie develops feelings for Dawn's brother Albert, with whom Dawn has a tumultuous and often violent relationship.

Similarly, complicated representations of traditional gender norms are portrayed by Tricia's friend Jan, when the duo are dyeing Dawn's hair. Describing how as children she injured Dawn's Uncle Hubert, "I beat the living snot out of him," she immediately follows with "yall want some cookies?

Them church people left a bunch of packs of cookies" (117). Jan's recounting of the events involves her admitting to her own violence, but she is both quick to point out her childhood reasoning ("Hubert stole my brand new fucking bicycle") and quick to resume her performative gender role as an adult cisgender woman. Jan then leaves the room, returning with the treats and "slamming two boxes of double-fudge sandwiches down" next to Dawn and then handing Dawn a drink shortly thereafter when Dawn admits to being thirsty (117). The act of "slamming" down an object may seem unladylike in its aggression, but the act itself is providing food desired by Jan's guests. Once Jan and Tricia finish cutting and dyeing Dawn's hair, Jan informs Dawn that she "look[s] like a guy" (118). This statement complicates Dawn's self-image and situates her in a place of gender fluidity rather than of performative gender identity and norms. Carissa Massey notes that the influence of constructing one's appearance to match typical gender binaries affects all Americans, but particularly in Appalachia where such "pressures ... are not lessened in a context of poverty," and "Appalachian women are indicted on their *inability* to act on [the pressures]" and are typified as "'trash' ... or desexualized altogether" (128, emphasis original). While this would certainly be problematic for anyone, it would clearly be damaging to the burgeoning identity of a teen who identifies as female growing up in Central Appalachia, particularly in a family of self-described "hillbillies." In discussing the gendered stereotypes of Appalachian "hillbillies," which Dawn denotes describes her family, Massey states, "If the hillbilly man is lazy, ignorant, and drunk then the hillbilly woman is aggressive, overly fecund, and masculine. For a cultural context that prizes women as feminine and men as masculine dichotomies, the Appalachian woman is often rendered as at least as unnatural or uncivilized as the man because she takes on the duties he lays aside and thus is stripped of the passivity and femininity desired of women by western culture" (130). Massey's description explains how Appalachian women are viewed as "Other" when compared to non-Appalachian women, and even to Appalachian women who embody alternate stereotypes (or perhaps embody no stereotype at all). While Jan may not have meant much harm to Dawn, her comment coupled with cultural influence is certainly detrimental and fraught with real-world implication.

The actions Appalachian women must take to achieve acceptance as their chosen gender, and the judgments Massey mentions at their perceived failure to do so, are prevalent throughout *Trampoline*. At the planning meeting, in preparation for the meeting with officials to discuss the fate of Blue Bear Mountain, several women were present and Dawn does not describe them very favorably: "April wore a homemade sweater ... that hung big on her,"

"Portia had leather patches across the shoulders of her sweater, like she was on a submarine," and then there was a woman with a "sticky-faced boy" (6). The only man described in their company was a gentleman with a "receding hairline" (6). Certainly there is some prejudice toward balding men in Western culture, so much so that there have been entire volumes devoted to the subject,[6] yet because of the patriarchal system of power the United States was founded upon and operates under, even a balding man has more power than a woman in an unflattering sweater. To further subtly emphasize the influence of a patriarchal capitalist system of oppression on the region, the meeting is held in the basement of the public library, an area decorated with "pictures of the USS Canard County in a glass case ... a navy ship that hauled tanks and trucks to Haiti and the Persian Gulf and Argentina til the navy sold it to Spain" (6). Images of this vessel were juxtaposed with interpretations of it such as "a model of the boat made out of sugar cubes spraypainted gray," an illusion to a particular weakness beneath the hardened exterior of both the vessel and the ideology (6).

In order to develop their agency in a land of oppression, we see many of Gipe's female characters engage in various forms of violence, either self-inflicted or against one another. Often scholarly research focuses on violence toward women inflicted by men, but over the past decade there has been more research into female intragender violence. One of the most prominent factors in female intragender violence is poverty, according to Hirschinger et al., which certainly afflicts many of the women in *Trampoline*. Early in the novel, Cora chases and assaults Dawn's mother and her own daughter, Tricia, with a broomstick in the Walmart parking lot for stealing her Social Security check. Later we see Evie attack several female bullies who are accosting Dawn. Hirschinger et al. note that most female intragender assaults were "by women they knew (88%), in outdoor locations (60%), and in the presence of others (91%)" (1098). Additionally, Hirschinger et al. discovered the demographic most "at risk for injury typically were young and socially active, used marijuana, and had experienced other kinds of violence," which also describes many of the female characters in Gipe's novel, particularly Dawn. By viewing *Trampoline* as a way to better understand the Appalachian region and its inhabitants, one can more thoroughly grasp the ways in which systems of oppression produce lateral violence that, essentially, makes it easier for the systems of oppression to remain in place.

In addition to lateral, female intragender violence, we also see women turning this violence inward in Gipe's novel, with a particular focus on self-destructive substance abuse. This may be most notable in the behavior of Tricia, Dawn's mother, who uses drugs and alcohol to cope with the death of her husband, Delbert, which occurred years earlier and was due to dangerous mining conditions. Interestingly, the self-destructive behaviors exhibited by female characters throughout the novel are often tied to their association with the natural world, frequently with comparisons between themselves and nonhuman animals, furthering the hypothesis that women and nonhuman animals are regarded similarly in Gipe's portrayal of Appalachia.

Tricia engages with the natural world by ascending a tree during a drug-induced bout of escapism. She later confides in Jan that "I had a dream Dawn turned into an owl" and she had climbed the tree "looking for the place she [Dawn] fell" (117). This connection between self-destructive behaviors and the nonhuman world can also be seen when Dawn shares "I went to my bed panting like a black dog in August" after falling ill, having binged on the snack bar's junk food in response to the stress caused by her mother and grandmother "having it out in the yellow stripes of the crossing zone" (8–9). Dawn's self-destructive response to familial stress is quite common, note Straiton et al. in a 2013 study that states, "Cultural gender scripts help shape which traits and behaviors, including self-destructive behaviors, are more appropriate for men or women. Conventional femininity is tied up with notions of dependency and indecisiveness. Interpersonal communication is central to the feminine gender role and self-harming is often seen as a way of communicating one's distress" (161). Thus, Tricia's experience links not only her substance abuse and her connection to the natural world but also the care and responsibility she feels toward her daughter. This ethic of care and inward-focused response to stress are both inextricably linked to the gender roles performed by cisgender women. We can expand on the ideas presented by Straiton et al. and draw a comparison between how these women treat themselves and other women and how the capitalist patriarchy in Gipe's Appalachia treats the natural world in addition to its female human inhabitants. As Engelhardt notes, "Along with race, class, and gender, which are also operating, nature too becomes an inseparable category of power and identity," one that is perhaps more visible on a large scale than a multitude of intimate, individual struggles (*Tangled Roots* 38).

Dawn describes a prime example of this intersectionality as she bears witness to its occurrence at the public meeting to discuss the fate of strip mining on Blue Bear Mountain:

> A woman I'd seen at Mamaw's meetings called the coal company out by name, said they'd told her mother they weren't going to strip mine her land, that they was just going to build a coal haul road across it

and that they wouldn't be out there even a month. She said they'd promised to build a road out to her family's cemetery—widen it. And then when her mother signed her rights away they'd strip mined the shit out of it—that's what the woman said—and they'd mined right up to the cemetery and probably would've mined right through it if she—the daughter—hadn't come back from Georgia. (12–13)

The connection this woman has with her land certainly embodies the idea of the feminist ethic of care. However, in order to protect her land, she has to stand up to systems of oppression that are trying to relegate both the woman in question and her land to a place of inferiority and victimhood. Gipe's nod to the idea of women as caregivers resounds throughout *Trampoline*, created as a cultural expectation among many of the female characters.

Decent Ferguson's exemplification of the feminist care ethic is mentioned in the "big-ass garden plot" that is larger than "her little house" (102). As it is implied that Decent lives alone, it is likely unnecessary for her to have a garden plot larger than her home. The implication of this is that she grows enough to support not only herself but also members of her community. Decent also exhibits this ethic in reaching out to Dawn, showing concern about Dawn's actions and offering support: "Why don't you talk to somebody about what's going on?" and "You don't think you need to talk about car stealing and jumping off mountains to somebody?" rather than turning her over to law enforcement or other patriarchal structures of power. Even when Dawn rejects Decent's outreach by saying "You're not helping me," Decent simply responds with "I'm sorry" rather than responding in a defensive ego-focused reply (103–4).

The representation of Decent's traditional Appalachian gender role also places her in the same social position as many of the women in the text. Gipe writes that "Decent Ferguson pulled out a sweater she had made" and that she rescued "quilts out of her last trailer fire," indicating her abilities typically associated with traditional mountain women. It is also noted that Decent has "pictures on her walls" and "there [are] always men in them" (105). The men are described as "black men with guitars and tambourines and groups of people wearing baseball gloves and shirts that said SPAM on them," which makes it difficult to know for certain whether these are simply celebrities or perhaps friends or family members. Regardless of the men's relations to Decent, it is notable that even as a woman who engages, whether consciously or subconsciously, with feminist ideals, she still is so influenced by men that they decorate the walls of her home. This exhibits that the patriarchal influence, even if cultural, still affects women in subtle yet powerful ways.

When discussing the feminist ethic of care, it is important to clarify that the definition is not essentialist. As Joan Tronto describes, men and women can both display care, though it is often directed differently, as Chaia Heller notes: "Within the sexual division of labor, women are assigned the direct service of 'caring for' children, the old, the sick, while men are credited for 'caring about' such romantic ideals as 'the prosperity of the family'" (233). However, as I mentioned earlier, Gagné notes that in rural Appalachia women often find themselves providing care in many of these realms and continuing to do so, often for a variety of reasons. Some women may genuinely enjoy and find satisfaction in providing care to others, while others may simply be continuing the gender role performance to avoid upsetting expected cultural norms.

Tricia, Dawn's mother, also displays care for the earth in her enjoyment of gardening as well as her affirmation that she stands with Cora and Dawn regarding the Blue Bear Mountain mining (though she admits that she is far less active in her support than they are—largely due to her drug-induced erratic behavior and addiction). Yet despite her occasional drug-addled behavior, readers should be aware that the feminist care ethic is displayed by Tricia's true self, as Dawn explains, watching her mother plant impatiens: "She picked at the roots delicate as a bird and set the flower in a hole. She troweled dirt in over the plant and patted it. Momma's hands moved like spider's legs over the flowers, the dirt, her tools" (153). The attention she pays to the flowers, as if they were her own children, is clear in the caution she takes in handling them. Her respect for even the dirt is noticed by her daughter. Moreover, the plants she is nurturing are not the healthy, robust plants that Hubert, lying, informed her that she'd won; they are, as the hardware store clerk informed her, "rootbound" and have "been here too long to sell" (150). Her willingness to take on the task of saving these plants also serves to exhibit Tricia's care and its associated gender role. We see a similar uphill battle, much like with Tricia, among nonfictional women as well, particularly among female activists working to halt mountaintop removal and environmental destruction in the coalfields.

In the associated scene in which Tricia receives the aforementioned plants, the clerk also exemplifies the shared source of oppression for both Appalachian women and the natural world they inhabit. He gives Tricia the plants for free, which at first seems kind, as though he has sympathy for her, given her travels and hope based on Hubert's falsified information. But it quickly becomes clear that the clerk's rationale for gifting Tricia the imperiled plants is self-motivated, as Dawn notices: "His eyes swam in his head as he looked Momma over.... It was like this with Momma. Some people... couldn't see her at all. Some, like the boy with the flowers, had to stare at her from every angle, like she was some fancy salamander or butterfly" (150). The clerk's obvious male gaze is meant to objectify Tricia, though his intentions do not seem to go further. When Tricia asks about repercussions for his wilted gifts, the gentleman explains that he's not concerned about consequences because he's "Quitting Friday" (150). While he is clearly not trying to impress her with his future plans, it is interesting that, as someone without regard to consequences, he could potentially give her any of the other available flowers, yet chooses to provide her with the ones that have lived out their capitalist usefulness.

Gipe's critique of this shared exploitation and commodification is one that we know, based on research, is a reflection of Appalachia's present-day reality. The intersections he reveals in *Trampoline* display the challenges faced by women living in Appalachia, who depend largely on the protection of the natural environment they inhabit, and yet this environment and its disenfranchised populations are struggling daily under a system that values coal more than human lives. What Gipe creates in *Trampoline* is more than a bildungsroman of an awkward fifteen-year-old trying to find her way; instead, Dawn and her cohorts illuminate the need for real and sustainable change in the hollows that are often overlooked.

NOTES

1. Engelhardt explains that the "working definition" is "a philosophy, formal or informal," that is anti-anthropocentric, engages with and critiques intersections of power (such as race, gender, class, species) and systems of oppression (such as capitalism and patriarchy), requires its activists to seek long-term, sustainable solutions to ecological crises, and is "not essentialist" in the notion that "women are not necessarily untied in sisterhood, nor are they equally oppressed, nor are they the only gender to have a role in enacting justice" (3–4).

2. "The people had to pay for it" refers to a bond passed by then-governor Paul Patton (a coal operator) that was funded by taxpayers to essentially "pay off" the coal company. As Gipe added, "If the mountain was not suitable for mining, then politicians should have told the coal companies to eat it, not pay them off. They got paid for what they would've gotten from the coal, without ever employing a single local person." The interview was conducted by Zackary Vernon on April 20, 2017, and published in the *Cold Mountain Review*, a publication of the Department of English at Appalachian State University (http://coldmountainreview.org/impulse-toward-terrain-interview-robert-gipe-zackary-vernon/).

3. See Shannon Elizabeth Bell's *Our Roots Run Deep as Ironweed: Appalachian Women and the Fight for Environmental Justice*, Joyce Barry's *Standing Our Ground: Women, Environmental Justice, and the Fight to End Mountaintop Removal*, and *Mountains of Injustice: Social and Environmental Injustice in Appalachia*, edited by Michele Morrone and Geoffrey L. Buckley.

4. It should be noted, however, that in situations of intimate partner violence, the killing of one partner's pet often is a precursor to the murder of that partner. See *Animal Maltreatment: Forensic Mental Health Issues and Evaluations*, edited by Lacie Levitt, Gary Patronek, and Thomas Grisso.

5. It should be noted that through a feminist lens, women who desire to embody traditional gender roles and make such a decision from a place of empowerment and agency are not considered to be victims of male oppression, at least where this single decision is concerned. Systemic oppression is a much larger matter.

6. See *Hair! Mankind's Historic Quest to End Baldness* by Gersh Kuntzman.

BIBLIOGRAPHY

Adams, Carol J., and Lori Gruen. *Ecofeminism: Feminist Intersections with Other Animals and the Earth*. New York: Bloomsbury, 2014.

Barry, Joyce. *Standing Our Ground: Women, Environmental Justice, and the Fight to End Mountaintop Removal*. Athens: Ohio University Press, 2012.

Bell, Shannon Elizabeth. *Our Roots Run Deep as Ironweed: Appalachian Women and the Fight for Environmental Justice*. Champaign: University of Illinois Press, 2013.

Bureau of Labor Statistics. "Table 18: Employed Persons by Detailed Industry, Sex, Race, and Hispanic or Latino Ethnicity, 2016." Current Population Survey, January 20, 2022. https://www.bls.gov/cps/cpsaat18.htm.

Cudworth, Erika. "Ecofeminism and the Animal." In *Contemporary Perspectives on Ecofeminism*, edited by Mary Phillips and Nick Rumens, 38–56. London: Routledge, 2016.

Davidov, Danielle, Stephen M. Davis, Motao Zhu, Tracie O. Afifi, Melissa Kimber, Abby Goldstein, Nicole Pitre, Kelly Gurka, and Carol Stocks. "Intimate Partner Violence-Related Hospitalizations in Appalachia and non-Appalachian United States." *Public Library of Science* 12, no. 9 (2017): n.p. https://doi.org/10.1371/journal.pone.0184222.

Duff, Betty Parker. "Stand by Your Man: Gender and Class in the Harlan County Coalfields." In *Beyond Hill and Hollow: Original Readings in Appalachian Women's Studies*, edited by Elizabeth S. D. Engelhardt, 152–69. Athens: Ohio University Press, 2005.

Engelhardt, Elizabeth S. D. "Nature-Loving Souls and Appalachian Mountains: The Promise of Feminist Ecocriticism." In *An American Vein: Critical Readings in Appalachian Literature*, edited by Danny L. Miller, Sharon Hatfield, and Gurney Norman, 337–52. Athens: Ohio University Press, 2005.

———. *The Tangled Roots of Feminism, Environmentalism, and Appalachian Literature*. Athens: Ohio University Press, 2003.

Gaard, Greta. "Ecofeminism Revisited: Rejecting Essentialism and Re-placing Species in a Material Feminist Environmentalism." *Feminist Formations* 23, no. 2 (2011): 26–53.

———. "Living Interconnections with Animals and Nature." In *Ecofeminism: Women, Animals, Nature*, edited by Greta Gaard, 1–13. Philadelphia: Temple University Press, 1993.

Gagné, Patricia L. "Appalachian Women: Violence and Social Control." *Journal of Contemporary Ethnography* 20, no. 4 (1992): 387–415.

Gipe, Robert. Interview conducted by David Joy on August 29, 2015. *Revolution John*,

August 29, 2015. https://revolutionjohn.wordpress.com/2015/08/29/the-man-who-is-drawing-my-next-tattoo-an-interview-with-robert-gipe-by-david-joy/.

———. Interview conducted by Zackary Vernon on April 20, 2017. *Cold Mountain Review*, Spring/Summer 2017. http://coldmountainreview.org/impulse-toward-terrain-interview-robert-gipe-zackary-vernon/.

———. Reading at Western Carolina University, Cullowhee, N.C., April 4, 2017, as part of the annual Literary Festival.

———. *Trampoline*. Athens: Ohio University Press, 2015.

Heller, Chaia. "For the Love of Nature." In *Ecofeminism: Women, Animals, Nature*, edited by Greta Gaard, 219–42. Philadelphia: Temple University Press, 1993.

Hirschinger, Nancy B., Jeane Ann Grisso, Donald B. Wallace, Kelly Farley McCollum, Donald Schwartz, Mary D. Sammel, Colleen Brensinger, and Elijah Anderson. "A Case-Control Study of Female-to-Female Nonintimate Violence in an Urban Area." *American Journal of Public Health* 93, no. 7 (2003): 1098–1103.

Kuntzman, Gersh. *Hair! Mankind's Historic Quest to End Baldness*. New York: Random House, 2001.

Levitt, Lacie, Gary Patronek, and Thomas Grisso, eds. *Animal Maltreatment: Forensic Mental Health Issues and Evaluations*. Oxford: Oxford University Press, 2016.

Massey, Carissa. "Appalachian Stereotypes: Cultural History, Gender, and Sexual Rhetoric." *Journal of Appalachian Studies* 13, no. 1/2 (2007): 124–36.

Morrone, Michele, and Geoffrey L. Buckley, eds. *Mountains of Injustice: Social and Environmental Injustice in Appalachia*. Athens: Ohio University Press, 2013.

Schnayerson, Michael. "The Rape of Appalachia." *Vanity Fair*, November 20, 2006. https://www.vanityfair.com/news/2006/05/appalachia200605.

Straiton, Melanie L., Heidi Hjelmeland, Tine K. Grimholt, and Gudrun Dieserud. "Self-Harm and Conventional Gender Roles in Women." *Suicide & Life-Threatening Behavior* 43, no. 2 (2013): 161–73.

Vance, J. D. *Hillbilly Elegy: A Memoir of a Family and Culture in Crisis*. New York: Harper, 2016.

Hidden Gems
Finding the New
in the Familiar

Ecosexuals in Appalachia
Identity, Community, and Counterdiscourse in *Goodbye Gauley Mountain*

CYNTHIA BELMONT

In the documentary film *Goodbye Gauley Mountain: An Ecosexual Love Story* (2013), filmmaker Elizabeth Stephens and her partner, prominent sex educator Annie Sprinkle, return to Stephens's hometown of Montgomery, West Virginia, in order to explore Appalachians' responses to the increasing encroachment of mountaintop removal (MTR) mining upon their environment and lifeways. Meeting with members of the LGBTQ+ community there, Stephens remarks, "We used to be lesbians, but now we're ecosexuals." Ecosexuality, an identity championed by Stephens and Sprinkle, invites an environmentalist reorientation of all other recognized sexual identity categories, which restrict the erotic to consenting humans' desires and actions, and presents a socially conscious alternative to the dominant strains of environmentalism, which historically neglect consideration of the interconnections between environment, gender, and sexuality. In ecosexuality, nature is seen as an active agent and erotic partner for humans, who are likewise drawn emotionally, physically, spiritually, and politically to its eroticism, which they celebrate and work to protect through diverse activist and educational endeavors, including performance and other art, such as street theater, photography, and pornography. In *Goodbye Gauley Mountain*, environmental activism within a philosophical framework of ecosexuality and seated in the rural justice context of a community's resistance to the destruction of its mountain home creates a powerful queer ecological counterdiscourse to mainstream environmentalism and antimining politics—a counterdiscourse that, in its departure from heteronormativity and its genuinely progressive approach to community building, should be of interest to ecofeminists, queer ecologists, and ecocritics.

Queer ecology, a hybrid movement, is conceived by its activist and academic proponents as "a cultural-political-social analysis that interrogates the co-relations between the social organization of sexuality and ecology," toward shaping a politics of sexuality that foregrounds environmental awareness and a politics of the environment that considers how sexuality is involved in our conceptions and treatment of the natural world (Mortimer-Sandilands, "Sexual Politics" 110). Queer ecology offers "a new practice of ecological knowledges, spaces, and politics that places central attention on challenging hetero-ecologies from the perspective of non-normative sexual and gender positions" (Mortimer-Sandilands and Erickson 22). Concomitantly, queer ecocriticism "embraces ... sexual pleasure and transgression as foundational to environmental ethics and politics, and resistance to heteronormativity as part and parcel of ... green strategy" (39), contributing to both the field of ecocriticism and the environmental justice movement (Hogan 232). Likewise, ecofeminism operates from the thoroughly intersectional understanding that "the ideologies which authorize injustices based on gender, race, and class are related to the ideologies which sanction the exploitation and degradation of the environment" (Sturgeon 260); further, "the democratic, ecological society envisioned as the goal of ecofeminism will, of necessity, be a society that values sexual diversity and the erotic" (Gaard 115), a society in which coalitions of queers, women, people of color, and "all those associated with nature and the erotic" are empowered (132). Operating in conversation with ecofeminist theory, literary and cultural criticism, and environmental activism, ecofeminist literary and cultural critics explore how the inclusion of feminist perspectives and marginalized voices enhances environmentalism's ability to address the social justice issues inherent in environmental issues and how attention to the environmental contexts of our social systems enhances feminism's efforts in striving for social change (Gaard and Murphy 12). In line with ecofeminism and queer ecology, Sprinkle and Stephens's vision of ecosexuality, which is intended "to make the environmental movement more sexy, fun and diverse," demonstrates how thinking in terms of both the environment and social change means recognizing the needs of multiple human and other-than-human communities and therefore provides opportunities for alliances between apparently divergent interests (Stephens and Sprinkle, "SexEcology"). Their Ecosex Symposiums, for instance, are designed to spark conversation between "artists, academics, students, activists, theorists, curators, ecologists, environmentalists, sex workers, art patrons, nature nymphs, country folk, city folk, herbalists, historians, pagans, scientists, media people, and others" and include presentations on topics such as "The Greening of the Sex Industry" and "conflict in the Middle East, genocide and olive trees" (Stephens and Sprinkle, "SexEcology"). Radical activist projects such as Stephens and Sprinkle's, which bring disparate agendas together toward the integration of environmentalism, social justice, and the arts, are rich ground on which to cultivate theoretical and activist connections between queer politics, feminism, environmentalism, and criticism.

Queer ecological and ecofeminist scholars argue that environmentalist discourse often supports a socially conservative status quo, such that its transformative promise is seriously compromised. As Di Chiro shows in "Polluted Politics? Confronting Toxic Discourse, Sex Panic, and Econormativity," U.S. environmentalism is contaminated by a history of embedment in capitalist/colonialist, patriarchal, heterosexist, and ableist institutions; therefore, what is needed in contemporary environmental theory and practice is "counter-discourses to these 'polluted politics,'" found in "research practices, environmental criticism, and social activism that ... profess allegiance to ecofeminist and/or environmental justice politics," challenging the norms of environmentalism (223). In the Foucault–Deleuze interview on discourse and power for *L'Arc* (1972), Foucault says, "It is this form of discourse which ultimately matters, a discourse against power, the counterdiscourse of prisoners and those we call delinquents" (Kay). The discourse of the "delinquent" is the discourse of the offending outsider—the deviant, nonconforming and non-normate, including queers—counterdiscourse that is essential to transformative politics since confrontational speech is a critical initial stage in challenging dominant power structures (Kay). Di Chiro explains that "while those bodies, communities, and environments that stray from the 'normate' may be hated, impoverished, and poisoned, ... seeing and knowing from non-normate positions may offer outsider views for imagining new, just, and sustainable ways of living" (225). Both the ecosexual and Appalachian voices of *Goodbye Gauley Mountain* are distinctly non-normate and in their mingling offer precisely this radical view. These voices thus offer an invaluable contribution to environmentalism and to oppositional discourse on mining, represented here by four other documentary films focused on community responses to the exploitative practices of mining companies: the well-known *Harlan County, USA* (1977) and recent *On Coal River* (2010), *The Last Mountain* (2011), and *Overburden* (2015). Coal cinema typically relies upon a strictly heteropatriarchal, anthropocentric vision of family, community, and the land—a vision that grounds these films' radical labor politics in retrogressive American values. An ecofeminist/queer ecological analysis of Stephens and Sprinkle's construction of an ecosexual identity and community that delights in the intimate frictions of complex ecological and social interests demonstrates how, in contrast, their approach to inclusiveness in environmental activism opens avenues for true coalition building that destabilizes normative environmental politics toward social and environmental justice.

In *Strange Natures: Futurity, Empathy, and the Queer Ecological Imagination*, Nicole Seymour asks, given the pervasiveness of eco-normativity, "Can a defense of 'nature' or 'the natural' ever be queer? Can one redefine those terms such that they effectively, and empathetically, accommodate both the queer and the non-human? And are there ways of being ironic and playful, those qualities often associated with queerness, while also being earnest and dedicated, those qualities often associated with environmentalism?" (viii). Sprinkle and Stephens's ecosexual activist/artistic projects accomplish just such apparently contradictory objectives, creating a counterdiscourse that refigures human/nature relationships, combats heterosexism and homophobia, blends playful irony with passionate dedication to social and environmental justice, and illuminates the limitations of hegemonic constructions of the normal within mainstream environmentalism. As a full-length documentary film that has been widely screened and reviewed, *Goodbye Gauley Mountain* has the potential to disrupt conventional views of nature, humanity, community, identity, sexuality, and environmental activism while providing an antidote to the toxicity of single-issue politics in the coal documentary genre.[1]

Ecosexual Counterdiscourse

Goodbye Gauley Mountain opens with an ironic content warning: "WARNING: This film contains environmental destruction, explicit ecosexuality, and performance art." Deploying the simultaneous lightness and edge of queer humor, this warning foregrounds the film's counterdiscursive approach by implicitly posing our culture's typical content concerns (based in an obsession with violence and a puritanical/prurient approach to sexuality), as well as its stunning lack of outrage regarding environmental issues, against this film's profound investment in and exposure of these issues, while suggesting that ecosexuality and performance art are dangerous in their subversive potential. Questioning the conventional discourse on what is dangerous, in Foucault's terms what requires "management procedures" (nudity? curse words? or, rather, pan-capitalism's brutal erasure of ancient ecosystems that sustain life?), and pointing to how contemporary culture neglects to consider the environmental/social implications of and connections between the stories it tells (and doesn't tell) about humanity, culture, and nature, the warning lays groundwork for a new story in which environmental politics, art, and the erotic comingle in order to repair the cultural fragmentation of bodies, land, and history—a story that reveals what is kept hidden (e.g., desire, sexuality, toxic sludge, clear-cut land, and elevated cancer rates in mining communities) by oppressive structures and institutions whose protectionism always serves dominant interests, particularly the interests of capital (Foucault 24). Foucault says, "The discourse of struggle is not opposed to the unconscious, but to the secretive. It may not seem like much; but what if it turned out to be more than we expected?" (Kay). Throughout *Goodbye Gauley Mountain*, devastating footage of MTR blasting, slurry ponds, bulldozed homes, and lush forest slashed to bare rock; interviews on mining companies' safety violations, exploitation of workers, and lies about the health risks associated with mining; and ironically charming hand-drawn cartoons and artwork illustrating with a disturbing homespun deftness the industrial and geologic processes involved in MTR and its effects are crosscut with scenes highlighting ecosexual/Appalachian attentiveness to, intimate connections with, and loving care for many forms of life, from insects to trees to dogs to humans to mountainsides. Following Stephens's intention that the film represents an ecosexual "process of engaged knowing," *Goodbye Gauley Mountain* explores the land as a beloved, eroticized, agentic, and victimized body whose secrets are both terrifying (as in stripped land, which is typically concealed from public scrutiny through strategic placement of MTR in poor communities and on terrain not easily viewed from the ground) and magical (as in the medicinal plants that grow in Appalachian forests) (Stephens). This exploration centralizes ways in which the inhabitants and their culture are the mountains, while the mountains are their inhabitants and therefore their politics and history, illustrating what Alaimo calls a necessary "sense of kinship, connection, and unraveling between dirt and flesh, word and world"; in this view, "political and ethical interests usually seen as separate are inextricably linked by the substantial transit across bodies and natures" (259). *Goodbye Gauley Mountain* employs many of the film techniques common to coal texts, comprising what Montrie identifies as the "'MTR documentary' recipe," including thematically relevant folk music, compelling beauty shots, footage of protest and heated confrontation with authorities, and a narrative arc spotlighting the heroism of ordinary citizens and concluding with a message of hope (274). Like *Goodbye Gauley Mountain*, all the other films under consideration here present an inspiring liberatory vision of working-class community resistance to corporate exploitation; the recent films share some locations and footage with Stephens's film as well. But *Goodbye Gauley Mountain*, whose perspective is queer, environmentalist, and feminist, is strikingly counterdiscursive with regard to its construction of gender. *Harlan County, USA* reinforces patriarchal/masculine control of economic and social systems since the featured miners, company representatives, and politicians are all men while the women are supportive of the struggle; likewise, following the standard division of labor, the physically challenging resistance actions in *Overburden* (trespassing, chaining) and the walk to D.C. in *On Coal River* are undertaken by men, while women handle communications and other organizing work as well as serving in support roles. All four films are thoroughly normative in their valorization of the heteropatriarchal family as the central unit of a community that is financially dependent upon heads of household whose masculine status as breadwinners is perpetually imperiled within the mining mono-economy. These films are also masculinist in their dualistic logic regarding mining conflicts,[2] wherein working-class citizen is posed against mining company, people are either for or against union/workers' rights (as in the stirring labor song from *Harlan County, USA* "Which Side Are You On?"), and conflicts of interest are neatly resolved through the emergence of consciousness, especially via protagonists' movement from mining employment to anti-MTR activism and on the occasion of tragic death, as in *Harlan County, USA*, where, as an elder says, "it took a young man's life to bring . . . the government, the union, and the operators together." *Goodbye Gauley Mountain* disrupts the dualistic imperative of politics as usual by highlighting the complexities and historicity of citizens' investments in the land, the economy, and their own well-being, for instance, the mining museum ride operator who, talking about how Appalachians can no longer hunt for ginseng out of season without getting fined while MTR companies are allowed to level entire mountaintops whenever they want, says, "The little man, he can't do it, but the big man can. They step on you every direction." This "little man" is deeply invested in the land and in mining; what he resists is being crushed under the juggernaut of contemporary global capitalism, wherein foreign companies own pieces of Appalachia, American coal is shipped to overseas markets, and whole mountains are topped for the profit of a few.

The film's compassionate treatment of the couple Roger and Cindy exemplifies Stephens's refusal to reduce complex positions to right and wrong sides. Roger, a mining equipment technician, is married to Cindy, Stephens's childhood best friend, despite their political opposition: she is anti-MTR, while he is a member of Friends of Coal, supports MTR, but also identifies as an environmentalist who believes that the mountains are sensate and imbued with spirit and is disturbed that Americans have no idea where their energy comes from, yet uses the biblical idea of dominion to justify an ethical position that humans can be "stewards" of the land while taking all the resources that the modern world requires. In their interview, Cindy and Roger discuss the delicacy of Stephens's position navigating among family members and friends whose views are antagonistic. Stephens and Sprinkle do not seem troubled by this position, however; rather, they invite everyone, of all persuasions, to participate in their ecosexual wedding to the mountains, footage of which closes the film (discussed below). Sprinkle says to Roger and Cindy, "We may disagree . . . , but we all love the mountains," and indeed the chief purpose of ecosexual activism is to share, across and through differences, appreciation for human connections to/embodiment as nature, in patience and hope that an ethic of empathy will grow therefrom. Regarding the apparent contradictions within perspectives such as Roger's, Deleuze asks,

> How is it that people whose interests are not being served can strictly support the existing power structure by demanding a piece of the action? Perhaps this is because in terms of investments, whether economic or unconscious, interest is not the final answer; there are investments of desire that function in a more profound and diffuse manner than our interests dictate. But of course, we never desire against our interests, because interest always follows and finds itself where desire has placed it. (Kay)

Ecosexuality precisely aims to encourage awareness of the diversity and earthiness of sexual desire so that interest in environmentalism will follow; this necessitates extending a far-reaching hand to the vast array of proclivities and emotions involved in our investments. *Goodbye Gauley Mountain* illustrates the value of an environmental politics that can admit to and accommodate the complexity of our stakes in environmental/social issues, resisting capitulation to an insufficient "which side are you on?" approach.

Goodbye Gauley Mountain is also counterdiscursive to other coal texts in modeling ecosexual empathy—a "queer empathy" that is "available to all"—in which intimate physical and emotional connections between species are illuminated and celebrated (Seymour 184). While Stephens's camera repeatedly lingers in close-up upon the brilliant specificities of plants and animals engaged in their livelihoods, such as a turtle strolling along, the delicate movement of insects upon wildflowers, the "sexy" lushness of tomatoes in a garden, a crayfish gazing up from a river bottom, and the faces of family dogs, reminding the viewer time and again that what MTR threatens is the kindred spirits who share Appalachia as home, *Harlan County, USA* approaches environmental connections only in illustrating the crushing poverty in which the miners live and in describing mining's threats to their health; meanwhile, its metaphoric uses of animals (e.g., mules) to explain how laborers are treated (vs. questioning why it is acceptable for humans to abuse animals in the first place) seats the film's resistance to oppressive social and economic structures within a hierarchical anthropocentric framework that can never present genuine solutions to problems with the mining industry since it does not acknowledge that the institutions and practices of domination over nature and marginalized human groups (such as labor) are mutually dependent and therefore must all be addressed for any to be undone. Foucault asks, "Isn't [the] difficulty of finding adequate forms of struggle a result of the fact that we continue to ignore the problem of power?" (Kay). *The Last Mountain* exemplifies this difficulty in its heroizing Bobby Kennedy, whose privilege of access to heads of state and romanticized history as a nature-loving child of the elite represent the film's apex of environmentalist dedication. In *The Last Mountain*, *On Coal River*, and *Overburden*, nature is viewed sensuously through appreciative long shots of birds in flight, rivers, and misty mountains, and physical connections to the Earth are emphasized via distress about MTR's corruption of the water supply and the community's extraordinary disease incidence, but these connections are rarely positive or inspiring ones. Aside from three long shots of a bear and deer in *Overburden*, these films never portray nonhuman animals or plants as individuals in place, with singular embodiments and shared embedment in ecosystems/communities, and their images of nature serve chiefly as establishing shots, providing context for what ultimately emerge as human problems— "crimes against humanity" as one activist in *The Last Mountain* says. Further, the main source of pathos in these films is MTR's threats to children (via poisoning and paternal death or joblessness), whose innocence and vulnerability are repeatedly emphasized, as in *Overburden*, which begins with the birth of a baby that serves as both a symbol of the community's fragile hopes and a marker of his grandmother's commitment to family as the motivation for her antimining activism. As Ed Wiley pleads in *The Last Mountain* regarding his daughter's exposure to pollutants at the school, "This is not an environmental issue. This is a little human being." He further explains, "We need to protect our mountains, but most importantly we do need to protect our children." This dualistic rhetorical move, positioning the land's interests as against and secondary to humans', anchors a narrative that places the problem with coal firmly in environmental justice for children and thus valorizes the figure of "the Child," which has been critiqued by queer theorists for centering environmental futurity in heterosexual reproduction.[3]

Ultimately, *On Coal River*, *The Last Mountain*, and *Overburden* are concerned with Appalachia as home for humans; the focus on burial in *The Last Mountain* and *On Coal River* exemplifies this priority. Both films crest emotionally with scenes of community activists visiting the cemeteries that house their ancestors and where they plan to be buried, emphasizing that this land is the people's final resting place. The tone of tragedy surrounding these scenes of contemplation of bodies' enmeshment in the Earth is the single note struck in these films' engagement with human/nature physical connections. None seriously considers the mountains as home to nonhuman creatures or MTR's threats to any other species, and the first two films' closing activist triumph is the relocation of Marsh Fork Elementary School away from a toxic sludge pond. Conversely, *Goodbye Gauley Mountain*, with its delicately weaving spider and swan cutting a wake across a pond, its bitter observation that MTR destroys all the animals in an area that then serves as a dumping ground for other (unwanted domestic) animals, and its reporting that Appalachia is "the second most biodiverse area in the western hemisphere after the Amazon," one acre of which contains "one and a half million living things," insists that resistance to MTR and environmental discourse in general must define community in terms of both human and other-than-human life and, likewise, that oppositional identities must involve a view of self as nature in community.

Ecosexual Identity

What constitutes a queer ecological identity? How can "ecosexual" be understood as an identification that is not only about the recognition and celebration of human erotic interconnection with the rest of nature but also about inhabiting a powerful political field in which the boundaries of environmental, queer, and feminist principles are dissolved? And how can ecosexual identity politics avoid the ontological pitfalls that have concerned numerous feminist, queer, and race theorists? Stephens and Sprinkle explain ecosexual identity: "For some of us being ecosexual is our primary (sexual) identity, whereas for others it is not. Ecosexuals can be GLBTQI, heterosexual, asexual, and/or Other. . . . We are everywhere. We are polymorphous and pollenamorous. We educate people about ecosex culture, community and practices. We hold these truths to be self-evident: that we are all part of, not separate from, nature. Thus all sex is ecosex" ("Ecosex Manifesto"). Ecosexuality is inherently politicized: according to ecosexuality theorist Reed, "As a cultural theory, ecosexuality draws from a wide range of scholarly fields including environmental studies, ecofeminism, and queer theory" (92). The editors of *Ecosexuality: When Nature Inspires the Arts of Love* explain that ecosexuality ignites new strategies for social change, recognizing that "we live in a time that demands integration between the erotic and the sacred, the ecstatic and the practical, emotion and reason, science and faith, energy and matter, body and mind, masculinity and femininity, the local and the global. At the vanishing point created by ecosexual love, all these elements . . . are components in an integrated, interdependent order" (Anderlini-D'Onofrio and Hagamen 6). Ecosexuals are "in love" with and "make love with" the Earth (via diverse emotional, sensual, and sexual forms of communion ranging from stargazing to aquaphilia to the identification of "espots"—especially sensual aspects of nature), which they conceive as their lover; therefore, following their pledge to "love, honor, and cherish" the Earth, they "work and play tirelessly for Earth justice and global peace," "embrace the revolutionary tactics of art, music, poetry, humor, and sex," and acknowledge the necessity of "public disobedience, anarchist and radical environmental activist strategies" in service of "sav[ing] the mountains, waters and skies by any means necessary," which includes buying green and local, rejecting consumerism, fostering community across difference, and practicing empathy with the Earth and its inhabitants (Stephens and Sprinkle, "Ecosex Manifesto"). As the "Ecosex Manifesto" shows in its categorizing, ecosexuality also represents an intersectional understanding of identity that is complementary with antiracist, feminist, and other radical politics, in which we must acknowledge that since our identities are composed of multiple positions, "the organized identity groups in which we find ourselves are in fact coalitions" (Crenshaw 491).

In *Goodbye Gauley Mountain*, Stephens and Sprinkle are exemplars of ecosexuality; Stephens is the central ecosexual ambassador, modeling an identity that is multivalent and self-consciously constructed in place. Early in the film she says, "Growing up queer in the heart of coal country, I knew that I would likely never be able to get a job there or want to marry a man who could. Instead of King Coal, I wanted a queen." Stephens here transforms the "King Coal" metaphor into a feminist play on words that emphasizes the masculinist, patriarchal nature of the coal industry. This move decenters the figure of the king (embodied in all the recent coal films, including this one, by Don Blankenship, owner of Massey Energy) by suggesting that submission to coal is optional (vs. required, as the industry would have Appalachians believe) and undermines the heteronormativity of coal culture by turning the king into merely one-half of a historically heterosexual equation whose queen is available for imaginative capture by the queer teen. In contrast, *Overburden* emphasizes only the economic tyranny of "King Coal," taking for granted his heteropatriarchal context; likewise, the heterosexuality of the stakeholders in all four of the other films is uncritically, even proudly, uncomplicated and situated within traditional social structures, particularly the family. In *Harlan County, USA*, murdered miner Lawrence Jones's grieving sixteen-year-old widow and baby supply a key empathetic connection, symbolizing the injustice of the death of a provider. In *Overburden*, Lorelei Scarbro's activism is at root on behalf of two valiant husbands/providers par excellence: her son-in-law Kevin, a miner against his will, who is repeatedly shown caring for his baby; and her deceased husband Kenny, killed by black lung disease, who saved her after an abusive prior marriage. Her daughter Nichole says that Kenny "gave us a life that we didn't have before—he showed my mom love that she never had." Scarbro's heterosexuality and maternal dedication are at the heart of *Overburden*'s story of activism, whose emotional appeal depends upon its normative center.

Stephens's sense of her sexuality, on the other hand, is complex and available for interrogation. Walking to a queer gathering where they will spread the word about ecosexuality, Sprinkle asks Stephens, "Were you always out, a gay person, as you grew up in West Virginia? When did you become gay?" "When did I become gay? Oh, in the eighties," Stephens replies (born in 1960, she would have been in her twenties then). This conversation, along with the couple's jocular claims "we used to be lesbians, but now we're ecosexuals" and "yes, we're ecosexuals, but we support gays and lesbians and bisexuals," denaturalizes and destabilizes monolithic and essentialized identities, particularly those involved in dualistic constructions such as queer/straight and gay/lesbian. Sprinkle and Stephens show, rather, an awareness of sexuality and sexual identity as discursive and historical, illustrating that, as Seymour says, "there must be a way to question 'nature' ... while still caring for the non-human natural environment" (10). There is in fact no room at all within ecosexuality for strictly bounded, deterministic identities given the enmeshment of body/spirit/passion/nature. In another scene, Stephens, learning tree-sitting skills, dons a climbing harness loaded at the waist with heavy gleaming carabiners; Sprinkle remarks, "I've seen you strap ... wear different kinds of straps, but none quite like this ... this is hot," to which Stephens replies that it is a "perfect combination of the machine shop and ... high lesbian culture." This exchange epitomizes the film's playfully earnest approach: it simultaneously eroticizes environmental activism and civil disobedience, re-embeds Stephens and Sprinkle within their lesbian history, locates their sexuality in a queer context that takes for granted the materiality and constructedness of sexuality and desire (given the reference to strap-ons), empowers Stephens as a bearer of the phallus, which is an absent referent here, and thus displaces maleness as a prerequisite for both penetrative sex and physically dangerous political action. It also counters the unwaveringly serious, often somber tone of the coal documentaries alongside which *Goodbye Gauley Mountain* stands—and of mainstream environmentalism which, as Morton notes, allows "scant space for humor, except perhaps a phobic, hearty kind" (279). Di Chiro explains that the environmental movement in the United States has consistently used visions of the normate "to determine which bodies and environments/landscapes embody the distinctly American values of productive work, rugged individualism, masculinity, independence, potency, and moral virtue, upon which environmental advocacy movements should be based" (224). While Stephens embodies masculinity, potency, and moral virtue in *Goodbye Gauley Mountain*, her appropriation of these values from a specific position of radical otherness queers them out of a hegemonic frame and into a distinctly nonnormate vision of environmentalism.

Wearing a colorful globe-print button-down over her butch all-black ensemble, Stephens exemplifies the queer, ecosexual world traveler—traveler of interior and exterior worlds that, in an ecosexual understanding, cannot in fact be meaningfully distinguished, whose identity means awareness that the parts of oneself may exist in tension but are not separate and are always mutually informative and located within history and culture. She thus epitomizes Haraway's definition of "ethical relation," which means—as opposed to an essentializing reduction of complexity—honest engagement "with other worlds, including with ourselves" ("Otherworldly" 179). Throughout the film, Stephens moves among stakeholders occupying conflicting and conflicted places while herself holding all at once the identities of ecosexual, urban intellectual (Stephens is a professor at UC Santa Cruz, and she and Sprinkle live in San Francisco), native of Appalachia, and daughter of a rural mining community, whose family has profited from mining since the 1600s, owning their own coal bit company during her childhood. Stephens's relationship to mining is complicated, and it centers *Goodbye Gauley Mountain* as a "good queer text"—in Seymour's terms, a text that "imagines a scenario in which a playful but politicized queerness literally grows out of, and effectively responds to, ecological devastation" (34). Stephens explains that observing operations in her family's machine shop as a child, she learned about coal production and also about how to "make do," "how to make something out of almost nothing," which was "extremely empowering" for "a young queer woman growing up in a man's world"; this queer historicity is a far cry from the linear pro-coal-to-anti-coal personal narratives found in the other coal texts. Touring the shop during filming,

Stephens asks if the workers still keep a pinup calendar in the back; indeed they do, and Stephens and Sprinkle admire the pictures of nude women, noting (with the support of photographs) that Sprinkle was once a pinup model herself—a scene underscoring connections between the masculinist institutions responsible for exploitation of the environment and those responsible for the limited conceptions of sexuality and the body from which ecosexuality departs, and implicating Stephens and Sprinkle as participants therein. This practice of engaging with one's "other worlds" is further demonstrated as Stephens and her cousin, historian Patricia Spangler, expose their own white privilege and complicity in the historical erasures of Black lives by making visible through a montage of archival photographs the murderous racism of Gauley Mountain's labor history, wherein many Black migrant workers died of silicosis while digging the Hawk's Nest Tunnel under the very ground on which Stephens's family and the rest of the white community later enjoyed blissfully ignorant "idyllic summer days" at a golf club. This practice is, as Spangler says, "painful"—a difficult and necessary reckoning with history that the other coal films, given their unitary agendas, cannot accommodate. *Overburden*, for example, also uses images of vintage photographs to document mining history in Appalachia, but these pictures do not include consideration of race and merely contextualize mining companies' control over their workers. Stephens's reckoning with history informs her understanding of home, complicating the nostalgia of the film's theme songs "West Virginia, My Home" and "The West Virginia Hills" in favor of an ethical, emotionally honest relation to place and community.

Visiting Lindytown, a ghost town bought out by Massey Energy in order to make way for MTR, in which everything is vacant, gutted, and/or on the verge of being bulldozed, Stephens stops to admire a tree full of ripe peaches that no one will ever eat; the peaches are lush embodiments of the land's fecundity and also tragic markers of an absence that is the outcome of the triumph of capitalism over mutually nourishing human/nature relationships. Stephens says, "I don't know if it really matters where I was conceived or not, but to have the privilege of at least knowing that and ... being able to go back there as a place that I can still consider home ... I think that the places people are born are genetically imprinted on their psyche and on their DNA and on their hearts. And so all of the people that had connections here, they've just been absolutely erased." Home video clips of Stephens's childhood play during her voiceover of this line, so that the faces and memories of her personal history as an Appalachian—her genetic imprint—are conjoined with the history of Lindytown, its disappeared, place-imprinted residents, and their still-surviving (for now) imprints upon the place. Stephens's intimate linkage with the people and peaches of Lindytown exemplifies Butler's conception of embodiedness in *Undoing Gender*, in which "the very bodies for which we struggle are not quite ever only our own" (528) since the body is always *undone*—"Given over from the start to the world of others, bearing their imprint, formed within the crucible of social life" (528); in light of this, Butler argues that in our political endeavors we need to fight not only for rights and autonomy for all but also for a view of ourselves as "invariably in community, impressed upon by others, impressing them as well" (528). The conception of the embedded, multiple self, which defines ecosexual identity, necessarily includes the erotic: "The particular sociality that belongs to bodily life, to sexual life, and to becoming gendered (which is always, to a certain extent, becoming gendered *for others*) establishes a field of ethical enmeshment with others and a sense of disorientation for the first-person, that is, the perspective of the ego" (549). In a queer ecological understanding, "beings exist precisely because they are nothing but relationality" (Morton 275); queer ecology must then "espouse something very different from individualism, rugged or otherwise" (277), since ecology "demands intimacies with other beings that queer theory also demands, in another key" (273).

In its recognition of the inextricability of the body, nature, desire, history, discourse, and community, including the community of nature and the sense of the body as community, ecosexual identity as illustrated in *Goodbye Gauley Mountain* aligns with recent feminist theories of materiality. In Barad's "agentic realism," the material and the discursive are "reworked in a way that acknowledges their mutual entailment. In particular, . . . both materiality and discursive practices are rethought in terms of intra-activity" (138); "What is needed is a robust account of the materialization of all bodies—'human' and 'nonhuman'"—an account that considers the agentic properties of other-than-human entities and "the fullness of matter's implication in its ongoing historicity" (128–29). In Susan Hekman's analysis, "Language, bodies, technologies, and other elements interact to create 'collective assemblages of enunciation/utterance.' . . . This perspective has the advantage of bringing bodies and the material back into the discussion of social reality. It also serves another important function: it breaks down the division between the natural and the cultural" (114). Hekman's social ontology allows for the value of identity: while in much of postmodernism identity is viewed skeptically, as a naïve relic of modernism, in fact "bodies in social groups are not just bodies. They require an identity to make sense of their lives and to operate as human beings in a social setting" (113). Likewise, Hames-Garcia notes that identity categories are often viewed within the academy as "obstacles to transformative politics and as lacking substantial 'real' referents in the world" (309). But, he says, "history demonstrates the complex relationships that are possible among the affirmation of identity, the histories of oppression, and the articulation of freer, more egalitarian futures" (311): "it is often by exploring identities and fostering communal resistance that one can reveal the social conflicts produced by modernity and coloniality and begin to recognize possibilities that might lead to better ethical knowledge and progressive social change" (330). Crucially, unlike other queer constructions of selfhood, ecosexuality is an identity of inclusion versus exclusion. It says not "I am marginalized," "I am different," or even "I am distinct" but, rather, "I am inherently connected to and part of all of you, that is, of *everything*, and even my 'I' is in question" since, as Haraway explains, "human genomes can be found in only about 10 percent of all the cells that occupy the mundane space I call my body; the other 90 percent of the cells are filled with the genomes of bacteria, fungi, protists, and such," so that "to be one is always to *become with many*" (*When Species Meet* 3). Thus, the ecosexual approach to selfhood and identity runs counter to liberal and leftist discourse in which identities are seen as exclusive, additive, and/or oriented around individual freedoms, emphasizing instead the political potency in a recognition of *self as coalition, as community*—in coalition and community with others.

Ecosexual Community

Di Chiro asks, "Can we imagine... coalitions that can forge a critical normative environmental politics (we *all* should live in a clean environment; we *all* should have the right to healthy bodies) that resists appeals to normativity?" (203). And "can our coalitions be capacious enough to embrace and care for *all* community members (human and nonhuman) even in their 'irrevocable difference'?" (224). *Goodbye Gauley Mountain* offers a vision of such capaciousness in its enthusiastically embracing non-normate humans and other Others (e.g., animals and plants) and emphasizing that political convictions and alliances spring from shared emotion rather than from social uniformity, in this case a feeling of passionate love for the Earth. In *Everything in Its Path: Destruction of Community in the Buffalo Creek Flood* (1976), sociologist Kai T. Erikson discusses the marginalization of Appalachians, particularly in terms of their poverty and the exploitation of their land and labor by powerful capitalist interests: Appalachia "did not 'develop' according to prevailing American standards," and "no part of the country was more deeply hurt or more decisively changed by what Americans chose to call 'progress'" in the age of industrialization; Appalachians remain today a little-understood population associated with backwardness (71). Perhaps in an effort to counteract this association, the other coal films construct an "Average Joe" image of Appalachians, whose cultural uniformity, rather than their differences, is the point. This normative characterization is supported by numerous American flags in the mise-en-scènes, many shots of modest middle-class interiors, and footage of locals in ballcaps and sweatshirts going about their routines, particularly caring for children. Meanwhile, *Goodbye Gauley Mountain* highlights how Appalachians are non-normate in the depth of both their marginalization and their environmental investment, as well as being unique individuals whose quirkiness is distinctly regional. Paul Corbit Brown, a local photographer and activist, says, "Appalachians have often been looked down upon, and we have been considered illiterate, dumb hillbillies, uneducated, unimportant, and we've been considered disposable. . . . I believe that coal mining has become . . . a very protracted form of genocide." *Goodbye Gauley Mountain* recaptures the value of the "hillbilly" as a nonconformist, the principal example being Larry Gibson—"Keeper of the Mountains," "hillbilly saint," and "grandfather of the MTR movement," who is shown to be a highly non-normate figure and one worthy of profound respect; the film is in memory of him. Gibson was a passionate defender of the mountains and an expert MTR tour guide, having overcome lifelong marginalization based on a presumed disability; in the film he says that he was always seen as "Mr. Gibson's retarded son." His connection to the hills is profound: "If you go for a walk and listen, the land will talk to you. You can almost hear it breathe." He adds, "Perhaps if there's anything else in this world that I would love more than my wife, it would be the land." Gibson understood the land as an *agentic, communicative body* to be loved and cherished by humans, like all the bodies that Stephens and Sprinkle celebrate in *Goodbye Gauley Mountain*. The film's encouragement to loving care extends everywhere, from Sprinkle's explanation of the "deeply satisfying" feeling of gratitude experienced during "skygasms" and in viewing breathing as having "intercourse" with the air, to photographer Vivian Stockman's discussion of the value of the "cultural continuum" of generational ties to the land, as in women's passing down the knowledge of medicinal plants, to the relatives, friends, community leaders, and colorful countercultural figures who populate Stephens and Sprinkle's ecosexual wedding to the Appalachian Mountains.

Following a montage of footage of protests, sit-ins, marches, tree-sits, tree plantings, and so on that shows Appalachians walking their environmentalist talk, the film's climax, closure, and central community-building action is a wedding that unites the terms "sexy," "fun," and diverse" in honor of belonging to/in/as nature, epitomizing the dissimilarity between the queer, campy playfulness of *Goodbye Gauley Mountain* and the other coal texts' heterocentrism and dire, downtrodden tone. This wedding makes for a very different closure from the tidy, tangible—though provisional—political triumphs of *Harlan County, USA, On Coal River,* and *The Last Mountain* and the seamless conflict resolution of *Overburden*, wherein two women with opposing views see past their differences and come together after a momentous death. In *Goodbye Gauley Mountain* there is no suggestion of a sudden fix, resolution of contradiction, or end point to activism. The wedding to the mountains includes all local parties to whom the filmmakers have extended friendship as well as the ecosexual artists and supporters who travel to participate in Sprinkle and Stephens's many weddings to the Earth—large-scale queer performance art pieces inspired by Linda Montano's chakra-based work *14 Years of Living Art*, that employ the ritual of the wedding ceremony in ecosexual celebration of kinship with nature while challenging marriage's basic premises as an anthropocentric, heteropatriarchal tradition. A prominent feature of the weddings to the Earth is their inclusiveness, for instance, the use of social media for organizing. Even the vows, which include "Do you ... promise to educate yourselves and others about environmental issues?" and (in the case of the wedding in *Goodbye Gauley Mountain*) "Do you promise to speak out, act up, and raise hell about mountaintop removal?," are collaborative; at the wedding to the mountains, "anyone in attendance could make vows promising to lower their electricity usage, to speak out against mountaintop removal coal mining and to love and cherish the earth" (Bechtol). This wedding, which was conceived as "an artistic protest volley" (Imbrogno), and *Goodbye Gauley Mountain* are but two facets in Stephens and Sprinkle's ongoing activist response to MTR, which includes photo shoots, protest, 3D artworks, and the couple's attendance at Mountain Justice Summer Camp (Stephens and Sprinkle, "Save the Mountains"). Their weddings are models of successful coalition politics, as environmental, queer, and sex-positive agendas are linked in art activism. With these ceremonies, whose meaning is made through the creative, politicized participation of unlikely and unprecedented assemblages, the traditional insularity of the heterosexual marriage contract is transformed into a protean radical collectivity's shared promise to live responsibly within the pan-species community of the Earth.

The ecosexual weddings resonate strongly with Heller's anarchic ecofeminist imperative that we "explore the idea of 'allied resistance,' a radical alternative to the romantic protection of nature" and to the narrow view of community, exemplified by the other coal texts, as the necessary flattening of differences in service of labor concerns and protection of the traditional family (228). As *Goodbye Gauley Mountain* demonstrates, allied resistance means recognition of the social complexity that people bring to consideration of the environment, as opposed to the traditional environmentalist tendency to bury this complexity under the amorphous, monolithic label of "humanity." Catriona Mortimer-Sandilands also refers to "the necessity of affinity politics in formulating and enacting ecological actions and visions"—"the need to look deeply at social relations to locate our understandings of nature. In this context, sexuality, as a powerful mode of social identity ... is surely ... part of this nexus" ("From Unnatural" 31–32). Acting in terms of a social relationality that moves the non-normate to center stage, as Sprinkle and Stephens do with their wedding performances, is a means of surpassing environmentalism's historical organization of nature "through contrasts," where "outdoorsy and extraverted, heterosexual, able-bodied" are assumed, "disability is nowhere to be seen," and "physical wholeness and coordination are valued over spontaneity" (Morton 279). In their article on the wedding featured in *Goodbye Gauley Mountain*, "On Becoming Appalachian Moonshine," Stephens and Sprinkle say, "While we applaud and support the hard work of our environmental activist friends, our networks include artists, sex workers, academics, drag queens, queer folks, and others whose voices do not necessarily fit into the existing environmental movement" (66). Thus, Sprinkle's career-long validation of physical and sexual differences, as shown in her "post-porn modernist" performances,[4] extends to include new allies in affective, erotic, and political engagement with nature, "towards different kinds of relational practices and possibilities" (Stephens and Sprinkle, "On Becoming" 61).

A notable feature of Sprinkle and Stephens's articulation of marriage is their deployment of faux-naif humor to undermine heterosexual privilege and rights discourse: the wedding to the mountains represents not uncritical investment in a politics of individual rights extended to queers or in the institution of marriage as a solution to social problems but, rather, a reconception of marital commitment as collective responsibility to the Earth. In *Goodbye Gauley Mountain* Sprinkle explains, "You know they say that if they let the gay people marry that they'll start marrying everything, they'll marry their dogs, they're gonna marry trees." Stephens finishes, "And we're out to prove them right." This appropriation of homophobic rhetoric ironically contradicts the illogic of its assumptions that acceptance of queer marriage means acceptance of nonconsensual/predatory sexualities (e.g., pedophilia and bestiality) and that "true love" can exist only between human heterosexuals, while opposing gay and lesbian politics as usual in the United States, where, until recently, marriage equality dominated the

LGBTQ+ agenda. Sprinkle asks Stephens, "Do you think that more queer people need to get involved in the environmental movement?" Stephens's answer displaces marriage as the central issue for queer politics: "Well I can tell you what, if queers don't have water, they're not going to survive. You know, you can survive without being married, but if you don't have drinking water, you're dead." In an ecosexual marriage to the mountains and the community, human love necessarily includes loving care for the environment, as humans are inseparable from both human society and all the rest of life.

Further challenging heterosexual privilege, the queer ecological aesthetic of the weddings to the Earth disrupts the "sanctity" of marriage, which has been used by conservatives to attempt to maintain marriage as a sort of nature preserve for endangered heterosexuals. *Goodbye Gauley Mountain*'s wedding includes a purple-underwear-clad interpretive dancer, many costumed participants including the singing animal quartet Tony's Circus, Larry Gibson's homily on the destruction of the mountains intercut with B-roll footage of MTR, and dramatic homemade purple-and-silver mountain-and-moon-themed wedding garb ornamented with suggestive details such as Stephens's huge, spiky silver codpiece and the twin silver moons adorning Sprinkle's bust. In its striking departure from the staid respectability of the traditional wedding, which brackets out the erotic and deemphasizes the political contexts that its respectability naturalizes (e.g., the patriarchal exchange of capital, the household as locus of consumer culture, the reproductive imperative), this performance reminds us that in fact "all weddings are performance art" (Imbrogno). Sprinkle and Stephens's merrily anarchic, parodic, yet sincere appropriation of the wedding ceremony answers Morton's call for a queer ecological alternative to conventional environmentalism's approach to loving nature, which "strives to rise above the contingency of desire. Loving Nature thus becomes enslaved to masculine heteronormativity, a performance that erases the trace of performance: as the green camping slogan puts it, 'Leave no trace'" (279). Heller explains how conservationism traditionally constructs love as a matter of constraint—"a holding back, a repression of a destructive desire" (227); she would like to see instead "a 'postromantic' concept of 'authentic love,'" "drawing from the anarchist imperative for the release of creative and cooperative potential within society" (228). Sprinkle and Stephens enact this release of potential in their role as guides and healers leading us down their wedding aisle—out of guilty, self-punishing, misanthropic worship of an untouched, "virgin" Nature that mirrors our self-denial and into erotic activist intimacy with nature, where even stripped, gutted mountains count as subjects of desire.

Haraway asks us to consider how we might conceptualize the "radical otherness" that is at the heart of ethical relating; "That problem is more than a human one; . . . it is intrinsic to the story of life on earth" ("Otherworldly" 178). In its practice of respect for multiplicity and for the agency and individuality of all species, Stephens and Sprinkle's ecosexuality certainly works in this direction. It may be argued, however, that their anthropomorphizing the Earth through the metaphor of lover contradicts this appreciation of otherness. For instance, in *Goodbye Gauley Mountain*, as Stephens prepares to enact a tree-sit, she playfully reappropriates the "tree-hugger" pejorative by stating that trees "like to have their tops hugged as well as their bottoms." But this assumption cannot (yet?) be validated by communication from trees and thus perhaps moves ecosexuality toward anthropocentrism. This issue, which is centrally about Haraway's question "What is inter-subjectivity between radically different kinds of subjects?"—a question of relevance to any relationship between living things—is somewhat ameliorated by the consistently campy, self-conscious approach that Sprinkle and Stephens bring to their eroticizing nature. In the scene in which they propose to marry a mountain, they kneel to kiss the actual ground, literalizing the "lover" metaphor, but when they rise, their faces covered in dirt, their evident delight is *about* the symbolism as much as it is about sensuality, and it also includes their passion for working on behalf of that ground ("Otherworldly" 178).[5] Haraway says, "I want to learn to strike up interesting intercourse with possible subjects about livable worlds"—it would seem that that is exactly what Stephens and Sprinkle are doing (184). Overall, they build through their empathetic ecosexual identity politics a model of what Haraway calls "queer confederacy," rooted in deep knowledge and love of place and community (161). Haraway argues that such a "knowing love" "could not be innocent; it did not originate in a garden. But neither did it originate in *expulsion* from a garden. Not about secrets—of life or death—this knowing love took shape in quite particular, historical-social intercourse" (164). The disc jacket for *Goodbye Gauley Mountain* features a picture of Sprinkle lying naked in ecstasy upon a vibrant bed of artificial flowers, with Stephens standing over her, wearing hillbilly overalls and a look of rabid glee, watering Sprinkle's vulva with a watering can. Contesting puritanical conceptions of innocence, sin, and nature through a revisioning of sexuality as ecological diversity, Sprinkle and Stephens are radical gardeners, cultivating a relationship with/as nature that is serious, playful, deconstructive, and queer.

Goodbye Gauley Mountain's contribution to queer ecological practice and to coal cinema's earnest resistance to the mining industry's destruction of land and community is a vital one, especially given environmentalism's historical anti-eroticism and heterocentrism. Mortimer-Sandilands sees in Jan Zita Grover's memoir *North Enough* "a 'queer ecological' sensibility": Grover "focuses on dimensions of her experience born in the specific history of a queer community, and uses the resulting emotional resonances and conceptual links to live in nature in a way that reflects this queer experience. Simply put: Grover sees nature through queer eyes, and what she sees is important and unique" ("Unnatural Passions?" 3). This could well be a description of Sprinkle and Stephens's work—an enthusiastic, celebratory environmentalism based in their particular histories within queer, theater/art, and sex work communities and dependent upon their embedment in those communities for its development as coalition-based art activism. What they see when they look at nature is a sexual/life partner that should be recognized as such by us all and that, as with any partnership, merits our loyalty and support. As Heller says, "We must create an 'erotic democracy' that decentralizes power and allows for direct, passionate participation in the decisions that determine our lives" (240), for the task before us is "to care for each other and for nature in a way that truly expresses an authentic love for the natural and social worlds" (241). Sprinkle and Stephens's performative, collaborative, ever-desiring, not-so-secret garden is a fine place to start.

NOTES

This essay originally appeared in *ISLE: Interdisciplinary Studies in Literature and Environment* 25, no. 4 (Autumn 2018): 742–66. It is reprinted here with permissions from Oxford University Press on behalf of the Association for the Study of Literature and Environment.

1. See www.goodbyegauleymountain.org for information on the film's screenings, availability, reviews, and many awards.

2. On the connections between the logic of dualism and the domination of women and other marginalized groups, see Plumwood, *Feminism and the Mastery of Nature* (1993).

3. See, for example, Seymour's *Strange Natures* (2013) and mainly Lee Edelman's *No Future: Queer Theory and the Death Drive* (2004): "The consequences of ... an identification both of and with the child as the preeminent emblem of the motivating end ... of every political vision as a vision of futurity must weigh on any delineation of a queer oppositional politics. For the only queerness that queer sexualities could ever hope to signify would spring from their determined opposition to this underlying structure of the political" (Edelman 13).

4. See Sprinkle, *Post-Porn Modernist* (1998).

5. Sprinkle and Stephens are quite conscious of the risks and limitations of their anthropomorphism. See their article "On Becoming Appalachian Moonshine" (2012) for an excellent explanation of their philosophy regarding the weddings to the Earth, including the issue of anthropomorphism. Ecosexual anthropomor-

phizing is not exclusive to *Goodbye Gauley Mountain* or to Sprinkle and Stephens's work in general; it is found throughout ecosexual literature, art, and media. See, for example, Anderlini-D'Onofrio and Hagamen, eds., *Ecosexuality: When Nature Inspires the Arts of Love* (2015).

BIBLIOGRAPHY

Alaimo, Stacy. "Trans-corporeal Feminisms and the Ethical Space of Nature." In *Material Feminisms*, edited by Stacy Alaimo and Susan Hekman, 237–64. Bloomington: Indiana University Press, 2008.

Anderlini-D'Onofrio, Serenagaia, and Lindsay Hagamen. "Introduction: Time for Ecosexuality." In *Ecosexuality: When Nature Inspires the Arts of Love*, edited by Serenagaia Anderlini-D'Onofrio and Lindsay Hagamen, 1–20. Puerto Rico: 3Way-Kiss, 2015.

Barad, Karen. "Posthumanist Performativity: Toward an Understanding of How Matter Comes to Matter." In *Material Feminisms*, edited by Stacy Alaimo and Susan Hekman, 120–54. Bloomington: Indiana University Press, 2008.

Bechtol, Lucas. "'Sexecology' Creators 'Marry' Appalachian Mountains at OU." *College Green Mag*. http://www.collegegreenmag.com/sexecology-creators-marry-appalachian-mountainsin-ou-ceremony.

Butler, Judith. *Undoing Gender*. New York: Routledge, 2004.

Crenshaw, Kimberlé. "Intersectionality and Identity Politics: Learning from Violence Against Women of Color." In *Feminist Theory: A Reader*, 3rd ed., edited by Wendy K. Kolmar and Frances Bartkowski, 482–91. New York: McGraw-Hill, 2009.

Di Chiro, Giovanna. "Polluted Politics? Confronting Toxic Discourse, Sex Panic, and Eco-normativity." In *Queer Ecologies: Sex, Nature, Politics, Desire*, edited by Catriona Mortimer-Sandilands and Bruce Erickson, 199–230. Bloomington: Indiana University Press, 2010.

Edelman, Lee. *No Future: Queer Theory and the Death Drive*. Durham, N.C.: Duke University Press, 2004.

Erikson, Kai T. *Everything in Its Path: Destruction of Community in the Buffalo Creek Flood*. New York: Simon & Schuster, 1976.

Foucault, Michel. *The History of Sexuality*, vol. 1: *An Introduction*. Translated by Robert Hurley. New York: Vintage, 1990.

Gaard, Greta. "Toward a Queer Ecofeminism." *Hypatia* 12, no. 1 (1997): 114–37.

Gaard, Greta, and Patrick D. Murphy. "Introduction." In *Ecofeminist Literary Criticism*, edited by Greta Gaard and Patrick D. Murphy, 1–13. Champaign: University of Illinois Press, 1998.

Goodbye Gauley Mountain: An Ecosexual Love Story. Directed by Elizabeth Stephens. Performances by Elizabeth Stephens and Annie Sprinkle. Fecund Arts, 2013.

Hames-Garcia, Michael. "How Real Is Race?" In *Material Feminisms*, edited by Stacy Alaimo and Susan Hekman, 308–39. Bloomington: Indiana University Press, 2008.

Haraway, Donna. "Otherworldly Conversations, Terran Topics, Local Terms." In *Material Feminisms*, edited by Stacy Alaimo and Susan Hekman, 157–87. Bloomington: Indiana University Press, 2008.

———. *When Species Meet*. Minneapolis: University of Minnesota Press, 2008.

Harlan County, USA. Directed by Barbara Kopple. Performances by Norman Yarborough, Houston Elmore, and Phil Sparks. Cabin Creek, 1976.

Hekman, Susan. "Constructing the Ballast: An Ontology for Feminism." In *Material Feminisms*, edited by Stacy Alaimo and Susan Hekman, 85–119. Bloomington: Indiana University Press, 2008.

Heller, Chaia. "For the Love of Nature: Ecology and the Cult of the Romantic." In *Ecofeminism: Women, Animals, Nature*, edited by Greta Gaard, 219–42. Philadelphia: Temple University Press, 1993.

Hogan, Katie. "Undoing Nature: Coalition Building as Queer Environmentalism." In *Queer Ecologies: Sex, Nature, Politics, Desire*, edited by Catriona Mortimer-Sandilands and Bruce Erickson 231–53. Bloomington: Indiana University Press, 2010.

Imbrogno, Douglas. "The Professor and the Porn Legend 2: Got Purple?" *WestVirginiaVille*, December 3, 2010. http://westvirginiaville.com/2010/12/the-professor-and-the-porn-legend-2-got-purple/.

Kay, Joseph. "Intellectuals and Power: A Conversation between Michel Foucault and Gilles Deleuze." Libcom.org, September 9, 2006. https://libcom.org/library/intellectuals-power-a-conversation-between-michel-foucault-and-gilles-deleuze.

The Last Mountain. Directed by Bill Haney. Performance by Robert F. Kennedy. Massachusetts Documentary Productions, 2011.

Montrie, Chad. "Review of *Dirty Business, Low Coal*, and *On Coal River*." *Journal of Appalachian Studies* 17 (2011): 273–78.

Mortimer-Sandilands, Catriona. "From Unnatural Passions to Queer Nature." *Alternatives Journal* 27, no. 3 (2001): 30–35.

———. "Sexual Politics and Environmental Justice: Lesbian Separatists in Rural Oregon." In *New Perspectives on Environmental Justice*, edited by Rachel Stein, 109–26. New Brunswick, N.J.: Rutgers University Press, 2004.

———. "Unnatural Passions? Notes toward a Queer Ecology." *InVisible Culture* 9 (2005).

Mortimer-Sandilands, Catriona, and Bruce Erickson. "Introduction: A Genealogy of Queer Ecologies." In *Queer Ecologies: Sex, Nature, Politics, Desire*, edited by Mortimer-Sandilands and Erickson, 1–47. Bloomington: Indiana University Press, 2010.

Morton, Timothy. "Guest Column: Queer Ecology." *PMLA* 125 (2010): 273–82.

On Coal River. Directed by Adams Wood and Francine Cavanaugh. Performance by Ed Wiley. Katahdin Productions, 2010.

Overburden. Directed by Chad A. Stevens. Performances by Bill Price, Betty Harrah, and Lorelei Scarbro. Milesfrommaybe Productions, 2015.

Plumwood, Val. *Feminism and the Mastery of Nature*. New York: Routledge, 1993.

Reed, Jennifer. "From Ecofeminism to Ecosexuality: Queering the Environmental Movement." In *Ecosexuality: When Nature Inspires the Arts of Love*, edited by Serenagaia Anderlini-D'Onofrio and Lindsay Hagamen, 92–102. Puerto Rico: 3WayKiss, 2015.

Seymour, Nicole. *Strange Natures: Futurity, Empathy, and the Queer Ecological Imagination*. Champaign: University of Illinois Press, 2013.

Sprinkle, Annie. *Post-porn Modernist: My 25 Years as a Multimedia Whore.* Jersey City, N.J.: Cleis Press, 1998.

Stephens, Elizabeth. "Practice as Research: Goodbye Gauley Mountain: An Ecosexual Love Story." Elizabethstephens.org, n.d. https://elizabethstephens.org/par-goodbye-gauley-mountain-an-ecosexual-love-story/.

Stephens, Elizabeth, and Annie Sprinkle. "Ecosex Manifesto." Sexecology.org, n.d. http://sexecology.org/research-writing/ecosex-manifesto/.

———. "On Becoming Appalachian Moonshine." *Performance Research* 17 (2012): 61–66.

———. "Save the Mountains." Loveartlab.org, June 23, 2016. https://loveartlab.ucsc.edu/2016/06/23/save-the-mountains/.

———. "SexEcology: Where Art Meets Theory Meets Practice Meets Activism." Sexecology.org, n.d. http://www.sexecology.org/.

Sturgeon, Noël. "The Nature of Race: Discourses of Racial Difference in Ecofeminism." In *Ecofeminism: Women, Culture, Nature,* edited by Karen J. Warren, 260–78. Bloomington: Indiana University Press, 1997.

Seeing Queer Oddkin in
The Prettiest Star's Appalachia

CALEB PENDYGRAFT

Carter Sickels's LGBT novel *The Prettiest Star* (2020) follows twenty-four-year-old protagonist Brian Jackson back to Appalachia, to Chester, Ohio, after his having lived in New York City since he was eighteen. The novel is told from his perspective as well as from those of his mother Sharon and his sister Jess. Upon coming home, Brian grapples with his eventual death from HIV during the 1980s and living with his family during his final months. Brian's return to Appalachia oftentimes is met with resistance because his presence threatens the so-called natural order of things. Sharon makes this point clear when she reflects on her brother-in-law Wayne's ruminations on AIDS: "I remember not very long ago, Wayne said that people with AIDS should be sent to a far-away island, and every one of us, me, my husband, my nephews and nieces, we all agreed whole-heartedly. Protect the good from the bad, the normal from the abnormal, the innocent from the infected" (85–86). The disease is clearly designated in a binary context. On one side are the good, the everyday, and the innocent; on the opposite, HIV is synonymous with immorality, faraway places, and the abnormal. When HIV/AIDS, and by proxy queerness, is seen as outside Appalachia, it is implicit that queerness doesn't belong in the region. According to this logic, queerness cannot reside in the rural, small town but is sutured to the city and the metropolitan.

Such dualistic reasoning has spurred the emergence of queer ecocriticism, finding its footing with ecocritical scholar Greta Gaard's call for feminist liberation and queer theoretical alliances in the nineties. Since then, queer ecofeminism has "sustained attention to the ongoing re/inscriptions of the nature/culture binary in our understandings of sexed and gendered subjectivities (and embodiments)" (Merrick 218–19). That is to say that queerness lends itself to ecocritical analysis by further breaking down the dichotomies between sexed lines that exist concerning the natural world—often gendered as feminine, the ground on which to be conquered by white settler colonialism, and to be dominated by the cishetpatriarchy (Gaard 38–39)—and the cultured sphere, often gendered masculine and cast as the hierarchically superior to its binary opposite. While queer ecocriticism brings to the fore how the erotic—and by extension the sexual—also factors into these dualisms, it also asks us to consider what types of kinships are deemed viable. With regard to the topic of gay marriage, Judith Butler grappled with and categorically extrapolated the concept of kinship in queerdom at the turn of the millennium "as a set of practices that institutes relationships of various kinds which regulate the reproduction of life and the demands of death . . . kinship practices will be those that emerge to address fundamental forms of human dependency" ("Is Kinship Always Already Heterosexual?" 14–15). Returning to Sharon's thoughts, it's easy to see the connection between what types of kinships are thought of as acceptable, as naturalized in the setting of heterosexual Appalachia in the 1980s. HIV/AIDS, perceived by Sharon as urban outside force, threatens the "natural" ordering of Sharon's family kinships in rural Appalachia. When she interpolates herself in the "us" it becomes clearer that HIV/AIDS and queerness don't fit in the heterosexual familial bonds that exist between wife/husband, parent/child, and therefore what she understands as Appalachia. In short, queer ecocritical thought can brush up against these framings of typical kinship binaries and suggests that there are other types of bonds that can emerge. My analysis here offers a rethinking of how queerness can change our understanding and relationship with nonhuman objects, place, and nature itself, which may deviate in some ways from a typical ecocritical analysis, one that has "a commitment to environmentality from whatever critical vantage point" (Buell 11). Subsequently, an additional layer of analysis emerges from these relationships, an examination of how oddkinships can render new ways of seeing queerness in Appalachian environments.

The binaries that determine what is considered natural, such as those dichotomies that Sharon relies on to define her life, have shifted over time in Western culture and society. Philosopher Kate Soper, for instance, points out that historically "to invoke 'nature'" was a "means of policing behavior" (224). She argues that "it is very difficult to appeal to 'nature' for endorsement of any particular way of living or being," which, when placed next to Sharon's understanding of queerness in Appalachia, refutes the notion that queerness is inherently abhorrent in the mountains. While *The Prettiest Star* demonstrates how queerness and disease in the 1980s political landscape was thought of as unnatural and un-Appalachian, as I will show, Brian's relationship to Appalachia and to nonhumans—I'm thinking of his camera, the dishware that he is limited to by his parents, the food he encounters, his VHS archive—creates alliances that reveal that queerness can and does belong to Appalachian ecologies. What's more, this belonging also reveals to the reader how to see these Appalachian places in more nuanced ways. *The Prettiest Star*'s characters' narratology is a means of seeing queerness in Appalachia as co-constitutive productions resulting in new ways to imagine relationships to each other and the world. Sickels's novel provides ample instances of how unusual relationships that defy biological kinship are reconceptualized. That is to say that Appalachia is a queerly contestable region, and through examination of the novel we see that Appalachia may be considered always queer. Ultimately this chapter aims to break down—to queer—the binary of human versus nature, which is in large part to blame for the human exceptionalism that underscores much of our ecocriticism altogether. As such, I ask, what alternatives exist for kinship, and how do we permit nonhumans into our queer ecocritical analyses?

Defining Oddkin

Alternatively to kinship, throughout this chapter I deploy the term "oddkin," which underscores my queer ecocritical read of *The Prettiest Star*. Oddkin was coined by cultural theorist and scientist Donna Haraway in *Staying with the Trouble*, her polemical work on the Anthropocene. Oddkin requires us, she writes, "to make kin in lines of inventive connection as a practice of learning to live and die well with each other" (1). Oddkin is not based in genealogy nor predicated on biogenetics. What queer ecocriticism offers with regard to opening up binary thinking surrounding kinship, oddkin allows a space to explore new varieties of relationships. If biological kinships reinscribe the hierarchies that Gaard criticized decades ago, noting that "from a queer ecofeminist perspective, then, it is clear that notions of sexuality are implicit within the category of gender" (21), then oddkin can expose these hierarchies while at the same time permit new arrangements of genders and sexualities to emerge. Put simply, oddkin is queerly ecocritical because it is a "term for other-than-conventional biogenetic relatives" (Haraway 221). Convention here is a cornerstone of the purportedly natural order of the cishetpatriarchy that underscores Sharon's comments above, and ultimately the hierarchies challenged by feminist and queer ecocriticism. I define oddkin as entangled relations of humans and nonhumans that form beyond and in excess of mere biological familial bonds. Oddkin allows us to reframe relationships within the purview of ecocriticism and acts as an apparatus we can use to explore how queer ecocriticism can function for Appalachia.

However, I'm interested not just in the potential oddkinships that exist in/for queer Appalachia and in Sickels's novel. The arguments in this chapter are creating their own theoretical oddkin too: the oddkinship between queer and material ecocriticisms. Material ecocriticism sees the "world's material phenomena" as "knots in a vast network of agencies, which can be 'read' and interpreted as forming narratives, stories" (Iovino and Oppermann, *Material Ecocriticism* 1). At its fore, to put it simply, material ecocriticism acknowledges that things have agency: "The agency of matter, the interplay between the human and the nonhuman in a field of distributed effectuality and of inbuilt material-discursive dynamics, are concepts that influence deeply the ideas of narrativity and text" (Iovino and Oppermann, "Material Ecocriticism: Materiality" 79). How we interpret that agency in our stories, as I do throughout this chapter by examining the oddkins in *The Prettiest Star*, is to focus "on the way matter's (or nature's) nonhuman agentic capacities are described in narrative texts" (79). Oddkins make up the world of queer material ecocriticism.

Oddkin also recognizes that queer Appalachia is an odd pairing too. Recently the editors of a collection of essays, *Storytelling in Queer Appalachia: Imagining and Writing the Unspeakable Other*, define queer Appalachia this way: "Appalachia as a geographic, mythic, and cultural place is multifaceted and impossible to understand as a monolithic or singular. Queer identities and experiences are equally multifaceted and nonmonolithic; they are crossed by stereotyping" (Glasby, Gradin, and Ryerson 1). Ask most any queer Appalachian, including myself, if we agree here on all these points and I'd reckon we would. However, I believe that queerness, especially queerness in Appalachia, may have overlooked critical queer aspects. Queer Appalachia is queer because of queer folx from the region as much as it is *queer because of queer things and our relationships to them*.

I look to Carter Sickels's *The Prettiest Star* as a central textual example of how we can see this interplay between nonhuman actors, queerness, Appalachia, and queer people, and how this interplay can work to reconceptualize our relationship with the world. Brian's chapters in *The Prettiest Star* are written as though he is talking to his video camera. The agency of the camera along with the optics of queerness in the novel can exist only because of the presence of nonhuman actors. In turn, a queer materialist understanding of Brian's story emerges as well as how the reader can imagine the future of queer Appalachia. I seek to expand the thinking of queerness as a position from which to see Appalachian ecology and as an identificatory aspect of Appalachia, to include our understanding of queerness in Appalachia as emergent and enmeshed in a web of nonhuman relations. Queer materialist ecocriticism opens up future possibilities. My aim here is to show that the camera is a queer agent in the novel, creating an oddkinship with Brian and how one sees queerness in Appalachia. Overall, I see a queer materialist approach moving the narrative of nature in a different direction, embracing fluidity between human and nonhuman actors as critical to understanding life in Appalachia.

Coming to the Queer Appalachian Table

Shortly after Brian's arrival to the foothills of Appalachia, Sharon explains how she and her husband, Brian's father Travis, decide to prepare for their family meal: "We pass and reach for food, and fill our plates. Travis wanted to give Brian a paper plate and plastic utensils. You'll make him feel like a leper, I said. We compromised. He will not eat off disposable plates, but he'll have his own special set of silverware and dishes, his own cup" (55). At this point in history, the confusing and conspiratorial etiological discourse surrounding HIV/AIDS was rampant. There was speculation as to how contagious the disease was and how it spread. This particular moment in the novel underscores that point: Brian's parents negotiate between themselves as to how to deal with the disease as their son lives with them. Should they reveal to everyone that their son is living with HIV/AIDS (which hasn't happened at this point in the novel) by limiting him to disposable dishware, or should they discretely designate "special" dishware for his use?

This passage operates in a number of important ways. First, and perhaps most obviously, it becomes clear that Brian's queerness is feared as contaminant for Brian's parents, a queerness that is indistinguishable from disease. It threatens the Appalachian familial structure. The act of eating also becomes a spectacle that carries the potential to make Brian's queerness legible (seeing is a critical part of how oddkinships form in the novel, a point I make later on). The tension around eating a meal together isn't a matter of only concealing his queerness, either, but instead questions the degree to which the family's relationship begins to break down if Brian is exposed as having AIDS, and also how Brian being queer could infect his family, read here both literally and figuratively.

Next, I think this microcosmic scene of dinner plays a role in understanding the dining room table and all its objects as a site of Appalachian culture. We can understand dinner as a contained example of what life in Appalachia looks like. It also allows us to discuss who can sit at the table and in what capacity queerness is allowed to sit as well. Sharon describes the dinner and her son eating this way: "Brian continues to talk about the food of the world in his know-it-all way. He's both the son I remember and someone I've never met. His words sound flatter, and he talks faster. City-slicker. But it's more than that, the way he enunciates and stresses words. *Effeminate.* The word lands hard in my throat" (56). The relationship to food can also tell us about which environments are hospitable to queerness and which aren't. In this particular passage, Brian and his father, mother, sister, and grandmother all congregate at his parents' dining room table. Lettie asks Brian what he ate while he was away living in New York, and he responds, "Anything and everything. Indian, Chinese, Japanese" (56). Immediately his sister questions his choice of sushi, declaring it "gross" (56). Sharon narrates that "goulash used to be one of his favorite meals, but now I realize the canned tomatoes, ground beef, and macaroni are too simple, too Midwestern" (56). The nonhuman and non-"American" foodstuffs and Brian's queerness as foreign to Appalachia are linked. Brian's consumption of non-Appalachian foods demonstrates how he has formed queer relationships to the world around him while in New York. While it is important to be careful here not to conflate midwestern culture with Appalachian culture, Sharon's reasoning shows how the environmental overlap in the Ohioan foothills of Appalachia deem certain food relations acceptable or not. To experience oddkinship with non-Appalachian food further makes it clear that for Brian's immediate family queerness is thought of as unnatural.

What is interesting is that the binary of natural/unnatural is transcribed into gendered terms. If one aim of queer ecofeminism is "to probe the intersections of sex and nature with an eye to developing a sexual politics that more clearly included considerations of the natural world and its biosocial construction" (Mortimer-Sandilands and Erickson 5), then Sharon's framing of belonging to and staying in Appalachia is gendered masculine; when Brian leaves, he becomes an outsider, running the risk of being Othered. Brian is unnatural because of his effeminacy translated as queer. What's more, the urban and the rural emerge to reinforce this hierarchical thinking. To be Appalachian is not to be a "city-slicker." Also, implicit here is that Appalachians are static and fixed. They don't leave; they stay. The discourse surrounding Sharon's view of the Appalachian way of things is disrupted by Brian's presence. Brian is at once Appalachia and not—he defies, even queers, Sharon's worldview of Appalachia.

The disruption to the natural/unnatural, masculine/feminine, Appalachia/elsewhere, and straight/queer binaries that define Brian's exodus from and return to the mountains is captured in Sharon's comments. The queer disruption, whether a small shift in how dinner plays out or how Brian defies his mother's definition of Appalachian, functions to expose how Appalachia relies on these contradictions to exist. That's because Appalachia is a polymorphism anchored by geography: "Appalachia as a place has been so difficult to define that some have suggested that it is more akin to an idea than a geographic locale" (Straw 3). But rendering Appalachia as an idea oversimplifies it: "Appalachia is both a real place to those who live there and a sometimes mythic land to outsiders," and for those who do live in Appalachia, "how they identify themselves varies from person to person" (Clark and Hayward 1–2). Along these lines, narratives of poverty propelled by the Appalachian Regional Commission's (ARC) veiled visage of a philanthropic mission to save an entire region from poverty have also made it difficult to grapple with Appalachian identities (see Whisnant, esp. 126–55). But Appalachia isn't just one or all or always those things. Perhaps that's the point, though. There isn't a single way to define what it means to be Appalachian. Appalachia has been cast as one of America's Others for quite some time. You could say that its othered status was in part shaped by the ARC's influence, but mostly the othered status has been formed by outsiders' perspectives. After the Civil War, capitalism sunk its teeth into the region, marking Appalachia as a place to be saved with the promises of modernity, which should be understood as profit (Catte). Whether it's academics who come to study Appalachians (see Catte 38–39; Obermiller and Scott), corporations that exploit land for coal and other resources, or the government that subsidizes health care, welfare, and education (Whisnant; Davis and Baker), Appalachia in the cultural imagination is simultaneously set apart from America and deeply part of it. As Eller puts it, "We know Appalachia exists because we need it to exist in order to define what we are not" (3). A parallel can be drawn with Eller's point here to similar arguments about queerness.

Appalachia is queer. Appalachia is a queer place. Appalachian identities exist, but it's incredibly difficult to spell out what it means to be Appalachian. Appalachia is queer because "Appalachian" is just as slippery an identificatory category as "queer." The trickiness and contradiction that surround Appalachia as region and identity aren't the only premises to warrant its queerness, though. Whether queer theorists draw from Rich's compulsory heterosexuality or by way of Foucault's Repressive Hypothesis, there's a notion in queer theory that through queerness, straightness is propagated and reified as the norm. In other words straightness needs queerness to set it apart (Berlant and Warner; Butler, *Gender Trouble*; McCruer 6–9), just like America needs Appalachia to set its dominant culture apart. Although don't mistake me—I'm not implying Appalachia's queerness is the same type as sexual or gender nonnormativity (although it certainly can be). This doesn't mean that to be Appalachian is to be queer-read-as-nonstraight, either; homo-/trans-/queer-phobia and queer hate crimes are just as prevalent in Appalachia as they are elsewhere in the United States. It is in otherness, strangeness, indeterminacy, and resistance that Appalachia and queerness overlap. It's through our oddkinships that we are Appalachian, and in turn how we see the landscape of Appalachia emerge as queer.

Seeing Brian's Camera as Oddkin

The bulk of *The Prettiest Star* spans only a few months, from May 11 to roughly August 17, 1986. We gather Brian's narrative only through the lens of a camera. Each of his ten chapters is dated and stamped with a VHS icon; these aren't only journalistic entries or personal missives that document the end of Brian's life. These are documentary vignettes, logging the voyeurism of HIV/AIDS in Appalachia.

The opening of the novel constitutes the first and only time an omniscient narrator unfurls a scene: a metropolitan, realist account of New York City and of a man, Brian, who is traversing the streets early Sunday morning, April 20, 1986. Brian is told by Shawn, his late partner lost to AIDS, to "record everything" (3). Almost mantra-like, *record everything* becomes an impetus not only for the plot but also for Brian's characterization. And Brian often repeats it: "Record everything, Shawn said. For posterity. The camera will be my diary, my shrink" (58). Arguably the camera and Brian's relationship to the camera are much more than that. The act of recording underpins the last four months of Brian's life and inevitably asks readers of the novel to wrestle with what it means to witness and see queerness during the HIV/AIDS pandemic of the 1980s in Appalachia.

This opening is also important for establishing Brian's relationship to the New York landscape, as it reveals how his queerness mitigates his relationships to others but also his environment. The reader is told immediately that in New York, Brian sees "the park and empty lots and boarded up buildings with broken windows and graffiti-sprayed storefront metal gates. Sidewalks were littered with city souvenirs: an empty Coke can, a greasy paper plate, a crack vial" (3). The images of garbage and waste echo Sharon's understanding of queerness as "elsewhere" that I highlight earlier, but there is something implicitly valuable when we quickly come to learn that Brian found love in a seemingly derelict place. Even the juxtaposition between the trash and the "sky behind him" as "pink" and "silvery blue" (3) seems to indicate that what is thrown away can refashion our relationships with our surroundings but also how nonhuman things—in this instance trash—can queer our relationship even to ourselves. Additionally, the reader is told that this landscape is in stark contrast to the New York landscape that Brian experienced when he first moved there, before he contracted HIV: "His first couple of years in New York, this was a difference landscape—crowded with men sunbathing, shaking their hips to Donna Summer, writing poetry, checking each other out, finding dates and lovers and quick fucks down by the decaying edges of the docks" (6). The novel's omniscient narrator functions as a mouthpiece to indicate that New York experienced very real consequences of the HIV/AIDS pandemic—the disease ravished the community quite literally, especially in terms of experiencing the city as a sexual place. In a more nuanced way, though, this narration sets the reader up to look through the novel as Brian looks through his camera: How do we think about Appalachian culture as being thrown away or disregarded by American narratives more generally? Likewise, what can we learn from bringing cosmopolitan queerness back to Appalachia, as illustrated through Brian's return home? I'm not sure we ever find plain answers to these questions in the novel, but they bring to the fore how we, like Brian, should record Appalachian queerness and in the process pay attention to the oddkinships we develop along the way.

In order to understand how the camera is oddkin requires understanding further how material ecocriticism conceptualizes the world of things, namely agency. Karen Barad suggests that agency is intra-action, which "signifies the mutual constitution of entangled agencies" and "recognizes that distinct agencies do not precede, but rather emerge" (128). In simpler terms, a materialist view of agency resides in the space between actors, a space that is ubiquitous with potential, always moving and emergent. No longer do actors (i.e., humans) possess singular agency; agency is relational, meaning that it emerges from the actions between us and the world. Adding to this relationality, Jane Bennett describes this alternate view in "the form of an onto-story" (116) where things have "thing-power: the curious ability of inanimate things to animate, to act, to produce effect dramatic and subtle" (6): "Picture an ontological field without any unequivocal demarcations between human, animal, vegetable, or mineral. All forces and flows (materialities) are or can become lively, affective, and signaling.... This field lacks primordial divisions, but it is not a uniform or flat topography. It is just that its differentiations are too protean and diverse to coincide exclusively with the philosophical categories of life, matter, mental, environmental.... In this onto-tale, everything is, in a sense, alive" (116–17). Bennett recognizes that we need other ways of telling stories, "protean and diverse." A critical function of onto-stories, then, reveals to us that the world has already and always been a participant—we just haven't been looking for it. In other words, we don't have to imbue the nonhuman actors with agency because they've been here the entire time; onto-stories oblige us only to pay attention to nonhuman characters in our stories in new ways.

The camera, in this way of thinking, takes on far more relevance in the novel. The only means Brian has of seeing himself as someone infected, as well as seeing the disease itself, is through the mediation of his camera. The camera itself never speaks in *The Prettiest Star*. It isn't as though the camera has a voice of its own. We know the camera is there only because it is constantly being toted with Brian, as noted by his family, and the recording chapters themselves. The camera becomes an active participant in the novel not by contributing its own words but by enabling the testimony of Brian, the witnessing of queerness in Appalachia, and the experience of death.

Brian's first documentation on May 11 emphasizes how seeing his old life is necessary to record everything: "I had to get out of New York. Everything reminded me of Shawn. And death. I saw my reflection in the ghosts of men I passed on the streets. And here? In Chester? My parents told me no one knows and they want to keep it that way. Jess doesn't know, my grandmother doesn't. The word AIDS will never be said. The word gay will never be said. We'll live happily ever after in denial. Denial has helped me along so far.... Except look at me" (46).

The queer journey from the rural to the urban has a long history in queer literary theory. At the fore, Scott Herring's work goes to significant lengths to undermine the argument that queerness, in order to be fully embraced and lived, needs to find its way out of the countryside and into the city. I'd be naïve to think that at some levels this mythos doesn't still exist. We country and Appalachian queers recognize the seeming lie that there is such thing as a queer bucolic life. Brian's journey away from and back to Appalachia is significant in this passage because we witness him seeing his own queerness as well as his own mortality through the lens of the camera. The onus of his looking at other queers' mortality is enabled only by reseeing himself upon his return. Furthermore, as I expanded on in the last section, the camera is a catalyst to breaking down the binaries that exist around the rural/urban divide that his mother, Sharon, places on Brian by observing him at the dinner table.

Another critical point from the above quote is Brian's implication that speaking and seeing aren't always agential in the same way in Appalachia as compared to New York City, or perhaps even urban areas more generally. The act of disclosure, of coming out, is commonplace to queers and their queerness. Eve Sedgwick makes this abundantly clear in *Epistemology of the Closet*. Michel Foucault traces coming out to psychiatry and penal historiography. Yet there seems to be a refusal and impossibility to proclaiming queerness in Brian's narrative; queerness can be announced only through seeing. Because Brian's oddkinship with his camera is necessary for his narrative in the novel, and for his rationalizations with the inevitability of his disease, it also becomes queer.

Oddkinships are queer because they are capable of violating the human/nonhuman binary that exists in hierarchical thinking. As such, they possess queer agency. Feminist scholar Sara Ahmed, by way of philosopher Maurice Merleau-Ponty's phenomenology, argues that bodies extend into space in relation to objects they are directed toward (25–28). Yet when those bodies are oriented in ways that aren't apparent, or "straight", they are to be understood as queer: queer "is, after all, a spatial term, which then gets translated into a sexual term, a term for a twisted sexuality that does not follow a 'straight line,' a sexuality that is bent and crooked" (67). Ahmed notes agency as "a matter ... of how bodies come into contact with objects, as a contact that is never simply between two entities ... as each entity is already shaped by contact with others" (188). Harkening back to Adrienne Rich's notion of compulsory heterosexuality, queerness also fails to reproduce straightness. A queer agentalism then would see queerness as a complex web of bends and perhaps dead ends. Failure more generally has long been thought of as queer. Gender and sexuality theorist Jack Halberstam (2011) elucidates that queerness embraces "failing, losing, forgetting, unmaking, undoing, unbecoming, not knowing" and "may in fact offer more creative, more cooperative, more surprising ways of being in the world. Failing is something queers do and have always done exceptionally well" (2–3). To be queer and to queer both invoke a sense of failure, and the same should be considered when we discuss agency.

Brian is continually being seen. The moments in the novel when Brian's body is put on display as Other are legion. Sharon is constantly taking inventory of her son's embodiment. "I don't know how to be around him," she says. "How to look at him, how not to" (77–78). Queerness here is made legible on the body, yet refuses any utterance. What's notable is that when moments like this arise from other characters, but particularly from his mother, the camera is usually within the narration. Take, for instance, the moment when Sharon asks Brian, "So, really, what is it for? The video camera?" The dialogue unfolds: "'It's what I do.' 'Make movies?' 'Sort of. I document stuff, like my friends, and just things I see. I've made a few videos, like video art. Stuff that's, like, in progress. I really want to get you on camera.' 'I told you, I don't like to see myself on TV.' 'You'll get used to it,' Brian says" (51). Sharon's exclamation that she doesn't want to be seen on TV isn't a sentiment only she expresses. Most of the characters, including Brian himself, as I've pointed out, are reticent to being seen on camera. When Brian brings his camera to his Mamaw Lettie's house, he confesses that "nobody was pleased," and in Chester the response is very different from New York: "people duck, hide their faces" (63). Brian claims, "The camera is the elephant I'm trotting into the room. Or, maybe, I'm the elephant" (63). In many ways, Brian's parallelism between himself and the elephant speaks to my point above, that the camera, HIV, queerness, and Brian himself are enmeshed in a complex assemblage of how queerness is functioning in *The Prettiest Star*'s Appalachia, as something seen but not necessarily spoken about. During a conversation with his sister Jess, Brian makes this point a bit clearer. He tells Jess, "'I'm interested in documenting but also in capturing how random things are, and you know, like, there's not one way of being,' he says. 'The camera is my other set of eyes'" (67).

With the camera being another set of eyes for Brian, the reader is also permitted a new way of seeing the Appalachian landscape as queer. On July 16, 1986, Brian speaks to his camera about the creek behind his parents' house where as a kid he would "spend hours" "watching the minnows, the birds," and "after a hard rain the creek would rise" (138). He loves swimming, he tells the reader, detailing how in New York he would sometimes visit Coney Island, where he would swim in the "dirty and polluted water" (138). Harkening back to the first pages of the novel, the theme of contamination foreshadows how Brian sees HIV as polluting his idyllic life in New York. Brian explains how Shawn wanted Brian to "bring him here, to show him the places that made and undid me, the hills and trees and dirt" (140). He questions and fantasizes what it would have been like if he had brought Shawn home with him: "We'd fuck under the branches of a sweetgum, yellow stars falling around us. I'd make him a crown of bittersweet. His strong hands holding me down, his hot mouth on mine. All of it, happening out here, in the dirt and leaves of the place I tried so hard to escape" (140). Butler famously wrote, "We're undone by each other. And if we're not, we're missing something. If this seems so clearly the case with grief, it is only because it was already the case with desire" (*Undoing Gender* 19). Her passage obviously applies to Brian and Shawn's relationship, but I'd extend this statement even further to include Brian's relationship to nature and nonhumans. When Brian is able to be in nature by himself with the camera, he sees a number of connections between belonging to Appalachia, being queer, and the affective aftermath of partner's death. Brian is able to undo his previous understanding of Appalachia in this moment through his relationship with the camera by being out in places of his childhood. The harrowing image of sharing his love with Shawn isn't at the dinner table, or with his family; it is enacted on and with the land. Crowning his dead lover with a "crown of bittersweet" is in many ways a metaphorical turn of words because it's only after Brian has experienced the pain of queer death that he begins to undo his fraught relationship with his Appalachia heritage and belonging to place—bittersweet indeed.

Perhaps, too, the camera being his other set of eyes isn't purely metaphorical. Brian explains how "back in New York" he tried to capture "everyone and everything else" around him (58). He recorded the city and his friends, who "loved the attention" (63). At the novel's close, Brian details, "Before all of this, before I owned a camcorder even, before Shawn was sick, before we knew what was in our blood, before so many deaths, I was just living my life" (273). The simple act of living abruptly shifts once Brian has to face his own impermanence, his queerness, himself. Yet once the camera and Brian and HIV are in Appalachia, the camera takes on greater meaning, more agency. The camera is what Brian is; you could say it's his story. Even he admits that "talking to the camera like this is new thing" for him, but he "might as well" use the camera to "talk to you—whoever you are" (58).

Brian's interlocutor—this *whoever*—warrants unpacking. Seeing and saying are in tension with one another throughout *The Prettiest Star*, so exploring the camera as a queer oddkin that permits utterances where and when they are typically denied is significant. Speaking and looking carry with them threats throughout the novel. Coming out implies a locutionary event: queerness announced and heard makes it valid. A common dictum among Appalachian families when there's a queer in the bunch is to *just not talk about it*. "It," of course, is being queer. Sharon makes expressions like this all throughout the novel, thinking to herself whether she should "have known he was *that way*" (16). At first, Brian's disclosure, both of being gay and of having HIV/AIDS is not done in person, nor is it verbalized. Both instances are confined to letters sent to Sharon from New York. Even during the interactions with the letters, not speaking about their contents rings true here, as Sharon narrates: "A few years after he'd been in New York, he sent a letter. In it, he said that he was gay. I wept. . . . Maybe I had a few suspicions, but Travis and I certainly never talked about it" (79). Sharon doesn't even speak Brian's truth to Travis, Brian's dad. She explains that "the secret" of Brian being gay "became too heavy for [her] to bear, so one morning [she] left the letter" for Travis to find. She confronts Travis about whether he had read it: "'We should have gotten him help,' he said. That was it. He didn't want to talk about it. I know he would never accept his son as gay and I couldn't either.... A few months went by before I heard from Brian again. He asked if I'd read the letter.... 'I read it,' I said. That was it" (80). "Gay" is never uttered. It is denied the possibility of being heard. It's only through seeing Brian that "gay" is made visible to Brian's family and those in Chester.

So when Brian proclaims that he is talking to someone, there is an agential shift that occurs; the camera is revealed as being alive in its own way. Bennett may argue that the camera possesses thing-power and "manifest[s] traces of independence or aliveness" (xvi). This is to say, the camera has the ability to do things on its own. Not only does the camera allow Brian's queerness to be declared aloud, but it also begins to function as a character without dialogue in the novel at various points, which I extrapolate next.

By Brian declaring his audience a person, he is also giving the camera, in a wider sense, a person-status. When we attribute such animacy to an inanimate object, the hierarchical thinking I mentioned earlier also begins to break down in queer ways. Things are causal, in other words, affecting and creating new relationships with humans and the places. *Whoever* is at the same time both the human actors watching as well as the oddkin participating. Whoever, in this instance, is expanded to allow room for an entanglement of queer agents. Brian and the camera are co-constitutive in their queerness; they are inter-reliant on everything in the novel because they both record *everything*.

Brian discusses his relationship with the camera in his recordings frequently. Perhaps the most significant video entries are those during which he spends time chronicling how he came to own the camera and how videography emerged as an important aspect of his life:

> Shawn told me to document everything, the good and bad. He was scared our lives would be forgotten.
>
> When he first gave me my first camcorder, I didn't know what to do with it. It was a hefty, bulky thing he got from a dying friend who was giving away all his possessions. At first I just recorded Shawn making funny faces, or Annie [Brian's friend] telling me about her latest crush. Then I started to fool around—teaching myself how to take different kinds of shots, about lighting and editing. Rewind, pause, record, like making a mix tape.... I started thinking about art school. Thinking I had a future. (87)

It's apparent that Brian's identity begins to be tied to what he can see through the lens. Running in tandem to this point is Brian's relationship with seeing time through the lens. He can manipulate his observations, editing the film, maneuvering what is seen and how it's seen. He is so entwined with his camera that he considers making "a future" out of it. He "wanted to capture the joy, the life" (88) of queerness in the city: "Drag queens sashaying down the street. Glitter, rainbows, feathers" (87). On some levels, the oddkinship between him and his camera allows Brian to fall prey to the mythos of queerness being linked only to urbanity. When he talks to the reader and to his camera, Brian almost equates the city to happiness, to gayness in the most literal sense.

It isn't until HIV/AIDS becomes a sweeping force in the city and Brian is faced with the reality of his partner dying that the camera's agency tethers him to Appalachia. Brian confesses, "But, Shawn—he wanted me to document the harder stuff. Even wanted me to record him in the hospital, dying. I couldn't do it. I didn't understand then, but I think I do now. The world is ignoring us. We've got to document, even if it's just me talking to the camera in my parents' basement. At least I'm here. A face, a voice. The world wants to silence and disappear us. Well, here I am. Look at me" (88). Brian's oddkinship with his camera is an assertion of his queer environmental presence—his situatedness in a specific place, an assertation of his right to exist and not be erased from his Appalachian home and environment. Earlier I mentioned how the novel opens with description and contrasting details of New York as a place of queer revelry and death, and here we see a contrast with how the camera enables refusal for Brian. He can refuse a world that wants to silence and erase him through such oddkin. To just talk, as a face *and* a voice, imbricates a host of agential ties in this instance. Brian sees the connection between the city and the rural conflate. His parents' home, his family, his voice, the camera, Chester, Ohio, HIV/AIDS all are interlocked in these few moments. To proclaim to the camera and to the viewer, and perhaps most importantly to the reader, "Look at me," is simultaneously asking us to witness and to listen. It is this web of relationships, signified through the lens of the camera, that demonstrates how onto-stories involve multitudinous actors, which in turn make oddkin. It is through his queer relationship to his camera that Brian is able to relate to Appalachia, a nonhuman that enables his queerness to emerge entangling everyone and everything in the novel, including us, the reader. The camera in *The Prettiest Star* allows us to gaze into a time when queers were not able to survive in a world as they are now. The camera reminds us, too, that if we pay attention to our relationships to nonhumans, we can find our queer worlds full of oddkin, which ultimately render queerness a natural part of Appalachia. To this end, Brian's sexuality is arguably a natural part of Appalachia.

Oddkin Futures in Queer Appalachia

Brian and the camera demonstrate, as I've argued, a type of relationship that queerly goes beyond normal, biological, even human-human relationships. In this way, oddkin possess the queer agency that queer materialist ecocriticism provides. Ways of being with others that exceed typical forms of kinship enable a means of looking at our world in all its precarity. Much as Brian's camera allows him to be queer in a place where queerness isn't meant to exist, queer materialism can help us look into our current stories by paying heed to the nonhumans that are enduring the current state of affairs alongside us. I recognize there is a level of contradiction that exists when discussing the future through looking at a novel set in the past. *The Prettiest Star* may not have at its core the impetus to imagine a queer utopia. It is a story about the inevitability of queer death. Yet isn't that what waits for us at the other end of the Anthropocene if we don't figure something out, and quickly? What we are left with as readers is the reminder that our stories live on. Moreover, it is the ability to see stories and be with stories that can give them queer potential. And if there is anything that Appalachians do best it's storytelling. *The Prettiest Star* allows us to see the queer possibility of Appalachia.

In fact, Appalachia has been queer all along, and what *The Prettiest Star* does is show us that despite the traumatic reality of HIV/AIDS, Brian and his camcorder, the videos, queerness can and does belong in Appalachia—it needs viable stories only where oddkinships are seen. I mentioned in the last section that when the novel begins the narrator has no name, telling us what Brian's life has been up until that point. The narrator also provides an imperative statement: *record everything*. I'd like to think that this isn't an omniscient voice, that what Sickels does is give voice to a character that permits the entire novel to unfold. What if the expository chapter is the mouthpiece of the camera imploring us to record everything, to see queerness where we are told we shouldn't, to live our queerness in Appalachia even in the face of the inexorable struggles such as what we face in the Anthropocene? What does it mean to bear witness, especially as queers? A possible answer is that to witness queerness requires us to see how our relationships to nonhuman objects are necessary for our stories to survive. In the novel, Brian's mother, I believe, comes to this realization at the precipice of her son's death when she finds his VHS tapes. One of the tapes is labeled "watch after my death" (255). Isn't that what we are doing with *The Prettiest Star*? Aren't we watching a queer story unfold after death? Isn't this what we're doing in the Anthropocene? I'm inclined to agree with materialist thinkers that "nonhuman beings are responsible for the next moment of human history and thinking" (Morton, *Hyperobjects* 210). Queer Appalachia with all its queer things has such agential possibility through storytelling with a multitude of queer oddkinships, and it's time to see them.

BIBLIOGRAPHY

Ahmed, Sara. *Queer Phenomenology: Orientations, Objects, Others.* Durham, N.C.: Duke University Press, 2006.

Barad, Karen. *Meeting the Universe Halfway: Quantum Physics and the Entanglement of Matter and Meaning.* Durham, N.C.: Duke University Press, 2007.

Bennett, Jane. *Vibrant Matter: A Political Ecology of Things.* Durham, N.C.: Duke University Press, 2010.

Berlant, Lauren, and Michael Warner. "Sex in Public." In *Publics and Counterpublics*, by M. Warner, 187–208. Brooklyn: Zone Books, 2008.

Bryant, Levi R. *The Democracy of Objects.* Ann Arbor, Mich.: Open Humanities Press, 2011.

———. *The Speculative Turn: Continental Materialism and Realism.* Melbourne, Australia: Re.press, 2015.

Buell, Lawrence. *The Environmental Imagination: Thoreau, Nature Writing, and the Formation of American Culture.* Cambridge, Mass.: Belknap, 1996.

Butler, Judith. *Gender Trouble: Feminism and the Subversion of Identity.* New York: Routledge, 2004.

———. "Is Kinship Always Already Heterosexual?" *differences: A Journal of Feminist Cultural Studies* 13, no. 1 (2002): 14–44.

———. *Undoing Gender.* New York: Routledge, 2004.

Catte, Elizabeth. *What You Are Getting Wrong about Appalachia.* Cleveland: Independent, 2017.

Clark, Amy D., and Nancy M. Hayward, eds. *Talking Appalachian Voice, Identity, and Community.* Lexington: University Press of Kentucky, 2013.

Coole, Diana, and Samantha Frost, eds. *New Materialisms: Ontology, Agency, and Politics.* Durham, N.C.: Duke University Press, 2010.

Davis, Donald E., and Chris Baker. "Fixing Appalachia: A Century of Community Development in a 'Depressed' Area." In *Studying Appalachian Studies: Making the Path by Walking*, edited by Chad Berry, Phillip J. Obermiller, and Shaunna L. Scott, 88–118. Urbana: University of Illinois Press, 2015.

Eller, Ronald D. *Uneven Ground: Appalachia since 1945.* Lexington: University Press of Kentucky, 2013.

Foucault, Michel. *The History of Sexuality*, vol. 1: *An Introduction.* New York: Vintage, 1990.

Gaard, Greta. "Toward a Queer Ecofeminism." In *New Perspectives on Environmental Justice: Gender, Sexuality, and Activism*, edited by Rachel Stein, 21–44. New Brunswick, N.J.: Rutgers University Press, 2004.

Glasby, Hillery, Sherrie L. Gradin, and Rachael Ryerson. *Storytelling in Queer Appalachia: Imagining and Writing the Unspeakable Other.* Morgantown: West Virginia University Press, 2020.

Halberstam, Judith. *The Queer Art of Failure.* Durham, N.C.: Duke University Press, 2011.

Haraway, Donna. *Staying with the Trouble: Making Kin in the Chthulucene*. Durham, N.C.: Duke University Press, 2016.
Harman, Graham. *Prince of Networks: Bruno Latour and Metaphysics*. Victoria, Australia: Re.press, 2009.
Herring, Scott. *Another Country: Queer Anti-urbanism*. New York: New York University Press, 2010.
Iovino, Serenella, and Serpil Oppermann, eds. *Material Ecocriticism*. Bloomington: Indiana University Press, 2014.
———. "Material Ecocriticism: Materiality, Agency, and Models of Narrativity." *Ecozon@: European Journal of Literature, Culture and Environment* 3, no. 1 (2012).
Joagose, Annemarie. *Queer Theory: An Introduction*. New York: New York University Press, 1996.
McRuer, Robert. *Crip Theory: Cultural Signs of Queerness and Disability*. New York: New York University Press, 2004.
Merrick, Helen. "Queering Nature: Close Encounters with the Alien in Ecofeminist Science Fiction." In *Queer Universes: Sexualities in Science Fiction*, edited by Wendy Gay Pearson, Veronica Hollinger, and Joan Gordon, 216–32. Cambridge: Cambridge University Press, 2008.
Mortimer-Sandilands, Catriona, and Bruce Erickson, eds. *Queer Ecologies: Sex, Nature, Politics, Desire*. Bloomington: Indiana University Press, 2010.
Morton, Timothy. *Dark Ecology: For a Logic of Future Coexistence*. New York: Columbia University Press, 2015
———. *The Ecological Thought*. Cambridge, Mass.: Harvard University Press, 2010.
———. *Hyperobjects: Philosophy and Ecology after the End of the World*. Minneapolis: University of Minnesota Press, 2013.
Obermiller, Phillip J., and Shaunna L. Scott. "Studying Appalachia: Critical Reflections." In *Studying Appalachian Studies: Making the Path by Walking*, edited by Chad Berry, Phillip J. Obermiller, and Shaunna L. Scott, 141–67. Urbana: University of Illinois Press, 2015.
Pearson, Wendy Gay, Veronica Hollingr, and Joan Gordon. *Queer Universes: Sexualities in Science Fiction*. Liverpool: Liverpool University Press, 2008.
Rich, Adrienne. "Compulsory Heterosexuality and Lesbian Existence." *Signs* 5, no. 4 (1980): 631–60.
Sedgwick, Eve K. *Epistemology of the Closet*. Berkeley: University of California Press, 2008.
Sickels, Carter. *The Prettiest Star*. Spartanburg, S.C.: Hub City Press, 2020.
Sontag, Susan. "Notes on 'Camp.'" In *Against Interpretation, and Other Essays*, 275–92. New York: Farrar, Straus and Giroux, 1966.
Soper, Kate. "Unnatural Times? The Social Imaginary and the Future of Nature." *Sociological Review* 57, no. 2 (2009): 222–35.
Straw, Richard Alan. "Introduction." In *High Mountains Rising: Appalachia in Time and Place*, edited by Richard Alan Straw and H. Tyler Blethen, 1–6. Urbana: University of Illinois Press, 2004.
Whisnant, David E. *Modernizing Mountaineer: People, Power, Planning Appalachia*. Knoxville: University of Tennessee Press, 1994.
Wilchins, Riki Anne. *Queer Theory, Gender Theory: An Instant Primer*. Bronx, N.Y.: Magnus Books, 2004.

Trail Magic
Seeking Guidance
along the Journey

Raven, Woman, Man
A/Religious Ecocritical Reading of
Jim Minick's *Fire Is Your Water*

THERESA BURRISS

In his debut novel, *Fire Is Your Water* (2017), set in mid-1950s Appalachian Pennsylvania, Jim Minick introduces readers to a centuries-old healing tradition known as *brauche* in the Pennsylvania Dutch dialect, powwowing in its English form. Drawing from his own family lore, Minick presents two characters, Mark Hoover and Ada Franklin, who hold this power, a power stemming from a deep belief in and commitment to Christianity. In his review of David Kriebel's text *Powwowing among the Pennsylvania Dutch: A Traditional Medical Practice in the Modern World*, James Higgins explains the origins of the practice: "Powwowing emerged from two distinct strands of experience: the power of a belief in God and the ineffectiveness of what passed for medicine until almost the end of the nineteenth century. These two factors are inimical to understanding the practice of powwowing" (312). According to Judith Offner in "Pow-Wowing: The Pennsylvania Dutch Way to Heal," these healing practices originated centuries ago with Pennsylvania Dutch ancestors living in the Palatine region of Europe (480). The term *braucher* became powwower after the Pennsylvania Dutch "consulted with Native American shamans to learn the unfamiliar herbs and other healing materials of their new environment" (481). Minick further explains the practice must be passed down from generation to generation through opposite sexes. Hence, Uncle Mark Hoover, a minor character who learned to powwow from his grandmother, Ida, passes the tradition onto Ada Franklin, his niece and one of three main characters in the novel. All powwowers possess an innate gift to heal, however, which is cultivated and strengthened through instruction in chanting specific prayers over the injured or sick, nonhuman and human alike.

In fact, Ada's first healing occurs when she is only ten years old after a sparrow flies into a window above her while she sits outside. As the bird is on the verge of death, Ada cradles it. "'Help this little bird, Lord,' Ada whispered. As she stroked its back, her hands grew tingly and her fingers buzzed with warmth" (19). Thus, from the start of the novel, Minick establishes the interconnectedness of nonhuman and human and the value placed on nonhuman life. As Garrard explains, "The boundary between human and animal is arbitrary and, moreover, irrelevant, since we share with animals a capacity for suffering that only 'the hand of tyranny' (ibid.) could ignore" (147). Minick continues to describe Ada's first healing experience: "The sparrow's heart fluttered in her palms, and slowly it lifted its neck and closed its beak. For a moment, the shiny eye peered into her, and the rest of the world blurred to just Ada and this speckled sparrow" (19–20). Clearly, Minick debunks traditional Western belief systems that posit the human against the nonhuman, the spiritual against the corporeal, as Ada identifies this small sparrow as a sentient being.

Indeed, great significance exists in the telltale sign of Ada's tingling hands, an embodied spiritual experience, and gets to the heart of an emerging and quickly evolving ecocriticism influenced by various Christian tenets. Joshua Mabie specifically addresses frictions present in both Christianity and ecocriticism, independent of one another, yet demonstrates how they complement one another: "Just as scholars of Christianity have resisted an oversimplified understanding of human dominion over creation as a warrant for environmental destruction, ecocritics have rethought and in many cases rejected the strict biocentrism that comes across as a form of anti-humanism" (282). Minick's *Fire Is Your Water* incorporates many signature characteristics of a Christian ecocriticism, whereby tenets of the religion, such as human stewardship of creation, merge with an ecocritical valuing of the intrinsic good of that creation, independent of humans.

Despite an overarching Christian theme centered on powwowing, Minick borrows from the thirteenth-century Persian Muslim poet Rumi for the title of the novel, with a line from Rumi's poem "The Question" serving as the novel's opening epigraph: "If you are a friend of God, fire is your water." Moreover, Cicero, a sassy-talking raven that speaks directly to readers, a first-bird point of view as it were, begins the novel by recounting the Cherokee tale of how raven feathers became black "by trying to fetch fire" (1). Quite purposefully, Minick eschews traditional Western dualisms, including spirit/body, religion/nature, and human/nonhuman, further aligning his work with progressive Christian ecocritical thought, traditional Eastern religions, and Native American spiritual beliefs. Thus, he avoids reductive religious singularity by incorporating several belief systems, all with a focus on the element of fire.

When asked why he included a talking bird, Minick explained that he eventually came to understand that Cicero "wanted to talk." Clark discusses the difficulty of presenting nonhuman agency in literature: "As the inhabitant of undeniably real worlds, alien to us and not fully comprehensible, the animal's gaze into the human realm may seem profoundly to shake it, refusing it the illusion of totality or of self-evidence in its modes of coherence" (191). Unafraid of challenging human illusions of superiority, Minick also asserted the need to take chances, to experiment with characters in ways that push the imagination.[1] Again as Clark suggests, "Given that all human representations project a human measure of some sort, it soon becomes debatable where 'anthropomorphism' stops.... All human knowledge must needs be anthropomorphic in some way" (193). Clark goes on to cite Eileen Crist, who "defends anthropomorphism as a genuine source of understanding: 'in the hands of impeccable observers of animals the anthropomorphic perspective deserves serious attention, for it discloses the nature of animal life with the power and internal cohesion that real worlds possess' (*Images of Animals* 7). She believes that scientific evidence for the commonality of humans and other animals gives credit to anthropomorphism as a pragmatic shortcut for understanding animal life" (193–94). Even the arresting book jacket and front and back cloth covers of Minick's novel display the feisty raven's personality as the bird has stolen the O from the "Your" of the novel's title. Such ravening, or hungering, represents a key theme in the novel's main characters, whether they are yearning for healing, as in the case of Cicero, recovered faith, in the case of Ada, or maternal love, in the case of Will Burk, Ada's love interest. Moreover, from beginning to end, both fire as threat and fire as promise thread throughout the novel, with Cicero having the first and last say on the story.

Indeed, Cicero provides an ominous foreshadowing on the very first page in his recounting of the Cherokee tale: "Then a huge flame blasted up and scorched me black. I barely made it back across the water" (1). As Cicero continues the fire creation story by crediting the spider with carrying the spark across the water in her "baskety web," the raven establishes one of the key tensions in the novel: "That's how fire came into the world—a good thing, I guess, though I'm not always sure" (1). Doubt, as well as acknowledged and unacknowledged needs to be rescued, manifests itself throughout the novel in the three main characters, Cicero, Ada, and Will, who navigate a unique love triangle heated with emotion, including intense jealousy. Additionally, the characters demonstrate ecocriticism's "fundamental premise that human culture is connected to the physical world, affecting it and affected by it" (Glotfelty and Fromm xix)

Despite Ada's and Cicero's fear of or disdain for each other, respectively, this woman and bird are linked in mysterious, at times spiritual, ways, perhaps because of their mutual love for Will Burk. In yet another love twist, Ada's old boyfriend Jesse attempts to shoot Cicero with his shotgun one day while working on the newly constructed barn because the bird swoops close to his head after Jesse pretended to shoot it with his masonry trowel. Cicero barely escapes but is slightly injured from the pellets. And though Ada seemingly loses her powwowing abilities during the fire that destroys her family's barn, perhaps due to her intense fear of fire and evidenced when she cannot heal her mother's singed hands after they have released the trapped animals, Ada learns otherwise as she spies Cicero "huddled under a pine tree" and then calls to him. "Immediately, she felt tingling in her fingers. *Could it be?* She tried to calm her breathing. The raven wouldn't let her get near. She knelt in the pine needles and called his name again. The tingling intensified.... But just her fingers tingled, not her whole hands. Ada closed her eyes and recited the chant for stopping blood. She repeated it twice more and then opened her eyes. The tingling slowly faded. Cicero stood on his good foot and hopped toward the orchard. When he reached the open grass, he spread his wings and flew away" (175). In this scene, which is reminiscent of her first time healing the sparrow, Ada regains her powwowing ability with Cicero, another bird, who confirms in his own chapter that Ada did indeed heal him. Much later in the novel, when Ada describes to Will her healing of Cicero, she even acknowledges that "'maybe he somehow healed me'" (229).

Nonhuman animals enable Ada to discover and, in the case of Cicero, regain her very Christian-inspired healing. Cicero acknowledges, a bit begrudgingly, "Somehow she found me. She kept her distance, there under that pine. As soon as she said my name, I got a weird feeling over those pellet wounds. Warm, like water. Like the time Will took me to that man who held me and whispered over my stump and bandaged my wing. That kind of funnybone sparkling. And then the pain was gone" (176). "That man" Cicero mentions is Ada's Uncle Mark, who taught her to powwow. Although the terms "creation care" and "reconciliation ecology" did not exist during the 1950s, both Uncle Mark and Ada practice these faith-based principles as healing servants. The authors of "Reconciliation Ecology: A New Paradigm for Advancing Creation Care" explain, "Service is a prevalent and critical theme in Christianity.... This notion of serving is fundamental to our identity as Christians.... And the model of servanthood Jesus provides is expansive—encompassing all of creation" (Warners, Ryskamp, and Dragt 222). As a Christian servant, Ada calls upon God and utilizes her gift to heal Cicero, a representative of Nature damaged by human hubris and spite.

During a rare lunar eclipse, which Will anticipates with great excitement as he works the evening shift at the gas station, Ada and Cicero share an eerie feeling when they view the spectacle, Ada from her bedroom window and Cicero from Will's car parked at the garage. "Ada looked back at the moon, and what emerged made her clutch her throat. . . . All of it flushed to glow orange-red, like a giant dying coal. The intensity of color made it look alive, burning even. Ada hugged herself. She was silly to think it, but somehow, this red moon could mean nothing good" (224). Similarly, Cicero remarks, "It looked too big. It looked like a red eye. It looked like something dead. And I didn't like it one bit" (225). Once Will sees the spectacle, even he uses similar descriptions, although he does not possess the same foreboding as Ada and Cicero. He exclaims, "'It looks like it's on fire. . . . Like some owl flew up there with a torch in its beak'" (222). However, only Ada and Cicero possess a primal connection with their premonition. Their psychic unification persists throughout the novel, although the two communicate in more traditional ways as well.

Later in the novel, when Cicero flies to Ada's farm, apparently searching for Will, she offers dog food to him and then explains, "'Will is OK.' . . . Cicero stopped eating, looking at her. 'Will is OK. He's in the hospital. He'll be there for a while.' Cicero looked away. . . . Ada folded her arms. 'I just wanted you to know.' Then Cicero said, 'OK.' 'OK,' Ada repeated. 'OK,' the bird echoed" (311). Later, when Ada visits with Will in the hospital, she shares that she saw Cicero that morning: "'He didn't make any noise for the longest time until I repeated that you were OK. Then he looked at me and said, "OK." It was like he understood.' 'I think that bird knows way more than we do,'" Will replies (313). This exchange stresses the intelligence of nonhuman animals, thereby avoiding the worst of anthropocentricism and its consequent hegemony. Therefore, the text aligns itself with anti-Cartesian philosophers, recognizing the arrogance and ignorance of Descartes, who "hyperseparated mind and body, and denied to animals not only the faculty of reasons, but the whole range of feelings and sensations that he had associated with thought. As a result, he saw animals as radically different from, and inferior to, humans. They were bodies without minds, effectively machines" (28). Garrard attributes Val Plumwood with the term "hyperseparation," an understanding that in Western thought, "'reason' has so often been called upon to hyperseparate both men from women and humans from animals." Garrard goes on to claim, "[Plumwood] does not argue for a rejection of either science or reason, but rather a qualification of the philosophies that would polarise reason and nature in opposition: whereas scientific 'objectivity' decrees that any talk of intention or purpose in nature constitutes unscientific anthropomorphism, Plumwood advocates for a recognition of both similarity and difference in the human-nature continuum" (28). Such "both/and" positioning aligns with deconstruction, whereby simple binarisms are revealed as social constructions in the Euro-patriarchal master narrative to enable those in power to maintain that power. Minick demonstrates "both similarity and difference in the human-nature continuum" with Cicero, the raven, Ada, the woman, and Will, the man.

Toward the end of his work, Minick reveals how Ada and Cicero align philosophically as well. Throughout the novel, Cicero expresses an intense fascination with words, offering astute commentary on semiotics: "I was such a fool to fall in love with [words]. Such a fool to think they could say exactly what I mean. They never touch the truth of a thing, they only point *toward* it.... It's like language became its own little demon-god. It doesn't want you to shut up. Demands that you chatter on and on. When do we stop and just listen? In a quiet world, what would we find? More miracles. Maybe more gods" (306–7). Similarly, when Ada sits in Will's hospital room as he sleeps, she reflects on the barn fire and her desire to "drink that fire. How odd this sounded now, yet it was true. She had been thirsty for fire" (337). Then she recalls the psalm, "'Be still, and know that I am God.' Be still. Be quiet. Just listen. Don't doubt. God's Word won't lie" (337). Both raven and woman recognize the power of silence and what may be discovered there, despite their different ways of coming to this recognition.

While Ada possesses a deep, authentic Christian faith, she is a complex, multidimensional character. After the barn fire, she experiences severe doubt, not only with the apparent loss of her powwowing ability but also with her belief in God's presence. Her Uncle Mark is the one who has to heal her mother's hands because Ada cannot. She attempts a prayer, "*Thank you, God, for helping Mama and Uncle Mark and for bringing Papa home safely.* Ada prayed for Nathan, too, on his long journey across the ocean. But she wondered whether those words really mattered" (22). At the crux of this faith crisis is the question of how a Christian healer heals herself. In addition to her doubts, Ada expresses fears, the most significant being a fear of fire.

Notably, Ada begins to heal herself in Nature as she seeks peace from her internal torment. Readers witness Ada's beginning transformation as she hikes to gathers herbs in a cove: "Her lungs filled with the lushness of this deep hollow, the air cooler, the shade more dense. This place was more holy than any church. These plants a congregation of old friends" (124). Clearly, she recognizes the sanctity of the natural world and even elevates it beyond a human-constructed church. Moreover, Ada begins her quest to overcome her fear of fire in this same scene as she and her dog, Lucky, trot off to the nearby stream. "That good tired she loved came over her, so she leaned against a birch, but something flashed up the slope. Something moved in that spicebush. A bird? For a moment it looked like the whole bush sparkled" (124). When Ada looks directly at the bush, she sees nothing. Then, from her peripheral vision she witnesses a rhododendron alight: "Again, when she faced it, the flickering ceased" (124). At this point, Ada recalls how Moses could not look straight on at the burning bush and wonders if these signs are from God to begin to heal her. "All around her, the water danced like fire. It flared with shimmering flames. Eddies swirled with color. Fish darted like sparks. The fire was everywhere, her feet in a lava stream yet not getting burned. . . . Then all of it disappeared, and the stream became just a noisy gurgle, the bush just a tangle of green. Briefly, the tips of her fingers tingled, but she couldn't be sure. She knew what she'd witnessed, though—a fire burning in this flinty water" (125). Not only does Minick connect Ada to the biblical Moses in this scene, thereby emphasizing her Christian disposition, but he also ties Ada intimately, deeply to Nature. Ada's brief, intense experience illustrates a Christian ecocriticism that refuses competing beliefs in the Holy Spirit, as represented in the burning bush, and the spirituality of the natural world. Instead, both are sacred and holy. Eco-poet Gary Snyder provides insight into such a connection by citing the twelfth-century Zen Buddhist philosopher Dogen: "To see a wren in a bush, call it 'wren,' and go on walking is to have (self-importantly) seen nothing. To see a bird and stop, watch, feel, forget yourself for a moment, be in the bushy shadows, maybe then feel 'wren'—that is to have joined in a larger moment with the world" (130). Ada surrenders herself while sitting on the stream bank to become one with the burning water, to join "in a larger moment with the world," which initiates her healing as evidenced in the slight tingling of her fingertips.

In seeming contradiction to her traditional spirituality and faith, Ada owns an amulet, which she purchased through the mail based on an advertisement she read. Ada believes the amulet holds great significance: "The black stone fell into her palm, cool, dark, and shiny. The size of her thumbnail, it had a white streak of quartz like a lightning strike. The first time she'd held it, she'd known it had special power" (115). Thus, Ada sees no incongruity between her Christian and earth-based spirituality. When she realizes she apparently lost the amulet when jumping over a fence, she becomes quite distraught. Readers follow her train of thought: "It was her lucky stone she'd kept in her pocket for the past five years, through school and waitressing and even the barn fire. Did it work? She never could tell. Maybe it had saved her from the burning timber, or maybe God had done that. Either way, now that tiny weight was gone" (212). Readers recognize the importance of that tiny weight for Ada and come to understand the compatibility of its power and God's power in her life. In many ways, Ada's connection to the black stone exemplifies Merleau-Ponty's phenomenological "encounters with the 'flesh of world'" (Garrard 36). Garrard cites David Abram in explaining this concept: "To touch the coarse skin of a tree is thus, at the same time, to feel oneself touched *by* the tree" (36). Therefore, Ada loses this intimate connection to the amulet.

Of particular interest is the measure Ada and her family take after their new barn is raised. While Cicero is an agnostic raven, Will comes across as an avowed atheist, primarily due to the death of his mother at his birth, thereby establishing a central conflict throughout the novel between believers and nonbelievers. Will's exchange with Uncle Mark exemplifies the conflict as Uncle Mark asks Will, "'Do you believe in the Lord, Will Burk?'" (159). After responding in the negative, Will shares, "If God exists, he's out in the woods for me. He's in this bird. Not in no church" (160). The ecocritical commentary comes through unmistakably here with Will's equation of God with woods. Will's skepticism of such faith is apparent when he finds a piece of paper with odd block lettering tacked above a door in Ada's family's new barn. Confused by the words, he queries Ada, "What does 'ROTAS' mean, Ada? And 'SATOR'?" A bit taken aback by the tone of Will's voice, Ada calmly responds, "It's a hex sign to protect the barn. Daddy asked Uncle Mark to put it there last week" (243). Given Will's areligious nature, he is quick to criticize what he deems as mere foolishness and, after saying so, storms out of the barn to leave Ada standing alone. At first Ada longs to pursue him, yet "another, deeper part of her made her wait," which readers may interpret as not only her faith in God but faith in allowing life to unfold organically, without desperation or coercion.

Not only does Cicero and Ada's relationship defy Cartesian hyperseparation, so does Cicero's and Will's. From the very start, as soon as Will rescues Cicero from his entrapment in the tree downed during a fierce storm, "He knew he should fear the raven, especially that stout beak, but he didn't. For some reason, the bird felt like an old friend" (96). Some innate relation does indeed bind Will and Cicero. After Will's fiery confrontation with Ada in the barn, he returns home that night subdued, a condition Cicero finds unsettling because it defies Will's normal state of being. Cicero recounts the brief albeit existential exchange.

> "What do you know about God?" he asked. "Ada is a purty girl" came out of my mouth just like that. God of all rootknots and rank weeds, why the hell did I say that? "You're right about that," he said. . . . I wanted to say, *God is a black feather*. I wanted to say *God is a shining black feather that rides the wind*. But a single black feather can't do diddly, can't do more than float wherever the fucking wind decides. What's-her-name would've probably said that wind is also god. And maybe she'd be right. But back then, with Will so lost, language failed me, again, the words silent as feathers, loose and blowing away. (245)

In the world of Cicero, black feathers constitute the very essence of raven-hood, how the birds establish their physical existence. Yet one black feather possesses little to no power and remains at the whim of the wind. Minick's metaphorical comparison between failed words and loose feathers demonstrates the miscommunication that can occur between even the most spiritually connected human and nonhuman animals.

Such a breakdown in communication turns tragic. While Cicero's intuition is so profound that he is able to predict events before they occur, he cannot articulate what he senses despite his love for Will. In the hospital, Will asks his Aunt Amanda if she has seen the raven since the accident. She has not and notes, "'He was there right before the fire, wasn't he?' 'He was, and he acted funny that whole morning. . . . It was like he knew. That sounds crazy, but I think he did'" (299). While Will does not understand Cicero's attempted warnings, neither does Ada, who reflects on the last time she saw him before the fire: "Cicero had come directly toward her with those long agitated caws. *I thought he was attacking me. But he came to warn me*" (303). Thus, readers witness the limitations of communication between nonhuman and human animals, which seem to be attributed to human ignorance, no matter the good intentions of the humans.

In a different vein of exposition, the novel severely critiques humans with ill intentions, revealing the hypocrisy of some Christian-identified individuals. Both Ada and Will, regardless of their different beliefs, endure strikingly similar confrontations with sanctimonious characters full of condemnation. For Ada, the confrontation is with the Hopewell community's relatively new preacher, Reverend Zigler. For Will, the confrontation is with his new boss, Buddy Dickson. Ada constantly tries to avoid Zigler and his moralizing. As she holds her special amulet in her hand, she reflects, "Their new minister called it idolatry to believe in amulets, but he also disavowed her healing" (116). Interestingly, Ada reflects on her first encounter with Zigler as she climbs the mountain behind the family farm after the barn fire. On the mountain, she runs into Uncle Mark, who warns her to watch for snakes, and she remembers, "She'd met a copperhead here last year, sunning itself on the path.... The memory called up Reverend Zigler, their minister of two years. His venom" (121). Ada knows to respect the copperhead's self-defense, yet equates the snake's deadly venom to the preacher's self-righteous condemnation. While her parents are in town running errands, Zigler stops by unannounced, claiming he called ahead of time. Although Ada does not want to talk with him, propriety dictates and the two settle on the porch. After small chitchat on Zigler's part, he pointedly remarks,

> "I called on Denton Atwood this morning." [Ada] slowed her rocking. "He told me how you healed his arthritis. Said you chanted over his knees and the pain stopped." . . . "Is that true?" "Yes, it's true," she replied. . . . "That's what I feared. Your powwowing, Ada Franklin, is the work of the Devil. Only the Lord heals, only He has that power. . . . Before I came to this parish, I had heard about you and your uncle, heard you could stop bleeding and heal burns, and even then, I was afraid for your souls, afraid you served the Devil." He leaned forward, placed his hand on her knee. "But the Lord forgives, Ada. You can start anew, you can leave this Devil's work, you can." (122–23)

Outraged, Ada stands her ground and counters his criticism by proclaiming that God provides her with the healing, that it is God's power that dispels the Devil and his evil through her. Nevertheless, the next Sunday Zigler preaches in church about only God and Jesus possessing the ability to heal: "Anyone who claims otherwise bears false witness before the Lord" (123).

Not content with this public admonition, Zigler challenges Ada yet again. As she seeks time to practice the piano alone in church during the week, she stumbles upon Zigler, who takes advantage of the situation. Asking her to read some of John Newton's work, Zigler interrupts her to emphasize, "Satan overruled by a power unseen.... That's what can happen in your life, Ada. Satan is behind your powwowing." Ada counters, as she did before, that it is only through God that she heals, for the Devil cannot. Zigler retorts, "'Oh, but he can pretend.' 'I could do nothing without the Lord. Not even pretend.' 'But Satan comes as a wolf covered by a sheepskin, remember?' 'I think I smell a wolf right now.' 'I think you smell yourself'" (164–65). Through this exchange, Minick demonstrates the imperialism of dogmatic Christianity through the character of Zigler, who is threatened by Ada's healing power he does not possess and therefore cannot control. Throughout the novel, Ada poses more of a threat to Zigler than even Uncle Mark, for Zigler does not confront the elder male powwower of the family. A woman, however, young, pure in intention, and overtly dedicated to the Church and the natural environment, unhinges the preacher. In many regards, this male/female power dynamic exhibited by Zigler and Ada is symptomatic of traditional Western ideas of Christianity, where dominion is valued at the expense of whatever happens to be in the way, regardless of the quest.

Just as Ada must bear Zigler's condemnation, Will continually endures the zealotry of Buddy Dickson, his boss at the Blue Mountain Service Plaza. On his first day at the station, Will is under inquisition: "Fifteen steps from the pumps, Buddy Dickson paused. He faced Will, his dark eyes intense. 'Will Burk, are you saved? . . . Do you know Jesus as your personal savior?'" (26). When Will does not respond immediately, because he is holding in his impulse to retort "Hell no," Dickson punishes him by making him sweep the entire parking lot in the heat of the day. As Dickson conjures the memory of Will's dead mother, who "knew the way to heaven," he presses on with his obsessive rant. "I'm worried you don't, Will Burk. It has bothered me to no end that Sam [Will's father] let you wander into the dark depths of hell" (27). Such relentless moralizing by Dickson threads its way throughout the novel.

Even when Will is in the hospital recovering from life-threatening injuries, Dickson is unyielding in his pursuit to save Will's soul, as if this were his only mission in life. After giving Will a book on the birds of the Bible, Dickson launches into his rote speech: "You know, when I heard how bad you were burned, the first thing I thought was he's not saved. Will Burk is on Death's doorstep, and he might go to Hell. Might never see his mother or his father" (316). After Dickson deposits a Gideon Bible on Will's table and then leaves his room without saying another word, Will cusses Dickson in an internal dialogue that grows existential.

> Sure, it'd be nice to know what happened when you died. But no one knew. That's just how it was. So we made up stories to fill in the emptiness. . . . Heaven, the story. Hell, the story. God, the story. They might exist. They might not. Who knew? No reason. This was all there was, folks. And damn Dickson for thinking he knew more. Cicero knew more, that was for sure. From the day he hatched, he understood that *this* world was heaven, not the next world or the last one, but this one. He didn't fly around worrying about the future of his soul or about the sky falling. He just flew through that sky, sure of it. (317)

Will continues to share his thoughts on Cicero as he recalls all the Bibles and religious pamphlets Dickson has gifted him over the past months. Will smiles to himself over how "Cicero loved every one of them. He ripped the pages, shredding the onion-skin paper, and he made confetti of the pamphlets. When he flapped his wings, he made a biblical snowstorm, the words floating around the room" (317). Although Minick has fun with Cicero's destruction of the religious texts, he taps into Heideggerian ecophilosophy through Will's thought processes. According to Garrard, "Responsible humans have an implicit duty to let things disclose themselves in their own inimitable way, rather than forcing them into meanings and identities that suit their own instrumental values" (34). Will rails against the blind faith of Dickson and instead honors the completeness of Cicero, honoring Cicero as he inhabits his own being.

Acknowledging philosophical and moral problems with some of Heidegger's polemics, Garrard later cites Merleau-Ponty as one of Heidegger's heirs, who wrote against the "residual anthropocentrism of his mentor, emphasising instead that 'humans are enmeshed in the wild realm of the "actual world" as flesh of its flesh.' . . . Merleau-Ponty's phenomenology has encouraged ecocritics to highlight the sensuous pleasure of encounters with the 'flesh of world,' as distinct from the Puritan self-denial often wrongly associated with environmentalism" (35–36). Minick scorns Puritanical sanctimoniousness in the intense religious disputes between Ada and Reverend Zigler and between Will and Buddy Dickson. Through the "flesh of world" according to Cicero, readers understand the ecocritical necessity of embracing the material, while appreciating Merleau-Ponty's view of language as "gestural and emotionally expressive as well as conventional and denotative" (Garrard 36). Minick's characters reflect the complex, sometimes contradictory, relationships of the corporeal reality of nonhuman and human animals, social constructions, language, and ideologies.

Without a doubt *Fire Is Your Water* gestures toward an inclusiveness of both the nonhuman and the human, particularly as Cicero, Ada, and Will become intimately entwined over the course of the story. The novel represents a reconciled Christian ecocriticism encompassing the strengths of the religious tradition as it engages with and makes meaning of literature focused on the sacredness of the natural environment. The three characters are linked not only physically but also through the unconscious, whether via a dream uniting Cicero and Ada or via Will recovering in the hospital, "flying, black wings bright. Cicero chortling beside him, the wind gusting in great waves" (283). Cicero provides the most acute commentary on semiotics, namely meaning making, throughout the novel, beginning with a deep fascination with words, diving into a cynicism over their failures, and then resurfacing with an acknowledgment of their power. He admits, "I was wrong about what I said earlier—words are not all lies. . . . I just wish you people using these precious little stones would tell the damn truth more" (340). Indeed. And this is the admonishment Minick leaves with his readers, with Cicero, the high-spirited raven, delivering the message.

NOTE

1. Jim Minick, interview by Theresa Burriss, Radford, Va., July 10, 2017.

BIBLIOGRAPHY

Clark, Timothy. *The Cambridge Introduction to Literature and the Environment.* New York: Cambridge University Press, 2011.
Garrard, Greg. *Ecocriticism.* 2nd ed. New York: Routledge, 2012.
Glotfelty, Cheryll, and Harold Fromm. *The Ecocriticism Reader: Landmarks in Literary Ecology.* Athens: University of Georgia Press, 1996.
Higgins, James. Review of *Powwowing among the Pennsylvania Dutch: A Traditional Medical Practice in the Modern World. H-Net,* February 2017. http://www.h-net.org/reviews/showrev.php?id=47857.
Kriebel, David. *Powwowing among the Pennsylvania Dutch: A Traditional Medical Practice in the Modern World.* University Park: Penn State University Press, 2016.
Mabie, Joshua. "The Field Is Ripe: Christian Literary Scholarship, Postcolonial Ecocriticism, and Environmentalism." *Christianity and Literature* 65, no. 3 (2016): 279–97.
Minick, Jim. *Fire Is Your Water: A Novel.* Athens, Ohio: Swallow Press, 2017.
———. Personal communication with the author, July 10, 2017.
Offner, Judith. "Pow-Wowing: The Pennsylvania Dutch Way to Heal." *Journal of Holistic Nursing* 16, no. 4 (1998): 479–86.
Snyder, Gary. "Language Goes Two Ways." In *The Green Studies Reader: From Romanticism to Ecocriticism,* edited by Laurence Coupe, 127–31. London: Routledge, 2000.
Warners, David, Michael Ryskamp, and Randall Van Dragt. "Reconciliation Ecology: A New Paradigm for Advancing Creation Care." *Perspectives on Science and Christian Faith* 66, no. 4 (2014): 221–35.

"Forest Christian," a Poet of the River Lands
Wendell Berry in Appalachia

LUCAS NOSSAMAN

> This is a poet of the river lands,
> a lowdown man of the deepest
> depth of the valley, where gravity gathers
> the waters, the poisons, the trash,
> where light comes late and leaves early.
>
> —Wendell Berry, Sabbath I (2013)

Eco-spirituality, which seeks an open-ended relationship to the world and its visible and invisible forces, has been for some time now an important stream in the broad flow of ecocriticism.[1] Yet this subfield of ecocriticism can leave ecocritics with the sense that if a writer espouses a commitment to one religion over others, he or she is in some way limited or prone to narrow judgments. For example, while in *Slow Violence and the Environmentalism of the Poor* Rob Nixon relies on Wendell Berry's thinking, Nixon nonetheless worries that some American environmental writers tend toward "transcendentalism" rather than "transnationalism," and he relegates Berry to a group he calls the "bioregionalists" (238). Though Nixon does not directly address Berry's Christianity, he takes issue with his commitment to a local rather than a more global perspective. But a single religion, much like a single region (however much it inevitably overlaps with other bioregions or ecosystems with varying features), should not prevent ecocritics from recognizing a writer's contributions to the environmental cause or even to concerns of "transnational" environmental justice. In the case of Berry, much hope resides in the middle ground he inhabits between environmentalists concerned with justice and evangelical Christians, who by default often claim to be anti-environment. In particular, his Sabbath poetry, a fresh take on an old convention, imagines the potential for Christianity to be once again an earth-friendly religion. Through an unassuming artistry, the Sabbath verse invokes the Christian commitment to specific places and the cause of justice for neighbors, including those living far off, who have been affected by global capitalism's "creative destruction" of ecosystems.[2]

If one insists on being technical about region, Berry is actually not an Appalachian writer. He lives in the Kentucky River valley or, as it is sometimes called, the Outer Bluegrass region, but he daily perceives his relation to Appalachia by the pollutants and toxins carried through the mountains to his lower section of the river on his farm in Port Royal, Kentucky. He has long been opposed to strip mining, participating in public protests against the destruction of forest land, and he has long insisted that "the mentality that exploits and destroys the natural environment is the same that abuses racial and economic minorities" (Berry, "Think Little" 72). His Christian faith leads him to be attuned to the marginalized in both human and nonhuman communities. In the riverside cabin where he writes, the "long-legged house," as he calls it, he observes the effects of what we often "cannot see: the steady seeping of poison into our world and our bodies" ("Preface" 3). Or as he puts it in the poem quoted in my epigraph, Berry considers himself

> a poet of the river lands,
> a lowdown man of the deepest
> depth of the valley, where gravity gathers
> the waters, the poisons, the trash. (Sabbath I, 2013, in *This Day* 3)

From this vantage, it is impossible for him to ignore the relation to his mountain neighbors or to not feel with grief the ecological loss that is only part of a much larger crisis of land and people. It is thus vital for him to speak not of the "land alone or of the people alone, but always and only of both together."[3]

Yet here we return to the critical dilemma concerning Berry. Does this commitment to his local community in Port Royal and to his particular religious inheritance, Christianity—even as he recognizes other places and religions—encourage escapism and introspection rather than multicultural engagement and political action? In other words, are Berry's writings irrelevant to the contemporary environmental movement as it seeks a more "transnational" perspective? According to Nixon, "The concentric rings of the bioregionalists more often open out into transcendentalism than into transnationalism." Nixon fears that "placed" writers committed to a region will conceive of themselves as "spiritual" or "mystical" and, as a result, will downplay the sense of responsibility to other nations and people group (238). In using fairly nondescript words like "spiritual" and "mystical," though, it seems that Nixon has internalized most religions as dualistic. According to this view, it would seem that Christianity permits its members, because they are journeying toward heaven, to endure passively earth's travails and ignore any sense of impending environmental crisis. On this point, Berry would certainly agree that some Christians have been complacent, irresponsible, and impoverished readers of their own sacred text. But he also wonders if this understanding does justice to Christianity. He thinks a better reading of the Bible might correct the tendency for some evangelical Christians to declare themselves to be by default "anti-environment."[4]

This essay argues that Wendell Berry's poems and essays demonstrate that he mostly concurs with ecocritics in their understanding of pollution and ecological destruction as an issue of economic inequality and injustice on a global scale. However, his writings also represent an important middle place between evangelical Christians and more secular ecocritics concerned with environmental justice; for the latter, in turn, sometimes downplay the important roles of religion and region in constructing a responsible response to land abuse and destructive capitalist economics. Berry's Sabbath poetry in particular imagines what a commitment to a single land community involves in the long term. He envisions good work as done with a sense of the "whole": in Christian thinking, the harmonious Creation knit together by sacrificial, Christ-imitating acts of care.

Nixon's more convincing point than what he argues about global thinking has to do with what he calls "slow violence." The concept applies especially to Berry's Appalachia, though Nixon does not emphasize this connection. Slow violence underscores how ecological destruction often "occurs gradually and out of sight." It is a violence "of delayed destruction that is dispersed across time and space, an attritional violence that is typically not viewed as violence at all." But how might an individual *see* such a slow violence in order to respond to it? Nixon points to the work of imaginative writing to render the invisible visible, to challenge "perceptual habits" (2), and to traverse a "time span that exceeds the instance of observation or even the physiological life of the human observer" (15). In other words, one needs both to be situated in a specific temporal-spatial context *and* to transcend it through the work of imagination. Berry has remained long enough in his region of the Kentucky River valley to see and imagine the pollutants and toxins floating down the Kentucky River from strip mining and the ecological misuse of the region's rolling hills that has created gullies and washouts. In his early writing especially, pollution and land abuse of the local ecosystem frustrate the sense of pastoral reflection: "And now I find lying in the path an empty beer can. This is the track of the ubiquitous man Friday of all our woods. In my walks I never fail to discover some sign that he has preceded me. I find his empty shotgun shells, his empty cans and bottles, his sandwich wrappings. In wooded places along roadsides one is apt to find, as well, his overtraveled bedsprings, his outcast refrigerator, and heaps of the imperishable refuse of his modern kitchen" ("Native Hill" 195). One can hear echoes of Thoreau's "Slavery in Massachusetts" (1854): "The remembrance of my country spoils my walk. My thoughts are murder to the State, and involuntarily go plotting against her" (108). Even in 1965, for Berry there was no escaping the insidious effects of global capitalism. His writings were and are tinged with an awareness of there being no unpolluted place. For more than fifty years he has worked to cultivate his family's farm in an ecological way despite awareness of this disruption.

Based on his early writings, it might seem that Berry himself agrees with the critique that while Christianity encourages an awareness of sin, it provides little in the way of active response, encouraging spiritual escapism or perhaps desperate prayer. But as Berry observed in 1991,

> Work done in gratitude,
> Kindly, and well *is* prayer.
>
> ("Sabbath IX: The Farm," lines 195–96, in *This Day* 119)

Rather than turning away from his religious tradition, since the 1980s especially Berry has sought to map out a Christianity that encourages ecological care and kindly work, an active biblical response to the crisis that he has largely discovered on his own.[5] He continues to take issue with the modern evangelical church and its refusal, often enough, to acknowledge any kind of crisis of land and people. Yet he has called himself a "forest Christian."[6] What I take this phrase first to mean is that he identifies not only with the Bible's insistence on respect for God's creation but also with a Christian tradition of English poetry, starting most clearly with Chaucer and Spenser, which prioritizes Nature as God's "vicar."[7] Second—and even more practically—forest Christian refers to the fact that he feels most alive, most evidently a confessing Christian, while in the forest. For him, the Bible is "best read and understood outdoors": he often takes Sunday walks, meditating on Christian teachings in the woods rather than attending his local Baptist church.⁸ Ultimately, it is through his efforts to tend and properly imagine his farm with care that he most clearly senses that

> It is only the Christ-life,
> the life undying, given,
> received, again given,
> that completes our work. (Sabbath XIII, lines 12–15, in *Small Porch* 68)

How then might a forest Christian be better equipped to respond to issues of economic inequality and environmental injustice? Berry the forest Christian is also a poet of the river lands. On his Sabbath walks he encounters the problem of how to rest, and in walking from forest to river, he cannot help but be aware of the pollution covering the earth and haunting the human mind in this age. Even so, mere awareness of his connection to regional and global neighbors is different from the politically engaged response that Nixon seems to prize. My reading of the Sabbath poems insists that we recognize those passages in which the ecological crisis of Appalachia is an issue with global ramifications. In these passages, we see Berry refusing industrial solutions to problems caused by a worldwide lack of restraint in technological progress. He turns instead to an ecological ethic of care that he derives from the practical neighborly love that Christ taught and embodied. For Berry, this ethic means staying in Appalachia, doing good work in his hill country, *even when*, as his "Mad Farmer" puts it, one is made aware of the

> blasted mountains, the killed children, the bombed
> villages haunted already by the hurting bodies
> of their dead. (Sabbath XXI, lines 20–22, in *This Day* 397)

He insists on getting the word out in essays and the models of form in poetry as a responsible response to economic and environmental injustice. Though the Sabbath poems have always been concerned with the forest, Berry's emphasis on the watershed and his place as a river poet perhaps manifests even more vividly his faith and regional commitments. In this way, humility, the "lowdown" life of Christ, determines the shape of his Sabbath meditations in Appalachia.

❦

Gary Snyder was likely the first to fear that Berry's Sabbath poems would be unsavory to more secular environmentalists: "I can enjoy the poems, but not the theology" (54). After Snyder read the manuscript of the first Sabbath lyrics, he questioned the theological assumptions behind the project, the way Berry seemed to be skirting the line between a sort of quietism, a hearty acceptance of Christianity, and a radical reworking of the theological tradition. In the Sabbath poems, Berry indeed matures from naturalizing Christian vocabulary to a more precise understanding of what an ecological Christianity entails in the long term. Memorably, in the fourth poem from 1979, Berry writes, "The bell calls in the town," and

> I hear, but understand
> Contrarily, and walk into the woods, (lines 5–6, in *This Day*, 11–12)

conveying his rejection of institutional Christianity and his attempt to naturalize the Bible's teachings to correspond with the "strewn remnants of the primal Sabbath's hymn" he hears in the woods (line 36, in *This Day* 12). This naturalizing of Christianity, I argue, is problematic: Berry repeats the old pattern of finding the New World to be an Eden, even as he tries to remind himself that here is no "perfect garden." By the early 2000s, Berry is more pronounced in his need to clear out the old theology for a more rigorously Christian ecology. Witness Sabbath VII from 2008:

> If I'm a theologian
> I am one to the extent I have learned to duck
> when the small haughty doctrines fly overhead,
> dropping their loads of whitewash at random
> on the faces of those who look toward Heaven. (lines 13–17, in *This Day* 321)

For Berry at this point,

> Christmas
> night and Easter morning are this soil's only laws,

and he calls the reader to

> look down, look down, and save your soul
> by honester dirt, (lines 19–20 and 18–19, respectively, in *This Day* 321)

rejecting theological abstraction but cultivating faith in Christ's teachings as affirmed by the events of Christmas and Easter.

But to back up a little in the Sabbath project, Sabbath IX from 1991 indicates his desire to place his farm at Lanes Landing in a larger context, in which the forest ecosystem is the measure of his clearings:

> But make your land recall,
> In workdays of the fields,
> The Sabbath of the woods.

> Although your fields must bear
> The barbed seed of the Fall,
> Though nations yet make war
> For madness and for hire,
> By work in harmony
> With the God-given world
> You bring your days to rest,
> Remain a living soul.
> In time of hate and waste,
> Wars and rumors of wars,
> Rich armies and poor peace,
> Your blessed economy,
> Beloved sufficiency
> Upon a dear, small place,
> Sings with the morning stars. (lines 409–26, in *This Day* 125–26)

In this poem, the "primal Sabbath's hymn" is carried into the reality of wars, global inequality ("poor peace"), and the madness of limitless technological progress. The lines are more precisely measured compared to earlier Sabbath poems and the diction exact enough to carry both the fierceness of Berry's rejection of certain forms of dualistic Christianity and the affirmation of a "God-given world." I read this poem, which operates in Virgil's georgic mode, as a marked transition in the Sabbath project, for Berry is beginning to recognize the ecological principle of Sabbath rest for his land.[9] Yet at this point (1991) it is unclear how the Gospel teachings of Christ fit into the picture.

In part, what Berry is wrestling with in the early Sabbath lyrics is how to be content. He himself is unsure of what he wants or what would count as peaceable living:

> What more did I
> think I wanted? Here is
> what has always been, (lines 21–23, in *This Day* 201)

he tells himself in Sabbath VII from 1999. Following Nixon's critique, we might read this struggle as emphasizing a place of privilege, Berry with his stand of woods in which to contemplate the Creation, which the poor lack and which poorer nations are stripped of through the destructive practices of global capitalism. But we can also read these lyrics as preparation for a greater engagement with the economic problem of land abuse and pollution in Appalachia and beyond, an engagement that occurs in later poems. Moreover, the question arises in these personal lyrics of just what is required to be content: what counts as an abundant life? In Sabbath VII from 1999, he realizes how easy it is to refuse the "lesson" of

> how small a thing
> can be pleasing, how little
> in this hard world it takes
> to satisfy the mind
> and bring it to its rest. ("Sabbaths 1999 VII," lines 2–6, in *This Day* 201)

Here we can draw parallels to Berry's discussion of John 10:10: "I am come that they may have life, and that they might have it more abundantly" ("Burden" 133–34). Unless there is a consensus of what an "abundant life" entails, an agreement about the pleasure small miracles can bring—flowers by the roadside, birds on the telephone wire, squirrels on the rooftop—the goal of achieving "environmental justice" becomes synonymous with getting the marginalized to a place of technological advancement. Elsewhere, Berry speaks of the "two kinds of oppression" of forcing people off the land only to fill in the labor with migrant workers ("Prejudice" 111). Technological solutions often multiply the economic problem, transferring the labor to people from whom it can be extracted even more cheaply. Consequently, the problem of form in the Sabbath lyrics is more complicated than it might seem at a first glance, for Berry strives to imagine the kind of rest that is not an evasion from work but rather a rest that renews work by understanding what rest is from an ecological perspective. As he puts it in the introduction to his collected Sabbath poems, the problem is how "to come to rest in the presence of time, error, and mortality ... in knowing of all that human beings have done and are doing to damage the given world, and in knowing one's own complicity in that damage" (*This Day* xxii). Finding the means to speak of rest in the midst of this knowledge, to imagine wholeness without evading hard realities—this is the task Berry puts before himself.

Rest in the Sabbath poems, as a result, is a confrontation with his place, the way that the global economy, which runs ceaselessly, disrupts even the *thought* of rest in a place. This confrontation with the world as it is, we will see, is the way of the Incarnation, a connection Berry increasingly recognizes in the later lyrics. Berry's woods are by the "loud road"; they admittedly are woods where "you can still see the marks of cropland erosion now mostly healed and healing," and so it takes patience to hear the birds singing in the trees, perhaps patience until the

> last
> of the dire machines has passed,

> burning the world, and the burning
> has ceased.
>
> (This Day xxi; Sabbath IX, 2005,
lines 14–17, in This Day 269)

But the forms of poetry, Berry finds, can serve as forms of renewal to prepare him to address larger issues of his region and nation. Brief, arresting moments of beauty, tainted as they are by the ongoing crisis, are possible for the mind working to heal.

Yet in the later lyrics Berry is more concerned with the economic problems he encounters in the Sabbath meditations, going beyond moments of beauty to a practical response also born out of his Christianity. In "A Forest Conversation," Berry describes the economic dilemma of logging in Appalachia and the reason why families often feel forced to clear-cut their woods:

> "We need money," a forest-owning family decides. "We'll sell our trees." "The environment" being in fashion, the family takes comfort in the thought that after the marketable trees are gone, many smaller trees will remain as the "next crop." And so they sell their "standing timber" to a logging company, whose representative comes in and marks every tree that can be sold.
>
> And then, all too often, a sawyer and a driver of a mechanical skidder, employees of the logging company, arrive with, inevitably, the single purpose of cutting and removing the marked trees as quickly, which is to say as cheaply, as possible. The logging company is in every sense an absentee, and of all short-term economies in forestry, the absentee logging company's is the shortest. (23)

According to Berry, "The woods is left a shambles, for nobody thought of the forest rather than the trees" (24). In his opinion the woods, fragmented through small landholdings designated for competing purposes, ought to be respected as a whole, and clearly that has not been the case in the Appalachian region, where too often strip mining "destroys the forest virtually forever" ("Compromise" 22). Who or what can teach us to respect the integrity of the woods in the face of supposed economic realities of profit margins and "job creation"? Berry turns to English pastoral poetry and the Christian tradition of Nature as God's vicar as a means of integrative thinking, beginning as they do with "sympathy" for the land and people rather than economics in the abstract.[10]

One critic has emphasized the kind of creed Berry believes, in his words, "that the world was created and approved by love, that it subsists, coheres, and endures by love, and that, insofar as it is redeemable, it can be redeemed only by love."[11] That was written in 1995; by the early 2000s, Berry recognizes that Christ's teachings are essential and intimately practical when it comes to living out this "indwelling" love, so that by 2014, in his long essay concerning the origins of "dame Nature," he can speak of the inextricable connection between Christ's teachings about loving neighbors and enemies, and the biblical passages that call for care of creation. He believes the practical application of Nature as God's vicar is congruent with the Gospel teachings of Christ, which impress on him the sense that all of life is holy if we learn to perceive it aright: "This neighborly love [of Christ] cannot be a merely human transaction, for you cannot love your neighbor while you destroy the earth and its community of creatures on which you and your neighbor mutually depend" (Berry, "Presence" 108).

As a result, in later poems about the forest, such as those included in the sequence titled "A Small Porch in the Woods" from the 2014 Sabbath poems, we see him returning to the wholeness, the sense of a "holy" life, a healthy forest strived for. This sense of holiness now calls for a practical response:

> Loving the forest,
> you enter it to walk and watch.
> As you observe its manifold and comely life,
> it enters familiarly into imagination,
> and so into sympathy. By sympathy
> the mind in the forest is made at home.
> From knowledge of the forest comes
> at last knowledge of forestry:
> what, without permanent damage,
> can be spared and carefully removed,
> leaving the forest whole. This learning
> "takes decades. That's all there is to it."

(Sabbath VIII: A Small Porch in the Woods,
2014, sec. 10, lines 14–25, in *Small Porch* 26)[12]

It is rare for a poet to slide from sylvan reflection to forestry, but Berry is not satisfied to glean from the Bible the idea of harmony with nature. He is interested now in the practical sympathy of the Good Samaritan, loving the forest and the people who take their living from it, a sympathy he believes cousin to divine love indwelling in the natural world. The blend of religious reflection and practical love hinges on a carefully chosen vocabulary: "loving" the forest in all its "manifold and comely life," "imagination" and "sympathy," and "whole." For Berry, these words carry religious connotations further explained in his essays, though sometimes precisely and directly stated in the Sabbath poems, as in the point about wholeness in Sabbath XIII from 2015:

> It is only the Christ-life,
> the life undying, given,
> received, again given,
> that completes our work.
>
> (lines 12–15, in A Small Porch 68)

In *The Unsettling of America*, the etymological relationships of health, wholeness, and holiness capture his imagination and suggest not only spiritual but also ecological healing: "It becomes clear that the health or wholeness of the body is a vast subject, and that to preserve it calls for a vast enterprise" (103). Especially in the later poems, the forest becomes a place for Berry to imagine the web of relationships between his Christianity and the ecological principles of good use. In this effort, Sabbath rest is an immensely useful concept, allowing him to stand apart from his work and refresh his sense of the "whole."

In the Sabbath poems, Berry has also consistently written about the Kentucky River and the creeks of his native community that drain into it. Especially in the post-2000 lyrics, the watershed becomes a place for him to contemplate the economic problems of water use and to perceive how the fate of his land is connected to the fate of his region. As a means of contrast, consider one of his early river lyrics—there is a longing for wholeness unanswered by the farming practices of Berry, at least from what we can gather from the poem:

> Bottles and wrappers of expensive
> cheap feasts ride the quieted current
> toward the Gulf of Mexico.
>
> And now the breeze comes down
> from the hill, the kingfisher returns
> to the dead limb of the sycamore,
> the swallows feed in the air
> over the water.
>
> (Sabbath IV, 1985, lines 8–12, in This Day 66)

From the Kentucky River in the mountains to the Ohio River, then following the Mississippi, trash journeys slowly, often imperceptibly, to zones of waste. What strikes us is the shift with "and now"—a sudden transformation, the miracle of Sabbath wrought from beyond any human making:

> Out of the frenzy of an August Sunday
> the Sabbath comes. The valley glows.

> A raincrow flies across the river
> Into the shadowy leaves. The dark falls.
>
> <div align="right">(Sabbath IV, 1985, lines 18–21, in <i>This Day</i> 66)</div>

With this conclusion, what is the poet to do but watch and wait for such moments of transformation, from an August Sunday to a holy Sabbath, moments that are "religious" and yet do not seem to provoke a practical response? In the later lyrics, Berry goes beyond observation and passive worship of the divine miracle of renewal in nature. For, truth be told, if one is always dependent on these mystical moments of transformation, a depression follows—"The dark falls"—in the knowledge that moments of heightened awareness are fleeting, short-lived.

Yet neither are practical responses a complete guarantee of joy—this is where Christianity comes into play with its hope of eternity, not as escape from travail but as extension of the kingdom of heaven Christ taught about for this present life. Paradoxically, as Berry grows more cognizant of these teachings, he is, it seems, brought down to the level of the watershed, the "lowlife" he perceives as connecting him to Appalachia. Critics have noticed this sense of humility in his poetic, which to some extent is present even in the early lyrics.[13] But the practical nature of humility, to be aware of one's close proximity to the soil and yet still make a living from it, is more explicit in the post-2000 poems. In general, the river poems are less frequent—probably because his Sabbath walks tend toward the forest—but on rainy days, and perhaps days when rest seems to come more by staying put than taking a walk in the woods, Berry reflects on the creeks, branches, and the river near the long-legged house.

In Sabbath III from 2000, he reflects on God's "timeless life" passing into "this world," "as timely as a river" (lines 1–2, in *This Day* 207). For Berry there is a message of incarnation in the river, along with the passing of life to death, divine in its cycle. But more than adhering to a sense of natural cycles, he believes that like the river,

> we are completely filled
> With breath of love, in us
> Forever incomplete.
>
> <div align="right">(lines 13–15, in <i>This Day</i> 207)</div>

The river teaches about beauty, about embodiment and the change it brings in time, while it also evokes the "breath of love," the breath of Christ on his disciples after the Resurrection. The religious allusion, though, invokes a practical meaning—see the need for the life of the river, but recognize through love your limitation, the sense of incompletion ("forever incomplete") in your work of ecological healing. The farm has limits, as it is shaped by the river's transformations and by the growth and change of the nearby forest. While the forest poems at times tend toward the heavens by an airy contemplation of the treetops, the river poems flow downward, following the way of love to the lowest of spots. This agrees with Berry's preference for Nature, "a more lowly presence" compared to the concept of the Trinity in the Christian faith, for Nature is "holy yet familiar, matronly, practical, concerned, eager to teach." Though orthodox Christians might wince at this somewhat dismissive judgment about the Trinity, clearly Berry is working against the duality of body and soul present in some forms of Christianity, and he seeks to recover the full implication of the Incarnation for the Christian practice of Jesus's teachings ("Presence" 115).

In a 2002 Sabbath poem dedicated to Denise Levertov, a Catholic poet, Berry meditates on the lowly presence of the river, recalling at the same time Christian humility through the word "flesh":

> To know what flesh inherits
> learn the art of the little boat,
> leave the solid footing,
> row out upon the water.   (Sabbath VI, lines 22–25, in *This Day* 229)

Like Peter stepping out of the boat toward Jesus in the storm, the poet must act on faith and take the way of humility to see "what flesh inherits." Here Berry is reflecting on Levertov's attention to organic form and natural detail, and he wonders what the water would teach: sometimes it instructs one about peace, sometimes about death, sometimes about ignorance and unknowing. It can be a place for small miracles, like a fish leaping out, or a yellow warbler "in the curtain of wild grape along the steep shore." These miracles, though, do not remove the poet in transcendental rapture from natural life but rather return him to his concern for the river as "bedeviled by the engines / of the utterly displaced," to watch for many years and "imagine it, rising, light drawn, invisibly, / up into the air. (lines 65–66 and 73–75, in *This Day* 231)

Staying close to the water's surface, the poet attempts to imagine what it would mean to live in the watershed as a peaceable creature. This is no small task, for as other river poems attest, the poisoned waters can change one's perspective and language in an instant.

In observing the effects of pollutants traveling down the mountains from strip mining and pesticides draining from industrial-style farms, Berry knows the Kentucky River is no safe zone. But the proper way of imagination is *through* this river, not beyond it in a kind of Platonic transcendence of the world. In Sabbath III from 2006, called "The Book of Camp Branch,"

Berry recognizes that "here is / no 'fortification against time'" (lines 21–22, in *This Day* 285). Although this longer meditation begins by seeming to prioritize his "native stream," the close proximity to his birthplace and his family history, the poet discovers that

> the language too
> descends through time, subserving
> false economy, heedless power,
> blown with the gas of salesmanship,
> rattled with the sale of needless war. (lines 91–95, in *This Day* 288)

Camp Branch joins the downward flow—the water seeks the "level that is lowest," flowing toward the gathering place of the trash and toxins at the lower end of the Kentucky River as it opens up to the Ohio (line 141, in *This Day* 289). His poetry, consequently, must join these "tumbling waters," or else the work will be false, an escape from reality:

> The song changes by singing
> into a different song.
> It sings by falling. The water
> descending in its old groove
> wears it new. The words descending
> to the page render the possible
> into the actual, by wear,
> for better or worse, renew
> the wearied mind. This is only
> the lowly stream of Camp Branch,
> but every stream is lowly. (lines 128–138, in *This Day* 289)

The farm drains into the river, but the river also shapes the farm: the relationship is akin to a marriage, "for better or worse." As Berry describes the interaction in a 2003 interview, "Living downstream from somebody is a predicament, and you would ask certain things of the upstream people if you had the power to do it. You would be interested in what they do with their sewage, and the way they manage their mountain sides, and so on" (Grubbs 155). But rather than denounce his neighbors in this poem, the poet seeks to participate in the changing nature of the river, and thus become a "stone rolled away," an allusion to the Resurrection. We see here Berry's refusal to propose, at least in this poem, large-scale political solutions that would force his upriver neighbors to change. Through love of his place, and then even of his enemies who have damaged the river, the poet begins to participate in the song of Camp Branch:

> It flows as deep in its hollow
> as it can go, far down as it has
> worn its way. Passing down
> over its plunder of rocks, it makes
> an irregular music. Here
> is what I want to know. Here
> is what I am trying to say. (lines 14–20, in *This Day* 285)

The enjambment, the tumbling from line to line like water over rocks, keeps a kind of music, however "irregular" it may be. The utter commitment to "here" is not so that Berry can discover the "secret" meaning of nature's riddle. What he seeks to know and seeks to say is song itself, not sense only: the poet desires participation in the reality that is his native stream and its inextricability from the river and the Appalachian region. To be a "forest Christian" and river poet is not to escape to an otherworldly, "spiritual" realm; it is to face and oppose—as Berry has done over his long career—mountaintop removal, pollution, and industrial agriculture by way of a particular, cultivated love for a place. "People inevitably destroy what they do not understand," Berry wrote in 1972, insisting on small acts of conservation and kindly use to combat the wrongs of corporate greed ("Think Little" 77). "The Book of Camp Branch" turns to the place for a clearer understanding of the fate of all waters when they are kept to their natural paths. The economic implication is that this requires kindly use, whereas the thoughtless attempt to farm the rolling hills creates gullies and washouts. Reckless farming hardly requires the landowner to be

> walking and thinking, balanced
> on unsure footholds
> in the flowing stream. (Sabbaths 2006 III, lines 106–8,
> lines 91–95, in *This Day* 288)

When Berry is attuned to the watershed, he uses the terms of humility and lowliness, drawn from the figure of Nature as God's vicar and from the practical love of Christ. Indeed, the latter source seems most at play in these later lyrics concerned with the watershed.

Perhaps Sabbath XX from 2013 best illustrates his identifying as a river poet and "forest Christian"; here he is registering his region's devastation through the Christian teachings he inherits. In this poem he calls himself "The lowlife poet moreover / is the poet of a 'backwater,' / a 'boondock,' a 'nowhere,' / where life starts, yes, / from low down." ("Sabbaths 2013," lines 1–5, in *Sewanee Review* 562). His "nowhere," which he says is his only "where," the "only consciousness he has," puns on the Christian concept of creation *ex nihilo*, the miracle of life as totally from God's delight. Identifying with this nowhere, a place in marginal Appalachia, gives him the proper perspective to attest to miracles. It grants him the "lowdown" perspective to witness what is not of his making or art:

> from high up, from the soil,
> the sunlight, the falling rain,
> joining Heaven and Earth.

(Sabbaths 2013 XX, lines 6–8, in *Sewanee Review* 562)

With scare quotes around "backwater," "boondock," and "nowhere," Berry seems to understand that some readers will take issue with his local and therefore limited perspective, stumbling also on the notion that only from his vantage can Heaven be glimpsed, while others elsewhere suffer the insidious effects of global capitalism, even while other writings by Berry attest to this being no safe place: Sabbath II from 2007 says that one

> [goes] from the corrupted nation
> to the ruining country.

(lines 6–8, in *This Day* 299)

The question looms, should the poet "move on" to a broader perspective, a "transnational" meditation of sorts beyond the boondocks? Yet he insists that,

> .... this lowly where
> is reached by every visible
> flicker of the universe, to which
> it is central, for it is the center
> of the poet's half-lighted mind,
> the only consciousness he has.
> So it is his limitation
> that gives due honor
> to this place............

(Sabbath XX, 2013, lines 13–21, in *Sewanee Review* 562)

The qualifying phrase starting with "for" is Berry's reminder that what we experience is going to be limited, perhaps even biased in unforeseen ways. But the phrasing of light and the universe's center recalls T. S. Eliot and Dante, for if the poet as a pilgrim of sorts remains humble, in this case attuned to the watershed, he or she may indeed imagine how

> on that Point
> depend all nature and all of the heavens,

as Dante put it (canto XXVIII, lines 41–42, 554).[14] And like Dante's pilgrim falling away after the beatific vision in *Paradiso*, Berry says it is his

> limitation
> that gives due honor
> to this place.   (Sabbaths 2013 XX, lines 19–21,
> in *Sewanee Review* 562)

Speak no more than necessary, enough to point to the witnessed miracle; for him, humility is more important than "transnational" awareness, the humility of the Christ hymn in Philippians 2: "in lowliness of mind let each esteem other better then themselves . . . Let this mind be in you, which was also in Christ Jesus" (3, 5). With the grace of lucid phrasing, this Sabbath poem works in the Christian tradition while capturing Berry's longtime insistence on the overlooked, often discarded places and the need for practical, ecological kindness in them.

This by no means excludes the need for political action. Instead, it is precisely by acknowledging these "nowheres" and the people for whom the nowhere is central—in other words, by recognizing what Nixon calls the "vernacular" rather than the "official landscapes"—that we might begin to preserve our sanity in political action (16).

In Sabbath I from 2013, Berry recognizes that his

> . . . poems
> are creatures of the shore that the river
> gnaws, dissolves, and carries away.

The poems themselves are

> leavings, sheddings, gathered
> from the light.   (lines 16–18 and 22–23, in *This Day* 3)

This stepping out of the poetic practice, in recognition of the limitations of what a poet can accomplish, reveals Berry's deep respect for place and the Creator's work in it. Humility returns him to the quiet, often unrewarding work of the land, the effort to recover Christian neighborliness toward the forest and the watershed. The poet watches the river for "ripples, flashes, signs" not as a mystic, but as a citizen of his place and region. To be a citizen requires he clean up his own trash, the vanity of poetic practice to strive for lasting glory, praise for the well-wrought artistic creation. Berry has said that during his Sabbath walks, his mind "becomes hospitable to unintended thoughts: to what I am very willing to call inspiration. The poems come incidentally, or they do not come at all. If the Muse leaves me alone, I leave her alone. To be quiet, even wordless, in a good place is a better gift than poetry" ("This Day: An Introduction," in *This Day* xxi). The thought recalls Eliot in *Four Quartets*:

> The poetry does not matter
> It was not (to start again) what one had expected.[15]

In general, though, Berry's point in Sabbath I from 2013 would irk ecocritics taking a more hardline secular perspective, for evidently religion leads here to a form of renunciation: the poet seems to withdraw from the task of advocating a response to the environmental destruction that trashes the river. The renunciation, if it is such, would ignore all the injustice and inequality surely reigning elsewhere in favor of a "recollection in tranquility" clearly not available to all. But for Berry, to take up strident resistance in the public sphere is to risk replicating the industrial mind by proposing big political solutions to what are often practical, close to the ground issues. As the record shows, Berry is not opposed to political action—why else would he continue to advocate for the fifty-year farm bill?—but he does remain skeptical of political action as an ultimate solution to our crisis.[16] In an essay on civil disobedience, he notes that "it is a mistake to make your opposition conditional upon winning. . . . I am in this struggle with the firm intention of winning, but I don't forget that I first wrote against strip mining in 1965. If I had required even reasonable expectation of victory, I would have given up long ago" ("About" 107).

And so Berry returns to his Christian faith. He believes in the ecological implications in Jesus's teachings as a radical means of renewal. Ultimately this turn to religion calls upon a whole faith community and suggests that small-scale communities elsewhere, including churches, can take up the practices Berry illuminates in his poems and essays. In Berry's Sabbath project, Christianity becomes a means of confronting a world of illusions, but it is also and finally the end goal: the Sabbath poems look forward to a heavenly kingdom that would fulfill the good work done on earth.

In *Laudato si'*, Pope Francis says there is a need for "true wisdom, as the fruit of self-examination, dialogue and generous encounter between persons" concerned for the environment (28). Recognizing that a spectrum of solutions exist in response to the crisis, Francis knows that dialogue is essential among groups with varying commitments. For the most part, the environmental movement has consisted of an urban or suburban population concerned about wilderness and political solutions addressing climate change, and with this background and focus, Berry's rural, Christian perspective, on the margins of Appalachia, is easily ignored. The broad appeal of a figure like Pope Francis demonstrates that people of faith can play a role and can bring a further range of responses to the table of environmental action. The Sabbath poems reveal Berry's self-identification as a "forest Christian" and a poet of the river lands, and his burden has been to figure out how Christian reflection can remain practical, rooted, and moreover, sensible to those of a more secular mind. The result is a fresh form of ecological Christianity that acknowledges the "whole" of nature as God's vicar, and the lordship of Christ as the bearer of practical, neighborly love.

NOTES

1. See, for instance, the various "pathways" invoked in Katie Rigby's "Spirits That Matter: Pathways toward a Rematerialization of Religion and Spirituality": ecocriticism in relation to Daoism, Buddhism, Aboriginal spirituality, Christianity, and (post-Christian) feminist spirituality, and any mixture of these.
2. Berry derides the euphemism in "Our Deserted Country," in *Our Only World*, 147.
3. Berry, "Local Economies to Save the Land and the People," in *Our Only World*, 58.
4. See in particular Berry's essay "Christianity and the Survival of Creation," in which he addresses the issue of dualism in Christianity. There is still some debate over whether Berry holds consistently to Christian faith or not. Phillip Donnelly contends that Berry's occasionally imprecise use of theological terms serves to "communicate his [agrarian-environmental] vision to Christians who might otherwise dismiss out of hand, or misunderstand, his relationship to Christian tradition" (292). D. G. Hart gently criticizes Berry for failing "to see how the ways of the institutional church, no matter how flawed in practice, actually resonate with his call for sensitivity to the interrelatedness of body and soul, the created order and the world of the spirit" (134).
5. See Berry, "The Gift of Good Land" (1981). Ellen Davis's *Scripture, Culture, and Agriculture: An Agrarian Reading of the Bible* (2008) was a "pleasure" and "a help" (ix), as Berry noted in his foreword to it. For a useful chronology of Berry's engagements with Christianity, see Bilbro, "When Did Wendell Berry Start Talking Like a Christian?"
6. For the phrase "forest Christian," see the March 11, 1983, letter to Gary Snyder in Wriglesworth 107 and the 1983 interview with the *Bloomsbury Review* included in Grubbs 19–26.
7. See Berry's "The Presence of Nature in the Natural World: A Long Conversation."
8. See Berry, "Christianity and the Survival of Creation," 103, and "This Day: An Introduction," in *This Day*, xxi–xxvi.
9. Marc Hudson places Berry's Sabbath poetry in the "Christian Georgic tradition" (184), while Laird Christensen calls "The Farm" "surely one of our greatest georgic poems" (173).
10. Berry, "A Forest Conversation," in *Our Only World* 48.
11. Bilbro, *Loving God's Wildness* 138–40; Berry, "Health Is Membership" 89.

12. The final line is a quote from Troy Firth in "A Forest Conversation," 48.
13. See especially Norman Wirzba, "The Dark Night of the Soil." Harold Bush also notes Berry's "humble understatement" in "Wendell Berry, Seeds of Hope," 302.
14. The pilgrim's Lady continues, "Observe the circle nearest it, and know / the reason for its spinning at such speed / is that Love's fire burns it into motion" (lines 43–45). In this vision, divine love keeps the world intact.
15. Eliot, "East Coker," in *Four Quartets*, 184.
16. Berry, "For the 50-Year Farm Bill," in *Our Only World*, 159–65.

BIBLIOGRAPHY

Alighieri, Dante. *The Divine Comedy*. In *The Portable Dante*, translated and edited by Mark Musa. New York: Penguin, 1995.

Berry, Wendell. "About Civil Disobedience." In *It All Turns on Affection: The Jefferson Lecture and Other Essays*, 103–9. Berkeley, Calif.: Counterpoint, 2012.

———. "The Burden of the Gospels." In *The Way of Ignorance, and Other Essays*, 127–37. Berkeley, Calif.: Counterpoint, 2005.

———. "Christianity and the Survival of Creation." In *Sex, Economy, Freedom, and Community: Eight Essays*, 93–116. New York: Pantheon, 1993.

———. "Compromise, Hell!" In *The Way of Ignorance, and Other Essays*, 21–27. Berkeley, Calif.: Counterpoint, 2005.

———. *Conversations with Wendell Berry*. Edited by Morris Allen Grubbs. Jackson: University Press of Mississippi, 2007.

———. "The Gift of Good Land." In *The Gift of Good Land: Further Essays, Cultural and Agricultural*, 267–81. New York: North Point Press, 1981.

———. "Health Is Membership." In *Another Turn of the Crank: Essays*, 86–109. Berkeley, Calif.: Counterpoint, 1995.

———. "A Native Hill." In *The Long-Legged House*, 170–213. Berkeley: Shoemaker & Hoard, 2004.

———. *Our Only World: Ten Essays*. Berkeley, Calif.: Counterpoint, 2015.

———. "Preface." In *Waste Land: Meditations on a Ravaged Landscape, Photographs and Essays*, by David T. Hanson, 3 vols. New York: Aperture Foundation, 1997.

———. "The Prejudice Against Country People." In *Citizenship Papers*, 107–12. Berkeley: Shoemaker & Hoard, 2004.

———. "The Presence of Nature in the Natural World: A Long Conversation." In *The Art of Loading Brush: New Agrarian Writings*, 103–75. Berkeley, Calif.: Counterpoint, 2017.

———. "Sabbaths 2013." *Sewanee Review*, 122, no. 4 (2014): 552–62.

———. *A Small Porch: Sabbath Poems 2014 and 2015. Together with The Presence of Nature in the Natural World*. Berkeley, Calif.: Counterpoint, 2016.

———. "Think Little." In *A Continuous Harmony: Essays Cultural and Agricultural*, 71–85. San Diego: Harcourt Brace Jovanovich, 1972.

———. *This Day: Collected and New Sabbath Poems, 1979–2013*. Berkeley, Calif.: Counterpoint, 2013.

———. *The Unsettling of America: Culture and Agriculture*. San Francisco: Sierra Club Books, 1977.

Bilbro, Jeffrey. *Loving God's Wildness: The Christian Roots of Ecological Ethics in American Literature*. Tuscaloosa: University of Alabama Press, 2015.

———. "When Did Wendell Berry Start Talking Like a Christian?" *Christianity and Literature* 68, no. 2 (2019): 272–96.
Bush, Harold K. "Wendell Berry, Seeds of Hope, and the Survival of Creation." *Christianity and Literature* 56, no. 2 (2007): 297–316.
Christensen, Laird. "Spirit Astir in the World: Wendell Berry's Sacramental Poetry." *Renascence* 52, no. 2 (2000): 163–81.
Davis, Ellen F. *Scripture, Culture, and Agriculture: An Agrarian Reading of the Bible*. Cambridge: Cambridge University Press, 2008.
Donnelly, Phillip J. "Biblical Convocation in Wendell Berry's *Remembering*." *Christianity and Literature* 56, no. 2 (2007): 275–96.
Eliot, T. S. *Four Quartets* (1943). In *Collected Poems: 1909–1962*. San Diego: Harcourt, 1991.
Grubbs, Morris Allen, ed. *Conversation with Wendell Berry*. Jackson: University Press of Mississippi, 2007.
Hart, David Bentley. *The Beauty of the Infinite: The Aesthetics of Christian Truth*. Grand Rapids, Mich.: Eerdmans, 2004.
Hart, D. G. "Wendell Berry's Unlikely Case for Conservative Christianity." In *The Humane Vision of Wendell Berry*, edited by Mark T. Mitchell and Nathan Schlueter, 124–46. Wilmington, Del.: ISI Books, 2011.
The Holy Bible: 1611 Edition, King James Version. Peabody, Mass.: Hendrickson Press, 2010.
Hudson, Marc. "Instantaneous and Eternal: Wendell Berry's Sabbath Poems." *Sewanee Review* 123, no. 1 (2015): 182–91.
Nixon, Rob. *Slow Violence and the Environmentalism of the Poor*. Cambridge, Mass.: Harvard University Press, 2011.
Pope Francis. *Encyclical on Climate Change and Inequality: On Care for Our Common Home*. New York: Melville House, 2015.
Rigby, Katie. "Spirits That Matter: Pathways toward a Rematerialization of Religion and Spirituality." In *Material Ecocriticism*, edited by Serenella Iovino and Serpil Oppermann, 283–90. Bloomington: Indiana University Press, 2014.
Thoreau, Henry D. "Slavery in Massachusetts." In *Reform Papers*, edited by Wendell Glick, 91–109. Princeton, N.J.: Princeton University Press, 1973.
Wirzba, Norman. "The Dark Night of the Soil: An Agrarian Approach to Mystical Life." *Christianity and Literature* 56, no. 2 (2007): 253–73.
Wriglesworth, Chad. *Distant Neighbors: The Selected Letters of Wendell Berry and Gary Snyder*. Berkeley, Calif.: Counterpoint, 2014.

Conflict and Resolution
Eco-environmentalism in Charles Frazier's Antiwar Novel *Cold Mountain*

SYLVIA BAILEY SHURBUTT

Poet, novelist, and storyteller Ron Rash, in his poem "Signs," writes about the significance of the natural world to Appalachians; the lines are immensely insightful in understanding the central focus of the fiction of his friend Charles Frazier:

> My older kin always believed
> in looking backward to explain
> the here and now, always a sign
> present in the past each time
> a barn burned down, a life was lost.
> So like boys turning over stones
> to find what dark had hid from day,
> they'd turnover in their minds
> the way the mare turned from its stall
> as if she smelled hay smoldering,
> a living hand so damp and cold
> it seemed already in the grave.
> And so I learned to see the world
> as language one might understand
> but only when translated by
> signs first forgotten or misread.

When disillusioned Confederate soldier Inman steps through his hospital window to begin his long and dangerous journey home, in Charles Frazier's 1997 novel *Cold Mountain*, he understands that this journey will be the "axle" of his life (71). Wounded in both body and soul, Inman is far more than a war-weary Odysseus trekking his way homeward: he is coming to terms with a deeper understanding of his connection with the land and those who "tenant" it and the relationship of the two in terms of survival. That understanding is Inman's "roadmap" for discerning our human place in this physical world, an understanding that counters the disharmony of the man-made conflict and destruction that augers the chaos and despair of war and other human disasters. This essay explores that journey toward enlightenment, both Inman's trek homeward to North Carolina and his love Ada's parallel journey of discovery about her own place in the natural world. The philosophic and environmental lessons of Charles Frazier's uncommon antiwar novel offer a moral imperative to the reader about honoring and respecting the Earth on which we live, as well as honoring each other as the human caretakers of the planet.

Cold Mountain has had a range of interpretations, with each scholar contributing to our understanding of the complexity of its structure and the depth of its ideas. Some of the more engaging studies of the book include McCarron and Knoke's exploration of the animal topology, double characters, and parallelisms in the text ("Images of War and Peace: Parallelism and Antithesis in the Beginning and Ending of *Cold Mountain*") and Piacentino's study of the cross-racial bonding and the exploration of "other-directed sensitivity" (113). Terry Gifford has written about the importance of landscape in what he calls the "post-pastoral" qualities of *Cold Mountain* and its connection to the work of Cormac McCarthy, while Ava Chitwood has attempted to discern the philosophical context for *Cold Mountain*, interpreting the book as a tension between Homeric and Heraclitean ideas, with the work of Heraclitus offering a counterbalance and tension against the heroic epic—Heraclitus being a fourth-century pre-Socratic philosopher who challenged humankind to understand and discourse with nature.[1] Each critic is insightful, and each brings to light some facet of the rich and thoughtful tapestry of Frazier's Civil War tale, but it is clear from looking at all of Frazier's work that the physical landscape itself plays the most significant role in conveying his ideas about the humans who inhabit the natural world, bringing war and destruction on each other and on the environment around them.

Cold Mountain, written in the tradition of Stephen Crane's *Red Badge of Courage* and Ernest Hemingway's *A Farewell to Arms*, is one of the great antiwar novels in American literature. That said, it is clear from the beginning Frazier was immersed and enthralled in the splendors of the natural world. In a 2016 interview published in volume 9 of the *Anthology of Appalachian Writers*, he says this about the influence of place on his thinking:

> During the time I was working on my [PhD] dissertation I lived in Colorado and spent a great deal of time hiking, biking, and skiing. I was also writing a trekking guide for Sierra Club Books on Ecuador, Peru, and Bolivia, and walking hundreds of miles a year in the northern Andes. So I was more immersed than usual in the outdoor world, especially mountain landscapes. The dissertation ["The Geographic Possibility: Man and Landscape in Recent West Fiction"], in a sense, forced me to look more closely at the sense of place, the ways people and cultures are shaped by natural environments, about how landscape shaped the American personality and American literature. (43)

Like the work of Robert Morgan, Frazier's writing is more Naturalistic than Romantic, certainly in the brutal realism of the conflict it portrays, but there is a pointedly Romantic counterbalance throughout the book that is necessary for the resolution that Frazier offers through his theme of harmony between one's outer world and the corresponding inner world. This harmony entails coming to an understanding and appreciation not only of nature but also of one's neighbors and one's own humanity. For example, Inman is constantly refreshed and nurtured by reading a volume by eighteenth-century naturalist William Bartram, a book rich with bucolic descriptions, portraits of Native Americans, and a luxurious landscape that vastly contrasts with the devastation that Inman encounters as he walks across the war-ravaged terrain taking him back to Cold Mountain. Bartram's *Travels* offers Inman a fragment of humanity and natural harmony amid the hellish ravages of war. Reading Bartram provides a Wordsworthian interlude that sustains Inman in much the same way that he and Ada collect their Romantic "spots of time," moments in the memory that allow them to recall and survive particular low points on their respective journeys. An illustration is when Ada must part with her piano: she associates that moment with the Christmas gathering where she and Inman became aware that they shared a bond and connection with one another. Likewise, when Inman is physically recovering in the hospital and brooding over the loss of his sense of self and his fear that he will never heal spiritually from the horrors he has endured in four years of war, he remembers his Native American friend Swimmer and the connection that the white boys have with the Indian boys as they play a game of Lacrosse on the mountain bald. The memory has healing qualities. When Ada reads Inman's letter telling her he is coming home, she remembers the scene of his departure four years earlier when they said their tenuous goodbyes knowing they would wait for one another. These scenes evoke Wordsworth's philosophy of Hartlean Associationism, which is key to understanding the Romantic concept of the "spot of time"—those events, often associated with the physical landscape, that offer a sense of heightened understanding, events that freeze in the mind a sublime moment or image that will ultimately sustain us. Such images occur when Inman stops at the "gipsy" camp early on his journey and again with Sara, the young widow who feeds him and whom he reciprocates by butchering her hog, and, as it turns out, saving her from three Yankee soldiers who come to rob the farm. As Inman sits by the fire, he watches Sara, whose kindness and warmth reawaken his humanity: "The curve of the girl's back as she bent over the table seemed to Inman a shape not to be duplicated in all the time stretched out before him. A thing to fix in mind and hold, so that should he become an old man the memory might be useful . . . a consolation" (307). These images or "spots of time" not only bring the characters comfort but often initiate a flashback that paradoxically moves the narrative forward and structurally adds a new thread to the tapestry of the story and a new understanding of one's place in the natural and moral schemata.

As *Cold Mountain* opens, Inman is wounded and war-weary, recuperating in a Confederate hospital from a serious neck wound received at the Battle of Petersburg, where some of the bloodiest trench warfare of the Civil War has taken place. We get a sense of the utter devastation of that conflict through a narrative flashback recounting the battle, and it is clear that Inman is at one of his lowest points in the four years he has been a soldier. War has spiritually drained him, and certainly he no longer finds any glory in battle: "Inman's only thought looking on the enemy was, Go home" (13). He has a recurring dream of "scattered bloody pieces—arms, heads, legs, trunks—slowly [drawing] together and [re-forming] themselves into monstrous bodies of mismatched parts" (14). Every morning the dream comes to him, which puts him "in a mood as dark as the blackest crow," a mood he tries to counter by reading pages from his copy of Bartram's *Travels*. As an antidote, the image of Cold Mountain comes to him continually, "all its ridges and coves and water courses." Names like "Pigeon River, Little East Fork, Sorrell Cove . . . [are like] spells and incantations to ward off the things one fears most" (16). His Cherokee friend Swimmer's "creekside stories rush into his memory" of a restorative, celestial place in the mountains; and "reaching that healing realm, Cold Mountain . . . a place where all the scattered forces [of his broken self] might gather" becomes an obsession (23). Thus on the morning that Inman rises, dresses in his new clothes, and sets "his foot on the sill and step[s] out the window" (26), he is certain that "this journey" will change him forever (71).

Meanwhile Ada finds herself equally at a low point. Her father Monroe has died. He had moved them six years earlier from Charleston's amiable society to the mountains of North Carolina, both for his health and to pastor the savage, "heathenish" race of highlanders who settled around Cold Mountain. Ada is now alone at their "gentleman's" farm at the foot of Cold Mountain, unable to do anything practical other than paint a pretty picture and play Mozart on the piano; and the farm, never something that fully engaged Monroe and certainly not Ada, is falling quickly into decay, all the help having left. As much as she loved her father, Ada believes that he had done her a disservice in keeping her doll-like, a child: "Monroe," she thinks, "had shaped her into a type of monster," fit for little more than a decoration, certainly not for the business of life (65). A defining moment for Ada is when she is sent running to the house by the bantam rooster, who scratches her, wounding both her pride and her body. Doubtless, on the day she visits her mountain neighbors Esco and Sally Swanger, Ada needs help; she will not survive on the farm alone. While most expected her to return to Charleston after Monroe's death, that is not Ada's plan: she intends to remain at Black Cove, having no intention of returning to Charleston defeated and a failure. Ada tells Esco that she has received a letter from Inman, but she is fearful to read it. An old Celtic legend called up in his mind, Esco tells her to look into the well, and she will see the future, as water is the dividing point between the material and spiritual worlds—when she does so, Ada sees the figure of a "black silhouette" walking with "firm resolution." As she sees the image in the water, Ada feels faint; and as she walks back to Black Cove, strains of "Wayfaring Stranger" fill her mind to the rhythm of her walking. Ada has also had her own recurring dream, of her dead father's bones reconstituting and his animated corpse trying to speak to her "with great earnestness and urgency"; but try as she may, she cannot hear him (62–63). The two dreams are portents that the natural and human worlds are off-balance, disjointed, and skewed.

Mrs. Swanger finds the solution to Ada's dilemma and the decaying farm in the form of Ruby, who comes walking down the road one day to give Ada a hand. When Ada says she needs "a man-hand" for the job, Ruby assures her that will not be necessary, for the hardscrabble earth from which Ruby was formed had taught her to plow with a mule, know the signs of when to plant and harvest a crop, and how to barter their way to solvency and prosperity again on Monroe's farm. The narrator muses about Ruby: "[She] had a willing heart . . . had not spent a day of her life in school and could not read a word nor write even her name, [but] Ada thought she saw in her a spark as bright and hard as one struck with steel and flint" (67). Ada's impression of Ruby is accurate, and with a nod to equality and Ruby's assertion that "everybody empties their own night jar," Ruby transforms not only the fading farm but also Ada, into a woman of substance and independence, able to live in harmony with the physical world around her and with her neighbors. While it often goes against Ada's natural inclinations as a languishing southern belle, she accepts Ruby's instruction on the workings of the farm and on the workings of the seasons and the natural world around them; and by the novel's end Ada is a self-assured, competent human being, able to read both the natural and human worlds around her. However, she offers Ruby something as well, particularly in the evenings as the two sit together and Ada reads. As the evening light fades, they tell stories of their lives and a womanly bond forms that suits them both.

It is interesting to note that Frazier's research for the book took him to the "letters and journals of women of the nineteenth century." He speaks in a *BookBrowse* interview of his research for *Cold Mountain* and his particular interest in reading the letters of these women "to their husbands." These were women whose husbands had gone off to war leaving wives to manage the farms, wives who often experienced remarkable transformations. Frazier notes, "To follow those letters over the course of the war, to feel those women getting stronger, more confident—they had begun the war asking their husbands' permission for every decision that needed to be made. By about half way through the war, those same women were informing their husbands that decisions had been made." Frazier was profoundly impressed by "the process of self-mastery" of these wives left to run farms and find an accommodation with the natural world that would determine their fate and often their survival.

For Ada, Ruby's instruction is essential. She teaches her how one must learn to watch and listen to the "signs" from the natural world and live in harmony with that world, in the same way Native Americans did before the white man came to the mountains or Inman's Celtic forefathers.[2] Here, Ruby's instruction also reflects the older, Celtic wisdom that the earliest Appalachian settlers brought with them to America. As always, the Scots-Irish settlers were relegated to the hinterlands beyond the pale, which in the case of Colonial America were the Appalachian or Endless Mountains, as Mary Settle references them in *Beulah Land*. Ruby is representative of this ancient Celtic compatibility with the landscape, in a similar way as the yellow slave who assists "outlier" Inman after his foiled "execution" by the home guard, or as the goat-woman who treats Inman's wounds with herbs. Ruby is clearly cast in this Celtic mold, and Frazier gives her special insights and an intuitive quality that Ada will learn from. Ruby's very being is also overlaid with mythic inference, as her mother, in bitter reaction to her father Stobrod's shabby treatment, would insist that he had no part in Ruby's conception but rather a tall blue heron had spawned Ruby (194).

On a day when Ruby and Ada are inspecting the tobacco, they rest in the hayloft, and Ruby says, "You say you want to get to know the running of this land." Ada, of course, replies that she does. Ruby gets up and kneels behind her, hands cupped over Ada's eyes. "Listen," she says. "What do you hear?" Ada hears only the sound of the wind in the trees and says as much. "Trees, Ruby said contemptuously.... She removed her hands and took her seat again and said nothing more on the topic, leaving Ada to conclude that what she meant was that this is a particular world. Until Ada could listen and... tell the sound of poplar from oak... she had not even started to know the place" (288–89). Ruby's words seem to Ada composed of all verbs, "all of them tiring. Plow, plant, hoe, cut, can, feed, kill"; but as weary as Ada is with these tasks and learning the land, she knows "that anyone else she might hire would grow weary and walk away and let her fail. Ruby would not let her fail" (104–5). Eventually, however, Ada can do much more than identify the trees by the sound of the wind. She grows far beyond the callow and overly refined southern belle who replied so cavalierly to Inman on their last day together when he told her the story of an old Indian woman who had hidden in the mountains during the Cherokee Removal: "When Inman was finished Ada did not know what to say, so she said. Well, that was certainly folkloric" (252). Now, after Ruby's tutelage, Ada would not be so rude and dismissive, not of anyone, let alone someone she cares for. In learning empathy for the natural world, she has acquired a Wordsworthian universal sympathy for all.

If Ada's survival depends on her achieving compatibility with the landscape, being one with her physical world and understanding its myriad ways, Inman's task is no less complicated and in many ways fraught with more overt peril. When Inman steps out of his hospital window—and out of the war—he doesn't put its devastation behind him; and certainly more than once, "the horror, the horror" characterizes how far he has traveled from civility and from his own humanity during the years he has been away from Cold Mountain. At times only the words of his Native American friend Swimmer or Bartram or his memories of Ada can offer him solace; and his odyssey back to Cold Mountain allows him to encounter an array of persons who both impede and push forward his journey—they are representative of all that is best and worst in the world, and Inman's journey takes on the tenor of an elaborate allegory, with the mythic proportions of Joseph Campbell's paradigm of the monomythic journey of the hero. As Inman wends his way from Cape Fear westward, he encounters a land polluted and rank with the stench and disease of war and human destruction. On a dark night early in his journey, he comes upon a figure trying to toss a burden into the river: it is the venal "preacher" Veasey, whom Inman stops when he sees his burden is an unconscious woman. The woman is one of Veasey's parishioners with whom he has had an affair and she has become pregnant. When Inman thwarts the deed, Veasey explains he had no choice but to toss her in swirling water: "For one thing, there is my position. If we had been found out. I would have been run from the county. Our church is strict." Pleading with Inman, he confesses: "Believe me. I anguished over it through many a night" (118). Inman sets things aright, but his disgust with human waywardness is palpable.

For every brutal encounter on the journey—his betrayal by the redneck farmer Junior, his being taken prisoner by the ruthless home guard leader Teague, his treatment as an outlier and Confederate deserter, even his own brutality and ruthlessness as he returns to kill the treacherous Junior and his killing of the three Yankees who attempt to steal from Sara—Inman experiences equally the caring help of "others" who make his return to Cold Mountain possible. And from each of those who help him—the yellow slave, the goat-woman, Sara—Inman regains, as Ada does from Ruby, something of his own humanity. These "outcasts," who seem to Inman more connected to their natural environment than most, teach Inman tolerance and to look beyond the racial and gender prejudices of his times, and they serve as guides on his mythic journey. These outcasts willingly, sometimes risking their own safety, offer Inman sustenance and succor, all the more poignant as they are also associated in some way with the homeless, the classless, and the cast-out of society. For example, the gypsy group, with whom he dines and spends the night after his first encounter with Veasey, is composed of Indians, an Ethiopian, and gypsies, but their society and friendliness cheer Inman; and one of them, a beautiful dark-haired gypsy woman, reminds him of Ada, as does Laura, the girl he saves from Veasey and the young Confederate widow Sara. Each of these encounters, as well as individuals whom Inman himself offers help—such as the woman lamenting her dead daughter for whom he stops long enough to build a casket—teaches Inman sympathy and empathy, particularly so the yellow slave, who hides and nurses Inman after his "death and resurrection" at the hand of home-guard leader Teague... and the goat-woman.

Both goat-woman and the yellow slave are creatures of their natural surroundings. They are outsiders, removed from the conflict that has consumed Inman for four years, from which he now is attempting to escape. The days that Inman spends with goat-woman, a wise granny who uses natural herbs and ointments to heal his wounds, are particularly restorative for him, for both his body and his spirit. The two, high above the conflict and strife in the valley, share their stories as well as their mountain meals. Goat-woman is part of her natural environment, having lived alone with her goats since she ran away as a young girl from an abusive marriage to an old man her family saddled her with long ago. Like the gypsies, she lives in her caravan with her goats, free to travel wherever she wishes, gathering herbs, greens, and roots. And like Native Americans, she is not tied to the land through ownership. Inman observes that there are no mirrors in her wagon and that she is unconcerned with the vanities of the world which she only occasionally deals with in bartering her goat cheese for "taters, meal, lard, and the like" (273). She also sells natural brews for healing and the occasional pamphlet on "proper diet," a diet generally forsaking flesh for "bread of Graham flour and root crops" (273). As goat-woman treats Inman's wounds, he winces with the physical pain of wounds that don't want to heal, and she tells him, "That's just pain.... It goes eventually. And when it's gone, there's no lasting memory. Not the worst of it, anyway. It fades. Our minds aren't made to hold on to the particulars of pain the way we do bliss. It's a gift God gives us, a sign of His care for us" (277). As she shares her story with Inman, as she remembers the tale of her love for a yellow-haired boy before her family pawned her off to the old man she had run away from, her long-past "spots of time" associated with her first love appear to have sustained her over the years living alone in the mountains. When Inman tells goat-woman about Ada, whom he describes as "somewhat thistleish in comportment" but "very beautiful" (278–79), goat-woman responds, "Marrying a woman for her beauty makes no more sense than eating a bird for its singing" (279). However, Ada will be a different woman when Inman finds her again on Cold Mountain, just as he will be a different man.

Inman observes goat-woman's natural life secluded on the mountain bald: the way she walks—"she stepped with in-turned toes, a style of walking often said to be favored by Indians" (265)—the way she gathers most of what she needs from her natural surroundings, and even the gentle way she kills the "kid" for their evening meal, a thankful and appreciative dispatching different from anything Inman had ever seen before. He sees that she lives in harmony with the natural world around her, both with the animals and plants she encounters and even with the occasional people she comes in contact with. Inman thinks, "This would be one way to live . . . a hermit among the clouds. The contentious world but a fading memory. Mind turned only toward God's finer productions" (282). However, Inman has another destiny.

Before he leaves goat-woman, she asks him if the war was worth it—all the battles fought for the "big man's" slave? She asks as well whether Inman and his kind owned slaves. "No. Not hardly anybody I knew did," he answers. "Then what stirred you up enough for fighting and dying?" Inman admits, "Four years ago I maybe could have told you. Now I don't know. I've had all of it I want, though" (275). The goat-woman's genuineness and common sense make Inman feel regretful for his part in the war, an understanding about the war that Ada comes to as well when she calls down Mrs. McKennet, who cannot help glorifying the violence that to Ada now is "degrading to all" (182). The goat-woman's question to Inman causes him to articulate what he has felt increasingly about the war on his long journey westward: "The shame he felt now to think of his zeal in sixty-one to go off and fight the downtrodden mill worker of the Federal army, men so ignorant it took many lessons to convince them to load their cartridges ball foremost" (276). It is this empathy and understanding of the humanity of one's foe that moves Inman furthest along his journey; and the selflessness he cultivates is what will make salvation possible.

When Inman is ready to leave the goat-woman, he can offer her nothing but thanks for the healing she has afforded him. Rather, it is she who gives him a gift, one of her drawings of a blue-purple berry cluster in autumn; for she, like the yellow slave who helps Inman after his escape from Teague and who draws for Inman an exquisitely rendered map to follow homeward, is also an artist, inspired by the natural world in which both characters have learned to live without vanity or pride or the wish to dominate. Instead, both the yellow slave and the goat-woman have learned to accommodate themselves to their surroundings and have achieved a harmony with the natural world that augers a resolution for human conflict and strife. It is likewise significant that Inman must find his journey's end, as he learns from the yellow slave, through "indirection"—that is, by traveling first northward to avoid soldiers and home guard rather than directly westward toward Cold Mountain—as all great allegories teach.

When, after four years of separation, Ada and Inman finally meet again, each is unrecognizable to the other. Ruby and Ada have hiked up Cold Mountain to save Ruby's father Stobrod, who has been shot along with his young musical apprentice Pangle. The two women rescue Stobrod, who is too weak to haul down the mountain, and take him to a group of Cherokee cabins abandoned after the 1838 Removal. There they wait for Stobrod to come to a crisis point, while Ada goes out to shoot wild turkeys for their meal. When Inman and Ada encounter each other, there is no romantic falling into each other's arms. Inman sees a dark figure silhouetted against the snow. Thinking the figure is a hunter, he calls out, "I'm lost." And at this point he recognizes "Ada's face atop some strange trousered figure, like a mannish boy. 'Ada Monroe?' Inman calls out, 'Ada.'" But Ada does not answer, nor does she know the person standing before her in the snow. Inman is at the point of leaving and she shooting, when his calling her name slowly brings recognition. They are both wary. Inman thinks her "face firmer than he remembered, harder." At last he says to Ada, "I've been coming to you on a hard road and I'm not letting you go" (403–4). When she confesses she does not recognize him, he tells her, "Entirely warranted and in some way expected. . . . I'm no better than a rank stranger here. A wandering pilgrim in my own place. Such is the price I'll pay for the past four years" (405). With this, Ada tells him to come with her. It is interesting that when Ruby sees Inman, she tells Ada, "You don't need him," and Ada answers, "I know I don't need him. . . . But I think I want him." Ruby answers, "Well that's a whole different thing" (410). And thus the wayfaring stranger on his long pilgrimage to Cold Mountain comes to the final chapter of his journey, one that many readers took exception to after the book was published, but Charles Frazier could write this story no other way.

When Frazier's book was published, Frazier received no small amount of criticism from readers unhappy with its ending, and he admits in several interviews that he had pondered a good deal the ending. He told Susan Ketchin, "I don't feel like historical fiction should be constrained to what really happened, necessarily, but . . . I knew about the character [Frazier's great-great-granduncle Inman] from page one that . . . [he] was killed . . . shortly after he got home." To have ended the book any other way "would feel false." Despite the feeling that some readers may have had about the book's ending—that is, Inman's failure to reach Black Cove—this ending is not necessarily indicative of Frazier's ultimate rejection of the Romantic aesthetic of Nature and finding harmony with the natural world. Physically falling short of "home" does not necessarily indicate failure for Inman. This ending is more akin to what the Victorians call "success in failure." In terms of the organic quality of *Cold Mountain*, Frazier's ending is in keeping with how he had constructed the story from the beginning and how he integrated the central ideas in the book thematically.

Throughout the novel, Frazier builds parallel scenes and characters, all to drive home the book's concern with conflict and resolution, the mythic journey of the hero, and the role that understanding the natural world plays in both Inman's and Ada's "transformation" as "heroes" who achieve a sense of harmony with their physical environment. This theme is likewise in tune with the fatalistic Celtic and Native American understanding of a universal construct rather than with one emanating from traditional Western philosophy or theology. The animal symbolism and tropes associated with Inman forecast the exquisite ending as well. In the novel, Inman is associated with the crow, the heron, the bear, the drake, all things of the animate world that Inman comes to recognize he is part of. In the poignant scene leading to his death, Frazier references a frozen pool on the mountain bald, which prepares the reader for the violent ending of the story. After Ada and Ruby find Stobrod wounded on the wintry mountain slope, they pass the pool where they see three black ducks floating "motionless in the pool's center, their heads tucked against their breasts" (387). Inman passes the same ice-rimmed pool on his way to find Ada and Ruby, but now only "a lone drake rode the water at its center.... It seemed to look at nothing" (398). Just before Inman is confronted by Teague as he and Stobrod are riding down the mountain toward Black Cove, he passes by the pond once more, "frozen over and the ice... unmarked by a drake or even the carcass of one. It had drowned and sunk to the muddy bottom or flown away. There was no telling which" (438).

Essentially, in this book about a man's search for salvation and wholeness, for his humanity, Inman hesitates at the end to kill the white-haired boy, who confronts him after Inman has finally killed the ruthless Teague. He is loath to kill the boy—it jars his soul now and counters all that he has become by this journey's end, particularly after the nights he has just spent with Ada and the humanity he has regained. "Damn it, Inman said. I'm looking for a way not to kill you. We can do this so that twenty years on, we might run into one another in town and take a drink together and remember this dark time and shake our heads over it" (443). But the boy will have none of it, and his soul, like his cold blue eyes, is "empty" (444). However, in Inman's hesitation lies his salvation, as well as his bodily end. In this moment of human hesitation, a moment that brings his death, he is at last complete and whole, and his journey is over.

The final scene or epilogue in the book, more pagan and Celtic than Christian in its resolution, occurs some ten years later. Ruby has married the Georgia Boy, who had come for their help on the day Stobrod was shot and just stayed on. Three little boys now gather around a fire pit as the domestic scene of a picnic unfolds. Ada has a "tall slender girl of nine" by her side, Inman's gift from the days they had waited together for Stobrod to mend, making their plans for a life with each other in the cove—a life that Ada had insisted would include Ruby, the partner with whom she had bonded and who had helped her become a woman while Inman was gone to war. Stobrod, who survived and is transformed by both hardship and his music, plays a tune from the Scottish ballad "Bonnie George Campbell," which tells the story of a young man gone to war, whose horse returns without him. Ada's daughter sings the words to the ballad in a "voice clear and high and strong. Bear me away on your snowy wings" (448). The solstice is nearing, and a crescent moon stands close to Venus. Ada reads to the children from "Baucus and Philemon," a tale by Ovid of two old lovers who find an eternity together though separated by life, one of the literary transformations in the *Metamorphosis*. The scene is a tranquil one, one that reveals an unconventional family living together in harmony, having come to terms with their place in the natural world and with each other. The scene also suggests that Inman is with them as well and Ada's wounded heart has healed, just as the end of her right index finger has healed from an accidental severing of a few years prior—so neatly you would think "that was the way the ends of people's fingers were meant to look," Frazier writes (449). Gently elegiac in tone, the scene reveals a sense of peaceful resolution. Frazier concludes, "Time to go inside and cover up the coals and pull in the latch string" (449). Thus Charles Frazier provides fitting closure for the story of two "journeys" of heroic undertakings by people whose individual stories are also our own . . . stories about reconciling ourselves with each other and with the natural world that sustains us.

NOTES

1. Albert Way ("'A World Properly Put Together': Environmental Knowledge in Charles Frazier's *Cold Mountain*") and Oswald Chang ("Home, Journey and Landscape in Charles Frazier's *Cold Mountain*: The Mirroring of Internal Processes in the External World and the Literary Construction of Space") explore "landscape" as key to understanding Inman's and Ava's journeys in the book. Cedric Bryant looks at the book as an expression of "a resilient, eighteenth-century deistic rationalism" (591), while Emily McDermott explores the influence of Ovid, Christianity, and Celtic lore on *Cold Mountain*.

2. Marilou Awiakta has written about the similarity of early Celtic and Irish settlers and Native Americans in their attitudes toward the natural world: "They shared: devotion to family; love of the land; reverence for the Creator and the natural law; the egalitarian relationship between men and women; the sense of fierce independence and outrage at foreign invasions . . . [and] the love of ceremony and symbol. All of these combine in a quality of soul that relies on the inner life of the spirit to survive" (299).

BIBLIOGRAPHY

Awiakta, Marilou. *Selu, Seeking the Corn-Mother's Wisdom*. Golden, Colo.: Fulcrum, 1993.

Badley, Hannah, and Kristin Stover. "Interview." In *Anthology of Appalachian Writers: Charles Frazier*, vol. 9, 42–47. Charleston: West Virginia Center for the Book, 2017.

Bryant, Cedric Gael. "To Rise and Bloom Again: Resurrection, Race, and Rationalism in Charles Frazier's *Cold Mountain.*" *Mississippi Quarterly* 62, no. 4 (2009): 591–603.

Chang, Oswald Yuan Chin. "Home, Journey and Landscape in Charles Frazier's *Cold Mountain*: The Mirroring of Internal Processes in the External World and the Literary Construction of Space." *Nebula* 4, no. 4 (2007): 101–20.

Chitwood, Ava. "Epic or Philosophic, Homeric or Heraclitean? The Anonymous Philosopher in Charles Frazier's *Cold Mountain.*" *International Journal of the Classical Tradition* 11, no. 2 (2004): 232–43.

Frazier, Charles. *Cold Mountain.* New York: Vintage, 1997.

———. Interview. *BookBrowse*, n.d. https://www.bookbrowse.com/author_interviews/full/index.cfm/author_number/239/Charles-Frazier.

Gifford, Terry. "Nature's Eloquent Speech in Charles Frazier's *Nightwoods.*" *Mississippi Quarterly* 66, no. 4 (2013): 565–82.

———. "Terrain, Character and Text: Is *Cold Mountain* by Charles Frazier a Postpastoral Novel?" *Mississippi Quarterly* 55, no. 1 (2001): 87–96.

Ketchin, Susan. "Interview with Charles Frazier." *Journal of Southern Religion*, January 22, 2000. http://jsr.fsu.edu/Volume10/Ketchin.htm.

McCarron, Bill, and Paul Knoke. "Images of War and Peace: Parallelism and Antithesis in the Beginning and Ending of Cold Mountain." *Mississippi Quarterly* 52, no. 2 (1999): 273–85.

McDermott, Emily A. "Ovid, Christians, and Celts in the Epilogue of Charles Frazier's Cold Mountain." *Mississippi Quarterly* 64, no. 1–2 (2011): 179–97.

Piacentino, Ed. "Searching for Home: Cross-Racial Bonding in Charles Frazier's *Cold Mountain.*" *Mississippi Quarterly* 55, no. 1 (2001): 97–116.

Rash, Ron. "Signs." In *Among the Believers.* Oak Ridge, Tenn.: Irish Press, 2000.

Shurbutt, Sylvia Bailey, ed. *Anthology of Appalachian Writers: Charles Frazier.* Vol. 9. Charleston: West Virginia Center for the Book, 2016.

Way, Albert. "A World Properly Put Together: Environmental Knowledge in Charles Frazier's *Cold Mountain.*" *Southern Cultures* 10, no. 4 (2004): 33–54.

A New Overlook
Seeing the Forest Beyond the Trees

Wallace Stevens's "Anecdote of the Jar"
Modernist Poetics and the Industrial Logging of the Great Appalachian Forest

KEVIN E. O'DONNELL

Introduction; or, Can Appalachian Studies and Ecocriticism Refigure an Abstract Modernist Masterpiece as a Journalistic / Environmental Artifact?

Wallace Stevens is one of the great modernist poets of the twentieth century, and "Anecdote of the Jar" is one of his best-known poems. The poem has been widely anthologized and has inspired much commentary and discussion, as well as puzzlement. Notoriously oblique, opaque, and obscure, the piece is also playful, mystical, and vaguely comical. The first-person narrator places a jar on a hill in Tennessee. That act of placing the jar seems somehow to tame the "slovenly wilderness." The jar organizes the wilderness, which is then "no longer wild." Many readers have thus taken the poem as a kind of allegory for the creative act of the poet, whose Godlike gesture brings order and meaning to otherwise anarchic experience. The poem is therefore often held forth as a statement of modernist poetics.

Certainly, the poem invites readings along these lines, as I will discuss further. Yet I would also like to show how the poem can be read—over and above its allegorical meaning—in relation to a particular place and time.

Stevens most likely conceived the poem during a brief April 1918 visit to the East Tennessee town of Elizabethton, in Carter County, where he spent a day in his role as the head of the Surety Claims Department for the Hartford Accident and Indemnity Company. Stevens was in Carter County during the final frenzy of industrial logging of the great Appalachian deciduous hardwood forest. I show here how the poem dramatizes the mythic clash of forces that characterized the natural resource extraction that accompanied modernism in Appalachia.

For this reading, I use two critical lenses. Here I show how insights from both Appalachian studies and ecocriticism provide a surprising new perspective on Stevens's poem. Appalachian studies reminds readers to value local knowledge and to keep an eye out for the sort of economic colonialism that was so prevalent in the region during the latter half of the nineteenth century and first half of the twentieth. And Appalachian studies likewise provides a well-developed history of natural resource exploitation in the region. Indeed, a pretty substantial body of environmental history exists that is specifically about logging the great southern Appalachian forest, around 1880 to 1920. Ecocriticism, in turn, reminds us to consider the material relationships between humans and nature, and can inform a critique of natural resource exploitation.

My purpose is twofold: On the one hand, I propose a fresh take on a well-known poem. On the other, I use a reading of this poem as an occasion to retell the story of the reckless clear-cutting of one of the planet's great forests. That environmental history provides the context in which the poem was composed. In that sense, I read against the spirit of the poem as obscure, modernist allegory and reread it, instead, as a kind of journalistic artifact.

But First, a Typical Reading of the Poem, with Background Information and Vocabulary Notes

We can begin by reading the poem itself. The poem is, as I've said, generally taken as an account of an aesthetic act. The first-person narrator-poet here brings order to the scene by placing a jar.

> ANECDOTE OF THE JAR
>
> I placed a jar in Tennessee,
> And round it was, upon a hill.
> It made the slovenly wilderness
> Surround that hill.
>
> The wilderness rose up to it,
> And sprawled around, no longer wild.
> The jar was round upon the ground
> And tall and of a port in air.
>
> It took dominion everywhere.
> The jar was gray and bare.
> It did not give of bird or bush,
> Like nothing else in Tennessee.

William Blake, *The Ancient of Days Setting a Compass upon the Face of the Earth.* (See Proverbs, viii. 27). Frontispiece to *Europe: A Prophecy*, printed in 1794. Print colored by hand. Image from the Wikipedia article titled "Europe a Prophecy," July 2017.

Originally published in the October 1919 issue of *Poetry: A Magazine of Verse*, edited by Harriet Monroe in Chicago, this poem was included in *Harmonium* (1923), Stevens's first book of poems.

The poem evokes William Blake's etching of God placing a compass on the face of the waters. The compass is the *logos*, the ordering principle. So, too the jar. In this standard reading, the poem is an allegory about the ordering power of art and imagination. Yet perhaps in contrast to the Blake etching, the Stevens poem shows the ordering not as divine but rather as manmade and provisional.

In order to further elucidate the poem, it is necessary to examine a few words and phrases. The first is "anecdote." That word appears in the titles of this and four other poems collected in *Harmonium* (1923), Stevens's first book of poems. (The others are "Earthy Anecdote," "Anecdote of Men by the Thousand," "Anecdote of Canna," and "Anecdote of the Prince of Peacocks.") The jar poem, like these four others, does not convey an "anecdote," in the precise meaning of that term as a short conversational narrative. Rather, the poem presents an allegory. That is, the jar in the poem comes to stand in for an abstraction. So the word "anecdote" in the title is indirect, coy, perhaps comical and even self-deprecating. I take the title to be a gesture similar to the one later made by the surrealist painter, René Magritte, in his famous painting, formally titled *The Treachery of Images* (1928–29), produced ten years after Stevens first published his "Jar" poem. The Magritte painting depicts an image of a pipe, and below that image is the painted caption "this is not a pipe" (*ceci n'est pas un pipe*, in French). Stevens's title, like Magritte's caption, is a playful way of inviting readers to think twice about what they are reading.

Helen Vendler, the renowned American poetry critic and prolific Stevens commentator, has written that one rule for deciphering Stevens's work is to "mistrust titles" (44). Further, Vendler writes, "Stevens' strategies for freshness and originality are strategies of concealment, chiefly concealment of the lyric 'I'" (44). So Vendler encourages readers to investigate the "I" that has been concealed, to excavate the personal narrative underlying the obscure allegory of any given Stevens poem.

The second phrase worth discussing in the "Jar" poem is "of a port." This is an archaic term that I did not fully understand until I happened to be rereading a passage in the first chapter of Nathaniel Hawthorne's 1850 novel *The Scarlet Letter*—the "Custom House" chapter, wherein the first-person author/narrator, "Nathaniel Hawthorne," describes how he imagines his own progenitor, an ancestor from two centuries earlier, walking the streets of early Salem, Massachusetts: ". . .this grave, bearded, sable-cloaked and steeple-crowned progenitor,—who came so early, with his Bible and his sword, and trode the unworn street with such a stately port, and made so large a figure, as a man of war and peace" ("The Custom House, Introductory to 'The Scarlet Letter,'" para. 9, emphasis added). In the context of the jar poem, then, the phrase "of a port" suggests that the jar has a physical bearing, a peculiar sort of body language that one might attribute to a human being. One commentator on Stevens's poem, the poet Robert Hass, says his own grandmother was given to referring to her husband as "of a port," to describe, approvingly, his bearing and his substantial presence (Cook 68).

Wallace Stevens was a big man—six feet two inches tall and often close to three hundred pounds (his weight fluctuated over his lifetime). One of his coworkers—around the same time that Stevens wrote the "Jar" poem and visited Elizabethton, Tennessee—was Charles Beach, a young underwriter when Stevens was first hired in 1916 at the Hartford. Years later, in the 1970s, Beach recalled Stevens's demeanor and physical presence: "[Stevens] was such a big man physically that he impressed you, and you sort of stepped aside a little bit when he would come. He was a very charming man, very polished. And he conducted himself in such a way that would impress you" (interviewed August 1976, Farmington, Conn.; Brazeau 11).

So the jar on the hill can be likened to Stevens, himself, in his role as commanding insurance executive. Perhaps it reflects his view of himself as a well-dressed, important businessman, an emissary from the broader

Stock photo of a Dominion Wide Mouth Special canning jar.

world of commerce and finance, as he stepped into shabby offices to conduct business in Elizabethton, that provincial outpost on the edge of the Carter County wilderness on a spring day in 1918.

But before I get to that day, I would like to discuss a third phrase in the poem: "The jar was gray and bare." Helen Vendler and others take the gray jar to be a stone or ceramic jug. Roy Harvey Pearce, on the other hand, points to the Dominion canning jar—which was widely used as a moonshine jar. Perhaps, then, the jar was a nod to common notions about those East Tennessee hills to which Stevens's business had carried him, that spring, one hundred years ago.

Stevens in East Tennessee
Portrait of the Poet as a Traveling
Surety Bond Claimsman

Did Wallace Stevens write this poem while he was in Elizabethton? Or, more likely, did he conceive it at that time and write it sometime later? The truth is I do not know where and when he wrote the poem. However, the circumstantial evidence suggests that the poem arose from his experience on his brief business trip to East Tennessee in the spring of 1918.

We do know from his letters that he was in East Tennessee in late April 1918. And the first mention of the "Jar" poem in his published letters is from more than a year later, in August 1919. At that time, he refers—in a letter to Harriet Monroe, the editor of *Poetry* magazine, based in Chicago—to the "Jar" poem as a "new poem." The poem was then first published, two months later, along with a group of other poems, under the heading "Pecksniffiana," in Monroe's magazine in October 1919. A year and a half seems about the length of time one might expect for a poem to go from conception and composition to print.

Stevens had visited East Tennessee at least once before 1918—on a business trip in 1905. On August 10 of that year, he rode the Southern Railway passenger train down the great valley of Virginia and through upper East Tennessee. At that time he was only passing through. His journal shows that by the next day, August 11, he was in Covington, Louisiana. Yet according to his biographer, Joan Richardson, even before he had ever seen Tennessee, something about the state had a hold on his imagination. Months before his 1905 train trip, he dreamed of standing on "a green mountain—no trees, only grass" (Richardson 218). And as he approached Tennessee through southwest Virginia, he made an evocative note in his journal: "We are approaching Tennessee—green, hilly, sunny—cloudy place" (*Letters* 83).

When he returned thirteen years later, his business took him first to Chattanooga, on Friday, April 26. The next day he worked in a Chattanooga law office for twelve hours. Then on Sunday he traveled to Knoxville, arriving in the afternoon. He could not conduct business until Monday morning, so he walked through town all afternoon. He wrote about his walk in a letter to his wife that evening: "Out near the golf club, at the Western end of the city, there is a really swank view. The Tennessee River makes a great bend through woods and cliffs and hills and on the horizon run the blue ranges of the mountains. I saw no end of irises in people's gardens. There were peonies, tulip-trees, locust trees and an unknown tree, very large and spreading, covered with purple blossoms [this last was probably the princess tree or royal Paulownia (*Paulownia tomentosa*)]" (*Letters* 207).

The next day, for reasons not explained in Stevens's letters, he traveled one hundred miles east to Johnson City and secured a room at the Colonial Hotel, downtown. The following day he rode an "auto-bus" ten miles east, to Elizabethton. At the end of the work day, he sat down and wrote a letter to his wife:

> It is about four o'clock. I must wait until five for an auto-bus back to Johnson City, about ten miles away. It rains and rains and rains. Yet they have two fountains rattling loudly in front of the hotel. I have been visiting the sourest lawyers in the shabbiest offices. One of them

spoke of the contractors whose case I am handling as "a dark and black and damnable gang." . . . Here they spell Arthur, Arter, and so on. All this will give you some idea of the grandeurs of traveling in Tennessee. I noticed the other day that O. Henry, in one of his letters, asked, "Is it possible for anything to happen in Nashville?" Certainly not without outside help. This applies to the State as a whole. I have never been so concerned about a place. I begin to think of it as Pope thought of London: as a "dear, damned, distracting place." I slept last night, for instance, at the Colonial Hotel in Johnson City. The next room was separated by a warped wooden door that was an inch short at the top. Consequently, one could hear the least noise. Well, that room contained a baby, a small boy, a young man and his wife. They were from the country and I imagine did not know how to turn off the electricity. They snored and squalled all night with the light turned on full. What a nightmare it must have been for them! . . . This gives you an idea of my circumstances.

With love,
Wallace

(*Letters* 208)

Though I do not know the specifics of the case, I can tell you the nature of the work that Stevens was doing in Elizabethton. In April 1918, Stevens was thirty-eight years old. He had earned his law degree when he was twenty-three, then drifted in and out of law firms, along the way acquiring a background in surety law. In 1916, the Hartford Accident and Indemnity Company hired him to handle national surety operations at its home office, in Hartford, Connecticut. On April 1, 1918, the company established a separate fidelity and surety claims department, with Stevens as its head. (Stevens would hold the position until 1955, the year of his death.)

And what is surety, exactly? A surety bond guarantees that a principal will perform a contract. If the principal defaults, the surety company must step in and set things right. So a surety bond guarantees, for example, a contractor's satisfactory completion of, say, a sewer line or a road paving.

Bonding companies were new in the United States at the turn of the twentieth century. As Stevens's biographer Peter Brazeau points out, by the mid-1910s bonding companies had become an indispensable part of the way capital investments were guaranteed (5). The modern world was a scary place. 1918 was a year of global warfare, not to mention the global influenza pandemic. Surety bonds helped to reassure investors and thus promoted the flow of capital that fueled increasingly global economic activities. The bonding company executive was thus an ambassador of economic and technological modernism.

As head of Surety Claims at the Hartford in 1918, Stevens's job was to travel around the country evaluating claims, in order to decide whether and how to resolve them. For example, as one of his colleagues later explained, Stevens's job was "to check the financial position of the contractor, his assets, how far the job had progressed, what it would cost to complete the job by getting out other bids, and whether we should finance the contract to completion" (Brazeau 12).

Stevens remarked to his wife, around this time, regarding his work: "I go around to patch up trouble or else to cause it" (12).

Elizabethton 1918, in the Context of the Industrial Logging of Appalachia, ca. 1880–1920

Due to a long growing season and high rainfall, the mountains of southern Appalachia at the end of the nineteenth century held the most magnificent—and the most commercially valuable—forests in North America, and probably in the world (outside of the tropics). Beginning in the 1880s, the industrial logging of the great Appalachian forest began in earnest.

Northern and international "syndicates," or holding companies, purchased large tracts of land and logged them with relentless efficiency. Mechanized operations could reduce a stand of giant trees to an eroded hillside within a matter of weeks. In 1910, an article in the *Manufacturer's Record*, a newspaper for industrialists, reported that lumber companies gave "no thought ... to the effect which the cutting of timber may have on the mountain regions." Slash was left where it fell, usually to dry and catch fire. Some fires would smolder for years, reducing the earth to bare rock and mineral soil. Within three decades of the onset of industrial logging in the region, by around 1910, more than 90 percent of the trees in the southern mountains had been cut.

At the time Wallace Stevens visited Elizabethton in 1918, the timber industry was the only large-scale industrial activity in town. Carter County held some of the last virgin stands of hardwood in the nation. Within six years of his visit—by 1924—the last of the great trees in Carter County, and likewise in most of Appalachia, had been felled.

With the industrial clearing of its forests, rural Appalachia became what the historian C. Vann Woodward would later call a "colonial economy," its natural and human resources exploited by outside capital, its wealth expropriated by distant corporations and financial combinations (291). Ronald Eller's 1982 book, *Miners, Millhands, and Mountaineers: Industrialization of the Appalachian South, 1880–1930*, is now considered a classic work of Appalachian studies scholarship. The book has a chapter titled "The Last Great Trees," which tells the story of the logging of the region in a compelling fashion.

"Anecdote" as Allegory of Colonialization, Incorporation of Appalachia

Historian Alan Trachtenberg, in *The Incorporation of America: Culture and Society in the Gilded Age*, published the same year (1982) as Eller's book, provides some context for understanding the industrial logging of Appalachia. Trachtenberg describes how the post-Reconstruction American economic boom of the late nineteenth century was fueled by "tightening systems of transport and communication, the spread of a market economy into all regions." The spread of transportation technologies then gave rise to new economic relationships and social arrangements, "the remaking of cultural perceptions" and "new hierarchies of control" (3–4). Trachtenberg goes further in explaining what he means by "incorporation": "If in a literal sense incorporation refers to a specific form of industrial and business organization, in a figurative sense it encompasses a more comprehensive pattern of change" (4). The rise of the modern surety business was an essential part of this pattern of change. So too, perhaps, was the rise of modernist poetry.

Thus I suggest that in Stevens's poem the first-person "I"—the gesture of placing the jar—is an allegory not only for the creative act of the poet but also for the work of the insurance man—the act of modernization, the financial colonization of the Appalachian wilderness, the imposition of capital and market systems. The jar brings the wilderness—in this case, specifically, Carter County, Tennessee—under the influence of modern "hierarchies of control."

I read the poem this way because my sight has been conditioned both by Appalachian studies and by ecocriticism. In her introduction to *The Ecocriticism Reader* (1996) Cheryll Glotfelty defines ecocriticism broadly: "Simply put, ecocriticism is the study of the relationship between literature and the physical environment" (xviii). Further along in her discussion, she writes that "ecocriticism takes as its subject the interconnections between nature and culture, specifically the cultural artifacts of language and literature." Moreover, "If we agree with Barry Commoner's first law of ecology, 'Everything is connected to everything else,' we must conclude that literature does not float above the material world in some aesthetic ether, but, rather, plays a part in an immensely complex global system, in which energy, matter, *and ideas* interact" (xix). In this spirit, in this tradition that Glotfelty calls "ecocriticism," I read the Stevens poem as a kind of artifact, as a record of the social lines of force surrounding the great drama of human interaction with, and exploitation of, the natural environment in Appalachia.

This essay is an attempt to read Stevens's poem in the context of a complex global system, as Glotfelty would have it. I do *not* claim that Stevens was consciously composing a critique of capitalist colonialization. If anything, I read *against* what may have been Stevens's intentions. Never mind that his intentions are obscure—or, rather, it is clear that his intention was to obscure his intentions. In any case, I do not see Stevens as expressing an ecological consciousness here. Rather, his lyric poem expresses the cultural relationships complicit in natural resource exploitation. On the other hand, I do not see him advocating or celebrating those relationships. I do not condemn Stevens for being the exploiter and the colonizer. Rather, I see the poem as a beautiful representation of that pattern of relationships, that complex global system. I do believe that Wallace Stevens has, perhaps unwittingly, left us an artifact that contains a record or trace of the historical meaning of the business he was conducting in East Tennessee in 1918. That trace is visible to a reader with the proper critical tools.

BIBLIOGRAPHY

Brazeau, Peter. *Wallace Stevens Remembered: An Oral Biography.* New York: Random House, 1983.

Cook, Eleanor. *A Reader's Guide to Wallace Stevens.* Princeton, N.J.: Princeton University Press, 2007.

Eller, Ronald. "The Last Great Trees." In *Miners, Millhands, and Mountaineers: Industrialization of the Appalachian South, 1880–1930,* 86–127. Knoxville: University of Tennessee Press, 1982.

Glotfelty, Cheryll. "Introduction: Literary Studies in an Age of Environmental Crisis." In *The Ecocriticism Reader: Landmarks in Literary Ecology,* edited by Glotfelty and Harold Fromm, xv–xxxvii. Athens: University of Georgia Press, 1996.

Pearce, Roy Harvey. "The Last Lesson of the Master." In *The Act of the Mind: Essays on the Poetry of Wallace Stevens,* edited by R. H. Pearce and J. Hillis Miller, 121–42. Baltimore: Johns Hopkins University Press, 1965.

Richardson, Joan. *Wallace Stevens, a Biography: The Early Years, 1879–1923.* New York: Beech Tree Books, 1986.

Stevens, Wallace. *Harmonium.* New York: Knopf, 1923.

———. *Letters of Wallace Stevens.* Selected and edited by Holly Stevens. New York: Knopf, 1966.

Trachtenberg, Alan. *The Incorporation of America: Culture and Society in the Gilded Age.* New York: Hill & Wang, 1982.

Vendler, Helen. *Wallace Stevens: Words Chosen Out of Desire*. Knoxville: University of Tennessee Press, 1984.
Woodward, C. Vann. "The Colonial Economy." In *Origins of the New South, 1877–1913*, 291–320. Baton Rouge: Louisiana State University Press, 1951.

A Sense of Place
The Rhododendron as Regional Identification on the Covers of Appalachian Local Color Literature

STEWART PLEIN

The rhododendron, native to the Appalachian region, has a range that runs along the mountaintops and ridges of Virginia, West Virginia, North and South Carolina, Georgia, Kentucky, and Tennessee. Two forms are common, though others exist; the *Rhododendron catawbiense*, whose blooms are described as "showy pinkish-purple" flower clusters that appear in the late spring, and the *Rhododendron maximum*, or great rhododendron, the more common of the two. Its range extends well into the north beyond the Appalachian region, and its flower clusters range from white to blush pink, blooming in late spring to early summer. Both plants form dense shrubs of evergreen foliage that extends to the ground. The leaves also appear in clusters of three to six inches in length, pinnately veined and alternating on the branch. The undersides of the great rhododendron are rust colored, while the undersides of the Catawba rhododendron are a green that is lighter than the top and often tending toward white.[1]

As a native plant, the rhododendron is ubiquitous in the Appalachians. The beauty of its blooms and the impenetrable thicket the shrubs can form have been recognized and described for centuries, from the earliest naturalists and botanists who explored the Appalachians to the authors of local color literature who used it to create a sense of place, to the hikers and tourists of today who travel throughout the region.

Over time, the omnipresence of the rhododendron has come to represent the Appalachian region as a marker of identity, culture, and place.[2] As a representational image of Appalachia, the rhododendron is nonjudgmental. It is not an image of log cabins or tar-paper shacks; it is not a mountain man wearing a floppy brimmed hat holding a gun, an old crone with a corncob pipe, or a portrait of ragged, dirty children. The rhododendron, regardless of the color of its blooms, its range or form, is a thing of beauty that speaks of region without the accompanying visual commentary.

When the rhododendron is examined from a book arts perspective, it becomes clear that this plant was lifted to an emblematic status as a graphic indicator of regional identification as portrayed on the covers of nineteenth and early twentieth century local color literature. As an archetype, the rhododendron was translated by authors and artists into a symbolic shorthand used to capture a sense of place. The rhododendron became a standard representation of place on the covers of books. It was recognizable to readers at a single glance, whether they read the book or not.

For the purposes of this study, local color literature is defined as both fiction and nonfiction describing the Appalachian region during the late nineteenth and early twentieth centuries. Book history is an emerging field that examines the historical development of the book from the perspective of manufacturing as it evolved over time, technological advances, art and cultural impact. A particular focus on the study of publishers' bookbindings, the decorated covers of the late nineteenth and early twentieth centuries, when local color literature was at its height and topping best-seller lists, brings the use of archetypal design to the forefront (Hackett).

The data for this study were gathered from primary source material systematically indexed for the specific properties of botanical decoration and examined for the use of botanical features as a type of stylistic shorthand used to identify a region. The presence of a rhododendron or mountain laurel, blue grass, or towering tree was used by book binding designers of the late nineteenth and early twentieth century to elicit a response from the reading public plainly stating, without the use of words, the book's locale. These designs were effective marketing tools and were used as such by the publishers. While a book cover depicting tumbleweeds or cactus evokes the West and an image of maples with hanging buckets evokes New England, the use of flora native to Appalachia served as symbolic shorthand to convey region and to market the book to a specific audience (Plein).

In this context, a regional identifier refers to an image that is used to represent an association to or with the Appalachian region. One such example is the use of plants, such as the rhododendron, as a design element. Its repeated use on the covers of local color literature inextricably linked the rhododendron to the region through the literature of the local colorists (Plein).

By viewing the art of book cover design from this perspective, we can see botanical expression as a specific means used by the publisher, book binding designers, and artists to convey the idea of Appalachia as a separate and distinct region within the United States. Examination of native flora as a means of regional identification brings book cover art and design into focus. When viewed in this manner, we can see the cultural attitudes and ideas of the time expressed in a manner that relied on image rather than text, that made a region recognizable in a single glance from its distinctive and unique native flora.

In *Writing the Environment in Nineteenth-Century American Literature*, Petesheim and Jones ask a series of questions that address the inclusion of nature in literature, such as "how do we inscribe nature on a page?" and "how do we interpret the works of others who are inscribing nature?" and, most importantly, "when do literary representations of nature erase reality of the natural world, and when do they help us to better understand or investigate that world?" (xix). This study engages those questions as it examines the natural world of the local colorists.

The genre of local color literature itself was brought into being by what Shapiro describes as "the process by which a new reality or reality newly perceived is integrated into existing knowledge, the process by which taxonomic schemes are rearranged to make space for new knowledge." This research project relies on the same approach by taking known information and rearranging it to make room for new knowledge. Exploration of the subject of book covers in this context makes use of an underutilized resource for gaining historical insight into representations of the Appalachian region. Book cover design is an important, yet overlooked, tool in the continuing study and exploration of Appalachia as idea.

The prevailing idea or social construction of Appalachia has many different dimensions. The nineteenth-century idea of Appalachia was constructed from viewpoints and perspectives that lay "outside" rather than "inside," resulting in the prevailing stereotypes and depictions of the region.

Shapiro, in *Appalachia on Our Mind*, describes this "idea" as a means of categorizing and labeling Appalachia as "other" in depictions of the region as described by the writers and chroniclers of the region that I refer to as the big three: writers of local color literature, missionaries, and the tourists who documented their "idea" of Appalachia.

The rhododendron, as part of that idea, provides context, situating the reader within the region.

Exploration
Discovery versus Interpretation

In the eighteenth century, when Appalachia was the American frontier, naturalists such as William Bartram, André Michaux, and the Frasers were among the first travelers to experience the Appalachian region and write of its unique botanical treasures. At this time, the idea of wilderness was akin to a "mythology among Europeans that associated the forest with a dark, evil, and forbidding land alien to human habitation, whereas towns and cleared areas came to be regarded as suitable for civilized life" (Lewis 15). This European mythological approach to forests and unexplored territory was the prevailing attitude during the time of the great naturalists who came to this country to explore and categorize the riches of the dark and strange wilderness of the Appalachian frontier, and intrepid travelers were often frustrated by the tangled undergrowth and native flora of the Appalachians.

While this wilderness could inspire fear, it also moved others to note its singular beauty. Tennessee's Roan Mountain is recognized as the home of the purple rhododendron. When the rhododendron is in bloom, the mountain is covered with its purple blossoms. The French botanist André Michaux, who wrote of the *Rhododendron catawbiense* in 1803, years after seeing it for the first time on Roan Mountain, is credited with its discovery in 1796 (Ellison). One of his traveling companions, John Fraser, son of the famous botanist of the same name, offered this description of the purple rhododendron: "I shall never forget as long as I live the day we [John, Jr., and his father, John] discovered this plant. We had been traveling among the mountains, and one morning we were ascending to the summit of Great Roan [Bald Mt], N.C. in the midst of a fog so dense that we could not see farther than a yard before us. As we reached the top the fog began to clear away, and the sun to shine out brightly. The first object that attracted our eye, growing among the long grass, was *Rhododendron Catawbiense* in full bloom. There was no other plant there but itself and the grass, and the scene was beautiful!" (Ewan). Undeterred by difficulties, explorers such as Bartram, Michaux, and the Frasers traversed the Appalachian wilderness and used the landscape and flora they discovered on their journeys to define the region. Where many Europeans may have viewed such unexplored landscapes with fear, naturalists such as Michaux saw only opportunity to categorize and classify the botanical wealth and diversity of a new world. Bartram also "commented at length on the profusion of blossoming species, such as the rhododendron, and as others had done before him, he likened the mountains rising ahead of him to the waves of the sea" (Williams 84). Upon seeing the purple rhododendron in bloom, so moved was Bartram that he recorded his observations in his diary: "My imagination thus wholly engaged in the contemplation of this magnificent landscape, infinitely varied, and without bound, I was almost insensible or regardless of the charming objects more within my reach: a new species of Rhododendron foremost in the assembly of mountain beauties" (336).

Bartram, the Frasers, and Michaux all spoke of the native *Chododendron catawbiense*, whose beautiful, pinkish-purple flowers are striking in comparison to another native rhododendron, the common *Rhododendron maximum*, or great rhododendron, whose branches formed the impenetrably dense "laurel" (Kephart 295, 301) described by travelers and whose flowers are a creamy white shading to blush pink that bloom in June, much later then the early flowering *Chododendron catawbiense*.[3] Over a century later, Appalachian ethnographer Horace Kephart would echo these descriptions when he wrote, "In summer the upper mountains are one vast flower garden [with] the white and pink of rhododendron ... conspicuous above all else, in settings of every imaginable shade of green" (55).

Beginning in the middle of the nineteenth century, a new type of explorer sought to travel the region previously explored by naturalists and botanists. This new type of explorer tramped the highways and byways of Appalachia searching for a distinctive flavor in a region that seemed to their urban eyes as different and apart from their everyday lives and those of their prospective readers. Local color writers, such as John Fox Jr. and James Lane Allen, among others, sought to infuse their literary tales with an element of truth by steeping their stories with a rich and descriptive sense of place. This element of truth, the evocation of a sense of place, took a prominent position on the covers of local cover literature.

The presence of native flora representing the Appalachian region on the covers of books became an important design element. Books could now be stamped with the image of a blossoming rhododendron complete with tattered leaf as if nibbled by an insect or foraging deer—as seen on the cover of John Fox Jr.'s *Hell Fer Sartain* (1897)—to provide the reading public with a visual image that conveyed a sense of place and at the same time set the scene for the story.

Fox's collection of short stories is based in the Appalachian region. The final story, "The Purple Rhododendron," takes the reader to the highlands of Southwest Virginia and a tale of failed romance. In Fox's story, a young man

Cover of *"Hell fer Sartain": And Other Stories*, by John Fox Jr. New York: Harper, 1897. Berea College, Weatherford Collection.

named Grayson vows to climb a treacherous peak where a purple flowering rhododendron will be the first to bloom, encouraged by the cool sunshine of early spring. Grayson hopes to win back his love by bringing her a blossom of the purple rhododendron, a greater prize than the white. Instead, he falls to his death with a cluster in his hand.

In contrast to the naturalists who used botanical discoveries to define a region, the local colorists used landscape and flora to set a region apart from the rest of America. The history of the exploration of the Appalachian region, from naturalist to local colorists, forged a connecting chain that begins with discovery, recognition, and description during the first phase of botanical exploration and continued with an idea of landscape as a separation device in the later phase of regional exploration as local color writing.

Establishment of place through the description of landscape by local color writers proved to be a key element to the popularity of local color literature. Situating stories within the natural environment further placed the region's residents as "a people apart." In his essay, Sloman quotes Charles Brockden Brown's statement that "America has opened new views" for the novelist to "exhibit a series of adventures, growing out of the condition of our country" (1).

According to Shapiro, "The second 'discovery' of Appalachia ... took place in the new middle-class magazines that flourished in the years following the Civil War, in the context of an emerging literature of local color. Although this discovery occurred simultaneously with the systematic development of the natural resources of the region, it was the strangeness of the strange land rather than the economic opportunities which it offered that made Appalachia seem interesting and hence a suitable field for literary exploitation" (5–6). Shapiro also notes, "As literature, the work of the American local colorists is most closely tied to the travel sketches and descriptions of scenery written by the naturalists and physicians ... who sought to make knowledge of the climate, geography, resources, and natural history of America available to the scientific community" (9).

In the hands of local colorists, Appalachia was considered not as a land rich in botanical diversity but as a landscape to be idealized or criticized to match the author's point of view, as Shapiro explains: "The mid-nineteenth century writer and illustrator David Hunter Strother [pen name Porte Crayon] helped to perpetuate the notion that the Western Virginia mountain wilderness was threatening and 'impenetrable'" (5–6). John Fox Jr., in *The Trail of the Lonesome Pine* (1908), described the Appalachian region and idealized it as a place of beauty filled with natural resources waiting for exploitation.

The Gilded Leaf
Botanical Images as Book Decoration

From the earliest days, the cover of the book has been a ripe surface, ready to accept a gilded leaf stamped with an implement by hand, painted upon its surface, or printed on the page. The decoration of the book is subject to the technology and manufacturing processes of the time, but no matter the period, beautiful results could always be achieved. These delicate images of leaf, flower, and bud come down through the ages, and the simplicity or intricacy of the natural motif is still a marvel of ingenuity.[4]

The stamping on the book's cover of a solitary leaf, often referred to as the "Aldine Leaf,"[5] is one of the oldest and most recognized of the traditional book decorations. The Aldine or vine leaf, often placed on the title page of sixteenth- and seventeenth-century bookbindings or used to mark the end of a paragraph in the work of fine presses from the nineteenth century, has remained a standard device for the decoration of books.

In these early days, book production was spread across a variety of shops.

Aldine Leaf

The text was printed by the bookseller, who printed only as many copies as he thought he could sell and distribute to other sellers or lending libraries. The binder's work was performed in a separate shop. The binding of a single press run of books may have been spread across three or four binders, as shops were small and bindery work was purely a handicraft. Shops were equipped to handle only a short run of books at a time.

By the late nineteenth century, all of this had changed. As book manufacturing advanced in the industrial era, machinery took the place of hand tools, moving beyond the solitary leaf of earlier book decoration. Now the technology was available to quickly and repeatedly stamp an entire limb or a blossoming tree on a book cover in ink colors beyond the traditional gold and with leaves in a variety of shapes and sizes, mimicking those in real life. The development of manufacturing processes, including the introduction of steam to book production, paved the way for trained artists commissioned by the publisher to design and decorate the book's cover to match the text.[6] According to Chase,

> No experienced maker of book-covers would be willing to begin his design until he had become thoroughly acquainted with the contents of the book. Any stupid blunder on the part of the designer will not be forgotten by the publishers.... The designer who submits a cover for "In the Winter Woods" upon which he has utilized the graceful shape of the weeping willow, snow-laden though it be, makes himself ridiculous because the story concerns the Maine woods, with their evergreen-trees. A delicate pattern of lilies of the valley would be no more incongruous. (38)

The outpouring of local color literature demanded a similar treatment. From the first, botanical explorers and naturalists took their tasks seriously, exploring, cataloging, drawing, collecting, and examining the unique flora of the region. Local color writers relied on botanical images that would create the most interest and particularly images that would mark the region as unique, strange and different, a place set apart from urban America.

Rhododendron image from the cover of John Fox Jr.'s *Christmas Eve on Old Lonesome*, uniform edition, 1912.

In the titles and on the covers of their books, local colorists relied on plants to provide a sense of place. When local colorists arrived on the scene, the rediscovery of the region took another form and interpreted what it surveyed. Stylistic forms of representative interpretations heavily relied on the use of native flora to establish locale, for example, the rhododendron used on the cover of Fox's uniform edition of his works.[7]

The nineteenth century brought a combination of technology and art that could stamp a book's cover with a rhododendron or a mountain laurel, with a cone from a pine or hemlock, with bluegrass or corn stalks.[8]

Technology had evolved to allow for the mass production of books: "Books handsomely bound gilt, lettered, embossed and otherwise ornamented, no longer depend upon individual skill but are produced with extraordinary rapidity by the aid of machinery" (Chase 41). Better methods of distribution, from roads traveled by peddlers and subscription salesmen to river barges and railroads, could now place books in the hands of everyone, whether their residence was in a rural or urban setting.

James Lane Allen, according to Shapiro, after a lackluster turn as scholar and educator, decided to turn his hand to writing for a living. Henry Mills Alden of *Harper's* magazine reached out to Allen and encouraged him to write about Kentucky. Allen took Alden's advice and from this point followed the well-trod path established by others: tour the country, find your "little corner," make observations, gather material, and then return to write (Shapiro 26).

As Shapiro states, Allen's "plan was to publish a descriptive sketch, then re-work the sketch as background for a short story, thus guaranteeing the 'realism' of his stories while utilizing his material most efficiently" (26). This technique led to tremendous success for Allen. His essay, "Through Cumberland Gap on Horseback," was the result of this endeavor (Allen). Quickly published in *Harper's* in June 1886, "Through Cumberland Gap on Horseback" followed his first article for the magazine, "In the Blue-Grass Region of Kentucky," by a mere four months.

Allen's innovation, and one that had far-reaching implications for other local color writers, was his treatment of the state of Kentucky as a land split between the elites of the bluegrass and the "peculiar" people of the state's mountainous region. In doing this, Allen set the stage for "otherness," blazing the trail other local colorists would follow by describing/asserting Appalachia as "different and other" from the rest of America—rural versus urban—a distinct geographic region, home to a backward people with an outdated mode of living, set apart by its "exotic" and dramatic terrain, natural resources, and native botanical curiosities.

This very concept was used to great effect on the covers of his books. For example, the cover design for *Blue-Grass and Rhododendron* placed the overlapping elements of both plants on the book's cover, signifying the split Allen described in his earlier article, now published in book form, and foreshadowed the split other local colorists would imply between Appalachia and the rest of industrialized, urbanized America. As readers of *Harper's* magazine, everyone would have recognized this symbolic design immediately upon first seeing the book's cover. Where Allen saw Kentucky as a state split between two factions, local colorists adopted the same idea and used it to represent what they saw as a split between Appalachia and the rest of America. Allen is recognized as an influence on the work of Fox, who in turn interpreted Allen's idea of otherness, the split between the "two Kentuckys," and molded this idea into his own fiction.

As Baxter has said, "Charles Scribner's Sons first printed a staggering 100,000 copies of Fox's *The Trail of the Lonesome Pine* and (it was) simultaneously published in London... Soon, 200,000 more copies were printed. The novel was the third best seller in 1908 and fifth in 1909. After the first three printings sold quickly, the book was published nineteen more times. More than two million copies have now sold" (22). With this success, Fox "became the definitive source on southern mountain society in the public imagination" (Harkins 41).

With quite literally hundreds of thousands of copies in print, one can see the wide-ranging impact local color literature had on populations as diverse as those in urban America and abroad. It is not hard to see from these staggering statistics that local color literature had entered the mainstream and was the foundational literature for the spread of ideas about the Appalachian region as a place apart and the stereotypical treatment of its residents. Along the way, book covers with images of the rhododendron elevated it to a brand-like status for the region.

With this level of popularity in the literary marketplace, Fox and Allen brought a legitimacy to local color literature. Allen brought the idea of "otherness" and separateness to the genre through his concept of the "two Kentuckys," and Fox, following in the footsteps established by Allen, incorporated the tension of otherness between Appalachia and America, between elite and poor mountain white, to craft successful and popular fiction that survives to this day.

Most importantly, it was the book's cover art that was the tool used to signify this tension, as the essential element for establishing the story's setting, and providing that authentic "sense of place" so crucial to the tales of every local colorist. Perhaps one of the best uses of native flora to evoke not only locale but also the purported divide between Kentuckians of the highlands and their farmland neighbors, as reported in the nineteenth century, is the use of bluegrass and rhododendron in book design on the cover of two novels by Fox.

In *Through Cumberland Gap on Horseback*, Allen described the state of Kentucky as a land divided. In these two books by Fox, we can clearly decipher Allen's idea of the "Two Kentuckys" through the use of native flora portrayed on the covers of Fox's books. Both books depict highly stylized interpretations of the region's native flora and rely on an interweaving and overlaying of specific plants to identify the novels' setting as the state of Kentucky. In this instance the use of native flora serves another function as well—bluegrass and rhododendron highlight the tension Allen described in his book between the two regions of Kentucky.

Margaret Armstrong's design for the cover of *Blue-Grass and Rhododendron* (1901) is an art nouveau interpretation uniting the two plants, weaving them together to show unity, but supplanting one above the other to depict separation. Armstrong, a noted artist and amateur botanist, took the wild form of the plants and rendered them with an artist's sensibility to reflect not only the region through the identifying features of its native flora but the idea or concept of Allen's "Two Kentuckys" through the use of these plants on the cover of the book.[9]

Cover of *Blue-Grass and Rhododendron: Out-Doors in Old Kentucky*, by John Fox Jr. New York: Charles Scribner's Sons, 1901. West Virginia University. Scanned by the author.

Cover of *The Kentuckians* by John Fox Jr. New York: Charles Scribner's Sons, 1905. Berea College, Weatherford Collection.

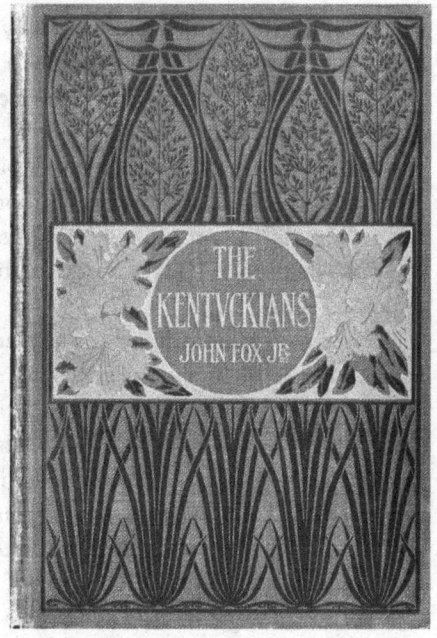

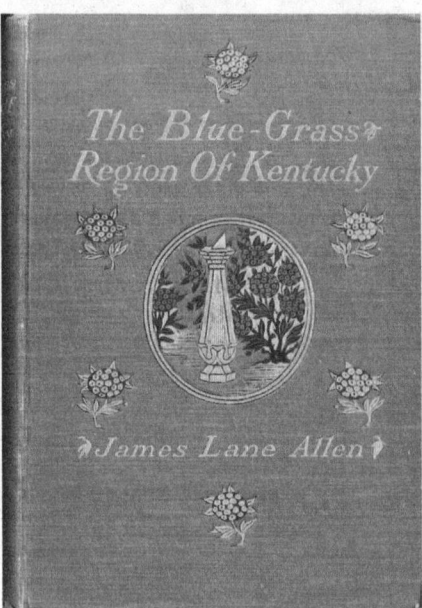

Cover of *The Blue-Grass Region of Kentucky, and Other Kentucky Articles*, by James Lane Allen. New York: Macmillan, 1911. Virginia Union University Archives and Special Collections.

These specific plants clearly identify the book's setting as Kentucky and notify the prospective audience, one that would surely be familiar with Allen's *Through Cumberland Gap on Horseback*, from either its publication run in *Harper's* magazine or later in book form. Interested readers would have been expected to instantly recognize the depiction of these two plants not only as representatives of locale but also as representatives of the tension Allen described as existing between the two "distinct" populations of Kentucky, the highlanders depicted by the rhododendron and the farmers of the bluegrass region.

Although the designer of the second book, Fox's *The Kentuckians* (1898), is unknown to us today, the same technique has been used successfully to convey the separate identities of Kentucky through the use of its native flora. Once again, the rhododendron has been placed in a superior position above the repeating fronds of a field of flowering bluegrass. These two plants, like their use on the cover of Fox's *Bluegrass and Rhododendron*, are used once again to convey the idea of region and tension between the residents of the highlands and those of the farmland of Kentucky.

The cover design for Allen's *The Blue-Grass Region of Kentucky* (1899) takes a slightly different approach to the same ends. This design, by an unknown artist, still incorporates the rhododendron as the hallmark of the highland

West Virginia University Press logo. https://twitter.com/wvupress. Used with permission by West Virginia University Press.

region of Kentucky. However, the use of bluegrass as an indicator of the farming region has been substituted with a sundial. The presence of a garden ornament indicates a level of comfortable living, such as that of a successful farmer, while the impressionistic representation of the rhododendron, both within the oval framework and outside of its borders, represents the concept of the "two Kentuckys." Within the oval frame, the rhododendron and sundial represent the farmers, while the scattered rhododendron sprays outside the oval framework denote the lesser status of the highlanders. Image as indicator of region also serves as evidence of the cultural attitudes and ideas of the day.

From Fox's *Hell Fer Sartain* to Allen's *Blue-Grass Region of Kentucky*, it is the biodiversity of the Appalachian region that creates a framework for exploration. From the early naturalists of the eighteenth century, whose description of new plant discoveries set the region apart from the familiar plants of the European continent, to the local color writers of the nineteenth century, whose discovery of the region and its botanical treasures was used as a descriptive device to set the Appalachian region apart from urban America, the natural diversity of the region has played a key role in its identity to the larger world.

The establishment of the rhododendron in the nineteenth century and early twentieth as a graphic indicator of place on the covers of local color literature addresses the questions posed by Petesheim and Jones (xix). As a form of expression in the book arts, the rhododendron was emblematic of Appalachia.

Even today, the rhododendron remains a powerful symbol of Appalachia, representing region, place, culture, and identity. A single spray of flowering rhododendron represents these ideals as the logo for the West Virginia University Press. Many of these botanical treasures, unique to the Appalachian region, were translated by authors and artists into a symbolic shorthand used to capture a sense of place. The image of a single plant, such as the rhododendron, could serve as a graphic indicator of regional identification, providing a sense of place to the cover of local color literature that was recognizable to the reader in a single glance.

Without these books as the foundation for scholarship, whether they are representatives of a bygone stereotypical view of Appalachians and the Appalachian region, or enlightening literature for urban Americans of the nineteenth century, much will be lost in the continuing study of the region. The lasting legacy of the sense of place determined in the pages and on the covers of nineteenth-century local color literature is still with us today.

NOTES

1. The Virginia Tech Department of Forest Resources and Environmental Conservation is an excellent resource for an overview of the rhododendron in the Appalachian region. "Rhododendron catawbiense," http://dendro.cnre.vt.edu/dendrology/syllabus/factsheet.cfm?ID=316; "Rhododendron maximum," http://dendro.cnre.vt.edu/dendrology/syllabus/factsheet.cfm?ID=81.

2. There are several different recurring motifs or images that have typified Appalachia—log cabins, stills, mountains, for example. Just as the thistle and shamrock are seen as a representation of Scotland and the fleur-de-lis represents France, the rhododendron is among those images that is representative of Appalachia. While there is a body of scholarship on these mountain tropes, such as discussed in McNeil's *Appalachian Images in Folk and Popular Culture* (1995), Harkins's *Hillbilly: A Cultural History of an American Icon* (2005), as well as Rehder's *Appalachian Folkways* (2004), the rhododendron has not been given its due. In my extensive examination of hundreds of examples of Appalachian local color literature, both fiction and nonfiction, I have found the prominent use of the rhododendron to be a regional signifier. As such, this statement is based on my own original research. My initial study of this topic was published in the *Journal of Appalachian Studies*.

3. Forest Resources and Environmental Department, Virginia Tech, "Rhododendron catawbiense," http://dendro.cnre.vt.edu/dendrology/syllabus/factsheet.cfm?ID=316; "Rhododendron maximum," http://dendro.cnre.vt.edu/dendrology/syllabus/factsheet.cfm?ID=81. See also Donald Hyatt's article, "Rhododendron catawbiense and Rhododendron maximum: The Elepidote Species of Eastern North America," for photographs and descriptions of these two native rhododendrons, http://www.donaldhyatt.com/articles/EasternElepidotes-03-illustrated.pdf.

4. For a good review of bindery practices, see the chapter on the binding trade in Philip Gaskell's *A New Introduction to Bibliography*, 146–49.

5. For an introductory discussion on the history and use of the Aldine Leaf as a typographical element, see the Collation blog post by Goran Proot for the Folger Library at https://collation.folger.edu/2013/06/the-single-vine-leaf-aka-the-aldine-leaf/ and the Booktryst blog post by Alastair Johnston at http://www.booktryst.com/2012/10/typographical-dingbats-explored-raising.html. For an image of an Aldine Leaf, see https://upload.wikimedia.org/wikipedia/commons/thumb/1/10/Aldine_typographique_%28Zapf%29.png/64px-Aldine_typographique_%28Zapf%29.png.

6. See Frank E. Comparato's *Books for the Millions* for an excellent overview of the development of the historical and technological manufacturing methods of the book.

7. A uniform edition is a collection of all an author's work similarly bound. Though each book can be purchased separately, the books have the appearance of being a set.

8. For an image from the cover of John Fox Jr.'s *Christmas Eve on Old Lonesome*, uniform edition, see http://www.djsawyerbooks.com/titles/000094.htm.

9. The fact that one of the most prominent book binding designers of the day, Margaret Armstrong, was responsible for the book's binding design is of equal importance. Armstrong was a descendant of a grand, old New York family. Not only was her skill recognized within the publishing community, as she designed for several publishing houses simultaneously, but she was also popular among readers, who recognized her designs by a monogram of her initials, MA. Her cover designs were so popular that they were credited by publishers in their catalogs as a selling point. Armstrong's cover design for Fox's *Blue-Grass and Rhododendron* indelibly created the necessary "sense of place" essential for any work of local color. For an excellent look at the life and career of Margaret Armstrong, see Gullans and Espey, *Margaret Armstrong and American Trade Bindings*.

BIBLIOGRAPHY

Allen, James Lane. "Through Cumberland Gap on Horseback." *Harper's New Monthly Magazine* 73, no. 433 (1886): 50–66.

Bartram, William. *Travels through North & South Carolina, Georgia, East & West Florida, the Cherokee Country, the Extensive Territories of the Muscogulges, or Creek Confederacy, and the Country of the Chactaws; Containing an Account of the Soil and Natural Productions of Those Regions, Together with Observations on the Manners of the Indians. Embellished with Copper-Plates*. Philadelphia: James & Johnson, 1791. http://docsouth.unc.edu/nc/bartram/bartram.html.

Baxter, Tamara. "The Trail of the Lonesome Pine at 100." *Now & Then: The Appalachian Magazine* 24, no. 1 (2008): 22.

Chase, John Cummings. *Decorative Design: A Text-book of Practical Methods*. Hoboken, N.J.: John Wiley, 1915.

Comparato, Frank E. *Books for the Millions: A History of the Men Whose Methods and Machines Packaged the Printed Word*. Harrisburg, Pa.: Stackpole, 1971.

Ellison, George. *Mountain Passages: Natural and Cultural History of Western North Carolina*, Gloucestershire: History Press, 2005.

Ewan, Joseph. "History of Exploring for Rhododendrons in Southeastern United States." *Journal American Rhododendron Society* 33, no. 4 (1979): n.p.

Gaskell, Philip. *A New Introduction to Bibliography*. New Castle, Del.: Oak Knoll Books, 2006.

Gullans, Charles, and John Espey. *Margaret Armstrong and American Trade Bindings*. UCLA University Research Library, Department of Special Collections, Occasional Papers no. 6. Los Angeles: University of California, Los Angeles, 1991.

Hackett, Alice Payne. *Fifty Years of Best Sellers: 1895–1945*. Ann Arbor, Mich.: R.R. Bowker, 1945.

Harkins, Anthony. *Hillbilly: A Cultural History of an American Icon*. Oxford: Oxford University Press, 2005.

Harney, Will Wallace. "A Strange and Peculiar People." *Lippincott's Magazine of Popular Literature and Science* 12, no. 31 (1873): 429–39.

Kephart, Horace. *Our Southern Highlanders*. New York: Outing, 1913.
Lewis, Ronald L., *Transforming the Appalachian Countryside: Railroads, Deforestation, and Social Change in West Virginia, 1880–1920*. Chapel Hill: University of North Carolina Press, 1998.
McNeil, W. K. *Appalachian Images in Folk and Popular Culture*. Knoxville: University of Tennessee Press, 1995.
Petesheim, Steven, and Madison P. Jones IV. *Writing the Environment in Nineteenth-Century American Literature: The Ecological Awareness of Early Scribes of Nature*. Lanham, Md.: Lexington Books, 2015.
Plein, Stewart. "Portraits of Appalachia: The Identification of Stereotype in Publishers' Bookbindings, 1850–1915." *Journal of Appalachian Studies* 15, no. 1/2 (2009): 99–115.
Rehder, John B. *Appalachian Folkways*. Baltimore: Johns Hopkins University Press, 2004.
Shapiro, Henry D., *Appalachia on Our Mind: The Southern Mountains and Mountaineers in the American Consciousness, 1870–1920*. Chapel Hill: University of North Carolina Press, 1978.
Sloman, Christopher. "Navigating the Interior: Edgar Huntly and the Mapping of Early America." In *Writing the Environment in Nineteenth-Century American Literature: The Ecological Awareness of Early Scribes of Nature*, edited by Steven Petesheim and Madison P. Jones IV. Lanham, Md.: Lexington Books, 2015.
Williams, John Alexander. *Appalachia: A History*. Chapel Hill: University of North Carolina Press, 2002.

What Lies Beyond the Summit
The Future of Appalachian Ecocriticism

Toward a Post-Appalachian Sense of Place

ZACKARY VERNON

In recent years, Ron Rash, Terry Roberts, and Charles Frazier have produced historical novels that complicate critical understandings of the U.S. South as both an actual material geography and, in Michael Kreyling's theorization, an *invented* cultural and literary space.[1] Rash's *The Cove* (2012), Roberts's *A Short Time to Stay Here* (2012), and Frazier's *Nightwoods* (2011) present fetishizations of rural, agricultural spaces that may be the result of lingering fantasies about Appalachia's agrarian past and anxieties about Appalachia's largely post-agrarian present. Although these novels glean material from past cultural productions, their allusions lack the parodic, intertextual qualities that so often mark postmodern and "postsouthern" literature. Instead, these novels appear more firmly grounded in historicity, by which I mean Fredric Jameson's explanation of the concept as the "lived possibility of experiencing history in some active way" (*Postmodernism* 21).[2] As a result of this sense of historicity, Rash, Roberts, and Frazier grapple earnestly—or at least more earnestly than is typical of so-called postsouthern writers—with how the sociohistorical shifts in Appalachia have impacted the region and its fictional representations. In this essay, I utilize these three novels as case studies that are representative of broader trends in Appalachian literature,[3] and I seek to determine whether postsouthern theory can be applied to Appalachia and whether Appalachian literature—despite its seeming historicity—may be more accurately labeled "post-Appalachian."

Much criticism in southern studies has been concerned with the decline of southern cultural and literary distinctiveness. For example, in *The Real South: Southern Narrative in the Age of Cultural Reproduction*, Scott Romine argues that proclamations about the demise of the South are part of a "standard account of globalization" (1). Romine identifies two common trends in the globalization narrative that, in the southern context, he attributes to cultural critics John Egerton and Edwin M. Yoder: "Both Egerton and Yoder place the Real Dixie in jeopardy, either as an absolute loss of culture under the homogenizing force of Americanization or as a simulation of culture—Dixiefication, not Dixie—that marks continuity itself as a fake." Debates about southern exceptionalism are by no means new; seminal scholars and critics, such as C. Vann Woodward and Allen Tate, highlighted southern cultural performativity and southern literary contrivances as early as the mid-twentieth century. The conversation has become more eschatological, prompting Lewis P. Simpson in 1980 to contend that we have entered a "postsouthern" era, and more recently Leigh Anne Duck has gone so far as to claim that the "New Southern Studies" is actually "southern studies without 'the South'" (qtd. in Bone 13).

Such declarations of the meaninglessness of "the South" and even the placelessness of the region may seem strange given that the South and southern literature have long been distinguished by their firm grounding in place.[4] Discourse about "sense of place" has been virtually ubiquitous in southern studies, particularly since Eudora Welty's 1956 essay "Place in Fiction," in which she notes, "It is both natural and sensible that the place where we have our roots should become the setting, the first and primary proving ground, of our fiction" (793). While there is nothing pernicious about Welty's emphasis on place, what is problematic about the politics of place in southern history is that notions of southern place have often been associated with agrarianism, as presented by the Southern Agrarians in their two manifestos, *I'll Take My Stand* (1930) and *Who Owns America?* (1936).[5] According to Martyn Bone, "Even now, the standard literary-critical conception of 'place' derives substantially from the Agrarians' idealized vision of a rural, agricultural society," which is "apotheosized in the subsistence farm" (vii–viii). One significant originary moment for this tendency to apotheosize the hardscrabble southern farm was Andrew Lytle's contribution to *I'll Take My Stand*, an essay titled "The Hind Tit," in which he glorifies the satisfying life of a subsistence-farming family, claiming, "It is in fact impossible for any culture to be sound and healthy without a proper respect and proper regard for the soil" (202–3).[6]

In part because of the critical influence wielded throughout the mid-twentieth century by the Agrarians (and later the New Critics)—for example, Allen Tate, Robert Penn Warren, John Crowe Ransom, and Donald Davidson—literary scholars have tended to yoke Welty's "sense of place" with Agrarian idealizations of rurality or what Richard Godden calls an "aesthetics of anti-development" (qtd. in Bone ix). The persistence of Agrarian conceptions of place is evident if we consider the abundance of scholars and critics who have used Agrarian ideology—regardless of whether they support or revile the Agrarians—as a sort of yardstick to determine the "southernness" of texts both old and new. Contemporary proponents of the concept of postsouthernism argue that this conflation of Weltyan sense of place with Agrarianism is anachronistic because Agrarian policies against industry, technology, and development are no longer viable in literature given that they are no longer feasible for the vast majority of the region.[7]

Although several prominent literary critics have discussed postsouthernism,[8] the neologism was first used by Lewis P. Simpson. In "The Closure of History in a Postsouthern America" (1980), Simpson states that the term "postsouthern" signifies a diminishment, if not the death, of southern exceptionalism, both in southern culture and in southern literature; the postsouthern, for Simpson, also reflects the flattening of regional diversity and the ascendency of national homogenization. Michael Kreyling's "Fee Fie Faux Faulkner: Parody and Postmodernism in Southern Literature" extends Simpson's theorization of the postsouthern, and for Kreyling postsouthernism is a way to imagine the postmodern tendency toward parody in the southern literary context. Thus, according to Kreyling, writers like Harry Crews and Barry Hannah could best be understood by studying their parodic relationships to Faulkner, and, more broadly, studying these types of parodic relationship demonstrates how writers negotiate and ultimately shed the Harold Bloomian "anxiety of influence" engendered by their southern literary forebears. In "Where Is Southern Literature? The Practice of Place in a Postsouthern Age," Romine builds upon Kreyling's thesis and argues that because a "real South" does not exist that contemporary southern writers can mimetically reflect in their work, they are left with only an intertextual mode of southern writing in which they feed off of older southern texts that actually had a "South" to reflect: "postsouthern literature can be delineated, as it were, only by its relationship to earlier writing that could image itself as Southern (capital S, no quotation marks)."

The concept of postsouthernism has been reenergized in recent years by Martyn Bone, whose *The Postsouthern Sense of Place in Contemporary Fiction* (2005) was the first (and to date only) book-length scholarly work to assess postsouthernism and the politics of place in the South. Although he undoubtedly drew on previous scholars such as Simpson, Kreyling, and Romine, Bone's primary aim is not necessarily to examine postmodern parody and intertextuality but rather to examine the South from a "historical-geographical materialist" perspective that enables him to consider the impact of capitalism on contemporary conceptions of southern place (x). Moreover, Bone's work extends beyond a privileging of place that is the result of lingering neo-Agrarianism and instead moves toward a nuanced sense of place that has more to do with the material cultures and geographies of place than with a commodified and fabricated sense of culture that is often imagined or invented.[9] Bone's emphasis on the "historical-geographical materialist" continuities of place is similar to Kreyling's and Romine's analyses of texts' parasitic, intertextual relationships insofar as all three of these approaches problematize the clearly delineated breaks between the southern and the postsouthern that some scholars have sought to identify.

In a keynote lecture given in the spring of 2012 at North Carolina State University, Bone argued that "the most conspicuous lacuna in existing definitions and discussions of postsouthernism [is] the failure to attend to the cultural productions of non-white southerners" (9). Striving not to fall into the trap of associating southern literature with *white* southern literature, Bone has explored in his more recent scholarship African American writers whose work may be read in the postsouthern vein; perhaps his best example of this is Alice Randall's *The Wind Done Gone* (2001), a postmodern, postsouthern parody of Margaret Mitchell's *Gone with the Wind* (1936). While I certainly appreciate Bone's efforts to analyze more nonwhite writers, I would also add that a second lacuna exists in theorizations of the postsouthern: the consideration of whether Appalachian writers fit into increasingly codified understandings of postsouthernism.[10] Appalachian writers are, after all, another group that has often been marginalized. In "Writing on the Cusp: Double Alterity and Minority Discourse in Appalachia" (1996), Rodger Cunningham argues, "Appalachia exists in a blank created by a double otherness—a *doubly* double otherness. For the region is not only an internal Other to the South as the South is the internal Other of America, but it is also the occupier of a simultaneous gap and overlap *between* North and South" (45, emphasis original). While it is imperative to acknowledge the distinctiveness of Appalachian history, it is equally imperative not to buttress outdated notions of Appalachian exceptionalism.[11] Much of southern Appalachia is part of the broader region identified as the South, and southern Appalachians often tend to embrace a southern as well as an Appalachian identity. According to a 2004 article by sociologist Larry J. Griffin, 74 percent of southern Appalachians identify themselves as "southern," which is a higher percentage of self-identifying southerners than in many places in the "peripheral" South (Virginia, North Carolina, Tennessee, Florida, Kentucky, Oklahoma, West Virginia, Arkansas, and Texas) (12–13). Overestimating the otherness of the South or the otherness of Appalachia within the South can be problematic because, as Herbert Reid argues, "a retreat to elemental group identity can lock us into a one-sided, hence reified and exaggerated, sense of Otherness" (164). Examining southern Appalachia as part the region commonly identified as the South will demonstrate how this particular portion of the region has at times developed differently—in terms of both culture and literature—than other places in the Deep South and the peripheral South.

Although my intention in this chapter is foremost to intervene in current postsouthern criticism and theory, my questions about the present state of Appalachian identity and sense of place are consistent with contemporary work that is being done specifically in the field of Appalachian studies. Several examples of the this type of work appear in the Fall 2010 issue of *Appalachian Journal*, which features "Appalachian Identity: A Roundtable Discussion," comprising short articles by Barbara Ellen Smith, Stephen Fisher, Phillip J. Obermiller, David Whisnant, Emily Satterwhite, and Rodger Cunningham.[12] This roundtable grew out of two sessions at the 2007 and 2008 Appalachian Studies conferences that were purposely organized to interrogate Appalachian regional identity. In the introduction to this roundtable, Smith states, "Here in the Appalachian region, deindustrialization, economic contraction, and forced migration undermine the viability of place-based communities, while the literal destruction of place through mountaintop removal proceeds apace" (57). A sense of incredulity regarding both the viability and the knowability of contemporary place-based Appalachian identity is echoed throughout the other essays in the roundtable. While Fisher offers what Smith calls one of the two "most favorable interpretations and endorsements" of Appalachian identity (Smith 56), he admits the impossibility of defining Appalachian identity in the present: "There is still no consensus as to what we really mean when we use the term 'Appalachian.' . . . In fact, I could make just as strong a case *against* Appalachian regionalism and identity as *for* it" (Fisher 58, emphasis original). Obermiller's essay, which is Smith's second example of a "favorable" endorsement of Appalachian identity, is similar to Fisher's in that it sidesteps the question of "ontological Appalachianness," instead stating that while Appalachian identity may be constructed, scholarship on the subject is most useful when it considers the "agency of identity, that is, how it can be used to create a better life by people *in* the place, or *from* the place, we call Appalachia" (63). Following Fisher and Obermiller, the essays in the roundtable by Whisnant, Satterwhite, and Cunningham provide even sharper criticisms of the notion of a coherent Appalachian identity. Satterwhite makes the point most directly when she states, "I have zero patience for insider/outside politics: I have no use for claims to authenticity or personal history with the region as evidence of authority and accuracy" ("Objecting" 68).[13]

While interest in contemporary Appalachian identity has at times been most robust among historians and sociologists, Satterwhite is one notable example of a scholar who has adeptly brought American studies as well as literary studies into dialogue with the question of Appalachian identity. For example, in *Dear Appalachia: Readers, Identity, and Popular Fiction since 1978* (2011), she "examines fan mail written in response to best-selling fiction set in Appalachia to understand how readers imagined the region and what purposes these imagined geographies served for them. Fan mail shows us that, from 1878 to 2003, readers who embraced best-selling fiction set in Appalachia conceived the region as a rooted, rural place populated by simple whites with a rich and colorful heritage protected from mass culture" (2). As thorough and convincing as Satterwhite's study is, it does not utilize recent postsouthern theory to explore the construction of Appalachian identity in literature. Furthermore, no postsouthern scholars have yet provided any sustained attention to the production of Appalachian literature and identity.

My argument intervenes in both of these critical veins—Appalachian studies and postsouthern theory—and my hope is that it will foster more discussion in each field and between these two fields that are necessarily linked. Examining Ron Rash's *The Cove* (2012), Terry Roberts's *A Short Time to Stay Here* (2012), and Charles Frazier's *Nightwoods* (2011) can facilitate a study of the relationship between postsouthernism and (post-)Appalachian culture and literature. Aside from the obvious connection between these three novels—i.e., they are all set in or around once-grand hotels in western North Carolina—the most significant link is a thematic preoccupation with an Appalachian past in which mountain inhabitants appear more substantively tied to the region's purportedly traditional forms of agriculture. While it could be said that Rash, Roberts, and Frazier all indulge in agrarian (lowercase "a," i.e., not necessarily Southern Agrarian) fantasies, each author also demonstrates a self-reflective awareness of this indulgence and each undermines Agrarian (capital A, i.e., Southern Agrarian) understandings of the rural, agricultural South.

Rash's *The Cove* tells the story of Laurel Shelton, a young woman living in a mountain cove outside Mars Hill, North Carolina, in 1917. Laurel is ostracized from her community because of a large birthmark on her back that leads the townspeople to believe she is a witch. After the death of her parents, which the locals attribute to a curse upon both Laurel and the cove, Laurel's only human contact comes from her brother Hank, who has recently returned from World War I after losing a hand, and Slidell, an eighty-one-year-old neighbor who is the sole member of the community willing to venture into the cove. Laurel's circle of acquaintances expands slightly after she finds an unconscious man in the woods who has been repeatedly stung by yellow jackets. The man has few belongings other than a silver flute and a letter saying, "The bearer of this note is Walter Smith. A childhood affliction has made him not able to speak. He wishes to buy a train ticket to New York City" (Rash 43). After Laurel nurses Walter back to health, he begins to work on the farm that Laurel and Hank have been struggling to manage, particularly since Hank lost his hand. Sharing a sense of alterity, Laurel and Walter form a bond that blossoms into a love affair. However, Laurel soon learns that Walter is a classically trained German flutist who has escaped from an internment camp in nearby Hot Springs that has imprisoned over two thousand German nationals.[14] Subsequently, Laurel and Walter's plans to wed are interrupted both due to Walter's status as an escaped internee and due to increasing political unrest as America escalates its involvement in World War I.

In *The Cove*, Rash complicates the Agrarians' idealization of the subsistence farm by demonstrating a collision of cultures that dispels notions of insularity, cultural purity, and autochthony. Although Laurel has designs to expand the farm's business model so that one day she can sell milk, eggs, and even livestock in one of the nearby towns, the homestead in the cove that she and Hank manage is essentially a subsistence farm, the likes of which the Agrarians, particularly Lytle, would have admired (Rash 20). Laurel's dreams of expansion demonstrate that the South, including Appalachia, was and is inextricably linked to national and even international networks of social and economic exchange. Additionally, Rash's depiction of the German-American cultural clashing throughout this novel can be read as an example of the increasingly widespread multinational and transnational shifts that occurred in the region throughout the nineteenth and twentieth centuries. Such cultural clashing in the first decades of the twentieth century undermines Donald Davidson's famous "autochthonous ideal," which Fred Hobson describes as the "condition in which the writer was in a certain harmony with the social and cultural environment, was nearly *unconscious* of it as a 'special' environment, quaint or rustic or backward, and thus was not motivated by any urge to interpret or explain" (80, emphasis original). Rash uses the collision of different cultures in *The Cove* to demonstrate the process by which people become aware of the unique and idiosyncratic facets of their own culture.

In particular, Rash uses music throughout the novel to convey not only the collision of cultures in this particular moment but also the fusion of cultures. For instance, one evening after a hard day's work at the Shelton farm, Hank, Laurel, and Walter are joined by Slidell and two musicians from the area who have heard that Walter is "a crackerjack fife player" (Rash

86).[15] As the two men begin to sing and play the dulcimer, they are joined first by Slidell on guitar and then Walter on the flute. Playing standards such as "I Am a Poor Wayfaring Stranger" and "Shady Grove," their styles merge and the sounds of their instruments "tightly wove . . . and then untangled" (92). As these two very different musical traditions converge—Walter's European classicism and the other men's old-time Appalachian style—there is also a cultural merging, and the musicians leave the session having each been influenced by the others. This scene would seem like an Agrarian fantasy, following Andrew Lytle's exhortation—"Throw out the radio and take down the fiddle from the wall" (244)—however, Rash complicates the scenario by highlighting a cross-pollination of cultures. While the Agrarians likely would have argued that an insular, agricultural community is the best breeding ground for autochthonous art, Rash seems to suggest that cultural merging actually catalyzes a more complex and interesting artistic expression.[16]

Terry Roberts's novel *A Short Time to Stay Here* is concerned with the same historical event as *The Cove*. Roberts's novel is set in and around Hot Springs, North Carolina, during World War I, and it deals much more directly with the German internment camp than does Rash's novel. Rash's characters are certainly impacted by the internment camp, but the central events of the narrative transpire in "the cove" outside the town of Hot Springs. Roberts's novel, on the other hand, is set principally at the Mountain Park Hotel, which was used during the war to house many of the German captives at the internment camp. The plot of the novel revolves around a man named Stephen Robbins, the hotel manager, who is made "Inspector General of the Hot Springs Internment Camp" after the 2,370 "aliens" are brought to the North Carolina mountains (9). There are two central narrative threads in the novel: the first portrays Stephen's attempts to keep the German prisoners in the camp and the murderous, jingoistic natives out; the second depicts Stephen's love-hate relationship with Anna, a documentary photographer who comes to the mountains from New York to capture what she assumes will be an interesting collision of cultures between the refined, cosmopolitan Germans and the inhabitants of the "Darkest part of the South" (Roberts 34–35).

Roberts's *A Short Time to Stay Here* is also similar to *The Cove* in that it resists a simple neo-Agrarian reading; however, upon first encountering the narrative, the complexities may not be fully apparent, given that Stephen, the narrator of the novel, often fetishizes a rural, agricultural sense of place. For example, he says that in western North Carolina "you wouldn't find anything you'd recognize except hard-scrabble farms, pastures, hard-use barns and smoke houses and corn cribs; steep fields of corn, wheat, burley tobacco.

Western North Carolina and eastern Tennessee in 1917 wasn't the 'rural, undeveloped South' of northern newspaper articles; it was a land far beyond. It was a place of the steepest mountains, the wildest river gorges, the meanest lives, and shortest winter rations in the country. It was deep, hard, lonesome, and—if you weren't starving to death—beautiful" (12). Descriptions of southern Appalachia such as this one appear repeatedly in the novel, and it is precisely this "authentic" Appalachia that Anna longs to capture in her photographs. Thus, she goes to the mountain cove where Stephen was born, "So that she could take her photographs of real mountain people, living as they had always lived" (89). Despite her desire to record this culture that still "followed the ancient course they had learned from the land" (133), "she had no clue just how dark, how cold, how rough the place—and the people—could be" (137). In these passages, one can see a tendency to romanticize both the "beautiful" *and* the "rough" Appalachia. In the context of the U.S. South, Romine calls this tendency "nostalgia" or "utopianism with a backward glance" (*Real South* 25). This nostalgia, Romine reminds us, continues in contemporary southern culture and can be applied both to the "detoxified Souths of which Andy Griffith's Mayberry is representative" and to the "'good old bad old days' Tony Horwitz identifies in *Confederates in the Attic*."

However, in *A Short Time to Stay Here*, a more sophisticated metacommentary addresses the difficulties of capturing the authentic mountain South. There are several scenes throughout the novel in which Roberts seems perilously close to perpetuating stereotypes about Appalachia before unexpectedly reversing and undermining this pattern. For example, when Anna shows Stephen a photograph of a rural woman, he immediately argues that it is "posed" (46). Anna then says, "That's why I need you—to help me understand what is real and what isn't in this hidden away, folded up country of yours. . . . And I hate the fake, the posed, the lie." Later, when Anna says, "I came here, where people live simple, natural lives," Stephen thinks, "She said this last bit as if reading from a tourist brochure" (47). Stephen's sudden awareness of the tendency to stereotype and commodify the people of southern Appalachia provides the narrative with an interesting irony, in that Stephen himself is often guilty of relying on tired stereotypes when describing his native habitat. More importantly, though, this awareness of the commodification of an Appalachian sense of place refutes readers' potential assumption that Roberts himself is guilty of employing the same stereotypes that his characters sometimes use.

At first glance, Charles Frazier's *Nightwoods* may appear to be less closely related than *The Cove* and *A Short Time to Stay Here*. While admittedly the plot and time period of Frazier's novel are vastly different, the setting and thematic preoccupations of *Nightwoods* are inextricably linked with those of Rash's and Roberts's novels. *Nightwoods* takes place at an abandoned hotel in the North Carolina mountains during the late 1950s and tells the story of Luce, a young woman who has become the guardian of her sister's two children after her sister is murdered by her second husband, Bud. The children, Dolores and Frank, are so traumatized by their mother's murder that they have seemingly lost the ability to speak, and the state workers handling the case assume them to be "feebleminded" (9). Out of a desperate attempt to regain agency in their own lives, Dolores and Frank often engage in and relish killing chickens and setting fires. In order to quell "whatever weirdness they shared and ignited between them" (4), Luce resolves that she will have "to be a teacher" to the children and demonstrate to them how and when it is best to comply with society's rules and mores. Under Luce's guidance, the children's reinitiation into society involves cultivating an intimate knowledge of agriculture and the natural world.

Frazier's *Nightwoods* is in some ways more of an agrarian fantasy than either *The Cove* or *A Short Time to Stay Here*. This may be surprising given that *Nightwoods* is set in the late 1950s, while the other two novels are set primarily in the late 1910s. Luce's anachronistic lifestyle in the novel is the result of her living alone in the decrepit old hotel outside her hometown. Luce has set up the hotel to be a subsistence farm, which enables her to produce most of what she needs to survive. Luce's closest neighbor and friend, Maddie, lives the same way: "In particular, Maddie, living in her own world like it had remained 1898 on and on forever. Or, to be generous, maybe 1917.... Early on, Luce viewed Maddie's homeplace as mostly imaginary, life still circling around hog killings, oil lamps, fetching water, outhouses, and all that other old business. Until Luce realized that these days, her life was a lot like that too" (12–13).

Throughout the novel, Luce engages in numerous types of behavior that Lytle and the Agrarians would have looked upon approvingly. For instance, in the three years that Luce has lived at the Lodge, "she had hardly missed any of the modern world" (24). Later, we also learn that Luce refuses to grow cash crops, instead focusing on subsistence agriculture, and that she "had limited use for cash money. Most of what it bought she didn't want. She was happy without modern conveniences, her desires being mostly impractical and lacking monetary value" (141).

Yet Luce's worldview and, more broadly, Frazier's *Nightwoods* are more complex than Lytle's romanticized Agrarian fantasy. While Rash complicates the Agrarian platform by revealing the transnational influences on Appalachia and Roberts complicates it by highlighting the potential commodification of Appalachian culture, Frazier extends the Agrarian platform by yoking it to a more complex environmental philosophy. For example, in addition to teaching Dolores and Frank about agriculture and "vegetable lore" (27), Luce frequently turns her attention away from the cultivated landscape of the Lodge in order to focus on the seemingly wild environments surrounding it: "Watchfulness was something Luce had mostly applied to nothing but the natural world. Birds and leaves and weather. An occasional deer or bear or screaming panther. Distant lights in the sky at night moving contrary to the expected. And the sweetness of it was simple: the natural world would go on and on just fine whether you watched or not. Your existence was incidental. Nature didn't require anything at all other than the bare minimum deal in return for life. Be born, die" (30). The seeming indifference of the natural world does not prevent Luce from having a significant emotional and psychological attachment to it. When asked if she ever gets lonely living by herself at the Lodge, "Luce said sure she got lonely, but there had been many reimbursements. Animals, for example.... A great deal of pleasure to be found in the growth of vegetables. And in the fall, birds passing over in waves, their calls singing of distance and other landscapes and the weird tones of Maddie's folklore songs from back in an older America" (142–43). Luce's sense of solidarity with the natural world evolves from possessing such a complete knowledge of it; however, her worldview takes into account not only nature but also agriculture and even popular culture: "So she tried to cull daily reality pretty harsh, retaining just landscape and weather and animals and the late-night radio" (24). Unlike Lytle, Luce does not disregard the proverbial radio; instead, she incorporates it into a new worldview that acknowledges the importance of agriculture and the environment without simply indulging in an atavistic Agrarian fantasy. This more inclusive worldview enables Luce to experience a local, material-geographical sense of place (as Bone would argue), while also acknowledging and enjoying the displaced, modern culture transmitted through the airways.

Rash, Roberts, and Frazier's preoccupations with the past are potentially problematic not only because they occasionally run the risk of indulging in agrarian fantasies but also because these preoccupations may prevent them from engaging in the cultural work of the present. That is not to suggest that historical novels cannot do important cultural work; they certainly can and do.[17] My question, rather, is why these three novelists—two of whom have proven themselves to be among the most important contemporary Appalachian literary figures—insist on setting so much of their work in the past. On one hand, it is significant that these writers are attempting to interject the voices of mountain people into a larger historical narrative that has, throughout parts of American history, relegated them to positions of less significance. If Rodger Cunningham is correct in his assertion that Appalachia has served as the "Other" for both America and the South, then it is crucially important to combat this position of "double alterity" by presenting Appalachian historical narratives to as wide an audience as possible. On the other hand, however, the use of the historical novel—the *repeated* use for Frazier and Rash[18]may suggest a longing for a cultural exceptionalism that no longer exists. Among certain readers and writers, Appalachian literature that is the most highly regarded generally eschews the present in favor of narratives about the past. According to Satterwhite, "Some best sellers emphasize rough-and-tumble life in a primitive near wilderness, and others emphasize peaceful if arduous agrarianism, but fans found in each a promise of the persistence of Appalachia as a place sheltered from both the ills and the advantages of 'civilization'" (*Dear Appalachia* 2).

Although the novels by Rash, Roberts, and Frazier complicate a reductive approach to agrarianism, they nevertheless present an Appalachian sense of place that reflects a yearning for a largely bygone Appalachia that was based more substantively on an agrarian cultural and economic platform. As a result, what sometimes transpires is a fetishization of a particular sense of place that is inevitably anachronistic. In *The Real South*, Romine argues that "efforts to locate culture turn out to dislocate it from the here and now—that is, to defer its imagined 'true' or 'authentic' existence to some nostalgic past or utopian future. ... Culture has a habit of not being where and when we are presently" (3). In addition, Romine contends that "the fake South ... becomes the real South through the intervention of narrative" (*Real South* 9). Therefore, the question of authenticity is rendered moot because what is actually authentic is irrelevant and only what a culture deems authentic truly matters (13). Regardless of whether the historical narratives presented by Rash, Roberts, and Frazier are "authentic," their very existence can tell us a great deal about how and why contemporary Appalachians are utilizing such narratives. Building upon Henry D. Shapiro's *Appalachia on Our Mind* (1978), Satterwhite makes a point similar to Romine's: "Fiction's narrative power invests meaning in a swath of geographic territory that becomes important for readers in search of 'culture' or 'identity' as grounding in a postmodern world" (*Dear Appalachia* 216).

So what meaning are these writers hoping to locate by employing the historical novel in this particular historical moment? Are they apprehensive about what they see as the increasing standardization of Appalachia? Can evoking the history of a place revive a lost culture? And if so, would that revived culture appear contrived and thus overly artificial?

Perhaps postmodern historicity will not be doomed to a never-ending cycle of simulacra if we are willing to forge new cultures and new works of art from our present material and ideological conditions. These new cultures and artistic forms may be at least in part engendered by the past, but they must not fall into the trap of idealizing and fetishizing the past. While the historical novel can be used to examine the region—be it the South or the post-South, Appalachia or post-Appalachia[19]I think it is important to take into account in a more direct way than Rash, Roberts, and Frazier do in these novels both the actual, material qualities and the artistic representations of place in the contemporary moment.

Just as I do not intend to universally discount the historical novel, I also do not mean to diminish the significance of historicity. Questions of historicity have been important for southern literary scholars during and after the Southern Renascence and in more recent years have become increasingly important for postmodern theorists. In the southern context, historicity has often been synonymous with Allen Tate's famous phrase "historical consciousness"—a mindset that he claims catalyzed the significant flowering of literature during the Southern Renascence (292). In "The Profession of Letters in the South" (1935), Tate argues that the strength of modern southern literature comes not from a link to the soil but rather from an alienation from it. Therefore, the southern writer's "historical consciousness" is temporary and functions to bring forth brilliant works of art only during a period of social and economic transition. In later essays, Tate would pronounce the death of the "historical consciousness" in no uncertain terms. According to Bone, Tate makes it clear that "unlike Lytle and Faulkner, emerging writers do not have the historical consciousness to gauge the modern destruction of the South (let alone an unmediated knowledge of the premodern South). Hence, not only southern literature but also southern literary criticism becomes, at best, a retrospective affair" (Bone 20). This argument echoes other southern literary scholars, such as Simpson, who posits "the closure of history," and Hobson, who asserts that certain postmodern literary characters "are products of a society that disregards history" (18).

Postmodern theorists have made arguments similar to these southern scholars. In *Postmodernism; or, The Cultural Logic of Late Capitalism* (1991), Fredric Jameson argues that a significant "symptom" of postmodern life is "the waning of our historicity, of our lived possibility of experiencing history in some active way" (21). Jameson implies that this disturbing deterioration of historicity is the result of a widespread historical illiteracy and a corresponding inability for postmodern people to understand the complications of the historical present. In *The Seeds of Time* (1993), Jameson applies this "logic of late capitalism" directly to local and regional cultures, contending that these cultures have been so inundated by corporations that it is "difficult to decide whether [they are] authentic any longer (and indeed whether that term still means anything)" (204–5). Jameson calls this process of acculturation "the EPCOT syndrome," in which "global American Disneyland-related corporations . . . will redo your own native architecture [or art, I would add] for you more exactly than you can do it for yourself."

Applying these theorizations to Rash, Roberts, and Frazier, we must ask whether the loss of the "historical consciousness" or the "waning of our historicity" is true for these writers. More broadly, do these trends accurately characterize Appalachia in the way that perhaps they characterize the broader region and nation? Are these Appalachian writers guilty of "the EPCOT syndrome," that is, of commodifying a fantasy of the past in their fiction in order to reach an audience that is obviously hungry for such a fantasy? Or is there something different about Appalachia that has made its inhabitants maintain their "historical consciousness" longer? Has the mountain South been insulated from cultural homogenization longer than other enclaves in the country, resulting in a lag time for the "historical consciousness"?

Although it is important not to reinscribe outdated myths about Appalachian otherness—its absence of a slavocracy, its frontier mentality, it geographical insularity, its cultural isolation—writers like Rash, Roberts, and Frazier seem to suggest that southern Appalachia (or at least parts of it) resisted homogenization longer than other areas of the South that were more fully inundated generations before with people and cultures from outside the region.[20] Even when writing historical novels, these writers draw from, if not personal, then at least familial stories, and thus they appear to readers to be more "authentic."[21] In an interview in 2006, Rash said this of his generation of Appalachian writers:

> We recognize something is disappearing. With human beings it's only when something is disappearing that you even know it. If it's always there, you don't notice it; it's when you're losing it. What's happening right now in the mountains, there's such a huge change, particularly because of an influx of people from outside the region, mainly retirees . . . who have moved in and are changing the culture. With the inability to maintain the small farm and that lifestyle, a lot of people have been leaving the mountains, trying to find jobs elsewhere. And it's been so rapid, but it happened a little later up there.[22]

If it is true that Rash, Roberts, and Frazier have, or at least are perceived to have, witnessed Appalachia during a period of accelerated change, then they may possess more in common with figures of the Southern Renascence than many other contemporary writers. In other words, they may have a stronger sense of historicity and a closer connection to social and economic transitions that have occurred in the mountain South. However, if contemporary Appalachian writers experienced in their younger lives an Appalachia that is quickly disappearing—particularly a rural, agrarian experience of Appalachia—then these present generations are likely the last to have access to this experience.[23] If historicity inevitably wanes, as Jameson has argued and as postsouthern literary scholars like Kreyling, Romine, and Bone have demonstrated relative to contemporary southern writers, then the question becomes whether Appalachian writers will follow a similar trajectory. I anticipate that the forthcoming generations of Appalachian writers will be more thoroughly post-Appalachian in their approach to regional subject matter, and either they will increasingly develop an ironic, parodic, and even parasitic relationship with past Appalachian literary forms and voices, or, in a desperate attempt to maintain historicity, they will rely on the commodification of Appalachian identity. Critics in Appalachian studies will then have to face the impossible postmodern task of deciding what, if anything, constitutes cultural and literary authenticity.

NOTES

A version of this article was originally published in the *Journal of American Studies* 50, no. 3 (2016): 639–58. Permission to reprint the article was granted by the journal's publisher, Cambridge University Press.

1. See Kreyling, *Inventing Southern Literature*. Kreyling's argument is similar to Allen W. Batteau's earlier study *The Invention of Appalachia*, which is more specifically about Appalachia rather than the South.

2. Rash's, Roberts's, and Frazier's historicity, or at least perceived historicity, seems to stem from their personal and/or familial connections to Appalachian history.

3. Due to space constraints, my analysis of contemporary Appalachian literature is necessarily limited. I do not provide a sustained discussion of Rash's, Roberts's, or Frazier's other literary works, nor do I venture into the works of other Appalachian novelists, poets, short story writers, or dramatists. Additionally, this essay may appear disproportionately weighted toward cultural and theoretical discussions rather than close analyses of the three novels in question. This is a deliberate choice, as my principal intervention in the fields of southern and Appalachian studies seeks to apply significant developments in "postsouthern" theory to Appalachian literature. Thus, I utilize Rash's, Roberts's, and Frazier's most recent novels in support of this intervention, and my primary purpose is not to fully explicate these novels or these writers' entire bodies of work.

4. Although not engaged specifically with the postsouthern debate, Douglas Reichert Powell can augment this critical conversation; he notes that "place cannot be destroyed, only transformed. As Delores Hayden points out, what is usually referred to as 'place destruction' or placelessness is usually more like a bad place" (168).

5. By "problematic," I refer to the Agrarians' well-known and well-documented reactionary attitudes toward race and class. The Agrarians are also guilty of promulgating many revisionist and apologist histories of the U.S. South. For more information on this topic, see my essay "The Problematic History and Recent Culture Reappropriation of Southern Agrarianism." For more on the Agrarians' conception of local culture and its ties to landscape, see Powell 148–52.

6. In the Appalachian context, the tendency to romanticize agrarianism far predates *I'll Take My Stand*. Wilma Dunaway explains, "Despite its origins among the country's wealthiest planters, the 'myth of the happy yeoman' was well entrenched by the early nineteenth century, and the southern mountains have been idealized in the contemporary period as one of the strongest bastions of such self-sufficient farmers" (*First American Frontier* 3). Building upon Dunaway's work, Emily Satterwhite argues, "Belief in a persistent frontier in turn permitted widespread faith that the region sustained a populace of Jefferson's beloved yeoman farmers shunted from more 'civilized' quarters of the nation" (*Dear Appalachia* 16). Recent scholarship in Appalachian studies has been devoted to deconstructing myths about Appalachia's cultural, economic, and geographic isolation. Examining rural cultures of the nineteenth century, Ronald L. Lewis states, "It is clear that much of Appalachia was neither unusually isolated, physically or culturally, nor was its population uniformly more homogeneous than that of other sections of rural America" (22). Cultural heterogeneity was particularly obvious in central Appalachia, which became heavily industrialized in the late nineteenth century: "Industrializing Appalachia was a matrix of cultural interaction among very diverse races and cultures" (37). See also Whisnant's *All That Is Native and Fine*, Dunaway's *First American Frontier*, and Satterwhite's *Dear Appalachia*. Yet despite these important scholarly interventions, popular perceptions of Appalachia largely remain the same as they have been since the late nineteenth century, imagining the region as a refuge for Jeffersonian ideals, at the heart of which is the small-scale, self-sufficient farm. Even if such idealized farms were never pervasive in Appalachia (Dunaway, *First American Frontier* 20), they live on in the American imagination and are common, as Satterwhite suggests (*Dear Appalachia* 2), in popular literature.

7. Increasingly, there are exceptions to the shift away from small-scale farming and toward industry and agribusiness. In the South and elsewhere, independent, family-owned and -operated farms—many of them organic and/or sustainable—are growing in number, making it not only possible but also popular to engage in a brand of agriculture that is functionally (if not ideologically) similar to the Agrarians' dream.

8. Outside of but relevant to this critical conversation is Powell's concept of critical regionalism, which examines "the conflicts and interactions that shape representations of identities in the context of a particular physical location, in order to connect these local interactions, by orders of geographical, cultural, and historical magnitude, to broader patterns of history and society" (152). Thus, Powell, like postsouthern scholars, argues against notions of a region that is or was culturally isolated, monolithic, or exceptional. As opposed to novels marked by displacement, Powell explores works such as James Still's *River of Earth* (1940) that consider "structural problems of injustice in dramatizations of economic and cultural struggle that are firmly emplaced, a novel that explores the possibility of devising alternative social structures using a commitment to a specific place as a central resource"

(171). Rather than possessing "the nostalgia and sentimentality that is attached to the concept of place," Powell argues that *River of Earth* provides "an unsentimentalized dramatization of the possibilities of a specific place" (171). Powell contends that this is particularly significant in the context of Appalachia, where place is all too often associated with "economic oppression" and consequently an "intense determinism" (171). "Nonetheless," Powell continues, "a commitment to inhabitation forged out of a working relationship to the land and to other people—not to some mystified, metaphysical 'sense' of place—augments the cultural and material resources that people use to counter unjust forces and pressures" (171). Powell's emphasis on location here is not wedded, however, merely to rural or agrarian places and is thus open to the full spectrum of heterogeneous places in the U.S. South and Appalachia. For more information on the link between place attachment and activist agency, see Stephen Fisher and Phillip J. Obermiller, cited below.

9. I particularly appreciate Bone's complication of sense of place because it seems to be more in keeping with significant theoretical work done in the field of geography. For instance, Doreen Massey asserts the need to reexamine the "view of place as bounded, as in various ways a site of an authenticity, as singular, fixed and unproblematic in its identity" (5). Instead, Massey contends that places are always "open and porous," and thus global forces, either cultural or economic, must be considered in relation to the local: "The identities of place are always unfixed, contested and multiple. And the particularity of any place is, in these terms, constructed not by placing boundaries around it and defining its identity through counter-position to the other which lies beyond, but precisely (in part) through the specificity of the mix of links and interconnections *to* that 'beyond.'" James L. Peacock makes a similar argument, although his is more specifically about space and place in the U.S. South: "Combine global scope and dynamism, and you get a global force field replacing what may have seemed a smaller, more localized, and less changeable space" (104).

10. Romine comes close to acknowledging this lacuna in the introduction to *The Real South*. After mentioning Fred Chappell, he states that "this project will have nothing further to say" about Appalachia (20).

11. For example, until relatively recently, many people, including scholars, believed that Appalachia possessed a certain racial innocence because it did not participate in the South's system of slavery (Satterwhite, *Dear Appalachia* 16). In 1996 Rodger Cunningham wrote, "The defining social fact of the Appalachian South is that, as a whole, it was never part of the slave/plantation economy, whence most of its other differences from the Deep South" (43). However, more recently, Wilma Dunaway has demonstrated that in the Mountain South "slavery flourished amid a nonslaveholding majority and a large surplus of poor white landless laborers" (*Slavery* 1). Furthermore, she asserts, "Southern Appalachia's largest group of unfree laborers were slaves who supplied long-term labor to one of every three farm owners and who accounted for one of every five agricultural laborer households" (4).

12. For another useful discussion of regional ontology, see the articles in *Journal of Appalachian Studies* 18, no. 1–2 (2012).

13. In an editorial published in *Appalachian Journal* following the 2010 roundtable, Tal Stanley also divides the roundtable between Fisher and Obermiller on one side, and Whisnant, Satterwhite, and Cunningham on the other. However, unlike Smith, Stanley makes this argument surprisingly personal, blaming the latter

group's disregard of Appalachian exceptionalism on their underdeveloped connections to place: "Fisher and Obermiller are of a place, not nomads, having not participated in the transient life fashionable in American higher education. Smith, Satterwhite, and Whisnant offer comments that often imply the values of a wandering, nomadic professoriate—values embedded in their critiques of 'insider' and 'outsider.'" Stanley's argument would now be impossible to maintain regarding Satterwhite, given that she was arrested protesting the Mountain Valley Pipeline that was slated to run through Montgomery County, Virginia, where she lives. In a series of interviews after her arrest on June 28, 2018, Satterwhite clearly states that her civil disobedience was motivated by a love of place.

14. For more information on this topic, see my interviews with Rash and Roberts, titled "Writing the Great War: Terry Roberts and Ron Rash Discuss World War I, the German Internment Camp in North Carolina, and the Historical Novel."

15. The use of the word "fife" rather than "flute" throughout *The Cove* is appropriate within the Appalachian musical tradition. Additionally, in the context the U.S. South more broadly, the fife has been associated with African music performed by enslaved individuals. The complicated history of the fife in the South further demonstrates the cultural heterogeneity that Rash highlights in this subtly handled scene.

16. For a fascinating analysis of the commodification of Appalachian musical traditions, see David Whisnant's study of the White Top Folk Festival in *All That Is Native and Fine*.

17. In the interviews mentioned in note 14 above, I spoke with Rash and Roberts about the uses and limits of the historical novel, and both held to an unwavering belief that *The Cove* and *A Short Time to Stay Here* speak meaningfully to the present. For example, they contend that by commenting on American xenophobia in the context of World War I, they are drawing clear parallels with various forms of xenophobia in the United States after 9/11.

18. I should note that some of Rash's fiction—for example, many of the short stories in *Chemistry and Other Stories* (2007), *Burning Bright* (2010), and *Nothing Gold Can Stay* (2013)—is set in contemporary Appalachia.

19. To avoid such strict delineations, we could also seek to identify a "late Appalachia" as Romine identifies the "late South": "I refer to the contemporary South as the 'late South,' a term that references simultaneously the condition of intensified continuity (as in 'late modernity' or 'late capitalism') and the condition of recent termination (as in 'the late C. Vann Woodward')" (*Real South* 2).

20. Although many scholars have highlighted Appalachia's significant cultural and economic ties beyond the region that extend back to the colonial period, Ronald D. Eller has pointed out that in Appalachia during the late nineteenth and early twentieth centuries "travel was nonetheless always difficult and ensured a relative isolation" (see Lewis 22–23). While travel was certainly not difficult during the childhoods of Rash, Roberts, and Frazier, such a sense of "relative isolation" probably existed for their forebears, which may have helped local, often agriculturally based folkways to endure.

21. Satterwhite argues that "fans, critics, and scholars of regional and ethnic literatures have demanded that authors write from personal experience. Fans of Appalachian-set fiction wanted to believe that it was 'true to life.' The authorial per-

sona therefore became key to the success of the fiction" (*Dear Appalachia* 8–9). For more information on Rash's and Roberts's personal and familial connections to their narratives, see my two pieces "Writing the Great War" and "The Role of Witness." In his review of *Nightwoods*, Wayne Caldwell notes that "the town [in the novel] is reminiscent of Andrews, North Carolina, where Frazier, absorbing details, grew up" (92). Furthermore, many critics have pointed out that Frazier was uniquely well suited to write *Cold Mountain*, both because it was set in his native landscape and because it was based, at least in part, on his great-great-uncle William Pinkney Inman, a Confederate deserter during the Civil War.

22. Zackary Vernon, interview with Ron Rash, Clemson, S.C., October 12, 2006.

23. There are many names that could be added to a list of significant Appalachian writers, including both the generation of Rash, Roberts, and Frazier and the generation preceding theirs—for example, Gurney Norman, Lee Smith, Jim Wayne Miller, Fred Chappell, Robert Morgan, George Ella Lyon, Jo Carson, Denise Giardina, Lisa Alther, Dorothy Allison, Chris Offutt, and many others.

BIBLIOGRAPHY

Batteau, Allen W. *The Invention of Appalachia*. Tucson: University of Arizona Press, 1990.

Bone, Martyn. *The Postsouthern Sense of Place in Contemporary Fiction*. Baton Rouge: Louisiana State University Press, 2005.

Caldwell, Wayne. "Book Review: Charles Frazier's *Nightwoods*." *Appalachian Heritage* 40, no. 1 (2012): 90–92.

Cunningham, Rodger. "Writing on the Cusp: Double Alterity and Minority Discourse in Appalachia." In *The Future of Southern Letters*, edited by Jefferson Humphries and John Lowe, 41–53. Oxford: Oxford University Press, 1996.

Dunaway, Wilma A. *The First American Frontier: Transition to Capitalism in Southern Appalachia 1700–1860*. 2nd ed. Chapel Hill: University of North Carolina Press, 1996.

———. *Slavery in the American Mountain South*. Cambridge: Cambridge University Press, 2003.

Fisher, Stephen. "Claiming Appalachia—and the Questions That Go with It." *Appalachian Journal* 38, no. 1 (2010): 58–61.

Frazier, Charles. *Nightwoods*. New York: Random House, 2011.

Griffin, Larry J. "Whiteness and Southern Identity in the Mountain and Lowland South." *Journal of Appalachian Studies* 10, no. 1/2 (2004): 7–37.

Hobson, Fred. *The Southern Writer in the Postmodern World*. Athens: University of Georgia Press, 1991.

Jameson, Fredric. *Postmodernism; or, The Cultural Logic of Late Capitalism*. Durham, N.C.: Duke University Press, 1991.

———. *The Seeds of Time*. New York: Columbia University Press, 1993.

Kreyling, Michael. "Fee Fie Faux Faulkner: Parody and Postmodernism in Southern Literature." *Southern Review* 29, no. 1 (1993): 1–15.

———. *Inventing Southern Literature*. Jackson: University Press of Mississippi, 1998.

Lewis, Ronald L. "Beyond Isolation and Homogeneity: Diversity and the History of Appalachia." In *Back Talk from Appalachia: Confronting Stereotypes*, edited by Dwight B. Billings, Gurney Norman, and Katherine Ledford, 21–43. Lexington: University Press of Kentucky, 1999.

Lytle, Andrew. "The Hind Tit." In *I'll Take My Stand: The South and the Agrarian Tradition*, edited by Louis D. Rubin Jr., 201–45. 1930. Baton Rouge: Louisiana State University Press, 1979.

Massey, Doreen. *Space, Place, and Gender*. Minneapolis: University of Minnesota Press, 1994.

Obermiller, Phillip J. "Thoughts on the Importance of Identifying Appalachians." *Appalachian Journal* 38, no. 1 (2010): 62–64.

Peacock, James L. *Grounded Globalism: How the U.S. South Embraces the World*. Athens: University of Georgia Press, 2007.

Powell, Douglas Reichert. *Critical Regionalism: Connecting Politics and Culture in the American Landscape*. Chapel Hill: University of North Carolina Press, 2007.

Rash, Ron. *The Cove*. New York: HarperCollins, 2012.

Reid, Herbert. "Appalachia and the 'Sacrament of Coexistence': Beyond Postcolonial Trauma and Regional Identity Traps." *Journal of Appalachian Studies* 11, no. 1/2 (2005): 164–81.

Roberts, Terry. *A Short Time to Stay Here*. Banner Elk, N.C.: Ingalls, 2012.

Romine, Scott. *The Real South: Southern Narrative in the Age of Cultural Reproduction*. Baton Rouge: Louisiana State University Press, 2008.

———. "Where Is Southern Literature? The Practice of Place in a Postsouthern Age." In *South to a New Place: Region, Literature, Culture*, edited by Suzanne W. Jones and Sharon Monteith, 23–43. Baton Rouge: Louisiana State University Press, 2002.

Satterwhite, Emily. *Dear Appalachia: Readers, Identity, and Popular Fiction since 1978*. Lexington: University Press of Kentucky, 2011.

———. "Objecting to Insider/Outsider Politics and the Uncritical Celebration of Appalachia." *Appalachian Journal* 38, no. 1 (2010): 68–73.

Simpson, Lewis P. "The Closure of History in a Postsouthern America." In *The Brazen Face of History: Studies in the Literary Consciousness in America*, edited by Simpson, 78–99. Baton Rouge: Louisiana State University Press, 1980.

Smith, Barbara Ellen. Introduction to "Appalachian Identity: A Roundtable Discussion." *Appalachian Journal* 38, no. 1 (2010): 56–57.

Stanley, Tal. "On Appalachian Identity." *Appalachian Journal* 38, no. 4 (2011): 356–61.

Still, James. *River of Earth*. Lexington: University Press of Kentucky, 1978.

Tate, Allen. *Collected Essays*. Denver, Colo.: Alan Swallow, 1959.

Vernon, Zackary. "The Problematic History and Recent Culture Reappropriation of Southern Agrarianism." *Interdisciplinary Studies in Literature and Environment* 21, no. 2 (2014): 337–52.

———. "The Role of Witness: Ron Rash's Peculiarly Historical Consciousness." *South Carolina Review* 42, no. 2 (2010): 19–24.

———. "Writing the Great War: Terry Roberts and Ron Rash Discuss World War I, the German Internment Camp in North Carolina, and the Historical Novel." *North Carolina Literary Review* 23 (2014): 30–47.

Welty, Eudora. "Place in Fiction" (1956). In *Welty: Stories, Essays, and Memoir*, 781–96. New York: Library of America, 1998.

Whisnant, David E. *All That Is Native and Fine: The Politics of Culture in an American Region*. 1983. Chapel Hill: University of North Carolina Press, 2009.

Woodward, C. Vann. *The Burden of Southern History*. Baton Rouge: Louisiana State University Press, 1960.

For Further Reading

John Lawson, *New Voyage to Carolina* (1709)
William Bartram, *Travels through North and South Carolina, Georgia, East and West Florida, the Cherokee Country, the Extensive Territories* . . . (1791)
John Fox Jr., *The Trail of the Lonesome Pine* (1908)
Effie Waller Smith, *Rhymes from the Cumberland* (1909)
Margaret W. Morley, *The Carolina Mountains* (1913)
John Muir, *A Thousand Mile Walk to the Gulf* (1916)
Emma Bell Miles, *Our Southern Birds* (1919)
Wilma Dykeman, *The French Broad* (1955)
Maurice Brooks, The Appalachians (1965)
Annie Dillard, *Pilgrim at Tinker Creek* (1974)
Ralph Sargent, *Biology in the Blue Ridge: Fifty Years of the Highlands Biological Station 1927–1977* (1977)
Gary Cummisk, "The Literary Naturalists of the Southern Appalachians" (MA thesis, Central Washington University, 1987), and "Appalachian Springs: Nature Writing and Environmental Views of the Southern Mountains" (PhD diss., University of Oregon, 1995)
Marilou Awiakta, *Selu: Seeking the Corn Mother's Wisdom* (1993) and *Abiding Appalachia: Where Mountain and Atom Meet* (1978, repr. 2006)
Robert J. Higgs et al., "Nature and Progress," in *Appalachia Inside Out*, vol. 1 (1995)
Joyce Dyer, *Bloodroot: Reflections on Place by Appalachian Women Writers* (2000)
Margaret Brown, *The Wild East: A Biography of the Great Smoky Mountains* (2001)
Donald Davis, *Where There Are Mountains: An Environmental History of the Southern Mountains* (2003)
Elizabeth Engelhardt, *The Tangled Roots of Feminism, Environmentalism, and Appalachian Literature* (2003), and "Nature-Loving Souls and the Appalachian Mountains: The Promise of Feminist Ecocriticism," in *An American Vein: Critical Readings in Appalachian Literature* (2005)
Kevin E. O'Donnell and Helen Hollingsworth, eds., *Seekers of Scenery: Travel Writing from Southern Appalachia, 1840–1900* (2004)
George Ellison, *Mountain Passages: Natural and Cultural History of Western North Carolina* (2005) and *High Vistas: An Anthology of Nature and Descriptive Writing from Western North Carolina and the Great Smoky Mountains*, vol. 1 (1643–1900) (2008) and vol. 2 (1901–2007) (2011) nature writing

Fred Waage, "Exploring the 'Life Territory': Ecology and Ecocriticism in Appalachia," *Journal of Appalachian Studies* 11, no. 1/2 (Spring/Fall 2005): 133–63

Thomas Rain Crowe, *Zoro's Field: My Life in the Appalachian Woods* (2006)

John Lang, *Appalachia and Beyond: Conversations with Writers from the Appalachian South* (2006)

Douglas Reichert Powell, *Critical Regionalism: Connecting Politics and Culture in the American Landscape* (2007)

Erik Reece, *Lost Mountain: A Year in the Vanishing Wilderness* (2007)

Appalachian Review (previously *Appalachian Heritage*) 37, no. 4 (2009) focuses solely on the Cherokee (and particularly the Eastern Band of Cherokee Indians) experience of western North Carolina and traditional Cherokee territory

Bradford Torrey, *Spring Notes from Tennessee* (2010)

Tom Lynch, Cheryll Glotfelty, and Karla Armbruster, eds., *The Bioregional Imagination: Literature, Ecology, and Place* (2012)

Shannon Elizabeth Bell, *Our Roots Run Deep as Ironweed: Appalachian Women and the Fight for Environmental Justice* (2013)

Neil Carpathios, ed., *Every River on Earth: Writing from Appalachian Ohio* (particularly "The Land" section) (2015)

Isaac J. Emrick, "Maopewa iati bi: Takai Tonqyayun Monyton 'To Abandon So Beautiful a Dwelling': Indians in the Kanawha-New River Valley, 1500–1755" (PhD diss., West Virginia University, 2015)

Dwight B. Billings and Ann E. Kingsolver, eds., *Appalachia in Regional Context: Place Matters* (2018)

Karida L. Brown, *Gone Home: Race and Roots through Appalachia* (2018)

Julia Spicher Kasdorf and Steven Rubin, *Shale Play: Poems and Photographs from the Fracking Fields* (2018)

Ian Marshall, ed., *Reading Shaver's Creek: Ecological Reflections from an Appalachian Forest* (2018)

Drew Swanson, *Beyond the Mountains* (2018)

Jessica Cory, ed., *Mountains Piled upon Mountains: Appalachian Nature Writing in the Anthropocene* (2019)

Lisa Hinrichsen, "Stuck in Place: Affect, Atmosphere, and the Appalachian World of Ann Pancake," and Jimmy Dean Smith, "Country Roads: Mountain Journeys in the Anthropocene," both in *Ecocriticism and the Future of Southern Studies*, edited by Zackary Vernon (2019)

Mae Miller Claxton and George Frizzell, eds., *Horace Kephart: Writings* (2020)

Katherine Ledford and Theresa Lloyd, eds., *Writing Appalachia: An Anthology* (2020)

Joe William Trotter Jr., *River Jordan: African American Urban Life in the Ohio Valley* (1998), *Pittsburgh and the Urban League Movement: A Century of Social Service and Activism* (2020), and *African American Workers and the Appalachian Coal Industry* (2022)

Contributor Biographies

Elisabeth Aiken received her PhD in literature and criticism from Indiana University of Pennsylvania and has taught at Saint Leo University since 2005. She specialized her master's degree and early career work in Irish and British literature, while her doctoral focus and subsequent scholarship is in American literature (primarily southern and Appalachian literatures) and the intersection and application of ecocriticism and postcolonial studies. She currently teaches a variety of literature, composition, and interdisciplinary courses. She has presented numerous times on topics related to land use, ownership, and cultural appropriation as represented within southern Appalachian literature. Her other research interests focus on the representation of race-related Supreme Court cases during the civil rights era in Central Florida. She has been an active board member of the Florida College English Association for several years, serving as president from 2016 to 2018, and recently assumed the post of coeditor for its scholarly journal, *Florida Scholarly Review*. She regularly holds membership in the South Atlantic Modern Language Association, Appalachian Studies Association, College English Association, and Popular Culture Association / American Culture Association, among others.

M. Joseph Aloi is the food hub marketing specialist for KISRA's Paradise Farms, where he coordinates aggregation and distribution as a member of the Turnrow Collective. He is a former university teaching fellow and recent PhD graduate in environmental philosophy at the University of North Texas. As a researcher, he tends to practice field philosophy at the intersection of philosophy with environmental and Appalachian studies. His dissertation, "Participation in the Play of Nature," is a Gadamerian approach to environmental aesthetics.

Cynthia Belmont is professor of English and gender and women's studies at Northland College, an environmental liberal arts school located on the South Shore of Lake Superior in Ashland, Wisconsin, where she teaches creative writing, literature, and intersections in feminism, queer theory, and environmentalism. Her most recent publications in ecofeminism and queer ecologies are in *Feminist Studies* and *Interdisciplinary Studies in Literature and Environment*.

Theresa Burriss has a BA (philosophy major / English minor) from Emory University in Atlanta, Georgia, an MS (English) from Radford University in Radford, Virginia, and a PhD (interdisciplinary studies: Appalachian studies / women's studies) from the Union Institute and University in Cincinnati, Ohio. She serves as Radford University's director of Appalachian Studies and the Appalachian Regional & Rural Studies Center, as well as director of academic outreach for the Southwest Virginia Higher Education Center in Abingdon. She teaches multidisciplinary graduate classes in Appalachian studies, Appalachian literature for the Department of English, and place-based education and critical theories classes for the School of Teacher Education & Leadership's EdD program. She was awarded a Fulbright Teaching & Research grant to teach Appalachian literature at Transilvania University in Brasov and conduct ethnographic research in the Jiu Valley, Romania's coal-mining region, for fall 2021. She has published literary criticism on the Affrilachian writers, including chapters in *An American Vein: Critical Readings in Appalachian Literature* (2005) and *Appalachia in the Classroom: Teaching the Region* (2013), for which she served as coeditor with Patricia Gantt. Her chapter "Ecofeminist Sensibilities and Rural Land Literacies in the Work of Contemporary Appalachian Novelist Ann Pancake" is included in *Literature and Ecofeminism: Intersectional and International Voices* (2018). For *Appalachian Reckoning: A Region Responds to Hillbilly Elegy*, she selected diverse Appalachian poets to contribute to the collection and provided her own photographs and contextual essay. She was appointed in 2020 by Governor Ralph Northam to serve two years on the Virginia Council for Environmental Justice. Additionally, she is the Virginia U.S. delegate for the Appalachian-Carpathian Mountain Initiative, a steering committee member for Opportunity SWVA, and a board member for Appalachian Sustainable Development. For over a decade, she has provided cultural sensitivity and responsiveness training for health care providers in the Roanoke and New River valleys and far Southwest Virginia.

Jessica Cory is an instructor in the English Studies department at Western Carolina University and a PhD candidate at the University of North Carolina at Greensboro, where she specializes in Native American, African American, and environmental literatures. She is the editor of *Mountains Piled upon Mountains: Appalachian Nature Writing in the Anthropocene* (2019), and her creative and scholarly writings have been published in the *North Carolina Literary Review*, *North Dakota Quarterly*, *Northern Appalachia Review*, and other wonderful outlets.

Cameron Williams Crawford received her PhD in twentieth- and twenty-first century American/southern literature from Florida State University. Her work has been published in the *Southern Quarterly*, *South Carolina Review*, and *Gender Forum*. She is also coeditor of *Telling an American Horror Story: Essays on History, Place and Identity in the Series* (2021). She is an assistant professor at the University of North Georgia in Gainesville.

Evan Gurney is an associate professor of English at the University of North Carolina, Asheville. He is the author of *Love's Quarrels: Reading Charity in Early Modern England* (2018) as well as numerous articles on early modern English literature.

Ethan Mannon is an ecocritic and associate professor of English at Mars Hill University—a small liberal arts institution twenty minutes north of Asheville, North Carolina. He teaches American and Appalachian literature, as well as composition, and directs the Honors Program. His publications include work on Robert Frost, Michael Pollan, Aldo Leopold, Harriette Arnow and Helena Maria Viramontes, and John Ehle.

Michael S. Martin is an associate professor of English, modern languages, and cultural studies at Nicholls State University, where he has recently received tenure and promotion. He specializes in antebellum American literature, Appalachian literature, and Native American literature. His writings have appeared in a variety of journals, including *Postmodern Culture*, the *Nathaniel Hawthorne Review*, and *Studies in American Indian Literature*.

Savannah Paige Murray holds a PhD in rhetoric and writing from Virginia Tech. She currently serves as a visiting assistant professor of rhetoric and writing studies at Appalachian State University, where she teaches courses in technical and professional writing and environmental rhetoric. Her research interests include ecocriticism, Appalachian literature, environmental rhetoric, and documentary film. More about her research in Appalachian grassroots environmental rhetoric can be found at her digital humanities project site, damfighters.com

Lucas Nossaman is assistant professor of English at North Greenville University. He has published articles and reviews on Sarah Orne Jewett, Wendell Berry, Henry David Thoreau, and Jonathan Edwards in *Christianity and Literature*, *Renascence*, and *Nineteenth-Century Prose*.

Kevin E. O'Donnell is a professor of English, and the director of the Environmental Studies minor, at East Tennessee State University. He is coeditor of *Seekers of Scenery: Travel Writing from Southern Appalachia, 1840–1900* (2004), and author of numerous publications regarding American studies, Appalachian studies, and environmental history. He lives in Johnson City, Tennessee.

Caleb Pendygraft earned his PhD at Miami University of Ohio and is currently an assistant professor at Massachusetts Maritime Academy on Cape Cod, where he administers within the writing program. He teaches writing, business communications, and literature. His research explores literacy, queerness, and new materialisms. Kentucky and Appalachia is home, and he is a proud cat dad and loves all things nature. He's the recipient of the Wilma Dykeman Fellowship and has been published in multiple Appalachian venues.

Stewart Plein is the curator of rare books and printed resources in the West Virginia & Regional History Center, the special collections unit of West Virginia University. She is also the managing director for the West Virginia National Digital Newspaper Project (NDNP) National Endowment for the Humanities grant in partnership with the Library of Congress. She received her master of library science from the University of South Carolina, her bachelor's degree from Emory & Henry College, and a certification in rare book librarianship from the University of Virginia's Rare Book School. Her research and publishing interests include book history, bookbinding design, and Appalachian studies, with a focus on stereotype on the covers of Appalachian local color literature. Her work has appeared in the *Journal of Appalachian Studies*, the *West Virginia History Journal*, the *Smithfield Review*, and the *Appalachian Curator*, among others. She works extensively with donors, gives lectures, provides book collection consultations, and teaches book history and rare book pedagogy sessions in the WVU rare book room and by invitation to groups and institutions.

Sylvia Bailey Shurbutt is a graduate of the University of Georgia, professor of English, and director of the Celtic Roots and Appalachian Studies curricular programs at Shepherd University in Shepherdstown, West Virginia. She is also director of the Center for Appalachian Studies and Communities at Shepherd. She is managing editor of the *Anthology of Appalachian Writers* (ISSN 1946-3103), an annual anthology of Appalachian poets, fiction writers, essayists, and photographic artists; and she is director of the NEH Summer Institutes Voices from the Misty Mountains and the Power of Place (2013, 2016, 2017, 2018) and 2020 WV BRIDGE Institute for Teachers. Her writing has appeared in the *Appalachian Review*, the *Journal of Appalachian Studies*, the *Journal of Kentucky Studies*, *North Carolina Review*, *Women's Studies*, *Women and Language*, *Essays in Literature*, the *Southern Literary Journal*, *Encyclopedia of American Literature*, and Scribner's American Writers and World Writers series, among others. She has chapters in *Feminism in Literature*, *Untying the Gender Knot* and *Destinations and Discoveries: Literary Travel Essays* and is author of books and articles about travel, writing, and Appalachia, including *Reading Writing Relationships* and *Silas House, Exploring an Appalachian Writer's Work*. She was 2006 West Virginia Professor of the Year and received the Appalachian Studies Fisher Award for Excellence in Teaching in 2020. She was the 2015 president of National Appalachian Studies Association (ASA) and 2016 conference chair in Shepherdstown.

Zackary Vernon is an associate professor of English at Appalachian State University in Boone, North Carolina. He specializes in American literature and film, and most of his work examines the intersections among environmental activism, philosophy, film, and literature from romanticism to the present. He is a coeditor of *Summoning the Dead: Essays on Ron Rash* (2018) and editor of *Ecocriticism and the Future of Southern Studies* (2019).

Laura Wright is the founder of the field of Vegan Studies. She is professor of English at Western Carolina University, where she specializes in postcolonial literatures and theory, ecocriticism, and animal studies. Her monographs include *Writing Out of All the Camps: J. M. Coetzee's Narratives of Displacement* (2006 and 2009), *Wilderness into Civilized Shapes: Reading the Postcolonial Environment* (2010), and *The Vegan Studies Project: Food, Animals, and Gender in the Age of Terror* (2015). She has edited and coedited numerous collections of essays, most recently *The Edinburgh Companion to Vegan Literary Studies* (with Emelia Quinn, 2022).

Index

activism, 16, 63, 130, 152, 154–55, 163–64; Appalachian tradition of, 5, 162, 286n8; class and gender in, 132, 140, 141n1; ecosexuality and 147–50, 153, 156–57, 165, 167

Affrilachia, 115, 121, 124, 127. *See also* Wilkinson, Crystal

agency, 275, 280; activism and, 286n8; gender and, 125, 137, 142n5; nonhuman, 50, 123, 166, 174, 179–81, 183, 185–86, 193; violence and, 125, 137

agrarian, 272–73, 282, 286n6, 286n7. *See also* agriculture; farm(s); plow

agriculture, 288n20; as permanent home, 30–33, 39, 278; enslavement and, 122, 287n11; environmental effects on/of, 73, 78, 218; gender and, 83; sustainable, 35, 286n7; tradition of, 64. *See also* agrarian; farm(s); plow

Aldine leaf, 258–59, 266n5

allegory, 231, 241–44, 249

Allen, James Lane, 256, 260–62, 264–65. See also *Blue-Grass Region of Kentucky*; *Through Cumberland Gap on Horseback*

allied resistance, 163–64

"Anecdote of the Jar," 241–50. *See also* artifact; jar; Stevens, Wallace

animal (non-human): as metaphor, 82, 140, 138, 154, 233, 236; birds, 18, 20, 25, 35, 52, 76, 93, 97, 103, 122, 154, 182, 192–95, 197–99, 201, 211, 236, 242, 281; dogs, 49, 125, 133, 138, 151, 153, 164, 197; human relationships with, 47, 52, 55, 73, 161, 192–95, 199, 202, 233; labor, 32; observations of, 93, 153, 179, 281; violence against, 133, 142n4, 155

antebellum, 81–84, 86, 88–89, 92–94, 96–99

anthropomorphism, 166–67, 167n5–168n5, 193, 196

Appalachia: as gendered, 87–88, 173, 176; boundaries of, 3, 6, 8, 287n9; communities of, 61–62, 159–61, 183; economy, 130–31, 134–35, 138, 206, 242, 280–81; environmental issues, 1–2, 32, 42, 62–65, 130, 147, 150–52, 156, 159, 166–67, 205–7, 210, 212, 248–50; history of, 61–65, 72, 88, 120–22, 127, 230, 254–58, 271, 283, 288n20; idea(s) of, 1, 6–7, 77–78, 79n1, 79n2, 98, 171–73, 180–81, 186–87, 274–77, 284, 285n3–4, 288n19; labor and work, 31–33, 42n1, 50, 56, 75, 132, 134–35, 156, 159, 280–81; landscapes of, 1, 3–4, 18, 20–21, 49, 53–54, 81–83, 86, 90–94, 96–97, 99n1, 211, 213, 218–19, 225, 241; mischaracterizations of, 5–6, 29–31, 115, 121–22, 136, 261–62, 266n2, 271, 279, 282, 284, 286n6, 286–87nn9–8, 287n11, 288n17, 288n21; outmigration from, 38, 176; politics of, 14–16, 102, 120, 162, 177–78; tourism, 36; transnational and global connections, 6, 102, 104–5, 208

Appalachian literature: as Georgic, 29, 32–33, 36, 41–42; environment and, 2–3, 5, 41, 45, 61–62; history of, 3, 7, 42, 106, 285nn2–3; importance of, 19; readership, 6, 78, 282; study of 5, 105, 271, 276; themes in, 1, 33, 45, 133, 135, 281; trajectory of, 9, 271, 285

Appalachian Mountains, 93, 96, 99n1, 102, 255; agriculture and, 31; deforestation of, 62; gendering of, 81–84, 88–92, 98–99, 116; literary history of, 2, 54, 97; settling of, 45–46; symbolism and, 85, 252; wedding to, 162

Appalachian region: diversity of, 1, 6, 8, 162, 171, 173–74, 259–61, 265, 273; economy, 36, 129, 132, 134, 177, 206, 212, 242, 248–49, 258, 275, 283–84, 286nn5–6, 288n20; environmental hazards and, 1, 7, 61, 71, 205–7, 212, 218, 248–49; geography, 14, 45, 61, 64, 97; labor and, 15–16, 22, 29, 273, 276; literature and, 5, 9, 39, 42, 42n4, 43n12, 83, 86, 89, 96–97, 205, 272–73, 276, 283, 288n14, 288nn17–18; living in, 6, 8, 14–15, 29, 76, 131, 137, 206, 220; portrayals and representation of, 1, 5, 8, 15, 30–31, 33, 86, 89, 98–99, 115, 252–57, 260–62, 264–66, 266n1, 271, 274, 286n6; reimagining, 2, 6–8, 214, 218, 220, 266, 285

Appalachian Regional Commission, 3, 94, 177

Appalachian studies, 286n6; Affrilachia and, 115; history of 3, 249; identity and, 275, 285; local knowledge, 242; literature and, 33, 39, 241–42, 249

Appalachians: environmental engagement, 147,

Appalachians (*continued*)
  152, 156, 225; mischaracterizations of, 6, 121–22, 176–77, 266n2, 274; mobility of, 31; oppression of, 8, 36, 161–62; storytelling and, 186, 282
Aristotle, 13–15, 18–19, 21, 25n1
Arnow, Harriette, 36, 38–39, 41. See also *Dollmaker, The*
artifact, 241–42, 249–50. See also "Anecdote of the Jar"; jar; Stevens, Wallace

Bartram, William, 1, 3, 227–28, 231, 255–56. See also naturalist(s)
Berry, Wendell, 204–22, 223n13, 223n16. See also Sabbath poetry
Bible: biblical, 244; as metaphor or comparison, 68, 197; idea of dominion, 153; in *Fire Is Your Water*, 201–2; in Wendell Berry's *Sabbath Poems*, 206–7, 209, 213, 222n5. See also Christian; Christianity
bioregionalism, 16, 61–62, 204–5
Birds of Opulence, 115–28. See also Wilkinson, Crystal
bluegrass, 205, 260–62, 264–65
Blue-grass and Rhododendron, 261–63, 267n9. See also Fox, John, Jr.
Blue-Grass Region of Kentucky, 261, 264–65. See also Allen, James Lane
bookbindings, 253, 258, 267n7, 267n9
Byer, Kathryn Stripling, 102–11, 111n2, 111n6

Casey, Edward, 16–17, 19, 21–22, 24
Celtic myth, 229–30, 237n1, 237n2. See also under water
Central Appalachia, 88, 129, 132, 136, 286n6. See also Kentucky; North Carolina; Ohio; Tennessee; Virginia; West Virginia
Cherokee, 228; language, 76; recognition of occupied homelands 50, 76; removal, 71–72, 231, 234; story of Nacoochee, 84–86; story of Princess Jocassee, 63–64, 73; story of Raven 192–93. See also Native American people(s); water
Christian, 63, 236–37, 237n1; ecocriticism, 192, 197, 202, 204–10, 212–16, 218–22, 222n8; in *Fire Is Your Water*, 191–92, 194–97, 199–202; in Wendell Berry's work, 204–22, 222n5, 222n8, 222n9. See also Christianity
Christianity: environmental stewardship and, 191–92;influence of, 237n1; service and, 194; Western ideas of, 200–1. See also Christian; Western thought; Christianity
coalition politics, 148, 150, 156, 161, 163, 167n3
colonialism, 63, 74, 82, 172, 242
contact zones, 63, 67–68
Cooke, George, 86–88, 98–99
Cove, The, 271, 276–80, 288n15, 288n17. See also Rash, Ron

Crapalachia: A Biography of Place, 14, 20–25. See also McClanahan, Scott
Crayon, Porte, 258. See also Strother, David Hunter
critical regionalism, 286n8
cross-racial bonding, 85–86, 99, 226
Crowe, Thomas Rain, 39–41. See also *Zoro's Field*

dam(s), 22–23, 62–75, 78
death: and the earth, 38, 53, 67, 110, 215–16; as a theme, 20; attitudes toward, 20–21, 23, 63, 67, 75, 84–85, 172, 180, 182–86, 201, 215–16, 236; human, 20, 51–52, 69, 126, 131, 138, 163, 171, 180, 182–86, 198, 229, 236, 247, 257, 276; metaphor and, 22–23, 69, 74, 110, 126, 232, 273, 283; mining and, 22, 152, 154, 157; nonhuman animals, 20, 25, 192
displacement: African American people and, 124; due to dams, 72; Georgic mode and, 33, 36, 38; reversal of, 39; systemic injustice and, 286n8; 'uninhabitants' and, 72, 79n2
Divine Right's Trip, 39–41. See also Norman, Gurney
documentary(ies), 2, 3, 147, 149–51, 158, 178. See also Sprinkle, Annie; Stephens, Elizabeth
Dollmaker, The, 36, 38–39, 43n12. See also Arnow, Harriette
Duke Power, 62–65, 69–74, 77–78
dwelling, 20, 29, 32–33, 38, 41

ecocritical spirituality, 197, 204, 222n1, 222n4. See also under Christian;
ecocriticism, 148; Appalachian literature and, 3, 6, 8, 32–33, 42, 45, 61, 242; history of, 2, 5, 45, 61, 173, 193, 204, 222n4, 249–50. See also ecofeminism; material ecocriticism; queer ecocriticism
ecofeminism: Appalachian literature and, 45; definition of, 3, 130, 148;
ecosexuality and, 155; queer ecological theories and, 148, 171, 176.
See also ecological feminism; feminist ecocriticism
ecological feminism, 105, 130. See also ecofeminism; feminist ecocriticism
ecosexuality: activism and, 147–48, 166; community, 161–67; definition of, 161; goals of, 153; history of, 155–57, 159; identity, 155–61; subversive potential of 150. See also Sprinkle, Annie; Stephens, Elizabeth
Ehle, John, 45–57. See also *Landbreakers, The*
eighteenth-century, 237n1; American nature writers/writing, 2, 227, 255; Appalachian life, 45, 49, 265; British and UK writers, 35–36, 84, 99n1; gendered landscapes, 90; travel, 48
enslavement; slavery, 63, 115–16, 120–22, 207, 287n11
Elizabethan, 102, 105–6

environmental justice (EJ): Appalachian literature and, 45; children and, 154; Christianity and, 206, 211; ecofeminism and, 130, 149; history of, 132; queer ecocriticism and, 148, 150; transnational, 204; women and, 131–32

erotic(s): activism and, 156–57, 164–67; agency and, 147–48, 160; celebratory nature of, 155; healing potential of, 151; ecological feminism and, 106–7; female pastoral archetype, 83–84; race exoticization and, 85–86; rural landscapes and, 102–4

ethic of care, 138–40

ethics, 7, 13–15, 19, 148

farm(s): Bluegrass region and, 264–65; in Charles Frazier's work, 228–230; in Gurney Norman's work, 39–40; in James Still's work, 36–38; in Jesse Stuart's work, 34–35; in Ron Rash's work, 65, 67–69, 74, 76; in Susan Fenimore Cooper's work, 94–96; in Wendell Berry's work 207–9, 214–18; pastoral agriculture, 31–32, 43n14, 90, 92, 99; subsistence, 272, 286nn6–7. *See also* agrarian; agriculture; plow

female pastoral 81–94, 98–99

feminism: critique, 95, 152; ecofeminism and, 129–30, 148–49, 171, 173; ecosexuality and, 155–56; ethic of care, 139–40; gender roles and, 142n5; materiality and, 160, 181; spirituality and, 222n1. *See also* ecocriticism; gender

feminist ecocriticism, 129. *See also* ecofeminism; ecological feminism

Fenimore Cooper, Susan, 94–98

fire: as passion, 223n14; in Charles Frazier's work, 228, 236, 280; in Jim Minick's work, 192–99; in John Ehle's work, 48–50, 55; in Robert Gipe's work, 139; industrial logging and, 248

Fire Is Your Water, 191–203. *See also* Minick, Jim

Fox, John, Jr., 256–58, 260, 263, 267n8. *See also* *Blue-grass and Rhododendron*; *Hell Fer Sartain*; *Kentuckians, The Trail of the Lonesome Pine*

Frazier, Charles: *Cold Mountain*, 2, 225–37, 237n1; *Nightwoods*, 271, 276, 279–285, 285nn2–3, 288–290nn20–21, 289n23

Fromm, Harold, 2, 45, 193–94

Gaard, Greta, 130, 148, 171–73

Gagné, Patricia, 132, 134–35, 140

Garrard, Greg, 2, 192, 195, 198, 202

gender: biases/prejudices, 232; construction of, 75, 129, 152, 160, 171, 172–73; diversity in, 5; identities, 90, 173, 181; landscape and, 89–90, 95, 98, 129; normativity/nonnormativity, 135, 178; neutral, 90–91, oppression, 3, 8, 102, 111n4, 141n1; race and, 122–26; roles, 95–96, 106, 116, 135–36, 138–40, 142n5, 148; sexuality and, 147–48; theories, 81–83, 86–87, 93, 97, 104, 110, 171, 176, 181. *See also* feminism; queer

Georgia, 84–88, 99, 139, 252

Georgic, 29, 32–42, 43n7, 43nn12–13, 210

Gifford, Terry, 30, 45–47, 51, 226

Gipe, Robert, 129, 141n2. *See also* *Trampoline*

God: and labor, 43n11; and spirituality, 108, 191–92, 195–201, 222n1, 222n5; as creator, 210, 212–13, 233; creation(s) of, 81, 198–99, 207, 212–13, 215, 218–19, 233, 243

goddess(es), 83–84

Goodbye Gauley Mountain, 2, 147, 150–53, 155–66, 167n5. *See also* documentary(ies); Sprinkle, Annie; Stephens, Elizabeth

Haraway, Donna, 158, 161, 166, 173. *See also* kinship

Harlan County, U.S.A., 152–54, 157, 163. *See also* documentary(ies);

Harmonium, 243. *See also* Stevens, Wallace

Harper's (magazine), 260–61, 264

Hartlean Associationism, 227–28

Hawk's Nest Tunnel, 22, 159

healing, 165, 191–94, 197–200, 211, 214–15, 227–28, 233–34; after loss, 57; land and place, 46, 211; mentally, 212, 233, 237; physically, 191, 194–97, 200, 233, 237; relationships with people, 119; spiritually, 227, 233

health, physical, 126, 132, 151, 214, 229

health, mental, 115, 119, 215

Hell Fer Sartain, 256–57, 265. *See also* Fox, John, Jr.

Hillbilly (film), 3. *See also* documentary(ies)

Hillbilly: A Cultural History of an American Icon (book), 266n2

hillbilly, 15, 122, 136, 162, 166

home: homeplace, 5, 20, 25, 29–30, 33, 38–39, 93, 132, 139, 182, 213; as part of community 92, 133, 147; damage to 133, 135, 151; displacement from 66–69, 72, 74, 76, 121, 151; nostalgia 159, 280; planetary home 45–46; and labor 38, 41, 47, 55, 277, 280; rural 37, 47–48, 99, 105, 124, 153, 155, 185, 261, 277; returning home 40–41, 118, 17, 179, 185, 196, 198, 225–28, 234–35; safety and 123, 185; yearning for 81, 159. *See also* place; sense of place

Homer: *Odyssey* 225–26, 231. *See also* journey; monomyth

human, 25n1, 32, 83–84, 160–62, 174–75, 191, 197, 206, 214, 244; community, 92, 148, 154, 164, 205, 229, 284; condition, 6, 29, 199, 248; culture, 45; degradation of environment, 3, 46, 54, 76, 141n2, 151, 208, 211, 213, 229, 232, 250; experience, 16–17, 95, 147, 195, 236; hierarchy of life, 3, 54–56, 75, 138, 141n1, 154, 173, 179, 192, 195–96, 199; identity, 54–55, 130, 160; relationships between humans, 50, 133, 147, 164–65, 172, 184, 186, 213, 226, 276, 284; relationships with nature, 8, 30, 32, 42, 42n1, 42n4, 46, 51, 55–56, 63, 77, 147, 150, 153–54, 159, 165–66, 181, 184, 202, 226, 234, 242; violence, 74, 133, 138, 232 humanity, 6, 8, 46, 150, 164; in *Cold Mountain* 227–28, 231–32, 234, 236

Jackson, Henry R., 85–86, 88, 90–91, 99
jar, 242, 245. *See also* "Anecdote of the Jar"; artifact; Stevens, Wallace
Jesus, 194, 200–1, 216, 220–21. *See also* Christian; Christianity
Jocassee Valley (Lake Jocassee), 7, 62, 65–66, 70–71, 73–75. *See also One Foot in Eden*; Rash, Ron.
journey, 7–9, 47, 66, 121, 180, 196, 206, 255; *Cold Mountain* as 225–28, 231–32, 234–37; nonhuman 214. *See also* Homer; monomyth

Kennedy, Philip Pendleton, 83–84, 88, 96, 98–99
Kentuckians, The, 263–264. *See also* Fox, John, Jr.
Kentucky: in Crystal Wilkinson's work, 115–16; in Gurney Norman's work, 39–40; in James Still's work, 36; in Jesse Stuart's work, 33–34; in Robert Gipe's work, 130–31; in Wendell Berry's work, 205–7, 214, 216–17; rhododendron in literature of, 252, 260–65; Southern theory, 274
Kentucky River, 207, 214–18
Kephart, Horace, 4, 256
kinship: alternatives to biological, 172–76, 178–79, 181, 185–87; Appalachian literature and, 42; celebration of, 163; with mountains, 151. *See also* Haraway, Donna
Kolodny, Annette, 87–88, 92–94

labor, 126, 246–49; as everyday nature, 54–56; damming and, 65; domestic, 92, 230, 277; environmental engagement and, 7, 75, 95, 115, 121–22, 166, 208–11, 215–17, 220–21, 230, 277; exploitation of, 22–23, 154, 161, 206–7, 287n11; gender and, 132, 134, 140, 152, 156, 158; Georgic mode and, 29, 31–32, 34, 36–37, 40–42, 43n11; industrialization, 259; politics of, 149, 163, 287n11; race and, 159; rural, 95, 103, 115–16, 121–22. *See also under* home; animal; Appalachian region
Land Breakers, The, 45–57. *See also* Ehle, John
Lanman, Charles, 83–86, 88, 90–91, 98–99
Last Mountain, The, 149, 154–55, 163
leisure, 30, 32, 36, 55, 75
letters: from Jesse Stuart, 33, 43n8; from Wallace Stevens, 245–47; from Wendell Berry, 222n6; in *Cold Mountain*, 227, 229–30; in *The Cove*, 277; in *The Prettiest Star*, 183–84
Lindytown, 159–60
local color: in Appalachian literature, 5, 258, 261–62, 265; markers of place, 8, 252–54, 256–62, 265, 266n2, 267n9; market for, 31, 257–58, 262
logging, 72, 212, 241–42, 248–49. *See also* timber industry

Magritte, René, 233–34

Man with a Bull-Tongue Plow, 33–35. *See also* Stuart, Jesse
Marlowe, Christopher, 102–7, 109–11, 111n3
marriage equality, 164
Maryland, 186
masculinity, 134, 156, 158
Massey Energy, 156, 159
material ecocriticism, 174, 179. *See also under* queer
materiality, 17, 74, 77, 99, 157, 160, 174
maternity, 37, 105, 176–77, 180–81, 186, 194, 196, 198, 201, 230, 280; in the work of Anna Maria Wells, 81–82, 90, 92–93, 98; in *Trampoline*, 131, 137–40; in *Birds of Opulence*, 115–19, 124–27
McClanahan, Scott, 14, 20–25. *See also Crapalachia: A Biography of Place*
Minick, Jim, 191–203, 203n11. *See also Fire Is Your Water*
mining, 24; history of, 159; hydraulic fracturing; fracking, 130; labor; work, 31–32, 36–38, 132, 134, 138, 152, 154, 158–159; land degradation due to, 21, 37, 39, 133, 149, 151, 154, 162, 166–67, 207, 212, 216; mountaintop removal, 62, 151, 147; protests against, 132–33, 140, 141n2, 147, 149, 152, 154, 162–63, 205; strip, 39, 130, 133, 138–139, 205, 207, 212, 216, 221; towns, 36–37; underground, 130. *See also* mountaintop removal; strip mining
Mississippi River, 3–4
mobility, 30–32, 36, 39, 41, 132, 134–35
modernism (literary), 33, 160, 241–42, 248–49
monomyth, 231. *See also* Homer; journey
Monroe, Harriet, 243, 246
mountaintop removal (MTR): activism and, 140, 141n2, 152–55, 162–63, 165; as type of environmental degradation, 5, 62, 218, 275; in Appalachia, 42, 147, 159, 275; in Appalachian literature, 1, 140, 218. *See also* activism; mining
multigenerational women, 115–17, 131, 134, 138, 162
Murfree, Mary Noailles, 30–31
myth, 90–91, 286n6; pastoral myth, 82, 91, 96, 98; of America, 98–99; of Appalachia, 9, 99, 121–22

Native American people(s): in *Cold Mountain*, 227, 230–31, 233, 235–36, 237n2; land use, 31, 233; Pennsylvania Dutch and, 192; spirituality, 191–92; stories (general), 88; story of Nacoochee, 84–86; worldviews, 235–36, 237n2; writing, 9. *See also* Cherokee; water: Native American stories of
naturalism (literary), 227
naturalist(s), 94, 227, 252, 255–59, 265. *See also* Bartram, William
nature, 46, 51–52, 85, 90, 129, 195–97; as oppressed, 3, 73–74, 83, 119, 130–31, 138; as resource, 41; as separate from humans, 3, 87, 155, 173, 196; attitudes toward, 2, 49, 51, 53, 75–76, 82–83, 89–90, 94–97, 116, 119–21, 125, 129, 138, 150, 156, 172, 176, 207, 212–13, 215–16, 227, 235, 281;

everyday, 29, 43n17, 54–57; feminized, 83, 129; human relationship with, 45–46, 53–57, 61, 91, 93, 116, 147–48, 150, 153–55, 157, 159–60, 162–67, 182, 218–19, 220, 226, 242; in harmony, 35, 40, 85, 210, 213; 227, 230, 233–35, 237n1; leisure and labor in, 30–32, 35–36, 68, 122; nonhuman, 29, 77, 174–175, 182, 192–193; preservation, 62; symbolism in 254; vs. culture binary, 42n1, 46, 150, 171, 173, 192, 196, 249; writers/writing, 3–6, 9, 82, 94–99, 99n1–100n1

neo-Agrarianism, 274. *See also* agrarian; agriculture; farm

New River, 21, 23–34

New York: as an Appalachian region, 99; in *The Cove*, 277–278; in *The Prettiest Star*, 171, 176, 178–80, 182–83; Margaret Armstrong and, 267n9; pastoralism and, 87; Susan Fenimore Cooper and, 94, 96

Nightwoods, 271, 276, 279–81, 288n21. *See also* Frazier, Charles

nineteenth-century: Appalachian life, 32, 64, 230, 277, 286n6, 288n20; Appalachian writers, 89–91; bookbindings, 253–54, 256, 258–60, 262, 265–66; brauche, 191; economy, 242, 248–49, 286n6; flooding, 70; logging industry, 248–49; nature writers, 2; poetry, 85; travel writing, 81–82, 99n1

non-human life forms; other-than-human life forms: absence of, 77; agency of, 160–61, 180–81, 193, 202; comparisons to humans, 138; deep ecology and, 77; human superiority over, 133; false dichotomies and, 42n1; Georgic mode and, 32; pastoralism and, 29–30; queerness and, 172–74, 176, 185; relationships, 55, 154–55, 178–79, 182, 186, 194, 199, 202; sense of place and, 42; value of, 3, 192, 195. *See also* animal

Norman, Gurney, 39–40, 289n23. *See also Divine Right's Trip*

North Carolina: as Southern, 274; literature set in, 6, 45, 47, 50, 79, 92, 226, 229, 276, 278–80; tourism, 36, 81, 99; writers, 6, 41, 79, 225, 278–80, 288n14, 288n21

Oconee Bell flower, 63, 67, 75

Ohio, 87, 171, 176, 185

Ohio River, 214, 217

On Coal River, 149, 152, 154–55, 163. *See also* activism; documentary(ies)

One Foot in Eden, 62–69, 71, 77–78. *See also* Jocassee Valley; Rash, Ron

othered (oddkinships): agency and, 181; dynamics of, 26n2, 42n2, 125, 140, 149, 160–61, 164, 232, 287n13; exploitation and, 15–16, 77–78; gender/sexuality and, 134–35, 140, 149, 160–61, 164, 176–77; relationships with, 13, 186, 232; struggles of, 8

Overburden, 149, 152, 154–57, 159. *See also* activism; documentary(ies)

pastoral: gender and the, 83–94, 98–99; Georgic mode and, 29–32, 39–42; landscape, 37, 54, 81–83 92–93, 96; lifestyle and, 36; reflection, 207; romance, 94, 102, 104–6, 111; writing, 7, 53–54, 212; theory, 5, 47, 81, 97

Pennsylvania, 6, 48, 89, 191

Pennsylvania Dutch, 191

phenomenology, 181, 202

philosophy: anthropomorphism and, 167n5; ecofeminist, 14n1; environmental, 14, 281; Hartlean Associationism, 227; Heideggerian, 202; hermeneutic, 16; of *travel picturesque*, 99; Western, 236

place, 45, 74–75, 85, 89, 99, 126, 171, 241, 258–59, 262; and ethics, 13–15, 19, 36, 39, 207–8, 210–11, 214, 217, 228; and identity, 6, 72–73, 77, 79, 276; as symbolism, 8, 71, 252–53, 256–57, 260, 262, 265, 266n2, 267n9; awareness of, 7, 14, 16–17, 29, 53, 73, 98–99, 156, 216; complexity/paradox of, 5, 21–23, 30, 56, 120, 123–24, 154, 158–59, 172–74, 177, 186, 218–21, 235, 237, 281–83, 285–86nn4–6, 287n9, 288n20; human relationship to, 8, 13–15, 17–22, 24, 29, 36–37, 40–41, 47–48, 52, 54–55, 63–64, 67, 79nn1–2, 88, 120, 127, 154, 159, 166, 182–85, 210–11, 226, 228, 231, 237, 246–47, 281–83, 285n2, 286n8, 288n18; importance of, 13, 16–18, 24–25, 38, 77, 94, 97, 117, 196, 205, 272–75; labor and work in, 32, 34–35, 40–42, 55, 278–79. *See also* home; sense of place

plow, 33–36, 38, 229, 231. *See also* agrarian; agriculture; farm

Plumwood, Val, 73, 167n2, 195–96

Prettiest Star, The, 171–87. *See also* Sickels, Carter

poetry, lyric: Appalachian female response to, 104, 107; ecological crisis and, 208–12, 214–15, 218; Renaissance, 102, 105, 111; Wallace Stevens and, 244, 250

poetry, modernist, 33–36, 244, 249–50

pollution; toxins, 5, 132, 205–8, 210, 217–18. *See also under* water

postmodernism, 39, 160, 271, 273–74, 282–83, 285

post-pastoral, 5, 7, 45–46, 48–51, 55–56, 226. *See also* pastoral

postsouthern theory, 9, 271–76, 285n3, 288n19. *See also* Roberts, Terry; Southern theory; Southern studies

powwowing, 191–92, 194, 196, 200

queer, 150, 152, 155, 157–58, 163, 167, 172–73, 175–76, 178–79; Appalachia as, 174, 177–78, 182, 185; agency/agentalism, 181, 184, 186; confederacy, 166; ecocriticism, 8, 148, 171–74, 176, 186; ecology/ecological sensibility, 147–49, 155, 160, 165–66; empathy, 153; materialism, 174, 186; people/identity, 148–49, 156–58, 161, 164–65, 167, 171–72, 174, 176, 180, 182–185; politics, 149,

queer (continued)
 158, 173–74; theory, 154–56, 160, 180. See also feminist; gender

Raising the Dead, 61–63, 69–71, 73–79. See also Rash, Ron
Rash, Ron: agrarianism and, 282; as Appalachian writer, 289nn22–23; historical novels and, 281–83, 288n14, 288n17, 288–89nn20–21; contemporary Appalachia and, 288n18; on Appalachian writers, 284; *One Foot in Eden*, 62–68, 70–72; *Raising the Dead*, 62–63, 69–71, 72–79; "Signs," 225; *The Cove*, 271, 276–78, 288n15; "The Trusty," 104
raven, 192–94, 196, 198–99, 203
reconciliation ecology, 194
religion: environmentalism and, 204–7, 213, 215, 221–22, 222n1, 222n4; Pennsylvania Dutch Christianity, 191–93, 201–2; symbolism of water, 63. See also Christian; Christianity
Rhododendron: as design element, 253, 260–62, 264–66; as metaphor, 197; as part of Appalachian landscape, 252–53, 255–57, 266n1, 266n3; catawbiense, 252, 255, 266n1, 266n3
River of Earth 36–38, 286n8. See also Still, James
Roberts, Terry: *A Short Time to Stay Here*, 271, 276, 278–80; as Appalachian writer, 289n23; historical novels and, 281–83, 288n14; postsouthern theory and, 285n3; the South and, 284

Sabbath poetry, 204–22; Sabbath I, 204–5, 207, 220–21; Sabbath II, 219; Sabbath III, 215–18; Sabbath IV, 214–15; Sabbath VI, 216; Sabbath VII, 209–11; Sabbath VIII, 213; Sabbath IX, 207, 209, 211–12; Sabbath XIII, 208, 214; Sabbath XX, 218–19; Sabbath XXI, 208
sense of place: African American people and, 127; bookbinding and, 267n9; labor and, 35, 42, 278; local colorists and, 260, 262, 266n2; material, 281; natural environment and, 227; in Appalachian literature, 252–53, 256, 265, 275, 279, 282; in pastoral romance, 106; Southern studies and, 272–73; theory and, 287n9. See also home; place
sexual assault, 118, 122–23, 125–27. See also under violence
Seymour, Nicole, 150, 153, 157–58, 167n3
Short Time to Stay Here, A, 271, 278–80, 288n17. See also Robert, Terry
Sickels, Carter, 171, 173–74, 186. See also *Prettiest Star, The*
slavery; enslavement, 63, 115–16, 120–22, 207, 287n11
Snyder, Gary, 197, 208, 222n6
South Carolina, 62, 64–66, 252

Southern literature, 9, 272–74, 283, 285
Southern studies, 271–72
Sprinkle, Annie: activism and, 149–50, 153, 162–67; anthropomorphism and, 167n5; ecosexuality and, 148–49, 153, 155–59, 166; *Goodbye Gauley Mountain* and, 2, 147; identity of, 147, 149, 167n4
Stephens, Elizabeth: activism and, 149, 151, 163–67; anthropomorphism and, 167n5; ecosexuality and, 148–50, 153, 155–59; *Goodbye Gauley Mountain* and, 1–2, 151–53, 162; identity of, 147
Stevens, Wallace, 35, 241–250. See also "Anecdote of the Jar"
Still, James, 36–39, 41, 286n8. See also *River of Earth*
strip mining, 130, 138–39, 207, 212, 216, 221. See also mining
Strother, David Hunter, 258. See also Porte Crayon
Stuart, Jesse, 33–36, 41, 43n8, 43n9. See also *Man with a Bull-Tongue Plow*
sublime, 29, 47–51, 87, 90, 228
substance use, 131, 137–38
surety bonds, 241, 247–49

Tennessee: agrarianism and, 278–79; "Anecdote of the Jar" and, 241–42, 249–50; as Southern, 274; cities in, 6; Mary Noailles Murfree and, 30–31; rhododendron and, 252; Roan Mountain and, 255; Wallace Stevens and, 244–47
Through Cumberland Gap on Horseback, 261–262, 264. See also Allen, James Lane
timber industry, 31–32, 64–65, 212, 248. See also logging
Trail of the Lonesome Pine, 258, 261. See also Fox, John, Jr.
Trampoline, 129–41. See also Gipe, Robert
trauma, 118, 122, 125, 186, 280. See also colonialism; sexual assault; violence
travel narratives, 82, 86. See also travel writing
travel writing, 30–31, 42n2, 82, 88–89. See also travel narratives

uninhabitants, 63, 79n2. See also displacement

violence: against animals, 133, 142n4; colonial, 74; domestic or intimate partner (DV or IPV), 125, 131, 134, 136–37, 142n4; environmental, 110; gendered, 83, 116, 125, 127–28, 134, 137–38, 150; geographical, 78; intragender, 137; racial, 115–16, 120, 125, 128, 234; self–harm, 138; slow, 61–62, 204, 206. See also sexual assault
Virginia: activism and, 287n13; Anne Newport Royall and, 89–90; as Southern, 274; enslavement and, 120; in *The Land Breakers*, 48, 54; John Fox Jr. and, 256, 258; rhododendron and, 252; Wallace Stevens and, 246; Thomas Jefferson and, 43n11

water, 52, 64, 70, 76, 87, 89, 165, 193–94, 197, 216, 218, 232, 236; and labor, 22, 280; and tourism, 72; as metaphor, 61–63, 66–69, 74–75, 90, 93, 105, 192, 243; Celtic myth of, 229–30, 237n1, 237n2; flooding, 67–69, 71, 73–74, 76–77; Native American stories of, 63–64, 84–85, 228; nymphs, 83–84, 99; pollution, 5, 37–38, 132, 154, 182, 204–5, 214, 217

watershed(s), 63, 65, 208, 214–16, 218–20

"Wayfaring Stranger," 229, 278

weddings to the Earth, 163, 165, 167. *See also* activism; *Goodbye, Gauley Mountain*; Sprinkle, Annie; Stephens, Elizabeth; *see also under* Appalachian Mountains

Wells, Anna Marie, 81–83, 90–94, 98–99

West Virginia: activism and, 133, 147; as Southern, 274; history of, 159; in *Crapalachia: A Biography of Place*, 14; queer identity and, 157; rhododendron and, 252; University Press, 265

Western thought: binaries, 172, 192; Christianity and, 201; environmental ideologies and, 236; femininity, 136; hyperseparation, 195; masculinity, 134, 137; separation from nature, 56. *See also* colonialism

wilderness: colonialism and, 3–4, 249; experiences of, 81–82, 241–42, 245, 282; gender and, 86, 88, 98–99; geography and, 73, 221; ideologies of, 56, 258; myth of, 3–4, 255; preservation and, 5, 42, 43n17

Wilkinson, Crystal, 115–28. *See also* Affrilachia; *Birds of Opulence*

Woodward, C. Vann, 248, 272, 288n19

working-class, 22, 39, 132, 151–52, 158–59

Zoro's Field: My Life in the Appalachian Woods, 39–41. *See also* Crowe, Thomas Rain

www.ingramcontent.com/pod-product-compliance
Lightning Source LLC
Chambersburg PA
CBHW011713290426
44113CB00019B/2659